The Happiest Kid on Campus

A Parent's Guide to the Very Best College Experience

(for You and Your Child)

Harlan Cohen

Published by Sourcebooks, Inc.
P.O. Box 4410, Naperville, Illinois 60567-4410
(630) 961-3900
Fax: (630) 961-2168
www.sourcebooks.com

Library of Congress Cataloging-in-Publication Data

Cohen, Harlan
  The happiest kid on campus : a parent's guide to the very best college experience (for you and your child) / Harlan Cohen.
       p. cm.
  1. College student orientation—Handbooks, manuals, etc. 2. Education, Higher—Parent participation. 3. College freshman—Handbooks, manuals, etc. 4. College freshman—Handbooks, manuals, etc. I. Title.
   LB2343.3.C617 2010
   378.1'98—dc22
                              2010009756

Printed and bound in the United States of America.
VP 10 9 8 7 6 5 4 3 2 1

For

Eva Kaye and Harrison

(two future happiest kids on campus)

and

Stephanie

(mom of the two future happiest kids on campus)

Contents

Acknowledgments

To my wife, Stephanie, thank you for all of your love, support, and edits. I love having you as partner on this journey. I adore you and treasure every minute of this wild adventure. Bread, oil, wine, and cheese (soon, I promise). To my children, Eva Kaye and Harrison Cooper, thank you for all the hugs, kisses, and smiles. They have been my fuel and inspiration. To my parents, Eugene and Shirlee—your unwavering love, support, and guidance continues to be a driving force. I'm so grateful for you both. Thank you for showing me how to be such a loving, supportive, and nurturing parent. To Marvin and Francine (aka the parents-in-law), thank you for your unwavering encouragement, love, and support—it means the world to me. To my brothers, Victor and Michael, sisters-in-law Irene and Rozi, and brother-in-law Dan—I'm so grateful to always have you all in my corner, and I deeply cherish our relationships. To Phoebe, Rae, Henry, and Ethan, thank you for making me the happiest uncle in the world. I love you all and will always be here to offer you advice 24/7 (but Ethan, you need to learn how to talk first).

Thank you to my always encouraging and enthusiastic agent Eliot Ephraim, my gifted (and very patient) editor Peter Lynch, my visionary publisher Dominique Raccah, and the entire team at Sourcebooks. Thank you to the entire team at King Features Syndicate for your support of "Help Me, Harlan!" Thank you to all the newspaper editors and publications who run my advice column and the readers who enjoy it (and don't always enjoy it).

A heartfelt thank-you goes out to the students, parents, and professionals who contributed to this book. You have been so generous with your time, thoughts, and wisdom. Please know that if your advice didn't make it into the book as a quote, your contribution shaped the content and form of this book. It's all in here. Thank you!

Thank you to all of the high schools, colleges, universities, organizations, and associations who have invited me to speak and share my message with your communities. As much as I love to share, I promise you, I always take so much away. So much of this is included in this book.

Thank you to the following organizations: FYE, NODA, NASPA, ACPA, AFA, AFLV, ACUHO-I, NACA, NASFAA, ACCA, ACHA, BACCHUS, ACP, and AHEPPP. Thank you to the Higher Education Research Institute (HERI) and the National Survey of Student Engagement (NSSE).

A heartfelt thank-you is extended to Cynthia Jenkins, Patrick Combs, Gary Tuerack, Erin Weed, Peter Bielagus, John Pryor, Linda Sax, President E. Gordon Gee, Debra Sanborn, Coach Bill Fennelly, Doug Bauder, Charles "Doc" Eberley, Judy Sindlinger, Michael Schultz, Josh Goldman, Ryan Lombardi, Cathy Bickel, Beth Saul, Brian Van Brunt, Mark Koepsel, Erika Lamarre, Janet Cox, Ron Martel, Pat Watkins, Tom Carskadon, Tom Jelke, Denise Rode, Eric Welgehausen, Edward Dadez, Kenneth Posner, Ana Di Donato, Judith Termini, Trina Dobberstein, Jason Bentley, Jamie Brown, Larry Dietz, Doug Bauder, Julie Payne Kirchmeier, Mark Amos, Nancy Hardendorf, Victoria Atkinson, Joanne Meyerhoff, Beth Oakley, Janita M. Patrick, Lauren Motzkin, Steven Butnik, and Angie Perzanowski.

A final thank-you is extended to the University of Wisconsin–Madison, Indiana University, the Indiana University School of Journalism, and the *Indiana Daily Student*. To the late David Adams, I miss sharing all the wonderful news with you. Thank you for always encouraging me to dream big.

Why This Book Was Written

Twenty years ago, when college students had problems, they were forced to find the answers themselves or turn to professionals on campus to find the answers.

Today cell phones, texting, and technology have made it easier than ever for students to reach out directly to parents the moment there is a problem. As a result, parents of today's college students are often filling the role of first responder. In order for a parent to know how to respond, that parent needs to have a baseline of what's normal and to be expected, as well as knowledge of the resources, support services, people, and places on campus where a student can turn to find answers and support. *The Happiest Kid on Campus* is a complete look at the college experience that answers this call and gives parents the information they need to guide themselves and their students through this amazing, emotional, and wild adventure that is the college experience.

WELCOME PARENTS

Thank you for picking up this book. And welcome to the "Welcome Parents" greeting.

I've been thinking a lot about what I've wanted to say to you. I've actually been practicing it. I like to say it out loud before I write it on paper. It makes it much more natural. A lot of times I'll practice while walking alone, sometimes in airports while traveling. If we crossed paths and you were listening, this may all sound familiar (next time please stop me and say hi).

The Happiest Kid on Campus has been a much bigger project than I anticipated. The short story of this six-hundred-plus-page book is that today's college parents are more involved and more important than ever before. Parents today have the opportunity to be more helpful, supportive, and loving than any college parents in the history of time. But they also have the opportunity to be more intrusive, annoying, and controlling than any college parents in the history of time (no, not you). College is no longer about saying good-bye; it's about talking, texting, Skyping, defining new roles, establishing new boundaries, and finding a new balance. Today's New College Parents are pioneers who are dealing with unprecedented challenges and are faced with new questions that don't always have definitive answers.

The goal of this book isn't to tell you what to do or what not to do (I know better). Instead, what I've done is share the latest research, trends, facts, and statistics that parents need to know to help answer their own questions and define their roles. I've also shared my approach to college success and offered suggestions based on thousands of interactions with parents, professionals, and students. In addition to my voice, you'll find tips, advice, suggestions, and anecdotes from some of the most respected, experienced, and insightful professionals in the field.

I look at this book as two books in one. The first part of the book gives you a baseline of what's normal and to be expected during the college experience and how you can help. The second part offers prescriptive advice from students and professionals on a variety of different issues you may encounter, in the same style as *The Naked Roommate: And 107 Other Issues You Might Run Into in College.*

Throughout the book you'll find references to *The Happiest Kid on Campus* website (www.HappiestKidonCampus.com), my Twitter address (@HarlanCohen or @HappiestKid), and the Facebook fan page (www.Facebook/HappiestKidonCampus). All of these places are intended to help you connect with other parents, professionals, and students who can answer your questions. I'm also interested in your feedback for future editions of this book.

About feedback: I know there are parts of this book that you'll love and some parts you won't love as much. If there's something that needs to be included or something you think I could put differently, I'm open to feedback. In fact, I'm depending on it. This book is a living project that will continue to grow over time. Regular updates and new editions are part of this experience. I look forward to including your voices as you make discoveries and think, "I wish I knew that…" That's when I hope you'll share. I want other parents to know what you will soon find out. You can send a note through the website or send an email to Harlan@HelpMeHarlan.com. Subject: Happiest Kid on Campus—2nd Edition. I value this new relationship and look forward to staying in touch through my website, Facebook, and Twitter (yes, you might even start Tweeting).

Again, thank you so much for inviting me to share in this experience with you.

P.S. A Note to First-Generation Parents

Welcome first-generation parents! (This means parents whose child or children are the first in the family to go to college.)

If your ears were burning, it's because your name has come up again and again during the research and writing of this book. (In the words of Willie Nelson, "You were always on my mind.") Here's one reason—according to a report by the National Survey of Student Engagement, "First-generation students are less likely to take part in enriching educational experiences such as study abroad, an internship, or research with a faculty member." But there's also new research indicating that first-generation parents who are involved can help a student find these enriching education experiences.

But to be involved and encourage your student, you need to know about the college experience. If you don't have your own college experience to draw upon, it may be a little bit harder for you. The good news is that you have more access to more information than you could ever want or need, and a book that provides more information than you will ever need. As you go through this experience, please let me know what I can do to help make this book even more valuable for you and other parents who are going through this experience for the very first time. All parents are important, but first-generation parents have unique challenges. I just wanted to let you know that I'm aware, college life professionals are aware, and we are all working to help make this experience the happiest for you and your child.

WELCOME COLLEGE LIFE PROFESSIONALS

First, thank you for all the support and encouragement you've given me while I've been researching and writing this book. I've had the most wonderful, engaging, and insightful conversations with so many of you. Whether it was at a conference, convention, workshop, event, via Facebook, email, or even Twitter—thank you!

My rule when doing research is that when I hear

something three times from three different sources, it's something I need to include in the book. Well, there's one idea that was expressed again and again from probably more than one hundred people—and that is the desire for parents to help their kids solve their own problems instead of parents solving their kids' problems for them. In your words, "It's the difference between a parent calling with a problem and a student walking into my office and saying, 'My mom and dad thought I should talk to you.'" That's what this book is about. It's about helping parents to support their children so that they can be better communicators with you.

It's also about helping parents work in concert with higher education. Not only will *The Happiest Kid on Campus* help you to support your student and be more understanding of your roles, but it will also help you to appreciate the new role of all college parents and support their needs.

I appreciate and value your feedback. As you read through this book, if you find something that needs to be shared that isn't included (a story, resource, or favorite statistic), I'd be grateful if you would send me a note. I'll do my best to include it in future editions. Send an email to: Harlan@HelpMeHarlan.com. Subject: Happiest Kid on Campus—2nd Edition.

Also, I'm currently compiling an extensive list of college, university, and department Twitter feeds and Facebook fan pages. If you would like to be included in the list, please follow me on Twitter: @HarlanCohen, @HappiestKid, @NakedRoommate, and become a fan of *The Happiest Kid on Campus* Facebook page (www.Facebook.com/HappiestKidonCampus).

Again, thank you for all of your help and support. I look forward to doing whatever I can to support your goals and the success of your students and institutions. Thank you!

WELCOME HIGH SCHOOL PROFESSIONALS AND GUIDANCE COUNSELORS

It's a pleasure to meet you. Thank you for all of your help and support during the research and writing of this book. Through my research, it's become much clearer to me that college success begins in high school. The more parents can appreciate the college experience and their role in it, the better they can be in guiding and supporting their students before they decide where to go to college. The before part is so crucial (clearly, I know you know this). So much of *The Happiest Kid on Campus* is centered on helping college-bound students take the time to map out a path and put together a plan that will enable them to create a life in college before ever setting foot on campus. Parents who understand the college experience can be much better partners in helping their children ask the right questions before deciding what's the right fit. A student who chooses a school for the right reasons and leaves for campus with a plan, patience, and reasonable expectations is set up for success. That makes for a happy student, a happy parent, and a happy high school guidance department.

I hope this book proves to be a valuable resource for you. I would love your feedback and suggestions on how I can make this book even more valuable for you and the parents in your community. I'm actively compiling an extensive list of college and university Twitter feeds and Facebook fan pages. Please feel free to follow my Twitter accounts, @HarlanCohen, @HelpMeHarlan.com, and @Naked Roommate, and Facebook fan page (www. Facebook.com/HappiestKidonCampus) and pass them along to parents and students. My goal is to provide an active link between students and parents and colleges and universities. Thank you for all of your help and support.

WELCOME STUDENTS

What are you doing here? (Eyes wide open, looking surprised.) This book is for parents... (Cleaning up the place.) I just didn't expect you here! (Now inviting you inside.) Of course, you're completely welcome! I mean, your name is in the title—this is *The Happiest Kid on Campus*.

First, let me thank you for contributing and sharing things that most parents never hear from their kids. Your stories, advice, and suggestions have been the driving force of this book. I look at this project as an opportunity for you to speak directly to parents. Rarely do parents get to listen to and engage in dialogue with thousands of college students from around the country and beyond (yes, there are Canadian students too).

If there's ever something you want to share with parents, please let me know and I will pass it along. Also, I invite you to follow me on Twitter (@HarlanCohen, @HappiestKid, @NakedRoommate) and become a fan on Facebook (www.Facebook.com/HappiestKidonCampus and www.Facebook.com/TNRfanpage). Please feel free to participate in any of the forums and discussions to help parents find answers.

At the end of the day, this project is about helping you be supported and as happy as possible. I look forward to staying in touch and doing whatever I can to help you have the happiest and most rewarding college experience. Thanks again for your continued support. It means the world to me.

A SHORT NOTE TO CANADIAN AND INTERNATIONAL READERS

Hi Canadian and international readers! I want to take a moment to acknowledge that use of the word *college* throughout this book. I do understand that *college* and *university* can have different meanings in different countries. Throughout this book, I use the terms *college* and *university* interchangeably. When I refer to college, I'm most often referring to your "university" experience. Just wanted to clear that up and let you know that I'm thinking about you.

ABOUT THE EDITORIAL CONTENT

The Happiest Kid on Campus is the product of over fifteen years of research and experiences. Included in this research have been visits to more than three hundred college campuses, hundreds of events with students and parents, and thousands of interviews. The tips, stories, and quotes were compiled during face-to-face and phone interviews; via written request forms and online surveys; via email, Facebook, and Twitter; through my websites (www.HelpMeHarlan.com and www.TheNakedRoommate.com); and through professional organizations that requested members forward their stories and tips. The latest facts, figures, and information were provided by the Higher Education Research Institute at UCLA using the CIPR Freshman Survey and Your First College Year Data (2005, 2006, 2007, and 2008 and *The American Freshman: Forty-Year Trends*), the National Survey of Student Engagement (2007, 2008), the BACCHUS Network, U.S. government websites, and several other sources cited throughout the book.

Please keep in mind that the tips and stories are in no way a fair and accurate representation of the entire student, professional, or parent population at each institution or of the institutions themselves. Due to the sensitive nature of some tips and requests from contributors to keep identities confidential, some names or years in school were changed or not included. The names of the institutions have not been changed. Also, the tips, stories, and quotes are not always direct quotes. Some tips, stories, and quotes have been edited for clarity and length. If you have any questions about the facts or sources, please feel free to send a note to Harlan@HelpMeHarlan.com. Subject: Happiest Kid on Campus Source Material.

ONE FAVOR TO ASK...

The Happiest Kid on Campus is an ongoing experience. The first edition is always the most challenging because I know there is so much that needs to be covered, but without question, there will always be something left out that should have been included. If you have feedback or a suggestion on what you would like included or changed in the next edition, I invite you to send me a note sharing your input to Harlan@HelpMeHarlan.com. Subject: Happiest Kid on Campus—2nd Edition. Thank you!

PART 1

A College Parent's Prerequisites

The New College Parent

"No matter what happens, remember that we are proud of you."

On a note my mom wrote to me when she
dropped me off my freshman year
—Gracie, junior, UC–San Diego

YOU ARE SO IMPORTANT (BUT YOU ALREADY KNEW THAT)

As your son or daughter walks through the college experience, you are literally in your child's hand. You are with him or her in class, during exams, while eating in the dining halls, studying at night, going to parties, coming home in the early morning, and sleeping over at a "friend's" room (just resting, nothing else). You are there on the very best days and the very worst ones too. All it takes is a push of a button and you can be there to comfort, guide, support, advise, elevate, empower, excite, motivate, love, and just listen. And more than ever, college students are calling, emailing, texting, and reaching out. You are more accessible, more present, and more involved in the lives of your children during their college years than during any other time of their lives.

I was recently speaking at a New Student Week event in front of an audience of five-hundred-plus first-year students (the new term for *freshmen*) who had been on campus for no more than three days. About forty-five minutes into the event, I asked the audience, "By a show of hands, how many of you have received a text from your parents during my event?"

More than half of the audience raised their hands. (It was actually closer to two-thirds, but I don't want you to think I'm exaggerating this early in the book.)

I had never asked this question before. I was floored by the answer (and after fifteen years as an advice columnist, it takes a lot to shock me). After my show, several students came up to me and shared that many of their parents had sent them multiple texts during my seventy-five-minute event. They didn't seem to mind. They found it amusing. Since then, I've asked this same question to several audiences, and each time I get a similar response. Apparently, this has become the norm.

According to a 2006 survey by the College Parents of America, one out of every three parents (34 percent) communicated with their child either daily or more than once a day. A 2007 report by the Pew Research Center reported

50 percent of eighteen- to twenty-four-year-olds are in touch with their parents on a daily basis. Now, this was in 2007. Factor in the fact that more than 50 percent of U.S. parents now know how to text and over 400 million people are on Facebook (one of the

People look at me cross-eyed when I tell them that we talk to our son on average every other week. Other parents tell me they talk to their kids every day. That's fine. Whatever works for you! He knows we'll call if something is really important, and we know he'll do the same. In between calls, I'll send him a text from work once in a while just to tell him I miss him.

—Mom of college sophomore (son)

fastest-growing segments is adults with college-age children), and you'll see that the information flowing between parents and students has reached levels beyond anything we've ever witnessed in the history of time. Is this good? Is this bad? It's just different.

I'm sure if you went to college, the idea of communicating with your own parents on a daily basis seems incomprehensible and completely over the top. When I was in college, making a call home would involve using a calling card or calling collect. I'd have to find a phone booth on campus or call from my room. Having a private conversation meant careful planning to find a private time to call. Not having instant access to my parents meant I was forced to work through situations on my own. Instead of calling Mom or Dad the moment a problem fell into my lap, I had to be the one to fix it and work through it. Leaving for school *really* meant leaving. My parents had to let go, and I had to let go. But now, given how accessible everyone is during the college years, it's not so much letting go; it's more just loosening and changing the grip.

Parents have always been important, but now it's reached a whole new level. Today's parents are hearing it all (or most of it), seeing it all (or most if it), and experiencing it all (or most of it) like no parents have before. At a minimum, a daily email, text message, or phone call can be a regular occurrence between kids and parents. Being a New College Parent who is so plugged in means you need to know so much more than any other parent before you. As one of today's push-button parents, you need to understand what's normal and to be expected so that you can put yourself at ease and help put your children at ease when they push that button and call, text, or instant message you.

BEFORE I DIVE DEEPER INTO THE BOOK, A QUICK STORY...

I do my writing in a lot of places all over the country. One night I was working on this book in the lobby of a busy hotel in New York at about 1:30 a.m. A mom sat down next to me and asked what I was writing. I told her I was working on a book for parents of college students. She responded with a question in a way that only someone from New York can put it: "What do *you* know about being a parent of a college student?" My answer was that I'm a dad, and I've been researching the relationship between students and parents for the past fifteen years. I've interviewed countless parents, students, and college life professionals, and I've had years of experience as a syndicated advice columnist. I thought I did a good job explaining. I was satisfied. I also mentioned that you don't have to jump off a bridge to know that it's a bad idea. You don't have to live something to know about it.

Then she asked me again, "But how do you know? You never sent a kid to college. You don't know what it's like to send a kid to college." Then her ride arrived and she had to leave. At first I was irritated. It was late. I was tired. But then I saw this interaction as a gift. Other moms and dads might be thinking this same thing. You might be thinking it. So here's the rest of the answer—the one I wish I had shared with her.

I'll never know what it's like to be you and go through what you will go through, but I have two small children, and I don't want to ever let them go. I love them so much, and they're only two and four years old. I can't imagine what it will be like to spend another sixteen and fourteen years with them and have to say good-bye. I want to break down just thinking about it.

Over the years, I've talked to so many parents who have struggled to be their best during this transition. I've talked to so many students who have so much to tell parents, but their parents are too emotionally involved to listen. And I've talked to so many college life professionals who are seeing both sides of the story.

My goal in writing this book is to take what I've learned over the years from all the moms, dads, college students, grads, college professionals, and researchers to help make this transition easier for you and as comfortable as possible for your child. This is a project born out of a love to help and support you. Not only do I intend to give you more than you will ever want to know about college life and the changing role of parents, but I will also provide a place for you to talk to other moms and dads who have been there and done that on the website I've created for parents (www.HappiestKidonCampus.com) and on *The Happiest Kid on Campus* Facebook page (www.Facebook.com/HappiestKidonCampus).

Thank you for inviting me into your world and allowing me to share this with you. Like all the books I write, this is a living, breathing project. I would love to share your voices and your stories in future editions. Please keep me in mind as you go through your journey and have stories and anecdotes you want to share. I would love to be able to pass them along to other parents as they enter this amazing journey.

This book is a gift to you. It's a gift to your students. And it's a gift for me when that day comes in fourteen years (I can't even think about it now). By then, I'll probably be able to have dinner with my kids via hologram. That could be fun.

LET'S DIVE RIGHT IN

If you're the parent of a current college student or soon-to-be college student and are reading this book, clearly you care. If you didn't care you'd probably be doing something else—like redecorating your kid's room and turning it into a place to store your old shoes. I imagine you want to be as supportive and loving as possible. Naturally, a lot of you are concerned about some part of the college experience. Even the most hopeful and positive parents have something on their minds. It could be safety, academics, the costs, the temptations, or some other issue. But let me tell you that what you think will happen and what's *really* going to happen can be two very different stories. To illustrate this, I'd like to start off with a drinking game. Actually, it's more like a drinking quiz (don't be alarmed; there is no real alcohol involved in this game).

A lot of you might be worried that your student will drink more than milk in college. You might be concerned that your kids will have "too" good a time. High schools have a zero-tolerance policy when it comes to drinking alcohol. The college world is a little bit different. Even the "driest" schools (dry = no alcohol on campus) aren't so dry. For some of you, this might make you extremely nervous. And now comes the game part (cue game show music, please). According to the American College Health Association, how many college students have never used alcohol in college?

    A.   **49.0 percent**

    B.   **23.1 percent**

    C.   **13.8 percent**

    D.   **3.1 percent**

    E.   **0.9 percent**

If your answer is **E**, you think 99.1 percent of students are drinking. In your world, just about everyone on campus is getting drunk. Buzz. Not true. E is not the correct answer.

If your answer is **D**, you think 96.9 percent of college students drink. In your world just three students out of every one hundred are sober (your student being one). Buzz. Not true. D is not the correct answer.

The correct answer is...

B. 23.1 percent of college students have never consumed alcohol.

The truth, according to the American College Health Association's 2008 report, is that nearly one-quarter of students had never had alcohol. Factor in 13.8 percent of students who didn't drink alcohol over the last thirty days, and that's more than one-third of students who haven't consumed alcohol in the past thirty days.

When students were asked how many of their peers had never consumed alcohol, students guessed that just 3.1 percent of students had never had alcohol versus the actual 23.1 percent. When asked how many students used alcohol in the last thirty days, respondents thought 94.3 percent of their peers were drinking when the actual percentage was 63.1 percent.

What we think is true and what is *really* true are two very different things. I'll get more into this in Tip #21, but one reason students drink is because they think everyone else is drinking, when in fact few people really are drinking.

This whole idea of expectations not being in alignment with reality isn't just confined to alcohol use. It's true of students making friends, finding their place, creating connections, balancing time, and making good grades. What students think will happen and what actually does happen can be two very different things. And it's the same for parents and the expectations that come along with having a student go to college. Try to abandon what you think you know and start fresh. Expect the best, but expect the unexpected. A student who embraces the unexpected can handle whatever comes his or her way. A parent who does the same can be a more patient, forgiving, flexible, supportive, and happier parent. And being a happier parent increases the likelihood of having a happy kid on campus.

YOU MIGHT KNOW TOO MUCH

Twenty years ago parents were lucky to hear about a child's problems during a weekly call; drama that unfolded on Monday was hardly important

PROUD PARENT MOMENT

My proudest moment was writing the final tuition check. That felt good.

—Father of two recent college grads

six days later on the following Sunday. Today a parent often hears about an issue as it unfolds in real time. Even worse, sometimes a student resolves the issue and forgets to tell the parent. So while the student has moved on to the next problem, he forgets to tell Mom or Dad. Meanwhile Mom and Dad are busy working to find a solution to the first problem, and the student has already moved on to the next problem. Drama unfolds quickly in college. Twenty-five years ago a child in college would talk to Mom or Dad once a week or less. Today some students are in contact with a parent several times a day. It's in the form of:

- Texting (if you don't know how to text, you'll soon learn)
- Talking on cell phones (family plans mean free long-distance calling)
- Writing on a Facebook wall
- Sending email (students barely check email anymore)
- Instant messaging (a great way to talk about a noisy, nasty roommate when the roommate is in the room)
- Video chatting (always examine the background of the shot)

A parent doesn't just hear about a messy roommate; now you get to see a live video feed of your kid's roommate's dirty underwear on your child's bed (yes, that's the new bedding you just bought under the dirty underwear).

Before you roll your eyes and think this is all crazy, it's important to understand that students are willing participants in this relationship. Some children like your being there. Some will never tell you to stop. Some will ask you to call them in the morning with a wake-up call (and you better not). When something happens in the life of a first-year student, many times they want their parents to be involved.

My roommate's mom gives her a wake-up call every morning. And then there's at least two more phone calls a day. But she doesn't seem to mind it. Her mom will even text her while we are at parties and tell her not to drink too much, which I think is a little strange. My mom and I talk about once every two days for about thirty minutes. If I sound homesick or upset on the phone (even though I would never tell her), she figures it out and there is either a card or a small package in the mail for me two days later. I know my mom misses me, but we made a deal that I wouldn't come home and she wouldn't come here for the first month. I am so glad we decided to do that. It has made it so much easier to become adjusted, and I feel like I'm not as homesick, because I get to spend weekends meeting people and making new friends instead of spending time at home with my old friends.

—Erica, freshman

When there's good news to share, this is fantastic. When it's not such good news, it's not so fantastic. Instead of your child working through the problem on his or her own, you might get a call, text, or email. They reach out to you because they can. Sometimes they just want you to listen. Other times they want help working through the situation. Sometimes they want *you* to swoop in and solve the problem.

The amount of information, the kind of information, and the way you're getting the information is something no parent before you has had to process. Whether you are hands-on or hands-off, you're always close enough to lend a hand. Whether your student lives on campus or commutes, you risk seeing things and hearing things that will pull you into this experience. And students love that you love to solve problems, so if you let them, they might be willing to let you solve it all.

Being so involved and so accessible means that parents need to know more. They need to understand the college experience. It means getting the right information from the right sources (there is a lot of misinformation out there). It means educating yourself and your husband, wife, or partner. It means getting comfortable with the uncomfortable. It means helping your student create a world of options. How a parent responds to the constant ticker tape of breaking news and emotions is a direct reflection of how much parents know and how comfortable parents can get with the uncomfortable.

GETTING COMFORTABLE WITH THE UNCOMFORTABLE

In chapter 3 I'll introduce something called the 10 percent rule. The 10 percent rule states that life is 90 percent amazing and 10 percent difficult. The problem is that too many times the 10 percent difficult can take up 100 percent of our time. The 10 percent difficult can come in the form of an unexpected bad grade, a crazy roommate, not getting into a fraternity or sorority, financial stress, homesickness, a broken heart, family issues, etc. A parent who is comfortable with the 10 percent can help minimize the drama and provide perspective. A parent who is uncomfortable with the 10 percent may increase the drama, blow things out of proportion, and get too involved. When both a student and a parent know the 10 percent is coming, the 10 percent doesn't have to take up 100 percent of anyone's time. Life can be 90 percent amazing, and the 10 percent difficult can be contained. In fact, the 10 percent can be filled with the most exciting, wonderful, and life-changing experiences—the very best ones. It's the 10 percent uncomfortable that leads us to meaningful conversations with ourselves and the people around us. It's what causes us to ask questions and find life-changing answers.

> My roommate had his girlfriend over for the night. I sent a text to my dad: "Should I go in to go to bed, or what?" He said, "Just do it." I then noisily said good night to the rest of my suitemates and entered the bedroom. Turns out they were asleep; they weren't doing anything. Phew.
>
> —Christopher, freshman

Uncomfortable moments in college are as normal and natural as breathing. In fact, to fight the uncomfortable is to fight breathing. It's just part of life. If your student is not having uncomfortable experiences at some point during college, then it's too safe an experience. Unfortunately, if there's one thing a parent doesn't like to experience, it's a kid feeling uncomfortable. And between video chats, texting, and cell phones, you can see it, hear it, and feel it. If you're not expecting it, chances are it will make you uncomfortable too. You might even panic and do something drastic.

Uncomfortable happens. And when it does, understanding what's normal, being an educated parent, and having read everything in this book will help you to get comfortable with the uncomfortable and handle it all.

A QUICK THOUGHT SO YOU CAN SLEEP AT NIGHT

I want to take a moment early in this book to address the idea that you might be

We had to call the police on two parents. One mom complained that the room was too small for a double. The other mother in the room told her to relax. That's when the demanding mother slapped her.

—Sophomore, resident assistant

scared or a little freaked out about all these changes. When it comes to how the college experience is portrayed in the media, it's all about tragedy, sex, drinking, danger, debauchery, debt, and drama. You don't see a lot of hidden camera shows exploiting "Students Who Study Too Much." The stories are all about madness, mayhem, and maniacs. And we have been through a lot. You've witnessed Columbine, 9/11, Virginia Tech, Amber alerts, sexual predators, and other bad stuff. It's coming at you twenty-four hours a day, seven days a week on cable news and via the flow of information on the Internet.

I can tell you with 100 percent certainty that *the vast majority of students have amazing, wonderful, safe, and healthy experiences* (I can't emphasize this enough). Most students make decisions they regret, but most of these decisions don't result in tragedy. The second half of the book explores the specifics of the college experience and includes campus safety tips and offers suggestions you can pass along to students. There's nothing wrong with parents who remind students to be smart when being stupid—actions like not taking open drinks from strangers at parties, not walking alone at night, never driving after drinking (even one drink), and being aware of date rape drugs are important. Those are all helpful suggestions. I think what will be even more powerful is the idea of helping your student know that he or she has a world of options. It's the student who lives in a world of options who can demand respect, reach out for help, make strong choices, and handle whatever comes his or her way. In my opinion, this is the key to having the most successful, safe, and meaningful college experience.

THE INSTITUTIONS THINK YOU'RE IMPORTANT TOO

Congratulations! You're no longer supposed to leave your kid alone. You are important. This doesn't mean you can't get carried away and become a:

> The hardest thing was for me to let go. Meaning to stop making her life easier, stop arranging things, stop making appointments, etc.
>
> —Mom of college senior

- Helicopter Parent (hovering and always fixing)
- Lawnmower Parent (mowing everyone down)
- Bulldozer Parent (destroying everything in your path)
- Blackhawk Parent (think extreme helicopter, armed and ready)
- Blue Angel Parent (zooming in unexpectedly but not hovering)
- Stealth Parent (secretly hovering from a distance without anyone knowing)
- Stroller Parent (wanting your kid to be independent, but not letting him walk alone)

- Psycho Parent (self-explanatory)
- In-Denial Parent ("not *my* perfect angel")
- Lion Parent (roaring and tearing everything up)
- Overinvolved Parent (wanting to attend too many campus events)
- Wolf Parent (traveling in packs, arguing in packs, and influencing each others' opinions)
- Mosquito Parent (always poking around and irritating people on campus)

As a result of increased parental involvement, institutions are working to educate parents to make them better informed partners during the college experience.

If you were to attend professional conferences for college life professionals and flip through the conference program today, you'd see educational sessions about parental involvement filling up the pages. More schools than ever before are creating programs and resources for parents (community colleges included). PhD candidates are writing dissertations analyzing the role of parents and how they can help or hinder student development. Professionals are publishing articles about parental involvement in academic journals. College newspapers are creating special publications for parents. Institutions are creating special parent and family programs to support parents' new roles. Orientation is no longer just to orient students. It's for parents too. Institutions want parents as partners.

For the colleges and universities, incorporating you

Parents and residence life professionals are indeed playing on the same team. Residence life professionals are talking a lot about parents being "major contributors" in our students' lives. Now, if the parents will get on board and understand that we are all working toward the same thing—the safety, security, and satisfaction of the student—life will be easier.

—Residence life coordinator (three years on the job)

into the mix isn't just good for student success. It's also good for business. The better educated a parent can be throughout this process, the better equipped he or she can be to work in concert with student affairs professionals and other college officials to support student success and wellness. Given that roughly one in three students will not return to the same campus their sophomore year (the number is lower at more selective institutions), the better informed a parent can be, the better equipped he or she can be to help a student engage in college life. And that means not transferring to another institution.

This idea of including parents and addressing their needs is coming across in ways that can't be captured in websites or brochures. I've actually observed campus officials and a vice president of student affairs offering their cell phone numbers to a gymnasium packed with hundreds of parents. In fact, the VP shared his cell phone number twice. The second time, he gave parents a chance to whip out their cell phones and program his number into their phones (some parents had a hard time programming the number in their phones and had to call their kids to get technical support).

When I saw this happening, I had to investigate. How could this man give out his number to a roomful of concerned parents? I approached him after the event and asked if he was lonely and needed friends. He laughed and told me that he's been giving out his cell phone number for several years. He rarely gets calls that bother him. In fact, as a father of college-age students, he understands where parents are coming from. When he gets a call, he directs the parent to the appropriate resource on campus or helps a parent get the right information to help his or her student take action. Most of the time a parent just needs to be heard or needs a contact name (not only do some professionals give out cell phone numbers to support parents, but they offer them to students too).

As I researched this book, I found several campus officials who willingly share their cell phone numbers with parents. It's a sign of the times. The reason institutions are creating special parent programs is because you have never been so important. Gone are the days of *in loco parentis* (institutions acting in place of parents). As Ohio State University President Dr. E. Gordon Gee put it in a conversation we had, the relationships parents have with the university can now be called *in loco amicus*, friends of the community and partnership.

THE BIG, COMPLICATED QUESTION FOR PARENTS

Here's the situation: research now says that parental involvement can be a good thing. But on the other hand, the research doesn't say how much and what kind of involvement. It's easy for a parent to take this information and totally lose control and feel like this is the loving thing to do. Linda Sax, associate professor in the Graduate School of Education and Information Studies at UCLA, sums it up like this:

The fact of the matter is that parental involvement that may be beneficial for some students may actually be counterproductive for others. Until research has addressed this issue more closely, for now parents are

probably best advised to think about how their inter-
actions with their college-age children can encourage
them towards healthy student development. How
can you help them promote independent thinking?
How can you help them promote self-reliance and
autonomy? In what ways do you need to "back off"
and let them learn through their mistakes? The
important message is to think carefully about what's
best for your child's development in the long run, to
be a source of support, and to resist the temptation to
solve all of their problems for them.

The big question for you is what level of involvement is appropriate, healthy, and helpful? How can a parent participate in the college experience and empower a student without overpowering that student? What's appropriate?

Some children need more help than others. Some need less than you think. This book is about helping you to figure out what's appropriate for your own child. The more you really know about this experience, the better equipped you'll be to judge. But to know what level is the appropriate level, you need to be calm, comfortable, and informed. This book should help. *The Naked Roommate* (my book on college life for students) should help. This book is more about what *you* need to know. *The Naked Roommate* is what students need to know. As a New College Parent, you need to know both sides of the story.

Our daughter received bad advice from an adviser and took three classes without the appropriate prerequisites. She nearly killed herself making a 3.5. She found out the error when she went to register this semester, and I ended up talking to the dean. I really hate interfering—particularly because I am a professor—but I think there are instances when it is appropriate that parents are parents, even for college-age students. There was really no way that we could have handled the situation differently—we didn't know she needed the other courses—but we did talk to the appropriate people to try to ensure that it doesn't happen in the future to another student.

—Mom of college junior

BEFORE YOU GET CARRIED AWAY...

Even if you feel the need to be involved, a challenge you may face is that the law doesn't always allow parents to get the information they want and desire. Your child is no longer a child in the eyes of the law. Therefore, once he or she turns eighteen, there's something called FERPA (Family Educational Rights and Privacy Act) (see sidebar on the next page) and HIPAA (Health Insurance Portability and Accountability Act) that kicks in. FERPA and HIPAA can be a real PIA (Pain in the Ass). Unless your eighteen-year-old student signs off and gives you access to his or her information, you may not be able to get all the information you were accustomed to getting for the past eighteen years. This means your child controls access to his or her grades, financial information, academic files, health information, etc.

Assuming your child is kind enough (or threatened by you enough) to allow you access to his or her information, what you do with the information is another question. Do you use the information to police your child? Do you use the information to help your student to fix the problem? Does having access violate the trust you have with your child? Will a student seek counseling for a personal problem involving depression, drugs, alcohol, sex, sexual orientation, gambling, sexual assault, or other personal problems if he or she knows Mom or Dad will have access to the file? Will a student avoid obtaining birth control, getting tested for HIV, or getting treatment because Mom or Dad will have access to medical records? Will a student avoid doing something he or she wants to do because getting help means Mom and Dad will have access to this information? At what age can a student be allowed to manage his or her life and choose what to share with Mom or Dad?

Forget about FERPA. This is about boundaries and trust. At this point in your relationship with your child, there should be an understanding that this time in life is about growing up. A parent who demands access is telling a child, "I don't trust you to take care of yourself." That doesn't exactly send the message of trust and respect.

SETTING BOUNDARIES CAN BE HARD

Given this new level of access and the relationships so many children have with their parents, this new stage in life is even more complicated. So many parents and students have friendships. Having your child leave for college means missing a friend. It also means not having your computer technical support team on location. When it comes to boundaries, as the parent, you must set them on yourself. For example:

1. You're driving in your car and hear your daughter's favorite song on the radio from a musical she performed in senior year. You want to call to say, "Hey, I was thinking of you." Can you call? Is calling intrusive? Do the rules change just because your daughter is no longer in high school?

2. The Internet goes down. You contemplate calling the Internet company to address the problem, but don't want to wait on hold. Besides, you've never had to deal with this before. You consider calling your son at college to offer you the technical support. If you're

Do not expect your son/daughter to tell you the truth, the whole truth, and nothing but the truth. Your child's RAs have condoms that they will give to residents on request for a reason. I may also think your daughter's roommate is crazy and needs some serious help, but I can't tell you this for a number of reasons.

—Residence life coordinator

helping pay for college, you might think the twenty thousand dollars in tuition is enough to warrant 24/7 technical support. Is this wrong?

3. You are on Facebook and see a kid's status update that mentions your daughter is hungover and missed class. You are irate because class is expensive and she isn't of age to drink. Plus, your daughter has been mentioning how she has been having problems in the class she missed. Do you call her and give her a piece of your mind? Do you let it go? Do you write on her wall and publicly humiliate her for all to see?

Parents of college students ten years ago didn't have the option to talk to their students when they wanted, where they wanted, and for so little money. Given the advances in technology, the inexpensive methods of communicating, the strong bonds parents have with today's students, and the fact that many students love and desire all this attention from their parents, the answers to these questions aren't so simple.

> Some parents think that we want them to be completely uninvolved, but that's not true. A lot of times it helps us to know they are there.
>
> —Emily, freshman

There are so many more questions that will come up during the college experience. I hope this book can help answer most of them:

-   What does it mean to be a supportive parent?
-   How can a parent be included without being intrusive?

- How often do you call, text, or video chat?
- What can a parent do to alleviate stress, not elevate stress?
- How can a parent trust a student's judgment?
- How can a parent trust a student to manage his/her finances?
- Should a parent be a child's Facebook friend?
- How do you tell a homesick child not to come home?
- Should you encourage your child to go Greek?
- What if your child has roommate issues?
- How do the rules change when your child comes home for break?
- What do you say or do if your child has gained or lost a lot of weight?
- How do you help a child who is sick at college?
- How do you help a child who is depressed at college?
- How do you know when a bad grade is due to the transition to college and not due to taking advantage of Mom and Dad?
- What's the best way to help your child choose a major? When is a major the wrong one?
- What happens if your child's GPA drops?
- What happens if you get a call that your child has been arrested for underage drinking?
- What do you do if your student is hospitalized after drinking?
- What about campus safety? How can you sleep at night after watching the news?

- How can you manage your own emotions?
- What if a college isn't the right fit for your child? What next?
- How does a parent deal with sex and alcohol being so accessible?
- How does a parent deal with a child coming out and sharing that he or she is gay?
- Should a parent ever call a professor, a child's roommate, or a future employer?
- What's the best way to take care of yourself?
- How do you manage your own relationships?
- How can you take care of your child?
- How can you help your child have the most amazing college experience?

There isn't one right answer, but there are answers.

This book is my way of trying to help you find the answers. The facts, statistics, stories, information, tips, and advice are about helping you have access to the most trusted, accurate, and compelling information so that you can formulate your own answers or reinforce what you already know. It's about giving you the essential information to help support your transition, your student's transition, and other college parents' transitions.

This book is organized into two parts. The first part is all about filling you in on the current state of the college culture—what's changed, what's the same, how to plug in to the flow of information on campus, how to connect to other parents, and some of the big issues you and your child will face during this first year. The second part of the book breaks down twenty-five different areas of campus life and offers prescriptive advice to help you point your child in the right direction should the unexpected and uncomfortable pop up its ugly head. The second part of the book highlights the voices of the students, top college life professionals, and leading experts. The first half tells you what's normal and to be expected, the second half gets into the nitty gritty. By the time you finish reading this book, I can promise you that you will know too much information—more than any parent has never needed to know or will ever need to know. It doesn't get any more complete than this.

As I mentioned at the top of this chapter, I love research and love sharing stories of people who have been there and done it. I want to get this book right and would love to hear from you if you think something could be better. Please reach out to me by visiting TheHappiestKidonCampus.com and NakedRoommate.com forums, *The Happiest Kid on Campus* Facebook page (www.Facebook.com/HappiestKidonCampus) and Twitter feed @HappiestKid (yes, you will soon be Tweeting). All of these are resources designed to help make life easier, more comfortable, and happier for you, and ultimately, for your student.

College: So What's Really Changed?

I want to start this chapter with one of my favorite lists. Every year (for the past twelve) Ron Nief and Tom McBride have compiled a list of what's changed over the years. Students entering college in the present year have never known a world without the things on this list. For example, for students entering college in 2006, *google* has always been a verb and "text messaging is their email." Here are twenty selections from the Beloit College Mindset List for the Class of 2013. To view the complete list of seventy-five entries visit www.beloit.edu/mindset. And a thank-you to Ron and Tom for allowing me to share this with you in the book.

Students entering college in 2009 lived in a world where:

- Women have always outnumbered men in college.
- There has always been a computer in the Oval Office.
- Salsa has always outsold ketchup.
- Magic Johnson has always been HIV-positive.
- Tattoos have always been very chic and highly visible.
- Rap music has always been mainstream.
- American students have always lived anxiously with high-stakes educational testing.
- State abbreviations in addresses have never had periods.
- Condoms have always been advertised on television.
- Desperate smokers have always been able to turn to Nicoderm skin patches.
- There has always been a Cartoon Network.
- Their folks could always reach for a Zoloft.
- They have always been able to read books on an electronic screen.
- We have always watched wars, coups, and police arrests unfold on television in real time.
- Madonna's perspective on sex has always been well documented.
- Smokers have never been promoted as an economic force that deserves respect.
- Elite American colleges have never been able to fix the price of tuition.
- The status of gays in the military has always been a topic of political debate.

- Migration of once independent media like radio, TV, videos, and compact discs to the computer has never amazed them.
- There has always been blue Jell-O.

WHEN YOU WERE EIGHTEEN

If someone were to tell eighteen-year-old you that your future child could snap photos, record video, and play thousands of songs on a cellular phone so small it could fit in a baby's hand, you would think that person was on drugs (and chances are, if you grew up in the '70s, he or she might have been on drugs.). In your day, parents drove station wagons to campus and played eight-track tapes on the car stereo. Computers were built to run businesses. College was seen as much more affordable; women lived in separate residence halls, students called home collect, blackboards were not digital, and a laptop was the top of your lap.

So much has changed over the years. I know it sounds like such a cliché (you won't find any other clichés other than this cliché referring to clichés), but it's true. If you spent time in college, just visit your old campus and look for the pay phone or phone booth you used to call home. Chances are you'll find an ATM or computer station in its place. If you walk around the student union, you'll see banners from clubs and organizations recruiting students to participate in public service and volunteer projects. This generation is one of the most service-oriented in history. Forget selfish, entitled teenagers—this generation wants to make a good living, but they want to make sure everyone around them is taken care of too. Everyone has a cause. They really do want to help.

> Today's college students don't even know what a mix tape is.

I should mention—while so much has changed, a lot is still the same. The buildings and big life issues are the same (although the buildings are now wireless and "green"). The college years continue to be a time of self-reflection, independence, experimentation, testing character, defining core values, and making choices surrounding careers, classes, relationships, drinking, drugs, sex/no sex, depression, faith, family, and friendship. The issues and emotions that go along with the college experience remain constant.

But technology, the costs of college, and several other contributing factors have presented unique challenges for this generation of students and their parents. It's easy to be so connected to one another but at the same time still find a way to feel so detached. By understanding the college world, the new challenges, and the dynamics, you'll be better equipped to help your child and yourself embrace these challenges and get comfortable with the uncomfortable that's part of the college experience. The more comfortable you can be with all these changes, the better sense you'll have of how to define your role in it all.

So what's really changed over the past thirty years? Let me bring you up to speed.

#1 THE COSTS HAVE CHANGED

College has always been expensive, but now it's gotten *really, really, really* expensive (and yes, I had one hundred really's but my editor made me delete ninety-seven of them. I had to fight for these three). Besides a home, a college education is one of the most expensive items a student will purchase. Unfortunately, you can't live in a diploma after graduation (it gets wet when it rains). Factor in the recent credit crisis and endowments falling in value 20 to 25 percent in 2008, and money for school has been a lot tighter and less available. So how much have prices changed?

COST OF TUITION OVER THE YEARS
National averages for published tuition from the College Board:

	Private Four-Year	Public Four-Year	Public Two-Year
1978–79	$ 9,903	$2,303	$1,095
1988–89	$14,857	$2,929	$1,483
1998–99	$19,825	$4,376	$2,098
2009–10	$26,273	$7,020	$2,544

COST OF TUITION + ROOM AND BOARD

National averages for published tuition from the College Board:

	Private Four-Year	Public Four-Year
1978–79	$15,434	$7,181
1988–89	$21,644	$8,270
1998–99	$27,580	$10,471
2009–10	$34,132	$14,333

I'll pause while you get up. I imagine this all made you fall out of your chair. The cost of attending a private four-year institution has *nearly* tripled over the last thirty years while the costs of attending a public four-year college *has tripled*. When you factor in the rate of inflation, tuition at four-year institutions has increased at a rate twice the rate of inflation over the past thirty years. As for two-year colleges, the price has more than doubled. The big price of college means more stress, more working students, and more students dependent on grants, scholarships, and loans.

On average, full-time students receive about $10,200 of grants and tax benefits in private four-year institutions; $3,700 in public four-year institutions; and $2,300 in public two-year colleges.

—Source: College Board

One changing trend has been the move from government grants to a shift in more private loans. In 2008, 66 percent of students received some kind of financial aid. With so many students seeking assistance, they must fill out the financial aid forms (this is as much fun as getting a cavity filled), apply for scholarships, and figure out where to go to school based on finances. This can all be overwhelming (but I don't need to tell you that).

As a result of the rising costs of colleges, more students than ever are not attending their first-choice school. In 1975, 79.7 percent of freshmen reported they were attending their first-choice institution. In 2006 that number reached an all-time low with 67.3 enrolled in their first choice (according to HERI, the Higher Education Research Institute). The result is more students in places they might not want to be. And that means having to work that much harder to find their place.

Even with financial aid, more students are planning to get jobs to help pay for college. In 2009, 49.4 percent of students reported that they would get a job in order to cover expenses (higher than at any time during the thirty-two years this question has been asked on the HERI survey).

As a result of these costs, enrollment in two-year public colleges and online institutions has been booming. With more students choosing two-year schools, transferring will become a rising trend in the coming years. As a result, more four-year schools are working harder to help support transfer students (transfers are the least likely group to engage in student life). The financial burdens may also be affecting how students see the importance of earning a degree. In 1976, 49.9 percent of students surveyed felt that making more money was an important reason to attend college. In 2006 that number moved up to 69 percent. Clearly, students want a return on their investment, or they just want to maintain the lifestyle they've been accustomed to living.

In fact, along with this new steep price of college, a new savvy consumer has been born. Twenty-five years ago a student attending college was first and foremost a student. Today the rising costs of college have turned students and parents into customers. And being a customer means expecting customer service.

Talk with professors who have been on campus for twenty-five years, and many will express how students back in the day would look at college as a time to learn. But many of today's students want to be taught and prefer to have the answers served to them. Some students think the professors are working for them—not the other way around.

When it comes to the world of residential living (formerly known as dorm life), there is a similar expectation of service and comfort among many residents. Given the prices and amenities, it's easy for students to expect it. But residence life professionals are not customer service representatives who believe the customer is always right—and that's because the customer is *not* always right. Parents sometimes think that because they are paying the bill, they are the customers and that therefore they are always right—wrong.

To sum this one up—the skyrocketing costs of college have changed the experience. More students than ever aren't able to attend their first-choice school, causing disappointment before college even begins. Picking a major and making grades isn't always a reflection of pursuing a passion; it's more about making enough money to pay down student loans and avoid long-term debt. While classes might take up fifteen hours a week, paying for those classes takes up more time than studying for them. The costs have also affected parents' attitudes. Having so much money tied up means feeling more invested in the experience. Parents want value and customer service. They want their kids to be happy. As a result, they make more calls and place more demands on the professionals serving their students' needs. Parents forget that the customer isn't always right. FERPA and HIPAA make it hard for the professionals on the other end of the conversation to tell the whole story, because the law is preventing them from doing so. This is one more reason why students need to make the calls and take care of themselves. Yes, a parent who is helping with college might be paying the bills, but the student has ownership over his or her college experience.

> **FIVE BIGGEST CHANGES FROM WHEN MY PARENTS WENT TO COLLEGE**
>
> 1. I submit assignments online.
> 2. Nothing you turn in for a grade is hand-written.
> 3. My parents can access my grades online.
> 4. I've met as many people from my college through Facebook as I have in person.
> 5. I get text message alerts from my school about what's going on around campus.
>
> —Rachel, sophomore

Forget that whole landing on the moon thing (although that had to be cool to see); we now live in a world where one person can have a thought, express it, and instantly share it with billions of people around the world all for free (and in his or her underwear). Technology has made it possible for students to create, share, and change the world. College proved to be a pivotal period of time for students like Bill Gates, Paul Allen, Larry Page, Sergey Brin, and Mark Zuckerberg (although some of them never completed college). What's amazing is how fast all this happened. Here's a quick thirty-year snapshot. Each of these changes has had a profound impact on the lives of college students and their parents.

Quick Snapshot of Technological Changes

A little over thirty years ago, on April 4, 1975, Bill Gates and Paul Allen founded Microsoft. In 1976 Steve Jobs and Steve Wozniak founded Apple computers. On October 13, 1983, the first commercial cellular call was placed from Soldier Field in Chicago. In 1989 the University of Phoenix founded their online classroom (there were twelve students), and Tom Berners-Lee invented the World Wide Web (the framework that harnessed the power of the Internet). In 1997 AOL introduced the Instant Messenger or IM (hello chatting). In 1998 AT&T introduced the Digital One Rate plan (eliminating roaming fees). On September 4, 1998, Stanford students Larry Page and Sergey Brin started Google. In June 1999 Napster was introduced and file sharing took off. In October 2001 Apple introduced the iPod. On April 28, 2003, Apple opened the iTunes store. In January 2004 MySpace was launched. A month later, in February, Mark Zuckerberg and cofounders launched Facebook from their Harvard dorm room. In February 2005 YouTube was founded (changing the way we broadcast and consume images). In 2008 Americans bought $21.33 billion worth of video game systems, software, and accessories (according to the NPD Group). In February 2010 Facebook reached 400 million active users, and Apple announced that more than two billion applications have been downloaded from its App Store. Then there's Yahoo, HDTV, word processors, PowerPoint, smartphones, video chat, online learning, and too many other innovations to include. And every single one of these inventions has had a direct impact on college students. In fact, college students are the ones creating so many of these changes.

PROUD PARENT MOMENT

When my son was in high school, he'd come home from school and close the door. We didn't talk much. Then he left for college in California. He went from a kid in Brooklyn who closed the door to someone who would email me with questions. He would ask me, "Mom, I have to hand in this article. What do you think?" What did I think? He cares about what *I* think!

—Shelly, mother of two

Technology is truly awesome. The idea that a parent can share in a celebration with a son or daughter, see a child's messy roommate's mess, or see a sick student's glazed eyes on a live video chat is mind-boggling. The reality that schools can contact thousands of students via text message to inform them of emergencies in seconds is remarkable. Being able to reach out to your children whenever you need to get in touch with them is a truly comforting and remarkable thing.

But while so much of this is good and comforting, there's a catch: it can also be unhealthy. Parents have to set limits on themselves, and students need to spend more time having face-to-face contact with new people instead of staying so close to all their friends at home. This brings up something you need watch out for—I call it the Fifth Wall of technology. The Fifth Wall is a virtual wall that can keep your child isolated from the world around him or her. You'll read a lot about how college can naturally be uncomfortable at times. That's just the normal, natural experience. Thirty years ago students couldn't reach out to all the people who made their life so comfortable at home. But now friends, family, and significant others from home are a push of a button away; it's never been easier for a kid to get stuck behind the Fifth Wall and miss out on the moments happening around him or her. While a student can physically be on campus, that same student can emotionally be at home, with friends from home, or with a significant other. It's hard to have life on campus when a student isn't "on" campus.

Technology's Impact on College Life

I can sum up the technology section with a question: How *hasn't* technology affected students' lives in college?

- Back in the day, a student would call home once a week from a dorm room landline or phone booth. Today a student can text, email, call (no landline needed), instant message, video chat, send a note on Facebook, or Tweet on Twitter (and the cost of the connection can be zero).
- Back in the day, a parent who wanted information would have to ask a student or call the institution. Today a parent can browse the campus website, read blogs by students, google keywords, participate in online forums and discussions, read the campus newspaper online, visit the school's Facebook page, and even follow the school president on Twitter.
- Back in the day, communicating with friends from home meant a student had to wait until Thanksgiving break or a visit from a friend to find out what was happening. Today students are plugged in to their friends' everyday worlds via Facebook news feeds, MySpace mail, texts, emails, IMs, video chats, and phone calls (no long-distance charges apply),
- Back in the day, there were ways to escape the constant social pressures and drama. Today social networking has made being part of the drama a 24/7 reality show. And when that means not being included (rejection is a part of everyone's life at some point), there's never a break from that social rejection.

- Back in the day, managing finances meant going to the bank, writing checks, and balancing a checkbook. Today students use ATMS, swipe debit cards, and check their balance from their cell phones. Parents no longer need to send money; they can just transfer it.

> Back in the day, I sure didn't have to worry about my students talking on the telephone during class! And between classes, students didn't walk at a zomboid pace, checking messages. All this communication is great, as long as it isn't done during class, but it makes for a very different campus life.
>
> —Professor, thirty-plus years in higher education

- Back in the day, getting help meant having to talk with someone or leaving a message. Today a student can google for help, find hotlines, join support groups, chat, and find endless information dealing with every possible physical and mental health issue.
- Back in the day, flirting would mean shooting a glance in someone's direction or asking a friend to find out if that person was single. Today a student can glance at a social networking profile, poke someone on Facebook, send a text, share a picture, or send a video message.
- Back in the day, having a roommate meant having to meet and judge your roommate in person. Today students and parents can observe roommates online via a Facebook or MySpace profile and judge a roommate before ever meeting that roommate.

- Back in the day, having a long-distance relationship meant not seeing someone or talking to someone for weeks or months (minus the occasional long-distance call). Today couples plan dates via live chats, talk on the phone for hours, text, and keep in touch on a minute-by-minute basis.

- Back in the day, going home meant posting a note on the ride board (if you didn't have a car) or spending hours on the phone with airline agents. Today it's a note on craigslist or a campus electronic bulletin board. When you want to fly somewhere, you comparison shop and get last-minute deals in a matter of seconds.

> ## HOW MUCH TIME IS SPENT ONLINE
>
> · Males spend an average of 29.20 hours per week on the Internet
> · Females spend an average of 27.23 hours per week on the Internet
>
> —Source: *Journal of Educational Technology Systems*, 2006

- Back in the day, being creepy meant following people around or making comments face-to-face. Today being creepy can be far less obvious with social networks revealing pictures, videos, and up-to-the-second personal information.

- Back in the day, registering for classes meant waiting in long lines (the perfect time to meet dates). Today it means going online and pressing buttons. Want to find out about a professor? Just google it, search www.RateMyProfessor.com, or send out a note.

- Back in the day, parents who wanted to talk to a child would have to wait until the student was in his or her room. Today parents just need to send a note, call, or learn to text. If a student doesn't answer, parents panic much faster.

- Back in the day, buying stuff meant going to lots of stores. Today it's going to the online store, looking on eBay, or shopping craigslist. Most of the time, shipping is free or less than the price of gas to get there and back. Wanting something means clicking a few buttons and having it delivered.

- Back in the day, traveling home in a car meant using a map. Getting lost meant driving for hours before realizing you were in the wrong state. Today students can plug in an address, and a talking computer takes them turn-by-turn. If a parent is concerned it's taking too long, forget having to worry—just call.

- Back in the day, you had to see it, hear about it, or be in a place with a landline to hear about real-time news. Today when it happens students can hear it, see it, and update the world about it (more on the news change later).

- Back in the day, playing video games meant Pong or going to an arcade. Today there's a virtual world where millions of people spend billions of dollars gaming (surprisingly, research says students who game work better in groups).

- Back in the day, confronting roommates meant having to talk to a roommate about a problem. Today students talk to everyone else but the roommate. And when it is time to talk, students prefer instant message or text.
- Back in the day, doing laundry in college meant using quarters and staying in the laundry room to watch the laundry finish drying. Today a student can swipe an electronic card, leave the laundry room, and get a text message delivered when his or her laundry is finished or when a machine becomes available (no more meeting friends or dates in the laundry room).

"IC students can monitor their building's washers and dryers without having to leave their dorm room through the College's Laundry View system... You can keep tabs on things through the website or via cell phone, and even get a text message when a machine becomes available or when the laundry is done!"

—From Ithaca College's *Fuse* student publication
(http://fuse.ithaca.edu/7219)

The impact of technology can be seen in how students interact with parents, friends, family, professors, and strangers. It can been seen in how students study, take notes, write papers, take exams, see lectures, check grades, and cheat (cheating has reached an entirely new level). It affects how they shop, get food, travel, buy and sell books, and even how they do laundry. As for this idea of letting go during the college years, technology has made it impossible. I've said it before and I'll keep saying it—the college years are no longer about letting go. They are about changing your grip and figuring out how you can be there to help support your child without doing it all for him or her.

#3 THE CLASSROOMS HAVE CHANGED

Remember taking pens to class? Remember sitting in class and feverishly taking notes? Remember getting bored and passing notes in class? Remember writing papers *on paper*? Flash-forward to today: Why use a pen when you can type on a laptop? Why print it out and kill trees when you can write it and send it to an electronic drop box? Why feverishly take notes in class when you can just record it and listen to it later? As for passing notes, all you need is a cell phone and a texting plan. The classroom has changed. Even goofing off in the classroom has changed (more in a minute).

Attending class is still the most important part of being successful in the classroom, but it's hard to be convinced to attend every single class when lectures are available online via a Podcast, on YouTube Edu (www.YouTube.com/edu), or on iTunes U. Maybe this is one reason why 70 percent of students "frequently" or "occasionally" skipped class (HERI 2008). Professors still lecture in the classroom, but instead of putting important points on a blackboard, the rooms gets dark and the PowerPoint slide show replaces all that chalk. Sure, a student can take notes in class, but having access to the digital notes makes it far less important. Missing class no longer means having to get notes from classmates; it means reviewing notes online or tracking down an audio copy of the lecture.

When bored in class, today's student has many options that you never had. There's still doodling and passing notes, but now there's texting, surfing the web, shopping, participating in online auctions, chatting, playing video games, or trying to get into a different class (one that isn't so boring) via the online registration system. A student with a love for learning can even take other online courses while in class.

Students having a hard time with the materials can approach a teacher without ever looking at that teacher. It can be an email, text, or call on a professor's cell phone. Some teachers give out their cell phone number or even respond to Facebook messages.

When it comes to work, research is done on the computer; spell check doesn't involve digging through dictionaries, just looking for words underlined in red. When turning in assignments, forget handing them to teachers; drop them in the electronic inbox. If you're late, forget telling the professor that your dog ate your assignment; say your hard drive crashed (that only works a few times). And if you hand in the assignment late, don't pretend it was on time and say you slipped it under the teacher's door (that doesn't work anymore). The digital time stamp on an inbox with the attached file makes it impossible to BS teachers like in the past.

Students looking to cheat have more options too. There's still looking on other papers, but they can also get answers texted, google answers on cell phones, and find readymade papers to copy and paste online. But the schools have a tech edge too—some schools run every paper submitted through programs like Turnitin.com and SafeAssign—these are programs that screen papers to see if work is original or if it's been plagiarized.

Life in the classroom has changed, but no matter what gadgets, gizmos, and apparatuses are available in the classroom, there's one thing that needs to be emphasized—a student needs to do the work, or there will be no more work to do, because that student will fail out. One thing there isn't a gadget (or an app) for is having the discipline to get the work done.

#4 PARENTS HAVE CHANGED

I have to hand it to you—you're an interesting generation. College students back in the late '70s were very busy changing the world. A large number of you were busy questioning authority, having sex before marriage, and experimenting with drugs (not all things I encourage students to do). You made it clear that women, gays, and people of different races all deserve rights (just not the right to marry). You also made it normal for students to have more than one set of parents (the "traditional" family is no longer a mom and dad). You put helmets on your kids, stopped spanking their tushies, and got MADD about drunk driving. You've also seen some bad stuff—assassinations, war, domestic terrorism, high school violence, the attacks of September 11, 2001, college shootings, kidnappings, and other tragedies. While violent crime has been going down for the past thirty years, the volume of bad news has gone up (see #7 News Has Changed below).

You are wealthier than your parents and have proven that a college degree has value. In general, your children have lived a nicer lifestyle than most of you lived at their age. You are parents who are involved and want to help your kids in every way. You sign them up for sports, music lessons, language classes, and anything else that can help them become well-rounded. You are used to communicating with your kids regularly and knowing where they are and who they are with. While you are free thinking and open to new ideas, safety is of the utmost importance. Most of your kids wear helmets, call you to check in, and are aware of danger.

So you know what *really* goes on with young adults. The idea that your child might drink might not shock you (though you hope he won't). The idea of a kid smoking pot might not shock you (although you hope your child won't). You are aware of the risks and have more information to consume you with worry if you let it. And it's understandable. You are so loving and so caring and so connected to your children. You want them to be comfortable. But because of that, you sometimes think things are much worse than they are.

So because parents are so involved, institutions are working harder to educate and incorporate parents into all aspects of college life. Still, a parent who wants to get information needs to seek out the information. How involved a parent needs to be to help a child thrive during the transition from teen to adult is unique to the child, the parent, and the dynamics of the relationship. The next chapter gives you all the access you need to get the information you desire (in fact, it gives you access to too much information).

Because of technology (cell phones, email, social networking sites, etc.), students seem to maintain their high school relationships (girlfriends/boyfriends) longer. There used to be a belief that high school relationships would end when students went home for Thanksgiving break. This is no longer the case, since high school partners talk at least once a day... if not several times a day.

—Gary Ireland, Dean of Students, North Central College

#5 STUDENTS HAVE CHANGED

Let me start this off by letting you know that your kids are so nice, so giving, so caring, and nurturing. They are the most compassionate and service-oriented generation in recent history. They love nature, they love working in groups, and some of them love communicating with their parents. All of this is so wonderful—they just need help learning to take the time to be more compassionate to themselves. While today's students spend so much time focusing on everyone else and the world around them, they sometimes forget to take time to work on themselves. I get it—it's easier to try to fix the world.

Today's students have been labeled "the Net Gen" or "Generation Y." Cell phones, computers, and handheld devices aren't technology, just a part of everyday life. Today's students are connected to the world, cared for by parents, and supported 24/7. There has never been a generation that has had more access to more help and support.

Today's students are used to being successful. They love to give of themselves, are good working in groups, and are better behaved than their parents. However, they are not as good at failing or receiving feedback that isn't positive. Only 1.3 percent of entering freshmen in 2006 report making a C average in high school—this is compared to 8.6 percent in 1966. Being imperfect isn't the norm. Students are used to being rewarded simply for participating. Trophies aren't given only to the champions—they are given to everyone.

Today's students have a different sense of danger as well. Amber alerts, security guards in high schools, and "lock down" drills have been the norm. "Stranger danger" doesn't just mean avoiding strangers; it means not answering instant messages, responding to email, accepting strange friend requests, posting cell phone numbers, or posting any private information. Today's students don't just get bullied at school; they also get cyber-bullied, text-bullied, and ridiculed on Facebook, MySpace, YouTube, and other social networking sites.

Sex and graphic images are as accessible as Elmo. Today's students have been peddled porn since they got their first email account. As for having sex, it's not taboo. Some parents buy kids condoms. But a lot of students are not having sex; in a recent survey, 33 percent of students reported that they had not had sex in the past twelve months. Many students had never had sex at all. The ones avoiding sex probably heeded the warnings and sent the news that one in four students have herpes or HPV (the virus that causes genital warts). As for the students who are having sex, condoms and candid conversations are the buzzwords. But that's harder to do when buzzed.

The Net Gen's encyclopedia is Wikipedia. Their card catalog is Google. They prefer Dictionary.com to dictionaries. They get answers in milliseconds. They believe in customer service and are used to being served. Many want to get answers without having to learn how to get the answers. Thus their brains are different from ours. Multitasking, video games, and technology have made students' brains more perceptive when processing images and receiving multiple streams of input. And there's research that says video games and social networks have made them more social—not less (go figure).

When it comes to college, preparation can start as early as elementary school. Colleges are more competitive. The process is intense. More applications to more schools means more risk of rejection. Students have more debt, more demands on their time, and more opportunities to disappoint those around them. Once accepted to college, more students on campus can mean more crowded living, bigger class sizes, and challenges getting into classes and graduating in a certain number of years. Between classes, jobs (almost half of today's students work), and creating a life, it's not a surprise that students are feeling more stressed, more overwhelmed, and more likely to reach out to counseling services than ever before.

The good news is that students now have access to more counseling, psychological services, and support groups. Hotlines, websites, and support services a few doors away are the norms on campus. Students looking for more support can find groups for any interest. From the GLBT (gay/lesbian/bisexual/transgender) groups to political groups (83 percent of students discussed politics in 2008), there are places for students.

When it comes to health, students don't just have colds and flu—they have ADD and ADHD, depression, eating disorders, addictions, and mental health issues. In fact, more students than ever before are

> **INTERESTING FACT**
>
> In 1987 Prozac was approved. Other drugs to treat ADHD like Ritalin and Adderall came about in the '80s. It wasn't until the '80s that the term ADHD became a recognized medical condition.

coming to school with disabilities. There's now an office on every single college campus receiving public funds to support students with disabilities. Students who have documented disabilities can register at the office and access support services (academic and emotional support), special accommodations (i.e., extra time for taking exams, private rooms for test taking, etc), and other programs to help them throughout their college experience.

When it comes to partying, today's college students like to have a good time, but most of them party responsibly. The drugs of choice are alcohol and marijuana. Half as many of today's students have experimented with alcohol compared to their parents' generation. When you did it, drinking was legal. Now that the legal drinking age is twenty-one, it's illegal for most new college students. When something bad happens, news travels fast. Schools are struggling to control drinking. The government is struggling to control drinking—specifically binge drinking. The National Institute of Alcohol Abuse and Alcoholism defines binge drinking as "a pattern of drinking that brings a person's blood alcohol concentration (BAC) to 0.08 grams percent or above." This typically happens when men consume five or more

> **FIVE BIGGEST CHANGES FROM WHEN MY PARENTS WENT TO COLLEGE:**
>
> 1. Online classes
> 2. Dramatic rise in cost
> 3. Luxury-style dorms
> 4. More options for eating in and out of cafeteria
> 5. Use of ID cards for meal plans, rec center access, etc.
>
> —Annalise, sophomore

drinks, and when women consume four or more drinks, in about two hours. The drinking culture is a problem, but the reasons that students drink are the bigger issues. I'll dive into those in Tip #21. I think I have answers— or at least an explanation and approach that can work.

When it comes to partying, today's college students like to drink, but not as much as their parents drank in college. Parents' perception is that more students are drinking than are actually doing it. Cable news, campus news, local news, and social networking make alcohol-related deaths become big news. The good news tends not to make headlines.

#6 THE RULES HAVE CHANGED

The past thirty years have seen a shift from colleges acting as the parent (*in loco parentis*) to students being responsible for their own actions. Along with this shift have come new rules. Some are more restrictive and others are less. The rules and student codes are constantly changing to reflect the culture, diversity, and needs of the community.

Campus violence has meant schools no longer give students the benefit of the doubt. If there's any suspicion, expect an institution to take action.

Campuses have codes of conduct that include a long list of rules, regulations, and judicial processes. There are too many to list, and each school has its own specific rules and regulations (you can check them out online), but the following are major common themes:

- **ZERO TOLERANCE:** There's no room for jokes anymore. When it comes to safety, zero tolerance is the rule. Lighthearted jokes about bombs are not looked at as funny. A frustrated roommate who talks about wanting to "kill" someone is greeted with a knock on the door from the police.
- **STUDENT RIGHTS:** FERPA and HIPAA mean parents need a student's permission to get school records and medical records. You might be helping pay the bill, but that and fifty dollars will only get you a sweatshirt with the school's mascot.
- **CRIME MUST BE REPORTED:** When you were in school, institutions could hide the bad things that happened on campus and handle it internally. Then came the Jeanne Clery Disclosure of Campus Security Policy and Campus Crime Statistics Act in 1990. Also known as the Campus Security Act, this law requires colleges and universities across the United States to disclose information about crime on and around their campuses. Because the law is tied to participation in federal student financial aid programs, it applies to most institutions of higher education, both public and private.
- **CAMPUSES HAVE GONE DRY:** The term *dry campus* mean the campus is alcohol free (but don't let that fool you). Students who drink and get caught can be expelled. Students who drink and drive with a .08 BAC can be arrested. Parents who buy alcohol for

the students can be arrested and go to jail (parents who drop off alcohol can go to jail). Mandatory alcohol education for students is now often part of college life. When it comes to getting busted, some schools notify Mom or Dad if there's an alcohol offense. Others just keep it between the school and the student. Many first-year students are now required to live on campus, because being on campus can be an integral part of student engagement.

- **VIRGIN VAULTS HAVE CLOSED (SOME, NOT ALL):** There used to be a time when men and women lived in separate buildings. The women's residence halls used to have nicknames like "Virgin Vault." Men weren't even allowed inside. Today men and women don't just live in the same buildings, but they also share hallways, bathrooms, and even bedrooms (new coed living has started). Visiting hours have become far more liberal. Visitors spending the night can be the norm.

RULES CHANGE

In 2009 Tufts University made it official—having sex while a roommate is present in the room is now officially against the rules.

- **ATHLETES NEED TO PERFORM:** The NCAA has created a long list of rules for students and coaches to follow. Students must take classes that put them on a graduation track in order to participate in athletics. If you have a student athlete, make sure he or she knows all the rules. Breaking rules can mean more than losing a spot on the team (we're talking about losing scholarships and/or getting probation).

- **CRIME DOESN'T PAY:** Students who are convicted of drug violations and other crimes can be refused financial aid.
- **SAFE SEX OR NO SEX:** Safe sex or no sex is the rule. The rule: if your child can't talk about HIV, herpes, genital warts, chlamydia, and the rest of the STDs with his or her partner, your child should not be having sex with that person.
- **SMOKERS OUT IN THE COLD:** There used to be a time when smokers were common. Now some schools forbid it altogether. The ones where students can smoke don't allow students to stand less than fifteen to twenty feet in front of the doorway when doing so.
- **HAZING:** Schools are vigilant about stopping hazing by any organization. Athletics, Greeks, and other organizations are constantly being suspended or having their charters revoked. See part 2, Tip #14 for the definition of hazing.

HAZING FACT

"According to the law, a person can commit a hazing offense not only by engaging in a hazing activity, but also by soliciting, directing, encouraging, aiding, or attempting to aid another in hazing; by intentionally, knowingly, or recklessly allowing hazing to occur; or by failing to report in writing to the dean of students firsthand knowledge that a hazing incident is planned or has occurred. The fact that a person consented to or acquiesced in a hazing activity is not a defense to prosecution for hazing under the law."

—Source: University of Texas at Austin

The trend over the past thirty years has been to protect students by whatever means possible. Every time a student is hurt or injured, there are parents who rally to make sure this never happens again.

#7 THE NEWS HAS CHANGED

- Headline #1: Serious violent crime levels have declined since 1993.
- Headline #2: Violent crime rates declined for both males and females since 1994.

Funny how the most positive headlines don't always make the news. The reality is that how we get the news, the amount of news we have access to, and how we filter the news we get have all changed dramatically. It used to be that news would happen on one day, and then the next day we would read about it. There would be local news and national news. There was no way for a parent to know what was happening on or near campus.

When it came to the people controlling the news, those with the ability to print, broadcast, and distribute it were the gatekeepers of it. Most of the time we had access to a few reliable sources. When we read the news, we trusted that the people reporting it were reporting facts. Seeing it in print or hearing it on the news meant it was true.

Fast-forward thirty years and everything has changed. News is reported where it happens while it's happening.

Forget waiting to get the facts—bits of information are texted, Tweeted, and broadcast on twenty-four-hour cable news, streaming local TV, network TV news, websites, personal blogs, and Facebook newsfeeds. The truth comes after the news is reported.

News is coming at us twenty-four hours a day and seven days a week. The worse the news, the more we hear about it. The good news takes more work to find (keep this in mind when you hear something bad about your student's institution).

Given the thousands of news outlets pushing out information, many times the facts are skewed or just wrong. There was a fake story that circulated about beer pong spreading herpes. Someone cited the CDC, and the story took off, causing undue panic. The problem about news today is that if you google a keyword, you can get an article from a reputable news source, a discussion thread, and a satirical blog in the first three results. Deciphering fact from fiction and reputable from reckless is something all consumers need to do today.

Parents can look for whatever news they want and find it. If you're looking for the good stories, they are out there. You just have to look beyond the not-so-happy headlines. When it comes to the headlines in your child's college experience, when you get the news that highlights all the drama, ask for a page-two or -three story. There is always good news to share. Sometimes you just have to pull it out of your child.

Thirty years ago a student went to college to get a degree
and get a job. Those who could go went to get an education. The idea of engagement was getting pinned and then
graduating with an MRS or MR. There wasn't all this
emphasis on the emotional experience and this push to get
students involved. These are new developments.

Today colleges are crowded. Enrollment is up and is
predicted to climb. In 1973, 17.1 percent of eighteen- to
twenty-four-year-olds were enrolled in a four-year college.
In 2008 the number jumped to 27.8 percent. Enrollment
in two-year colleges has seen a 4.9 percent increase to
11.8 percent over the same time period and is booming.
When it comes to the gender of college students, from
1971 to 2001, more women
were going to college in bigger
numbers. Women overtook
men in 1976 and have generally made up 55 percent of the
college population.

What a college looks like in
terms of diversity and population has changed dramatically
over the years. *The American
Freshman: Forty-Year Trends*
(Higher Education Research

The share of eighteen- to twenty-four-
year-olds attending college in the
United States hit an all-time high in
October 2008, driven by a recession-
era surge in enrollments at community colleges. Just under 11.5 million
students, or 39.6 percent of all young
adults ages eighteen to twenty-four,
were enrolled in either a two- or four-
year college in October 2008.

—Source: Pew Research Center
analysis of newly released data
from the U.S. Census Bureau

Institute) reports compelling data that paints the picture of diversity over the years:

- In 1971, white students made up 90.9 percent of full-time first-time new students. Over the years this number has declined to 76.5 percent in 2006.

- Asian Americans went from 0.6 percent of first-time full-time students in 1971 to 8.6 percent in 2006.

> There is much more of an effort made to welcome the incoming freshmen and get them quickly integrated into the community. There was no orientation for me or classes required just for freshmen to help us adjust. I think it's a great idea.
>
> —Sharla, mom of three kids

- Latino students went from 0.6 percent of first-time full-time students in 1971 to 7.3 percent in 2006.

- African Americans went from 7.5 percent of freshmen in 1971 to 12.5 percent in 1980 and then declined to 10.6 percent in 2006.

There's also been a dramatic increase in international students. College is now much more diverse (on most campuses).

When it comes to retention (students staying on campus beyond their freshman year), according to the College Board 26.6 percent of students attending public four-year colleges and 26.1 percent of students attending private four-year colleges do not return to the same college for a second year.

Some go home. Some go to other schools. Because so many students are leaving campus, schools are paying greater attention to trying to keep them on campus. Not only is doing so good for students, but it's also good for business.

One-credit college courses are being added to help students navigate the transition and engage in life on campus. Sometimes these courses are optional (strongly encourage your student to attend them). These College 101 classes often include upperclassmen or peer leaders who sit in on the class.

The focus on helping first-year students transition to college life has become so important that there are now entire conferences and associations devoted to this issue. There's the National Resource Center for the First-Year Experience and Students in Transition. There's also the National Orientation Directors Association. Many institutions are creating new positions and new offices to support first-year and transfer students. There's also been an especially strong effort to help first-year students and their parents.

This new awareness of the challenges facing first-year students is more evidence that students need extra support during this time of transition. The next trend that's starting to pick up steam is the need to support second-year students. But a student who can get comfortable with the uncomfortable first year can usually avoid a tough second one.

> TV lounges are no longer as popular, because students have cable in their rooms or are on their computers.
>
> —Elizabeth, Executive Director of Education and Outreach

#9 AMENITIES HAVE CHANGED

I love that there's a part of this book that talks about the amenities. The idea that institutions are touting amenities is a newer development. Thirty years ago, a degree was enough. Now there are multimillion-dollar recreation centers, dining facilities that rival Vegas buffets, and residence halls that can be newer and nicer than a student's home.

Organic food, elliptical machines, and state-of-the-art facilities are now part of the college package. It's about competition and amenities. New healthy food options; on-campus restaurants; and dining facilities with sushi, locally grown foods, and organic produce are things that students want.

When it comes to staying fit and working out, the recreation center (or gym) has fueled the college building boom. Millions of dollars are being poured into new facilities to offer students classes and ways to sweat it up. Some of the facilities are so modern they are beyond what any local health club can offer. Beautiful exercise equipment with built-in televisions are lined up along walls with dramatic architecture. Often there are indoor tracks, basketball courts, and volleyball courses filling the centers.

What you once knew as dorms are now residence halls (there's an important distinction). Residence halls are places where students can be part of a community. They eat together, learn together, and play together. Forget having a roommate; try having several suitemates. And as for the decor, we're talking granite counter tops, hardwood floors, new appliances, and private bathrooms (for suitemates to share).

I recently toured new residence halls at Arizona State

University and was in awe over the swimming pool, five barbecue pits next to the pool, a new workout room (with flat-screen TVs), several sitting areas (with more flat-screen TVs), a movie room, and two tanning beds. Of course, I've also been to schools that look and feel like they probably did thirty years ago, but even those have campuses that are wireless, green, and have million-dollar projects in the works to build residence halls and recreation centers.

Comfort is king. High-speed access is a must. Food so good you won't want to go home is the goal. The more comfortable a student can be on campus, the better the experience—or at least that seems to be the message communicated on the brochures, websites, and tours. Just be careful it's not *too* nice. If they get used to it, they'll never be able to live in an unfurnished apartment after graduation. And that could mean moving back home with you and living the good life one more time.

THE BIG "UNCOMFORTABLE" CHANGE

The last thirty years has been a time of dramatic change. How students communicate, work, play, study, shop, spend free time, find love, find lust, get news, pay for college, reach out for help, do laundry, and share their thoughts and ideas with the world has changed. Many of these changes have been about making life easier, better, and more comfortable.

What seems to get lost in the midst of all the changes is that no matter how much faster, better, and more beautiful it is on campus, life is uncomfortable at times. It's a natural and normal part of living. It's the uncomfortable moments in life that are gifts that lead us to the richest, most meaningful moments. A student who isn't allowed the room to feel uncomfortable never needs to learn how to get comfortable with the uncomfortable. And that means missing out on some of the most powerful life lessons.

Being so comfortable that students are shielded from the uncomfortable parts of life isn't a good thing. Never before has it been so easy for students to rely on so many people other than themselves to make life better and more comfortable. And if it's not relying on people, there are drugs, alcohol, video games, porn, gambling, and other forms of antiseptic diversion that keep them from feeling the uncomfortable parts of life. Because it's so easy to avoid the tough stuff, many students are not learning how to manage the difficult parts that come with going from teenager to adult.

A parent who understands the issues, obstacles, and changes that have taken place over the years is a parent who is likely to be more comfortable giving a child the space and time to learn how to get comfortable with the uncomfortable. In order to do so, a parent needs to know what's normal, natural, and to be expected. And that means understanding, appreciating, and accepting the stuff that is not mentioned in the brochures.

3

They Don't Mention *This* in the Brochures

Dear Harlan,

I am a freshman in college. I've been here for eight weeks. I wanted to leave home very badly. Weirdly enough, now that I'm here, I hate college. I am a very likable person and had an awesome group of friends back home. Here, I love my roommate but don't really have any other close friends. I know I'm supposed to "give it time," but I don't think I can. I just want to be back home with my best friend and boyfriend and my close friends from home. I'd rather be back in high school than here. What gives? When will it get better?

Freshman Blues

Dear Freshman,

It's getting better right now. Feel better yet?

No? How about now?

Hmmm, still no? Well, it's coming...

Here's the problem—no one ever tells students that college is 90 percent amazing and 10 percent difficult. When you don't know the 10 percent is coming, it can take up 100 percent of your time. That's when you get impatient, and that's when you want to run home or wall yourself away from campus via cell phones, texts, and other technology. You might not know it, but 65.1 percent of students admit feeling some sort of homesickness, and as many as 90 percent feel overwhelmed at least once during the year. The challenge for you is that technology has made it way too easy to hide from the uncomfortable times. Getting comfortable doesn't happen in two weeks, or even two months—it can take a good two years. Face the uncomfortable, embrace the uncomfortable, and turn the uncomfortable into a gift. Start working to get comfortable by turning to the people on campus who can help you find your place. Turn to counselors, resident assistants, upperclassmen, and professors. Then put yourself in rooms where you can meet people and share in group experiences (clubs, activities, and organizations). That's how you make friends, and that's how you find your place. And that's how

> you turn the uncomfortable into the very best and
> most comfortable time of your life.

THEY DON'T MENTION *THIS* IN THE BROCHURES

Ever notice that it rarely snows on campus in the pictures?

Take a look at the campus brochures or websites, and chances are you won't see students trudging through the snow on a cold winter day on campus (the University of Alaska is one exception). You also won't see it raining in Florida or students sweating in Arizona when school starts in August (temperatures can be 100-plus degrees). The pictures advertising college life capture the happiest, sunniest, and most wonderful moments. It's students playing, cheering, meeting people, making friends, learning, engaging, thinking, and being diverse. It's an idyllic world.

What you never see in college brochures and on campus websites are pictures of students crying hysterically, failing exams, fighting with roommates, sitting alone, feeling homesick, getting sick, or feeling hungover. These moments don't make the marketing materials.

In 2006 more than 56 percent of students applied to four or more colleges (according to HERI), the most ever. This means that even the most selective schools are now competing for the best and the brightest among the 18 million-plus college students out there. Naturally, the admissions process is about selling the college experience, making the best impression, and helping students get excited

I honestly didn't think that I would have any problems with college at all. I was looking forward to it almost all of senior year and the following summer, and I had been away from home for weeks at a time with no problems. In fact, I wanted to go to college far, far away from home (I ended up about five hours away). What surprised me was how much I missed home. Always having someone home to talk to or cook with, my favorite couch, the comfort of the routine developed over years past. The sudden change left me reeling a bit. I talked to my mom a lot. In fact, I still do. We are just really close.

—Meagan, sophomore

about life on campus. It's good marketing. There's a reason why campus tours feature the most beautiful spots on campus, the most impressive facts, the most famous alums, and tours of the newest and nicest residences and dining facilities. It's all about reflecting the very best the college has to offer. The only thing that can't be controlled is the cold, heat, snow, and rain.

And there's absolutely nothing wrong with wanting to impress prospective students. People don't go on first dates and start talking about their pimples, emotional problems, and relentless body odor—at least not people who want to go on second dates. Instead, we keep the not-so-impressive stuff out of view as long as we possibly can. Once we close the deal (i.e., when we get married), our partner can't help but see those pimples.

Once the tours end, acceptance letters go out, and school begins, students are often surprised that this idyllic world isn't 100 percent amazing. The truth is that college can be uncomfortable at times. Even the most beautiful and wonderful institutions can be challenging places to navigate once reality sets in. Days get shorter, the temperature changes, the snow (or rain) starts falling, the school work starts piling up, the roommate honeymoon ends, homesickness arrives, long-distance relationships become strained, the first round of grades hit, hangovers hit

harder, new best friends have yet to be made, high school friends are too far away, and the stuff not mentioned in the brochures starts to take its toll. Suddenly your child finds that college isn't what it was supposed to be.

Most students will have an amazing college experience 90 percent of the time. But most will also struggle at times (some more than others). It happens on all campuses. It's normal. Most of the time it's not a reflection of the institution, but rather the natural college experience. When the

uncomfortable arrives (and it will) and expectations don't meet reality, even the happiest kids on campus can get knocked off their feet. When a student looks around at other students on campus and sees that everyone else seems to be having the time of their lives (or are pretending to have the time of their lives), it will throw him or her. The reality is that making friends, passing classes, getting involved in new activities, managing time, handling romantic relationships, and juggling finances can be uncomfortable at times. Because no one ever tells students that uncomfortable is normal, most students assume they are doing something wrong when college isn't 100 percent amazing.

When a student starts to get uncomfortable, he or she starts to get impatient. As the days roll on, the stress builds, the pressure mounts, and impatience turns into desperation. This is when smart students do stupid things they regret. This is when the little annoyances of life become all-consuming. This is when a student loses perspective and confidence and the excitement wanes. This is when you are asked to fix it or make it all better.

Knowing what's normal and what's expected can be the difference between being a parent who elevates the stress and a parent who can alleviate it.

And a loving parent does whatever it takes to help his or her child feel more comfortable. It's in a parent's DNA. But before you drop everything to help, you need to know about the 10 percent rule. Knowing this rule will help you be more patient and help your college student put things in perspective.

THE 10 PERCENT RULE

Here's the rule: life is 90 percent amazing and 10 percent difficult. The 10 percent rule is that we should never allow the 10 percent difficult to consume more than 10 percent of our time. For most new students, the 10 percent difficult can happen early and often. It can often consume 100 percent of their time. If a student spends two hundred days on campus, twenty rough ones are more than enough. Anything more is too much.

There are three types of students in the world: those who run from the 10 percent difficult, those who welcome the 10 percent, and those with parents who shield them from it. The ones who run, hide, or are shielded never learn how to deal with the unavoidable adversity that's part of life. Those who learn to welcome it and how to work through it are able to thrive in any situation.

The 10 percent difficult in life is as normal and natural as breathing, but yet so many students (and their parents) fight it. The tough stuff can come in the first year, but it can also come up in the second, third, fourth, or fifth. A student who fights the difficult times becomes all-consumed. The little things get blown out of proportion. A college experience that doesn't give a student what he or she wants is intolerable. For these students, life isn't about living out a passion, but minimizing the pain. Excessive drinking and drug use can be tempting ways to medicate and deal with the 10 percent difficult if a student doesn't know it's coming or how to fix it. On the other hand, a student who accepts the 10 percent rule and knows that the uncomfortable times are a normal part of life in college can prepare for it and work through it. Working through it means asking tough questions and working to find meaningful answers. The process can be time-consuming, scary, emotional, and frustrating at times. But once a student accepts and embraces that college is supposed to be difficult sometimes, working through those times can build character, test values, and create a strong and confident adult. These moments are worth as much as if not more than any degree. I only wish that I had seen it coming when I went to college.

MY COLLEGE EXPERIENCE: I NEVER SAW IT COMING

Before I share the story of my first-year experience with you, I want to make it clear that my college experience was overwhelmingly amazing. It just so happens that my 10 percent BS came during the first few months of college life. I'm grateful to have experienced it and lucky I didn't have a cell phone, email, or the ability to stay more connected to my family, friends, and long-distance girlfriend. If so, I don't know if I would have been able to get to know myself so well and grow up so fast.

My college experience started when I was ten years old. I was in the backseat when we dropped my oldest brother off on the campus of Indiana University in Bloomington, Indiana. As we drove back home, my mom said, "I'll only cry to Indianapolis." As she puts it, "I sobbed to Martinsville, I cried to Indianapolis. And I whimpered all the way to Chicago." Three years later, my other brother went off to begin his college experience. He drove himself to campus and moved right into the fraternity house.

Five years later, my own college experience began. As the car rolled down the driveway, my stomach rolled too. I was anxious, excited, nervous, sad, and sick to my stomach. I knew this was the next step in my life, but to me it felt more like I was being pushed. Life was good at home. I had friends, a girlfriend, and people who liked me. When it came to researching my college decision, I didn't do a lot of it. I knew I wanted a big school experience, but didn't do enough research to know why. I decided to attend the University of Wisconsin in Madison. UW–Madison had a great reputation, and I thought it might be a good fit (whatever a good fit is for someone who doesn't know what it means to find a good fit).

What could go wrong?

After two and a half hours, we arrived on campus. My parents and brother stayed long enough to help move me in, not long enough to embarrass me. They said their good-byes and drove back to Chicago.

I watched their car leave and felt so incredibly alone. I had no cell phone to call them. There was no email to write, no text to send. I was on my own.

I headed up to my room to hang out with my roommate for the first time. We had talked on the phone once or twice to discuss what each of us would bring. He was relaxed about everything. The fact that he was so relaxed made me even more anxious.

We talked for a few minutes. He said his number-one goal was to not go into rehab like his older brother. Minutes later, he reached into his backpack and pulled out some sort of shrubbery. I wasn't familiar with this particular shrub. He offered me a hit. I told him I was full (I didn't know what else to say). The next week, he moved out. He wanted to be with someone who partied (not that this would help his goal of not going into rehab).

This wasn't the way things were supposed to be with my roommate. My roommate was supposed to be a best friend. He was supposed to be standing at my wedding. He wasn't supposed to move out after one week in college.

Not knowing anyone on campus and not having many options in terms of friends, I was left to make the most of the people on my floor. The people in my hall became my "friends." Even if they were the biggest a-holes in the world, they became new friends.

After a few weeks, I started hanging out with some of my new friends. When most of my friends decided to rush a fraternity, I decided to rush too. A few weeks later, rush ended and they all got bids (invitations to join)—everyone but me. The next day I was literally asked to leave the room when my "new friends" hung out, because I couldn't be with them while they discussed pledge secrets. They had fraternity events, date parties, and rituals that put me on the outside looking in.

I called my parents once a week. Usually we talked on Sunday nights, but there wasn't a firm time (my mom didn't want there to be a firm time, because if I didn't call she would think there was a problem). Occasionally we would talk more often, but mostly it was a weekly conversation. Long-distance calls were expensive. Finding privacy to talk was a challenge.

In academics I found relief from the constant social jockeying for position. In the classroom I knew my place. I knew my role. I didn't have to worry about talking to people, because part of the classroom experience was talking. I managed to excel in the classroom. In fact, my education was the best part of my experience. It was everything outside the classroom that was uncomfortable.

But in college, class is just a few hours a day at most. Taking 15 hours of classes leaves 153 hours a week to kill. Subtract 7 hours of sleep a night and that's 129 hours of time to fill. That's a lot of time to be uncomfortable.

No one told me it would be lonely at times. No one told me it would be so emotional. I didn't find my place at UW–Madison. In fact, I never felt more out of place. What was so frustrating was that all this was happening at a university where everyone was having the time of their lives. In my mind, I had to be defective, because the university was amazing and everyone else seemed so happy. It had to be me!

I had thought college was just supposed to be this magical, amazing experience. It was like being on a moving walkway—it was just supposed to be great. I expected college to be like high school, only with more freedom.

I expected to magically find friends, find my place, feel happy, and feel at home. Here's what no one told me:

- I had no idea what was normal and to be expected emotionally.
- I had no idea that homesickness was normal.
- I had no idea that not all roommates become great friends.
- I didn't know it would take time to find my place.
- I didn't know I would have to work to find my place.
- I didn't know I would have to take risks to find my place.
- I thought I would hook up more.
- I thought I would get into a fraternity.
- I thought my long-distance relationship would work.
- I didn't think it would be so cold.
- I didn't know I would get depressed at times.
- I didn't realize it would be difficult at times.

If only I had known this was normal, I wouldn't have spent so much time beating myself up emotionally. If only I knew to be more patient, I could have eased up the pressure on myself. If only I knew how to find my place, I could have taken action instead of being paralyzed with fear.

As my freshman experience got heavier, the only thing that lifted my spirits was my long-distance girlfriend. Her name was Alexis (still is Alexis). She was my high school sweetheart and she was still in high school. I loved her more than I loved myself (not hard considering I barely liked myself). I had no idea why she was so in love with me, but I didn't want to ask, because I was afraid she might think about it and break up with me. It was first love for both of us, and it was intense as it could be.

She visited me on campus once. We talked several times a week, but not for too long (it was too expensive). As my first semester dragged on, my long-distance relationship became heavier and harder to maintain. She was having the time of her life as a senior in high school. I was a bummer. Our relationship couldn't sustain the weight of my first-year transition. After a few months of us trying to make it work, Alexis's dad had a heart-to-heart conversation with her. He compared our relationship to a dying puppy, urging Alexis to shoot the puppy. Listening to her father's wise advice, Alexis called me on the phone. Then she shot the puppy. It was over.

After crying over this relationship, a weight lifted. I realized that my girlfriend wasn't always going to be there to make me happy. The guys on my floor weren't always going to be there to make me happy. My loving parents and older brothers weren't always going to be there to make me happy. I was the only one who was always going to be there for me. I was the one who had to make me happy. It was the first time in college that I realized that I was in charge of me. And this is when I took charge and college life changed for me. And what happened next? I transferred.

For me, transferring wasn't about giving up or quitting. It was about doing my first-year experience over again.

Even though my second semester in college was far better than the first, I still had lingering feelings from the rough start. I wanted a "do over."

Both of my brothers had attended Indiana University, and it was always a comfortable place (I didn't even realize why it was so appealing at the time). I thought I knew what I could expect there, because I was familiar with the campus. My parents supported my decision (they had never seen me so sad and wanted me to be happy). The next fall, I drove myself to Indiana and moved myself in. I didn't call this my sophomore year—I called it my second freshman year.

Amazingly, about 90 percent of the problems I had dealt with my first freshman year were waiting for me in my second freshman year—only the second time around I knew the secret. I knew what was coming. Instead of letting the 10 percent take up 100 percent of my time like it had during my first freshman year, I got involved on campus. I gave my roommate permission to not be my best friend. I approached my professors and gave them permission to know that I didn't know the answer. I was patient. I was kinder to myself. I put myself in rooms where I didn't know people. I surrounded myself with the type of people I wanted to get to know. I put myself in the right places to do the things I wanted to do. I knew what college was about. I knew how to win.

And that's how I learned how to become the happiest kid on campus.

WHEN PARENTS ARE UNCOMFORTABLE

Helping a student get comfortable with the uncomfortable is different for every parent. But until you get comfortable with the uncomfortable, it will be impossible for you to allow your child to have the freedom to work

THE TWENTY-FOUR-HOUR RULE

Most problems clear up in twenty-four hours. Before calling someone on campus or fixing a problem, give it twenty-four hours.

through these situations and grow. The challenge is that parents can't help but want to make life as comfortable as possible for their children. You worry. I worry too. When a kid gets uncomfortable, the knee-jerk reaction is to want to make it all better. That tends to mean fixing. Waiting for them to fix it takes too much time. Plus, it's hard to sleep at night. It's more efficient for you to get it done. But the only reason you know how to fix it is because you've been through so much in your life. This is what parents need to keep in mind when they feel compelled to fix it. This is their time to go through the things that will help them learn how to take care of themselves. Fixing it just means keeping them from learning how to take care of themselves. It also sends a message that you don't think they can do it. Here are two examples of loving parents with great intentions who got a little too involved (in my opinion):

MOM AND DAD WILL SAVE YOU #1

I was boarding an airplane and heading to a college event when I overheard a conversation between two women. A mom was telling a coworker how she had to do homework during the three-and-a-half-hour flight from Dallas to Boston. She explained that her daughter (a senior in high school) was sick and had missed a lot of school. She had gotten very behind and her mom offered to help. The homework was just "busy" work.

"It's not like I'm doing it for her," she said, as if justifying something she knew was wrong.

The mom had the study guide and was going to fill in the blanks. Then her daughter would use the guide with the answers to study. I chuckled to myself, imagining the daughter sending her mom study guides and papers in college. Then I imagined her in the professional world sending spreadsheets with the note, "Need to get this done or WE could get fired. Not cutting corners on this one!"

I wanted to ask the woman, "Why not have your daughter talk to her teacher and work out an arrangement?" Teachers can be sympathetic when it comes to dealing with medical issues. Why not help teach her daughter how to talk to her teachers now? Then once she gets to college she will already know how to help herself in the classroom. This loving mom had the best of intentions, but dealing with adversity and struggling with deadlines is part of life—not just high school. Considering that 80 percent of students feel stressed out in college, maybe if more students had more opportunities to learn how to manage the stress on their own in high school they'd be better equipped to handle it in college.

MOM AND DAD WILL SAVE YOU #2

I was recently presenting at a conference at the University of Notre Dame; there were

students from all over the Midwest in attendance. One of the RAs (resident assistants) shared a story about a resident on her floor. This particular resident was in her room when her roommate came home with a romantic partner. The roommate proceeded to have sex in the bed above the roommate. When the roommate in the bottom bunk heard what was happening, she did what anyone in this situation would do—she froze. After a few minutes, she did something else that anyone would do in this situation—she called her mom.

I'm imagining the conversation went something like this:

[Phone rings]

MOM: Hi, Sweetie! How are you?

DAUGHTER (whispering): Not so good.
My roommate is having sex on top of me.
What should I do? I need your help!"

MOM: I'll be right there...

Four and a half hours later, the RA heard a knock on her door. It was the mom. "My daughter called and told me her roommate was having sex. I was in the neighborhood and I want my daughter out of this room. NOW!" demanded Mom.

The next morning, her daughter was moved out of the room into a single.

I feel bad for this girl. Not because she was in the room while her roommate was having sex. I feel bad because she never had the opportunity to deal with it on her own. She was robbed of a gift. I'll offer some tips about how a student can manage these kinds of situations in the second half of the book (part 2, Tip #9)—but the point is that the student is the one who should have handled this situation. It would be as simple as saying something the next day about how uncomfortable this made her. They could have worked out a system. But instead, this girl was the victim—and Mom was the big hero. Mom took all the power instead of empowering her daughter. I understand why this happens.

Mom was uncomfortable, and her knee-jerk reaction was to want to make everything better. Her intentions were good and loving, but ultimately she robbed her daughter of a golden opportunity to grow and learn. This situation could have been a gift. But this student was put in an uncomfortable situation,

THE UNCOMFORTABLE RULE IN ACTION

Want to know how to help your student deal with ANY uncomfortable roommate situation? Turn to Tip #9, page 265.

and Mom was too uncomfortable to let her daughter try to fix it. For her, the precedent has been set. When things are uncomfortable, forget learning how to get comfortable with the uncomfortable. Call Mom and Dad. They'll fix it. They will make everything better.

GIVING YOUR STUDENT PERMISSION

Knowing that college can be uncomfortable at times doesn't mean all parents can accept this fact or allow their children to be uncomfortable. A lot of parents find themselves in uncomfortable denial. This is a place where parents can't stand to see a child uncomfort-

THINGS SOME PARENTS DO TO KEEP THEIR COLLEGE KIDS COMFORTABLE

· Lying to protect students from judicial reviews

· Doing their homework and writing papers

· Threatening lawsuits on a regular basis

· Calling employers to find out job information

· Calling kids' roommates to resolve situations

· Calling teachers when a student is sick

· Demanding roommate changes because they don't want their kids to live with gay roommates, roommates of different religions, roommates of a different race, or roommates who have different behaviors

· Driving to campus and doing laundry on a regular basis

able and will do whatever it takes to make things better. But in order to *really* give a kid room to work through uncomfortable situations, parents need to accept the 10 percent rule. This means patiently listening, guiding their kids when they need guidance, and intervening only if it's absolutely necessary. Just remember that college is 90 percent

Parents never cease to amaze me at the lengths that they go to "fix" their students' problems. I have lost count of the times that I have been threatened with litigation. I have had parents treat their students' roommates poorly, even going as far as threatening them with physical harm. I've seen parents cry, scream, and throw things. I can't tell you how many times students have apologized for their parents' behavior.

—Residence life professional, ten-plus years in higher education

amazing—it's just that kids need time to work through the 10 percent.

Here's an example of a father stuck in denial. A sophomore in college called her parents to vent. Her mom picked up and listened to her daughter vent. Mom wasn't trying to fix the problem; she was giving her daughter permission to be uncomfortable and work through it. Well, one day her dad picked up the phone and the daughter started to vent. Dad responded with, "How could you be having a bad time? I've been on campus and that school is beautiful. I went to college there too! What's the problem?" While his response seemed innocent enough, it really upset his daughter. What this translated to was something to the effect of "Campus is perfect. Therefore, you're wrong. I know because I was there too. The problem must be you." In other words, it was a parent who refused to give a student permission to be uncomfortable. And it's not just dads; there are plenty of moms who do this too.

There's no question that it's really hard to hear that someone you love is having a hard time—especially a child. A lot of parents don't want to hear it. They want to shut it down. They can't understand where it's coming from. But giving someone permission to be uncomfortable means not getting defensive, not passing blame or shutting them down. There's no one to blame when this is the natural and normal experience.

If you struggle to allow your child to be uncomfortable, think of it this way:

- A student who learns how to get comfortable with the uncomfortable when dealing with a challenging professor is a student who will gain the life skills to manage a difficult boss.
- A student who learns how to get comfortable with an uncomfortable situation with a classmate will gain the life skills to manage relationships with coworkers and peers.
- A student who can learn how to get comfortable with an uncomfortable situation with a roommate will gain the life skills to be a good roommate to his/her spouse.
- A student who can get comfortable with the uncomfortable and work through the bureaucracy of an institution and find answers can gain the life skills to create change and be a leader.

When it comes to the struggling part of the college experience, there are so many people who can help your child navigate the tough stuff if she seeks them out. There are professors,

My children are extremely resourceful and were able to cope with the transition without experiencing any issues.

—Mother of sophomore son and senior daughter

tutors, mentors, orientation leaders, counselors, academic advisers, therapists, doctors, nutritionists, alcohol educators, resident advisers, resident directors, gay/lesbian/ bisexual allies, law enforcement, spiritual leaders, crisis counselors, the dean of students, the chairs of the departments, the vice president, the president, and people participating and advising groups and organizations on campus. Help is available down the halls, across campus, on the other side of town, online, or a phone call away. Students today are enveloped with support and resources to help them get comfortable with the uncomfortable. The help is there. Students just sometimes need help to remember and a push to reach out.

I love when a student calls for an appointment and stops in and says, "My mom or dad said I should talk to you." Shows that the student and parents are engaging, but the parents are urging the student to take action for themselves.

—Professional, twenty-plus years working in the dean of students office

All that said, there are times when a parent needs to intervene, but more times than not, a student can fix it if he or she knows it's coming and knows who to talk to get help. If your child isn't sleeping, has poor grades, isn't showing an interest in things he or she loved, is skipping class, is exhibiting signs of depression (see Tip #23, page 550), or is in immediate danger, that's time to intervene. If you're ever unsure of when you need to take action, contact a professional on campus and ask for advice. You can share your concerns in the forums I've set up on my website and on Facebook.

Allowing a student to be uncomfortable isn't cruel and

She was lonely, scared, unprepared for a college workload (even though she was a good student going to a better school), dealing with expectations, living in a small space with a roommate, dealing with other people's habits, feelings, etc. She failed all her classes the first semester and half of the second semester. We were living and dying on an hourly basis with hysterical phone calls when things went wrong. The only thing that saved us was the fact that we decided to stay calm, not overreact, and encourage her to focus.

—Mom of college junior

unusual; it's necessary for a student to learn to grow up. The challenge is that the New College Parent has never been more aware of and more in touch with students dealing with uncomfortable situations. Twenty years ago, parents didn't have an all-access pass. Students didn't call parents on their cell phones from the bunk below a roommate having sex. Knowing so much puts parents in an entirely new position. You must decide what to say, when to say it, how to react, and where to direct them. You are a player in the drama. Often you are living it and hearing about it in real time. Once the call is made, your daily life consists of wondering if a problem has been solved. Just ask them to do you one favor—let you know when the situation is fixed so that you can move on too.

THE "OVERWHELMING" FACTS OF COLLEGE LIFE

According to a study by the American College Health Association:

- 43.3 percent of male students expressed feeling overwhelmed by all they had to do in the past two weeks

- 59.1 percent of female students expressed feeling overwhelmed by all they had to do in the past two weeks
- 77.4 percent of male students reported that they felt overwhelmed by all they had to do any time within the last twelve months
- 91.9 percent of female students reported that they felt overwhelmed by all they had to do any time within the last twelve months

When I look at these numbers, I see millions of students struggling to find answers and millions of parents wanting to do all they can to help. The irony is that the answer is to know that struggling is part of the experience. If everyone can expect it, plan for it, and embrace it when it shows its ugly face, it won't eat up so much time and energy. In fact, the 10 percent difficult will only take up 10 percent of our time. This leaves 90 percent to enjoy life.

P.S. If only more people in the world could live by the 10 percent rule, the world would be a much happier and more forgiving place.

More Information Than Any Parent Should Ever Want or Need...

WARNING!!!

What you are about to read in this chapter can make you the most informed and the most annoying overly involved parent on the planet. This chapter will enable you to know more than you need to know about life on campus. The information is here when you need it, should you need it. Please do not abuse it.

Parental discretion is advised.

Hi Harlan,

I'm looking for advice on what else to tell my daughter. She is in her first year of college. The first day in class, she shared textbooks with a young man who has since decided to pursue her. My daughter isn't used to this sort of attention and has been dodging him, though it is difficult since he is in three of her classes. When she asked me for advice, I suggested she be straight with him and say something like, "Look, I get the feeling that you are hoping a relationship will develop here, but it won't, and you are making me uncomfortable with all of this attention." Is there more I should be saying?

Helpful Mom

Hi Helpful Mom,

First of all, he might be interested in her textbooks (those things are expensive). Next I would tell her to give him permission to pursue her. There are going to be a lot of guys who like her and want to give her attention. If he asks her out, she can politely tell him that she appreciates his being so honest but she's focusing on being a student and isn't looking to date right now. If he continues, she can tell him that it's making her uncomfortable and she would appreciate his listening. If he still won't listen, then she can get campus safety involved. Your daughter will be pursued by lots of men. She just might have to get used to it.

FOR MORE DATING ADVICE, SEE TIP #18 IN PART 2

TAPPING INTO THE FLOW OF INFORMATION

Here's something you'll enjoy hearing: Did you know that 61.2 percent of college men and 59.8 percent of college women eat one to two servings of vegetables a day? But wait—it gets even better. A total of 25.9 percent of college men and 29.3 percent of college women eat three to four servings a day. A reported 4.8 percent of men and 5.2 percent of women eat five or more servings of veggies a day. That's a lot of vegetables—some students might be eating too many vegetables (and all you hear about are students drinking too much).

This section is not just about broadening your knowledge of vegetable consumption among college students; it's about helping you find more information than you will ever possibly want or need to know about life on campus. The best part—you will not have to rely on your son or daughter to get any of it.

About that warning at the top of page 93. Given the changes over the past thirty years, you're already more connected to your child in more ways than any parent before you. Being so connected means you want to be knowledgeable enough to connect your child to resources, support services, and help should your child need it. The risk in knowing so much is that you might want to share everything you know. You might want to call, email, text, and share all this good information with your student. Doing this will make you overly involved and completely irritating. It will probably cause your child to stop listening to you or to avoid you. Then you'll blame it on me.

To avoid being annoying, irritating, and overly involved, I would recommend sharing only as much information as your child wants you to share. Check with your son or daughter and ask before sharing. If you pass along email or text messages, check to make sure you haven't crossed the line. This is the easiest way to gauge if you're being too loving (i.e., annoying).

THE FLOW OF INFORMATION HAS CHANGED

Throughout your child's academic life, information has been coming to you from all directions. Between parent-teacher conferences, college nights, PTA meetings, athletic events, concerts, shows, dances, performances, permission slips, field trips, emails, phone calls home, and rides to and from school, you are getting the latest information. If your kid is sick at home or misses class, the school will call. Then there's all the news you get from your student while sharing meals, being in the same room, and needing your permission or money to do things. Information and conversations are all around you—the idea of having to actively seek out information instead of having it delivered to you is a new idea.

The good news is that you have access to more information than you will want or need. The not-so-good news is that it's easy to let all the information consume you if you don't have a balanced life (more on that in the next chapter).

Being informed and balanced should help you be a better resource should your child need support or help connecting to the right people on campus. (A bonus—when you read in the campus online newspaper that 350 students were arrested for underage drinking over the weekend you can text your child, "Anything you need to tell us?") Between the college websites, online newspapers, Facebook pages, Twitter feeds, blogs, forums, newsletters, interest groups, parent groups, and the occasional campus visit, you can know more than your son or daughter knows about life on campus. Just be careful not to use the information to become too involved.

The best way to use the information in this chapter is to know what's available and how to access it. I would recommend becoming familiar with the campus website, taking a walking tour of the campus, locating parent resources, signing up for a Facebook account, and messing around on Twitter. Knowing the support available on campus will help you rest easy. Also, finding a community of parents can help you find support when you need answers and someone else to lean on.

To make the technology portion of this chapter as easy and helpful as possible, I've set up a website devoted to helping you navigate the suggestions mentioned in the following pages. Please visit *The Happiest Kid on Campus* website at www.HappiestKidonCampus.com. On the site you'll find discussions, links mentioned in the book, video updates, and the latest information about what's changed since this book went to print.

This chapter is designed to give you more information than you will ever need to know about how to get more information than you will ever need to know. Let me explain. What's happened over the past ten years is that parents have more access to more information. If you're curious about the classes being offered on campus, you can browse the campus catalog of classes. If you're concerned about rules and regulations, you can read the entire student code of conduct on most campus websites. If you need to find out who are the best resources to help your child fix a problem, you can do a search and find the right people in the right places. The campus website is an encyclopedia of information that can be helpful to you and your child. Then there are social networking sites, third-party websites, college parents' forums, and resources to find support for anything and everything you or your child is dealing with. To help you see just how much is available, I've broken it all down for you.

1. COLLEGE NEWSPAPERS, LOCAL NEWSPAPERS, BLOGS, MAGAZINES, AND OTHER PUBLICATIONS

Get ready to wake up in the morning, sip your morning cup of coffee (or tea), eat a doughnut (you really should eat something that's better for you), and browse the latest college news on the computer, a cell phone, or video tablet (they are coming). Most college newspapers make it extremely easy to get the news online. Some even send you daily headlines and breaking news if you pass along an email address. A bonus that comes with reading the campus newspaper—you can also read if your student makes the police blotter.

If your child attends a smaller college that has a newspaper that publishes once a month or every other week, you should make reading the local newspaper part of your routine. Most local newspapers have a campus beat that can give you the latest and greatest information. And most local newspapers now have tools in place to make it as easy as possible to read up on the latest information and not have to click a bunch of buttons. Things like text-based services, automated email distribution, Twitter feeds, RSS feeds, and other gizmos can make it so you don't even have to visit the website to get the latest information.

In addition to the local daily and college newspapers, be

sure to check out the weekly alternative papers. You can locate the newspaper by searching the campus website, searching keywords on Google or Bing, and visiting Yahoo (they have a great section). The alternative weeklies can get a little edgy, so cover your eyes.

Once you're done reading the local news, check out the national news, online magazines, and blogs. I'm a fan of the education sections in *USA Today*, the *New York Times*, the *Washington Post*, *U.S.News & World Report*, the *Wall Street Journal Classroom Edition*, and many more. Again, you can use Google to search for all of these papers, and I'll include a list on www.HappiestKidonCampus.com.

Another great way to get the latest news, blogs, videos, and content delivered to you is to set up a Google Alert. This is a free service that gives you headlines from newspapers around the world based on keywords. Just go to www.Google.com/alerts. You'll be asked to enter keywords, your email address, the frequency you want headlines delivered, and a few other things. I'd suggest including the name of the institution or the name of the city as a keyword. Google Alerts can get you news, magazines, journals, blogs, and relevant videos having to do with your child's school or other college-related topics.

2. VISIT THE CAMPUS WEBSITE

The campus website is loaded. Dive in and get lost in the news, stories, and links leading to information about arts, culture, athletics, research, academics, community events, forums, publications, deadlines, bios, and much more. Watch videos from student reporters, read stories from first-year bloggers, participate in forums with other parents, and see where the links take you. Check out links for new students, current students, faculty, and staff.

Some key areas to explore:

- **STUDENT LIFE AREAS:** Find links to student orga-nizations and clubs (some schools boast hundreds of activities); professional or academic organizations; com-muter resources; cultural, religious, special interest, or residence hall organizations; groups for the arts, media and publications; and honors organizations. Discover how any student can start a club by taking a few steps. Investigate the Greek life section (Tip #14) if your student is thinking about joining a fraternity or sorority. Read staff bios of the campus support team and advisers who are running the groups.

- **ACADEMIC AREAS:** Visit the undergraduate studies area, degree programs, graduate studies, international programs, and online learning. Browse the list of majors. Explore the schools within the college and uni-versity (the business school, the school of journalism, the school of education, etc.). Find out about the honors college. Read about internships and programs abroad, and read bios of professors. Discover scholarship opportunities and research opportunities. Hear about the free tutoring, reading labs, and support available to students. Read about the academic organizations on campus. Find out who's been honored, what's being published, and how the institution is working to support research and an engaged student population. Click around and you might even find links to Facebook pages, Twitter accounts, and live-recorded lectures on YouTube Edu (www.YouTube.com/edu) or iTunes U (www.iTunesU.com)

- **CALANDAR OF EVENTS PAGE:** See what events are scheduled for parents' weekend (chances are your student will not even know). See the schedule of upcoming shows, lectures, and other activities (students love to say that nothing happens on campus, but there's a lot going on).
- **COUNSELING CENTER AND HEALTH SERVICES LINKS:** Read the bios of the therapists, counselors, and staff. See if there are hotlines, special services, and other resources that might be helpful should your student need a little direction or support.
- **CAMPUS HOUSING SITE:** Check out the staff, support, activities, leadership opportunities, and amenities. Look at the food services menu (you'll see there is "something" to eat). When your student tells you the food is terrible, you can say, "What about that new organic salad bar with locally produced vegetables and produce?"

3. WALK THE CAMPUS (BAREFOOT, IF POSSIBLE)

There's nothing like seeing it, feeling it, hearing it, touching it, smelling it, and walking it. Walk the footpaths (if they have them). Check out the student center, visit the residence halls, walk from the halls to the

> **ATTENTION VISITING PARENTS**
>
> SEE Tip #12 VISITING—Seeing It All, Hearing It All, and Smelling It All. There you'll find much more detailed information regarding the campus visit.

academic buildings. See the academic buildings. Step inside the classroom. Visit the library. Investigate the dining halls. Make sure to check out the recreational center (but don't work out while wearing black socks and sneakers).

Make sure to drop by the student union or campus center. When you go to the student center, you'll find banners celebrating special weeks of awareness and events sponsored by student organizations. Stop at the kiosks and read the leaflets and advertisements. Take a peek at the fraternity and sorority houses. Walk around the main downtown area and drive down the commercial streets to see what stores are available. And you must walk the big box stores. They are more popular than the student union.

Times to visit:

- **DURING ORIENTATION:** Take advantage of all orientations or any parent orientation programs. This is the ideal time to meet people and get a tour of the places your student will be spending so much of his or her time. Introduce yourself to the right people and other parents. If your student is uncomfortable or you don't want to ask in front of the group, you can always find a moment to talk to the people with the answers.

- **DURING PARENTS' WEEKEND:** Even if your student discourages you from attending, go. It's a time to see your student and the people who have supplied so much of the drama (feel free to bring statues and hand out awards for best actors and actresses on campus). See your student's friends. Meet a new boyfriend or girlfriend. Talk to other parents and make some connections. While it's not cool to "friend" your kid's Facebook friends, you can become Facebook friends with other parents. If you wait too long to make hotel reservations (if traveling), consider staying a town or two over. You can usually find a hotel thirty minutes away. Don't be surprised if your student wants to stay in the room to get away from campus. It's a nice break.
- **SPORTS WEEKEND:** It's one of the perks of being a parent. Just be careful not to sit in the student section and hog the beer pong table after the game.
- **A NORMAL DAY:** See the real world on a regular day. There's nothing like seeing campus on a typical class day—without the fans, hordes of parents, and fanfare that are part of special weekends on campus. The best way to approach this is to come in on a Thursday or stay a day later after a weekend visit. If your child has classes, you can at least drive through campus or take a walk (call it exercise) and get a feel for what's it's like

on campus. You can even get a sense of the energy by coming in on a Thursday and walking campus early Friday morning. If you live close to campus, see if you can take your son or daughter out to dinner and get there in the early afternoon. If you're picking your child up, get there early and take some time to explore. Make sure you go to the bookstore and buy your kid a gift. This way, if a friend of your child spots you on campus, it won't look like you were invading anyone's space. You were just buying a present—how loving of you!

4. GET YOUR FACEBOOK ON

WARNING: DO NOT FRIEND-REQUEST YOUR STUDENT (UNTIL YOU READ TIP #7 IN PART 2)

If you're not already on Facebook, you're likely thinking, "Ehhh, it's not for me." But think of Facebook like you think about your cell phone or television. Saying, "Ehhh, it's not for me," means saying that having access to one of the most helpful tools available is not for you.

While Facebook might not have been relevant in your life before this moment, having a child go to college makes it extremely relevant. This isn't about keeping tabs on your kid so you can scream GOTCHA! It's about taking advantage of a tool that will enable you to get information about much more than the school and to connect with other parents.

Just to be clear—this section of the book is not about

connecting with your student and having a friendship on Facebook. Part 2, Tip #7 will get into the details of how to approach this sensitive topic (Mom! You are forbidden to be on Facebook!). This section is about becoming familiar with Facebook so that you know why it's important and how it can help you be informed. If your son or daughter catches you reading about Facebook and forbids you to join, tell your kid to learn how to use the privacy settings. Not allowing a parent to participate in Facebook is like your child forbidding you from going to the mall. You can go—just don't hang out with your kids.

I should mention, if you're already on Facebook, please consider being a community leader on *The Happiest Kid on Campus* Facebook fan page (www.Facebook.com/ HappiestKidonCampus). I'm looking for parents who know their way around Facebook to help other parents get comfortable on Facebook. Once on the fan page you'll see information on how you can become a *Happiest Kid on Campus* parent guide to show other parents around.

So, What is Facebook?

Facebook's definition of Facebook:

> *"Founded in February 2004, Facebook is a social utility that helps people communicate more efficiently with their friends, family and coworkers. The company develops technologies that facilitate the sharing of information through the social graph, the digital mapping of people's real-world*

social connections. Anyone can sign up for Facebook and interact with the people they know in a trusted environment."

My definition of Facebook:

An amazing tool that connects parents to people, interest groups, communities, and a student's college. More than 400 million people are actively engaged in this community, sharing information that matters on a regular basis.

Why is it important for a parent to be on Facebook? Being on Facebook gives you access to:

- People
- Pages
- Groups
- Events
- Applications

PEOPLE: There are more than 400 million people on Facebook with whom you can connect. You can find other friends, old friends, acquaintances, family, coworkers, neighbors, strangers, and parents of college students on your child's campus and on other campuses. The way you connect is via a "friend request." Once a friend accepts your request, you can interact in a variety of ways. You can read your friends' status updates, see their profiles, view links to news stories that your friends post, see shared photos, watch shared videos, read shared blogs, and engage in a variety of other ways. You can also send email, engage in live chats, or post public messages on someone's wall (think of a big public bulletin board). Privacy settings can be changed to limit what certain people read, view, and post on your profile. NOTE: Your student can be your friend and restrict you in what you're able to see. As a college parent, having connections to other parents going through this same experience gives you an instant support group. If your child "friends" you, you'll be able to get a sense of what's going on in his or her life on an entirely different level.

PAGES: Facebook offers businesses, bands, schools, personalities, and political figures the ability to create pages to share information. Most colleges and universities either have pages or are launching pages. An institution's page can give you access to streaming news, blogs, videos, discussions, and relevant links. Often there are discussions and opportunities to engage with other parents and people who share an interest in the school. To help connect parents

CHECK OUT THESE FACEBOOK PAGES

Look up "Texas A &M University." (www.Facebook.com/TexasA&M). Texas A&M has one of the most active college pages, with over 140,000 fans. Their Facebook page has news, discussion threads, videos from YouTube, upcoming events, photos, information for new students, "Aggie" spirit postcards, and a very active wall where visitors leave comments.

For news, check out CNN's Facebook page: www.Facebook.com/CNN. Oprah has a great page too: www .Facebook.com/OprahWinfreyShow. For fake news visit www.Facebook .com/TheOnion.

of college students, I've sent up a page for you to communicate. Visit www.Facebook.com/HappiestKidonCampus. I've also included notes to help you navigate some of the other technology out there.

GROUPS: Think of groups as you would any particular interest group. A group can be "Class of 2013" or it can be "Parents Against Tuition Hikes." Groups can be serious or silly. Most groups are public, meaning you can be a fly on the

> **WANT TO SEE A GREAT FACEBOOK GROUP?**
>
> Looking for a group page to go to get started on Facebook? Type in "Class of 2014" in the search box and see groups populated by students in the class of 2014. Click on the tabs and make sure to check out the discussion threads.

wall and observe conversations without having to participate. Groups can be three people or one million people. And you can even start your own group if you're inspired.

EVENTS: Chances are you will not be invited to many college events, but you might be invited to parent-related events via the parents association or through people you connect with on Facebook. If you are invited to an event, you can view other people who are invited. This is an easy way to find new friends and people with whom you share common interests.

APPLICATIONS: Facebook applications allow you to share pictures, share videos, play games, share blogs, take quizzes, send virtual gifts, decorate your profile, remember birthdays, and engage with other users in a variety of ways. The idea that you can see pictures of your child's social life can seem really cool. That is until you see your underage son holding a red cup at a party with a half-naked girl on his lap, find out he's attending a "Legalize Marijuana" rally, and see a video of him wrestling with his roommate after waking him up at 3:00 in the morning. That said, you might also get to see pictures from an alternative spring break mission he took to Guatemala, photos from the first-place finish in the triathlon, and pictures from the dance marathon fundraiser that he chaired.

QUICK NOTE:

JUST IN CASE YOU WERE WONDERING: I don't work for Facebook or have any ownership (although I wish I had founded it). I just think it's a valuable tool that can help you connect with your child's school.

Why should a parent be on Facebook?
- You can connect to the institution
- You can connect to other parents
- You can connect to friends, family, and your student (but read part 2, Tip #7 first)
- You can connect to media, news, and entertainment

How do you sign up for Facebook?
Visit http://www.Facebook.com. You'll just need a valid email address to sign up. And it's all free.

Once you've signed up, visit www.Facebook.com/HappiestKidonCampus and you can find information to navigate through Facebook in the notes section (see the left side of the page for the notes link).

5. PARENT TWEETING (AKA WHY YOU NEED TO BE ON TWITTER)

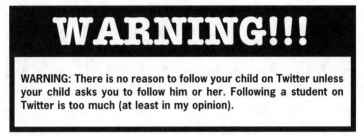

WARNING!!!

WARNING: There is no reason to follow your child on Twitter unless your child asks you to follow him or her. Following a student on Twitter is too much (at least in my opinion).

I know, I know—first I encourage you to jump on Facebook, and now I'm telling you about Twitter. I bet you want to take this book and shove it in a place inside my body that would result in my having to visit the health center to get it removed.

Some of you might be thinking, "Why should I care about Twitter? I don't care that you just took your shoes off and peed." But Twitter is not just about sharing shoes and pee.

More and more institutions and professionals on campus are using Twitter to broadcast important information and connect with students, parents, and alumni. If there is a crisis, a snow day, an important event, or breaking news happening on campus, Twitter allows you (and your student) to be informed. In fact, you can have access to information while it's happening from the people in the middle of the action. Beyond college life, leaders in industry and communication are increasingly using Twitter to listen and share with the world. It's a just a cool thing to know about.

What is Twitter?

Think of Twitter as a rapid current of fast-flowing information. It's a mechanism to broadcast what people, brands, businesses, governments, institutions, and news agencies want you to know. Once you're on Twitter, you can follow what's being broadcast, and you can share information, links to content, questions, or responses to other people's Tweets.

What is a Tweet?

A Tweet is a message limited to 140 characters. A Tweet can be about what someone is doing, what someone is reading, what someone thinks about a particular topic, or how someone feels. Tweets can contain links to newspaper articles, videos, photos, blogs, and other content. Tweets can include important, vital, and timely information. For example, when President Barack Obama announced his running mate, Twitter was one of the first places he made this announcement. When there was an uprising in Iran, a university student in Tehran was able to report on events and broadcast to the world via Twitter.

Here are some actual Tweets:

Tweets can be informative:

From @PresidentGee: president of The Ohio State University (http://Twitter.com/presidentgee)

Looking forward to talking with freshmen about leadership at today's First-Year Success program 8:45 AM Oct 26th from web

---

Ohio State Parent and Family Weekend 2009 kicks off tonight! Looking forward to meeting the parents. 7:09 AM Oct 16th from web

✻ ✻ ✻

Tweets can be newsworthy:

From @idsnews: *Indiana Daily Student* (newspaper at Indiana University) (http://Twitter.com/idsnews)

Rev. Jesse Jackson to speak at Bloomington MLK celebration http://bit.ly/4tWW35

From @USATODAYcollege (http://Twitter.com/USATODAYcollege)

10 colleges with the highest posted tuitions for 2009-10, is your school here? http://bit.ly/1xFTpq

From @USNEWSeducation (http://Twitter.com/USNEWSeducation)

10 Things You Didn't Know About College Grading: Read on for details you should know about how grading at uni.. http://bit.ly/3h1qYW

✻ ✻ ✻

Tweets can be delicious:

From @Stanford: Stanford University (http://Twitter.com/stanford)

Stanford: home to some of the best college food. I didn't know our chefs train in Paris! http://bit.ly/1Gtlwj3:33 PM Oct 16th

✻ ✻ ✻

Tweets can also be profound (or just funny):

From @VeryShortstory (http://Twitter.com/VeryShortstory)

I woke up to a quiet house and found a domino on the other side of the bed, the one-blank. Marla was giving notice; I was on my own now.

What else does a parent need to know about Twitter?

Twitter is unique because you don't need a computer or web browser to send and read messages. You can broadcast to the world and receive information via text messaging on your cell phone. SMS is a valuable way of communicating that means not having to depend on the Internet and cell phone calls to send and receive information. This is one reason that Twitter is emerging as a method of communication in case of emergencies.

How does Twitter work?

Sign up for a free account at http://Twitter.com.

Select a user name. Make it short and sweet.

Once you have a user name, you are ready to search. When using the search function, consider doing two searches. One that includes a space between the name of the school and the word *college* or *university* and one without (i.e., *Indiana University* and *IndianaUniversity*).

How accurate is the information in Twitter feeds?

Like anything where information is flowing so fast, it's hard to always know that what you're reading is in fact true. Many healthy celebrities have woken up from a long night's sleep having supposedly died on Twitter.

It's always suggested to make sure information from random people is substantiated.

6. CONNECT WITH PARENT GROUPS AND ASSOCIATIONS

Most colleges and universities have an office of parent programs. This office works as a central point to inform, support, and help answer parents'

"Harlan, all you've done is confuse me and make me want nothing to do with Twitter. How can I get a better handle on this?"

For a step-by-step demonstration, visit www.HappiestKidonCampus. I have set up links to how-to videos to help you get familiar with Twitter. I've also set up lists for you to follow to make this as easy as possible for you. Once you arrive on the site, I will direct you to the places to make this as simple as possible.

questions. Often there are parents' groups or associations. These groups are as much about you meeting other parents as they are about being connected to the institution. Make sure you ask about the parent associations and resources that are part of the institution.

Parent groups have been around, but now they are much more actively involved with campus life and plugged in to the information. Supporting parents and families have never been so important—in fact, many of these support services didn't exist fifteen years ago. Just recently a new organization was born out of a need to support parents because of their increasing importance and new roles. The group is called AHEPPP (Association of Higher Education Parent/Family Program Professionals), and it consists of leaders in the field. The vision statement of AHEPPP says it best:

Most schools have areas for parents on their websites. Often you'll be able to read parent news; get e-newsletters; and find links to forums, discussions, Facebook pages, Twitter feeds, and other tools to help you connect with other parents. Here's a quick snapshot of some of the things you might find on a parents website:

- Academic calendar
- Parents' weekend / family weekend information
- Links to tuition payment schedule
- Resources for off-campus living
- Information on campus safety, resources for students, and more
- Talking points on navigating finances during college
- Emergency notification information
- Online workshops and guides
- Alcohol education for parents
- Guide to healthy family involvement
- Information on HIPAA
- Campus vocabulary

Now that you're plugged in to Facebook and Twitter, you can also search for parent groups formed by the institution or created by other parents. If you can't find one out there, you can easily start a parent Facebook group. I will be more than happy to promote it and help enlist members to connect you with other parents. Just send me a note.

7. OTHER RECOMMENDED READING

While I hope you're enjoying this book (I should mention, you've barely gotten to the best parts yet), there are more books for you to check out. Each one offers a unique perspective that can give you deeper insight into the college experience beyond the first year. The titles included are books professionals and orientation directors often recommend. Sure, the first recommendation is my other book, but it comes highly recommended (wink wink). And honestly, it is the number-one book on college life, and parents write me all the time to share how much it's helped.

The Naked Roommate: And 107 Other Issues You Might Run Into in College (3rd ed. paperback) by Harlan Cohen

This is the book that's helped hundreds of thousands of students and parents. It's now being used as required reading in classrooms across the country. The Naked Roommate captures the college experience by using the voices of college students. Hearing about life in college through the voices of students will help reinforce the themes in this book and give you more opportunities to engage your college-bound child in discussion. In fact, it was the reaction from parents and their desire for information to help complement The Naked Roommate that inspired this book. At the least, flip through the pages when sharing it with your students.

> **Letting Go: A Parent's Guide to Understanding the College Years (5th ed.) by Karen Levin Coburn and Madge Lawrence Treeger**
>
> This is a wonderful book that goes through the college years. This in-depth book addresses many of the same issues I have, but with a focus more on understanding the trends, challenges, and emotions that parents will go through.
>
> **You're on Your Own (But I'm Here if You Need Me): Mentoring Your Child during the College Years by Majorie Savage**
>
> I've had the chance to visit with Marjorie and find her to be wonderful. She is in charge of parent programs at the University of Minnesota and is always working on new research to help connect parents with the best possible information. This book was recently updated and is one that student affairs professionals often recommend.

YOUR CONTINUING EDUCATION

Again, there's more information in here and out there than you will ever want or need. You don't need to know it all, all the time, but you need to know it's there if you ever need to access it.

As for the rest of this book, the final chapter in part 1 explores five things you can do to help your child as he or she prepares for the transition ahead. I think you'll find it an interesting, practical, and valuable approach. The second part of the book dives into twenty-five areas of college life in colorful detail (it might even make you blush at times). You'll hear some advice, lots of tips, and invaluable suggestions from students and professionals living life on and around campus. One thing that is very important to me is to give you prescriptive advice from experts you don't always get to hear from or have access to. I love the idea of students sharing stories and insight about the things they have done or not done with their parents. I also love sharing advice from professionals working in higher education—some have been on the job for more than forty years.

By the time you finish reading this book, you will know more about college than any parent has ever wanted or needed to know.

Helping Them Find Their Place (Before They Leave Yours)

My son is leaving for college in the fall. My wife and I are concerned that he won't be able to take care of himself on his own. When we leave it up to him, it just doesn't get done. We are always picking up the pieces. I know we probably haven't helped him, but now that we will not be there to do it for him, I don't know if he can handle all the responsibility.

Concerned Father

Dear Concerned Father,

I know students like this—they wear the same clothes for weeks and sleep on the same sheets for months. Then they meet a girl who doesn't like dirt. Suddenly the immature boy learns to shower, do laundry, and grow up. It's not because of you. It's because stinking gets old.

If he's ready for the next step, be clear about your expectations (he doesn't need to be at the top of his class, although that would be nice; he just needs to go to class). Make sure he, you, and your wife know how to access the resources, support services, and people who can support his transition. Before he leaves, have him put together a plan of where he'll find his place and how he'll find it. If he struggles, help connect him to the resources, people, and support services available on campus. Encourage him, give him room to grow and room to fall when he grows. Let his successes be his successes (not yours), and let his failures be his failures (not yours). Tell him he WILL make it and he WILL succeed. Avoid telling him he will fail or he's too immature to succeed. And whatever you do—never do his laundry for him. If he stinks during parents' weekend, buy him laundry detergent, a roll of quarters, and walk downwind. Trust that he'll figure it out before graduation.

POOF! THE PERFECT COLLEGE EXPERIENCE

The perfect college experience doesn't magically happen for your child. It can happen, but it usually doesn't just appear out of thin air. And here's why...

Let your student's successes be their successes (not yours) and your student's failures be their failures (not yours).

—Catherine M. Bickel, EdD,
Associate Director of Housing and
Residence Life, Ball State University

You have been the magic behind the scenes making it all happen for most of their lives. You signed them up for T-ball, baseball, soccer, gymnastics, dance, piano lessons, drama, and football. You arranged the play dates. You helped them get the extra help and lessons. You drove carpool. You celebrated the victories and picked them up when they were down. You helped create their world for them. This isn't a bad thing—this is what parents are supposed to do.

It happened at school too. Life just happened for them. They were required to perform in plays, they had to participate in team sports in gym class, they had to go on field trips, and at times they were forced to participate in after-school activities and fill leadership roles in organizations. Opportunities fell from the sky right into their laps.

And now, for the first time in most of their lives, it's not just all going to automatically happen. The moving walkway has ended, and most students don't know that they are in charge of taking the next step. There's a reason that one in four students don't return to the same school, that 90 percent get anxious, and two out of

WANT TO KNOW WHY...

so many college students choose to go to the same school as five of their friends from high school instead of a better school where they don't know anyone else on campus? Knowing no one means having to take risks and meet people, and that's just too risky for many students.

three feel homesick—this next step is more challenging than most of them imagine.

The next step is for them to do the work to find their place on campus. No one thinks about this part of college life. Up until now, college has been all about applications and acceptance letters. But by the time someone is accepted, the planning should have already started on how they will find their place on campus.

What does it mean to "find your place"? A student who finds his or her place is a student who has connected with campus, found new friends, and created a sense of community where he or she feels appreciated, included, desired, and supported. A student who finds his or her place is comfortable enough to make well-thought-out decisions in alignment with his or her core values and has the ability to help lead others to do the same. It's the power to say YES when something feels right and the power to say NO when it feels wrong.

If you're panicking because your student has done absolutely nothing to find his or her place, don't freak out. Some students can do this with little or no effort. They have interests and will pursue them once they get settled in. Then there are students who have friends with strong interests that will pull them along. A lot of times these students will take on their friends' strong interests, because this means not having to be the one to take the risks. I don't think that's the best option, but it's an option. Ideally, it would be nice if you could encourage your student to create a life that means stepping outside his or her comfort zone. That's where the idea of planning and supporting their planning can be helpful.

Now, you might be thinking this isn't relevant to your student, because he or she has a place waiting for him or her. A trombone player who played in his high school band and plans to play in the band in college will have a place waiting. A girl who has friends from high school already on campus in a sorority will have a place waiting for her. An athlete who has been recruited by a school and is living in the athletes' residence hall will have a place waiting for him.

EXCERPT FROM "HELP ME, HARLAN!" ADVICE COLUMN

I'm a full-time student with a part-time job. I'm getting to know people, but I'm not forging those "lifelong" friendships I always hear about. I'm in the marching band, but that doesn't seem to be too much help...

—Not Making Friends

But this doesn't mean that all these students will be comfortable in their places or that they will love the new friends they meet in these places. Sometimes having only one place can mean getting stuck in the wrong place or doing things that aren't comfortable, because a student feels like he or she doesn't have other places to go. This is why this is completely relevant to all students—we all need to know how to find our place. And this isn't just about college. Once a student graduates (I'm rooting for you), this approach can be used to help him or her create a life outside of college. Once we know how to find our place, we can create a healthy and balanced life anywhere.

But finding your place on campus isn't easy. Remember that one in four students will not return to the same school, that 90 percent get anxious, and two out of three feel homesick. Why do students have so much trouble finding their place on campus?

THE "GET INVOLVED" CHORUS

They say to get involved. "Get involved!" It's the most popular advice a first-year student will receive. This idea of getting involved is fantastic in theory, but it's kind of like telling a single person, "Get a date!". The problem for your child isn't the lack of options or opportunities—the challenge is being able to take the steps needed to get involved (or to get a date, more on this in part 2, Tip #18).

Getting involved on campus means having to take some risks. I'm not talking high-speed-chase kind of risks—I'm talking about students putting themselves into new and often uncomfortable everyday situations. Risks like walking into rooms filled with unfamiliar people, applying for leadership positions, trying out for teams, auditioning for roles, rushing to get into a fraternity or sorority, sitting with strangers in the dining hall—risks that can mean having to get picked, getting picked over, or being judged.

In all the new roles we play in life, it's as if we are standing in a crowded room wearing a very tight thong (yes, thong underwear). And in that kind of situation, it's hard to think clearly. It's impossible to listen to what people are saying, because we are consumed with what everyone is thinking. Our focus is covering up our insecurities and hiding the things that make us uncomfortable.

Most first-year students are uncomfortable in what I call "The First-Year-Experience Thong." The First-Year Thong makes it hard to walk into new situations and rooms filled with strangers. New situations are like the meat in the cafeteria—scary. Stand in the back of a classroom filled with first-year students on the first day of class, and you'll see that no one wants to be noticed when the professor asks a question.

So many first-year students are worried, uncomfortable, and sensitive. They are consumed with what everyone else is doing and thinking. Even the coolest ones aren't trained to take risks. One of my favorite interactions was with the starting quarterback of a major college football program. He walked me to my car and privately revealed how hard it was for him to take risks and talk to girls he really wanted to date. So instead of taking risks, he waited for the girls to approach him. The idea that he might be rejected and the rest of the team would know was enough for him to avoid taking risks. He didn't want the team to see him fail. I explained that as the leader of the team, if he could take a risk and show the rest of the guys that it's okay to take a fall, he could be a hero, because all the guys on the team who were holding back would then take risks and be more authentic.

Some schools advertise hundreds of clubs and organizations and talk about all the ways to get involved, but getting involved means taking hundreds of risks and possibly facing rejection hundreds of times. Of course, no one is going to get rejected hundreds of times (that would be too much), but a few rejections are all it takes for many students to give up and stop taking risks. That's when they have trouble. That's when they become spectators and followers. And that's when they may get desperate and do things they end up regretting (can you say, "Mom, Dad, I'm pregnant! You're going to be grandparents").

We love it when risks go as planned. But we hate it when they don't go as planned. The thing about being a first-year student is that around every corner there is a new experience, and that means having to take risk after risk. Emotional and social risks are literally everywhere in college:

- Leaving home and attending school = RISK
- Attending an orientation on your own = RISK
- Asking someone you don't know well to go with you to an event = RISK
- Living with a stranger = RISK
- Telling a roommate something that makes you uncomfortable = RISK
- Sitting at a table and eating a meal with people you don't know = RISK

- Walking into a classroom on the first day of class = RISK
- Talking to people you don't know in class = RISK
- Asking a question in front of the class = RISK
- Talking to a teacher and getting extra help = RISK
- Changing your major and telling your parents = RISK
- Telling your parent about a bad grade = RISK
- Asking someone on a date = RISK (especially while sober)
- Breaking up with a long-distance boyfriend or girl-friend = RISK
- Breaking up with a first love = RISK
- Not having sex with some-one who pressures you to have sex = RISK
- Saying no to a group of friends = RISK
- Refusing to take a drink from a stranger = RISK
- Refusing a drink from friends who are all drinking = RISK

> **WANT TO KNOW WHY...**
> so many students would rather email or text a roommate or a professor about a problem? Doing it face-to-face means possibly getting someone upset or angry, and that's just too risky for many students.

- Admitting you need help when you're sick = RISK
- Taking on massive debt = RISK
- Applying for a job on campus = RISK
- Rushing a fraternity or a sorority = RISK
- Starting a club or organization on campus = RISK
- Making new friends = RISK
- Joining a club or activity in which you don't know anyone = RISK
- Participating in a team sport = RISK

- Changing your appearance = RISK
- Transferring schools = RISK

Risks in college are everywhere. I've spoken to thousands of students, visited hundreds of campuses, and given students advice through my column for the past fifteen years, and I can tell you that almost all students struggle when it comes to taking risks. It's not that students don't want to do all of these things; it's just that doing all of these things means putting themselves out there emotionally. And when you're in the midst of the most dramatic change of your life, it's normal to feel vulnerable.

> Most students struggle when it comes to taking the everyday emotional and social risks needed to get involved in life on campus.

You might be thinking, "No, no, no, not my Noah." But yes, yes, yes, ah, your Noah. That gifted athlete who is out-of-control awesome on the court—he's also out-of-control insecure in the classroom, because he's too scared to get help, because he doesn't want to look stupid. That partying student who appears to be having the time of his life—he's secretly struggling with depression, but he won't get help, because he knows he's gay and getting help would mean having to face the truth. That debt-ridden student who is barely getting by financially—he's too proud to let anyone know and charges his way through college rather than face the truth. And that brilliantly gifted student in the classroom who had a 1600 on her SAT—she is too afraid to approach boys while sober, because she's never had a real boyfriend; getting drunk makes it so much easier for her to take risks.

This idea of supporting your child's journey to find his or her place isn't just about your child being comfortable—it's about him or her learning how to listen to what he or she wants and creating a life that reflects what he or she wants to be. What I find so interesting about the college experience is that it's easy for a student to graduate having taken few risks and rarely having left his or her comfort zone. He can live with a friend from home throughout college, take classes with his buddies, get the degree his parents want him to get, get recruited by a prestigious company, get married, have kids, and live a full life that appears to be happy and healthy, but never really make the effort to know himself (which is a risk). You hear a lot about those rare cases when a student slips through the cracks and graduates never learning how to read. But you don't often hear about students slipping through the cracks and never taking the time to learn about themselves.

College is all about us growing and developing into adults. We appreciate your support and input. You have to let us go and trust that you raised us to be good, functioning, responsible adults.

—Gracie, junior

FIVE THINGS THEY NEED TO DO TO FIND THE MAGIC AND FIND THEIR PLACE ON CAMPUS

As a parent, there are five things to keep in mind when guiding your student through the first year of college:

1. Finding their place takes planning
2. Finding their place takes patience
3. Finding their place takes accepting the truth
4. Finding their place takes training
5. Finding their place takes having the right people in their corner

Let me break down each of these five parts. I should mention, some of your children might naturally do some of these things. And some might not need to do all of these things to find their place. But if your child should ever have a hard time on campus, this will help you get him or her on track and headed in the right direction.

IT'S NEVER BEEN EASIER TO AVOID TAKING EMOTIONAL RISKS

Cell phones, the Internet, text messages, cheap transportation, and luxury living combined with easy access to alcohol, drugs, and other antiseptic diversions make it easier than ever to hide from the truth and avoid taking on the tough stuff that's part of living life in college.

1. FINDING THEIR PLACE TAKES PLANNING

If you want to build a house, you need blueprints. If you want to drive cross-country, you need a map (or a GPS). If your child wants to have a great college experience, your child needs to have a plan.

Most students spend more time contemplating how many pairs of shoes to bring than what will happen once they unpack their shoes. They think it will all just fall into place. I'll tell you a little secret (come in close)—it doesn't always just happen. Sure, a student can find any place on campus, but finding the *best* place takes some planning. Ideally, this whole planning process should happen during the application process, spring of senior year of high school, or during summer orientation. However, if you're reading this after the first week, it's not too late. In fact, life is always about stopping, evaluating, and making new plans. It's just a little easier to start making a plan before arriving on campus.

What happens to students who don't plan is that they get to campus hoping it will all just happen like always. When one or two weeks pass and the newness factor of college wears off, they start to get uncomfortable. They think something is wrong. This is when they start to feel out of place. This is when they start to settle for any old place or old comfortable places. This is when the homesickness kicks in and they want to hang out at your place. And that's not the best place to find their place.

Putting together a plan means figuring out what they're going to do on campus, who they want to meet on campus, and how to meet the people doing the things they want to do on campus (there's a nice worksheet at the end of this chapter to help them figure it out).

WHAT YOU CAN DO TO HELP: Encourage your child to find three activities or organizations that will allow him or her to find three different groups of friends.

Having more than one group of friends means living in a world of options. If one group of friends makes stupid choices, it's easier to not make the same stupid choice if you have other friends. Students make friends by participating in shared experiences. Activities and organizations are the best places to share some experiences. Before steering your child away from a bowling elective, remember that bowling will help him or her make friends (and get a personalized polyester shirt—bonus).

THREE AREAS WHERE STUDENTS CAN FIND THEIR PLACE
1. Spiritual (religious groups, public services, etc.)
2. Academic (professional clubs, leadership groups, etc.)
3. Social (athletics, Greek life, etc.)

Encourage your child to do things that feel comfortable that first year. There's nothing wrong with him or her using personal strengths to make connections. (See Tip #13 for a list of first-year-friendly ways to get involved.) Ideally, your child should start looking into what he or she wants to do on campus before applying to schools (I once talked to a student who was a debate champ but went to a school that didn't have debate—can you believe it?). He or she can also start this process the summer before school starts. Since you know more information than any parent should ever want or need to know from chapter 4, there's nothing wrong with sending your child a link or two if he or she is open to it. (Note: ask for permission, and then watch your child stare at you in disbelief that you're asking for permission.)

I got involved in the First-Year Experience at Central Michigan University by taking the one-credit course as a freshman, and then I became a mentor. I've taught for two years, and it is just amazing how much of a positive impact you can have on a student's college experience by being there for them during the rough transition.

—Brittany, junior

The best thing I ever did was get involved in Ski Club. My life revolves around snow sports, it is my addiction, it is my drug, it is what I use to escape the sh*tstorm that is my life. It gave me hope that I may fit in on my college campus and connected me with a guy who talked me into getting a job at my local ski resort. I now teach skiing.

—Dennis, freshman

2. FINDING THEIR PLACE TAKES PATIENCE

First-year college students all want to find their place right NOW! NOW! NOW! And most parents want them to find their places NOW! NOW! NOW! But when it doesn't happen fast enough, students and parents can both start to panic. This is when smart students do things they never thought they would do.

Alcohol and parties can make it easy to find new connections. All you need is a red plastic cup. Hooking up is another way to find fast connections. A lot of students have a great time and get carried away—but a lot of them don't even know how or why they got swept up in it. It's only after the bad grades, poor choices, and a lack of new friends that they realize this isn't as much as they thought it was at the time.

Finding the best place doesn't take two days, or two weeks, or two months—it can take as long as two years. (Parents forget this too.) A student who gives himself a couple of years (or at least one year at a minimum) to get comfortable with the uncomfortable will be set up for success. Too many students' problem is that they come to campus with big expectations but an unrealistic timeline. After a couple of months, if reality hasn't met expectations, they get disappointed and start to have doubts. But knowing it takes time, and your reminding your child that it takes time can mean more time for him or her to find a place.

WHAT YOU CAN DO TO HELP: Encourage him to give it a good year or two to get comfortable with the uncomfortable. Encourage him to create a world of options by getting involved. Remind him that college is all about creating a world of options. If he gets discouraged, remind him that it takes a couple of years to get comfortable in high school; it makes sense that it will take as long in college.

When he reaches out to you after a bad day and wants to run or hide, remind him that this is normal and get him back on track. Remind him of the 10 percent rule. If he has a plan in place, you can use the plan to steer him in the right direction.

If his friends are all having better experiences, remind him that his friends will have their turn too. Doing this work now will make everything better later.

In the meantime, encourage him to do something that isn't dependent on other people. Activities like working out at the recreational center, taking a cool elective, or participating in a spiritual organization can be helpful. Also, part-time jobs on campus can be the perfect fix—a great way to get involved without the social pressures. When you have to go to work at a coffee bar in the student center on Friday night, you can earn a few dollars and make a lot of friends while frothing a latte.

> ### THE PERFECT JOB
> If your child isn't all that social, encourage him or her to get a part-time job. Jobs in the library, the computer center, or in the student center can put students in the center of the action. If he or she is working on a weekend night, there is no pressure to make plans with new friends—the plan is to work. Taking a job in a social environment means making friends becomes a fringe benefit of the job.

3. FINDING THEIR PLACE TAKES ACCEPTING THE TRUTH

Accepting the truth means accepting the Universal Rejection Truth. The URT is a powerful and unavoidable force of nature and part of life in college. The URT says that not everyone we would like to appreciate, include, and desire us will always appreciate, include, and desire us. Many will, but many—not all.

While the Truth is as normal and natural as breathing, we are rarely taught to embrace it—in fact, most of us learn to run and hide from it at all costs. The Universal Rejection Truth is everywhere in college. Some common URTs:

- The URT of Roommates: not all roommates will get along
- The URT of College Friendships: not all people on campus will be friends
- The URT of Life Inside the Classroom: not all students will get A's
- The URT of Dating and Relationships: not everyone your kid wants to date will want to date your kid (I know, shocking!)

Fighting the URT of Dating and Relationships is the equivalent of saying, "I like you. You must like me. If you don't like me, I will hate you or avoid you." This way of thinking is called rejection denial. We love it when we are wanted, but we hate everything else.

Accepting the Truth when your child is looking to find her place means knowing that no matter

I found a job at our student union by luck. I have made a lot of contacts with fellow students, faculty, staff, and administrators. I've interacted with groups of people I probably never would have had the chance to. To me it's more than a job. It's a constant learning experience, and I grow every day.

—Jeff, senior

what she does, not everyone she meets will treat her the way she wants to be treated. Most of the time rejection will have nothing to do with your child. In fact, even the most attractive and comfortable students can meet a lot of resistance. You see it on reality TV—no one wants the strong, smart, attractive, and confident people sticking around. They are seen as a threat. The strong ones are some of the first to be attacked and misunderstood.

When she takes a risk, whether it be in class, with friends, or while trying to find a date, she needs to embrace the Truth and give people permission to not always respond the way she hopes they will respond. Those who can accept the Truth can live in a much more forgiving world. Those who fight the Truth or deny it end up angry at the world or just angry with themselves.

For example, an incoming freshman who loves singing auditions for the top college choir her first week on campus. She gets cut off in the middle of her first audition and doesn't make the choir. She storms off the stage in a huff. She's completely devastated. She wants to leave school. This has never happened to her before in her entire life. If she were familiar with the Universal Rejection Truth of Auditioning, she could give the world permission to react and find answers. If she refuses to accept the Truth, she's just left assuming either she's not as good as she thought or that the choral director is an a-hole.

Accepting the Truth means approaching the director and finding out the circumstances behind the rejection.

Only then might she discover that the director thinks her voice is beautiful but had to cut her off because first-year students are not allowed to join the high-level choir. He wanted her to join the freshman choir. He mentions that he would have said that to her, but she stormed off.

Going a level deeper, knowing about the Truth means doing more work to prepare for the risk. Instead of being afraid of rejection, a student can work to get the desired outcome. In this situation, the student could have looked on the campus website before the audition and found people in the choir. She could have contacted a self-identified leader of the singing group and sent a note via Facebook asking a few questions. She could have also contacted the choral director and sent a note with questions on how to audition. This research would not only have helped her prepare for the risk and know beforehand to audition for the freshman choir, but it would also have helped her to meet people and form new relationships that would be helpful far beyond the risk. But it all starts with being comfortable enough with the risk to reach out to the people who can help.

Uncomfortable students are so quick to judge and run. When something doesn't go right in the classroom, it's the terrible professor's fault. When something doesn't go right in a rela-

> I think of college as a hands-on/hands-off experience. The college student is hands-on and the parents are hands-off!
>
> —Ruth, mom of college senior

tionship, it's easier to hate someone or hide from someone than find out the truth. When a roommate relationship gets uncomfortable, the roommate is the problem. The problem isn't that things don't always go as planned; the problem is that most students refuse to allow it. And should they allow it, they have a hard time working through it, because they're so uncomfortable in their new role and can't handle anything less than an ideal situation.

WHAT YOU CAN DO TO HELP: Remind her that adversity isn't the end of the road—it's the beginning of a relationship and a search for answers. If she's not getting rejected at times, then she's not doing it right. It means she's playing it safe and not taking enough risks. Don't make success all about the outcome; make it about the experience of taking the risk. The better she can get at working through what comes after the risk, the better equipped she will be to take on any challenge that comes her way. College is a risk-taking training ground. It's a place to try new things and take on new challenges. It's a place where you can spend money on events, have the event flop, and not worry about losing your job. It's a place where you can write an article in the campus newspaper and get hundreds of people to respond. It's a place to apply for leadership positions, get the job and make mistakes and still be a leader on campus. Sure, it might not feel good to make mistakes, but this is the place for things to flop. Better a student flop in college and learn from the experience than flop beyond college. The opportunities to take academic risks, social risks, and spiritual risks are limitless. The only restrictions are those a student puts on him or herself (or those a parent places on the student). College is a risk-taking bonanza.

4. FINDING THEIR PLACE TAKES TRAINING

Yes, there might be hundreds of ways to get involved in life on campus, but that means being able to handle the hundreds of outcomes that happen following the hundreds of risks. A few risks gone bad, and most students give up or hide.

Training for the sport of taking risks means being able to take a risk and know that no matter what happens, you will be okay. It means taking lots of risks and learning from them. It means when you take a risk and someone rejects you, instead of fighting or running, you'll respond with, "Thank you for being honest. What can I do to participate in the future?" That's hard to do—especially during a vulnerable and uncomfortable time in life.

> A few risks gone bad, and most students give up or hide. They aren't good at taking risks.

When I present leadership sessions, I call the program "Training for the Sport of Taking Risks." Before a participant can begin training, the prerequisites are to embrace the Universal Rejection Truth and come out of rejection denial. This means giving the world around us permission to respond however it naturally responds and embracing the fact that not every action will work out as planned. The next step in training is to prepare for all possible outcomes. Of course, we want results to turn out as planned. But if not, there are things we must do to prepare for the sport of taking risks:

1. We must look in the mirror wearing a tight thong (figuratively or literally, it's up to you) and identify the things that make us uncomfortable. Don't BS yourself. Put on that figurative thong, turn on the lights, and face what makes you uncomfortable. Look at it with the lights on. And then move on to the next step.

2. Embrace what can't be changed and use it to your advantage, working to create a plan to change the things that can be changed.

3. Surround yourself with people who want you to win—not people who are threatened by your success. Ask these people to help you work through the tough questions if someone or something makes you uncomfortable.

> The hardest part for me was to be able to let go—meaning to stop making her life easier, stop arranging things, stop making appointments, etc.
>
> —Mom of college senior

Once we can accept the truth and train to take risks, we can handle whatever comes our way. If a risk doesn't turn out as planned, we can search for the answers. Because we've trained and are comfortable with ourselves and all possible outcomes, there's nothing we can't face following the risk. That's why it's so important to do the training.

WHAT YOU CAN DO TO HELP: This is a tough one, because there's only so much a parent can do. Training is about self-discovery. Training means looking in the mirror and examining what we love about ourselves and what we don't love. It's changing what we can change and learning how to embrace what can't be changed. It's putting on a physical thong and putting on an emotional thong. It can mean dealing with abuse, self-harm, eating disorders, drinking issues, unsafe behavior, and things your child can't talk about with Mom and Dad.

So your gift to your child is being supportive and encouraging and reminding him or her how proud you are of his or her journey. Connecting your child to professional support, campus resources, and people who can offer guidance while going through this process is incredibly helpful.

Also, getting yourself the best support and accessing the best resources available to you to help guide your child is valuable. During this process, your child might share things that make you uncomfortable, surprise you, or confuse you. Having a support system in place will help you to be better equipped to be a better listener and not react in a way that will scare your child off. This will enable you to connect your child with the experts (on and off campus) who can help him or her, and it will help you to reach out to parents and professionals who can support you.

5. FINDING THEIR PLACE TAKES HAVING THE RIGHT PEOPLE IN THEIR CORNER

I like to think that the college experience is like the sport of boxing (but without the punching). A boxer who enters the ring without understanding the sport or training is going to get knocked out after one or two rounds. But a boxer who enters the ring with a plan, trains, understands that the sport can be brutal at times, and has great people in his corner will be able to create the best and most satisfying college experience.

A student who wants to win needs to have people in his corner who want him to win. I'm sure you are a parent who wants your child to win; there's no way you would be reading this if you didn't. But there are a lot of parents who don't want their kids to win. There are siblings, friends of your children, and boyfriends and girlfriends who don't want them to win. Having them win can be threatening to others. Some parents see a child who is more educated as too independent or as thinking he or she is better than a parent. If a child has friends and siblings who aren't getting a college education, those people may feel less intelligent, less equipped to make a living, and jealous. It also means no longer having an excuse to avoid getting an education and settling.

Students who want to find their place need the *right* people in their corner. These are people who want them to win. The sport of taking risks can be brutal. Knowing the people in their corner want them to win means being able to hear not just want they want to hear, but what they need to hear. It also means asking for help, knowing that the people in their corner will not judge them but will help them find answers and connect to the right people, places, and resources. Those are the right people to have in their corner.

College campuses are filled with people who want students to win. Students should plan to identify at least five people who can be there to help them win. The people in their corner can be orientation leaders, peer mentors, orientation staff, professors, teaching assistants, student leaders, resident assistants, a residence life professional, therapists or doctors, members of support groups, spiritual leaders, or friends from home. A student who can come to campus with a plan, patience, and the right people in his or her corner will be set up for a happy, healthy, and awesome college experience that can exceed all expectations.

WHAT YOU CAN DO TO HELP: You are *the* most important person in your child's corner. As your son or daughter walks through his or her college experience, you are literally in your child's hand. You are with him or her in class, during exams, while eating in the dining halls, studying at night, going to parties, coming home in the early morning, and sleeping over at a "friend's" room (just resting, nothing else). You are there on the very best days and the very worst ones too. All it takes is a push of a button, and you can be there to comfort, guide, support, advise, elevate, empower, excite, motivate, love, and just listen. When you get the email, text, or call, understanding just how important you are, the changes that have taken place over the years, the stuff not mentioned in the brochures, all the resources and support services available on and off campus, and what it takes to help your child find his or her place will make you the best person to have in your child's corner.

EMBRACING YOUR ROLES AS THE NEW COLLEGE PARENT

A student's time in college is about so much more than earning a degree, graduating, and getting a job. It's about learning how to create a world filled with options and creating a life driven by passion. It's about working to understand and define oneself while embracing the adversity that comes with being a person of character and conviction. It's about having the confidence and courage to demand and command respect in one's personal, professional, and spiritual life. And most importantly, it's about having an amazing time and learning to love every single moment.

Your son or daughter can get there on his or her own, but to get there as safely and with as little regret as possible, it helps to have a mom or dad who understands the journey ahead and appreciates what it means to be the New College Parent. In part 2 we'll take a look at many of the common questions and concerns parents run into once a son or daughter leaves for college. I'll share advice from campus life professionals, leading experts on college life, students, grads, parents, and me. The goal in part 2 is to help you find the best approach to help your child be the happiest kid on campus and you to be the happiest parent in your neighborhood.

THE FOLLOWING EXERCISE IS FROM *The Naked Roommate's First Year Survival Workbook.*

(Feel free to share this with your child or use it as a guide when talking about the college experience.)

Naked Exercise #8: Finding Your (Best) Place on Campus

Your place is waiting to be found. You just need to look for it, but it takes work.

Imagine today is the last day of your college career (wow, that was fast!). Look back at your college experience, and write down the three activities or organizations that helped you find your closest friends and your most meaningful college experiences while on campus:

_____

_____

_____

_____

_____

_____

_____

_____

_____

_____

_____

_____

_____

_____

Mapping Out Your Path: Three Steps to Finding Your Place on Campus NOW

STEP 1. Identify activities, experiences, campus organizations, and hobbies that gave your high school experience meaning (sleeping and dating are not appropriate answers).

ACTIVITY/ORGANIZATION #1:

_____

_____

_____

How this helped you make friends: _____

_____

_____

How doing this made you feel: _____

_____

_____

ACTIVITY/ORGANIZATION #2:

_____

_____

_____

How this helped you make friends: _____

_____

_____

How doing this made you feel: _____

_____

_____

ACTIVITY/ORGANIZATION #3:

_____

_____

_____

How this helped you make friends: _____

_____

_____

How doing this made you feel: _____

_____

_____

ACTIVITY/ORGANIZATION #1:

_____

_____

_____

Why this is important you: _____

_____

_____

ACTIVITY/ORGANIZATION #2:

_____

_____

_____

Why this is important you: _____

_____

_____

ACTIVITY/ORGANIZATION #3:

_____

_____

_____

Why this is important you: _____

_____

_____

STEP 3. How will you get involved in each activity or organization? What makes you uncomfortable about taking the steps needed to get involved? Who are some people who can help answer your questions and help you get comfortable with the uncomfortable?

ACTIVITY/ORGANIZATION #1:

_____

_____

_____

How to get involved: _____

_____

_____

Possible obstacles: _____

_____

_____

Who I can contact to answer questions: _____

_____

_____

ACTIVITY/ORGANIZATION #2:

_____

_____

_____

How to get involved: _____

_____

_____

Possible obstacles: _____

_____

_____

Who I can contact to answer questions: _____

_____

_____

ACTIVITY/ORGANIZATION #3:

_____

_____

_____

How to get involved: _____

_____

_____

Possible obstacles: _____

_____

_____

Who I can contact to answer questions: _____

_____

_____

Enjoy the Intermission

There will now be a short intermission before part 2 of the book. Please take a moment to enjoy this brief break. Go to the bathroom, shift your weight to the other cheek, or enjoy some cool refreshments.

PART 2

Your College Experience (and Theirs)

Welcome to part 2 of *The Happiest Kid on Campus*. This section is designed to give you an in-depth look at college life tailored for you, the parents. Each tip is written in the same style as *The Naked Roommate: And 107 Other Issues You Might Run Into in College*. In fact, this book could be called, "The Naked Roommate's Parent," but I couldn't use "parent" and "naked" in the same title (not a good idea).

As always, if you have any questions or find that something is missing, please send me a note and I'll address it in future editions. Send an email to Harlan@HelpMeHarlan.com or on www.HappiestKidonCampus.com or via the Facebook page www.Facebook.com/HappiestKidonCampus.

Thank you. I hope this helps!

A Helpful List for Parents

From a student three months into his first year on campus
By Manas K., freshman and resident hall president at the University of Maryland

1. Everything doesn't have to be moved in on the first day.
2. Let me pick my own roommate. I'm the one living with him/her.
3. You have every right to join Facebook, but I'm warning you: you're not going to like everything you see.
4. Here's my schedule; please don't call me during class, because it's embarrassing. Anything else is fine!
5. I'll come home, but not every day.
6. I'll need you when I call you. I'm going to have hard times whether you like it or not.
7. You'll know I miss you when I tell you.
8. We share the same blood, but my sibling is not the same person. Please don't compare us.
9. I have the first-aid kit you made me. There's a nurse 24/7 whom I'll call if I need help.
10. Don't listen to everything you hear about frats/sororities.
11. Let's talk before you visit. Not all kids like surprises.
12. I'll look weak if I need my parents to talk to my roommate. I'll handle it.
13. I definitely appreciate your advice about choosing a major, but college has changed in the last few decades, and I'm sure I'll find what I love.

14. I'll talk to you if I need help.

15. Please trust me to make the right decisions regarding relationships. I'm a big kid.

16. If I don't come out to you first, please don't be offended. There are just other people who might be able to relate a little better.

17. Professors HATE parent complaints. Please don't send them angry emails or call if I fail my first essay.

18. Chances are, someone will notice if I have any disorders, and I'll get treatment here. Only call if I'm too gone to know it.

19. It's all inevitable in college. You've done what you could to prevent me from making stupid choices. The rest is up to me.

20. I'm in college now, but you don't have to let go of me. Just loosen the grip a wee bit. And read *The Naked Roommate*.

21. But at the end of the day—and please, never forget this—we love and miss you. And not just for the care packages!

TIP #1 THE SUMMER BEFORE

The Emotional Roller Coaster (Before the First Fall)

The Tip

A little road trip can leave all the anxiety in the rear-view mirror.

The Story

My dad and I were sitting in the living room one night watching television, and he was asking if I was nervous about leaving for college. I told him that it really wasn't the thought of leaving that scared me; I was more afraid of not knowing my way around or where anything was on campus. The next morning he came in my room around 8:00 a.m. and woke me up. He told me to get dressed, that we were going to the school. The campus is about an hour and a half from my house. It wasn't a very well-planned trip, so we didn't have a tour or anything lined up. Once we got there we found the dorm that I would be staying in. My dad did some searching and found an RA who was willing to show us around. After Meghan (the RA) showed us the residence hall, she volunteered to show us the rest of the campus. It worked out perfectly. While we were there, my dad kept making jokes about how he was going to come back to school because he didn't remember it being so cool. After the tour we ate in the dining hall, which has *amazing* food, and we started talking about my still being afraid. After spending the day with him there and getting to see the whole campus, I felt much better.

—Samantha T., freshman, Nicholls State University

* * *

THE EMOTIONAL GROUNDSWELL

I've been writing my "Help Me, Harlan!" syndicated advice column for the past fifteen years. Each summer before the start of college, there's a groundswell of letters from students sharing their deepest fears and anxieties. Rarely do these incoming students express their feelings to their parents. As a result, some parents get hurt feelings. Try not to take it personally. This question and answer tells the rest of the story:

Dear Harlan,

I leave for a large university in a month, and my relationship with my parents is becoming very stressful. I am the oldest child, and their stress is projected onto me, which only adds to any stress I have on starting this new life. I'm very excited about college, but they claim that the way I express my excitement is making them feel forgotten and irrelevant. I want and need my independence, but I am starting to feel guilty for the way I feel. Any advice?

Discombobulated in Milwaukee

Dear Discombobulated,

If you express your excitement with a tear-away calendar on your bedroom door counting down "X DAYS UNTIL I CHECK OUT OF THIS MOTEL I'VE CALLED HOME FOR EIGHTEEN YEARS AND DO WHATEVER, WHENEVER, WITH WHOMEVER I WANT WITHOUT YOU EVER KNOWING! HA! HA! HA!" they might have a reason to feel forgotten and irrelevant.

Here's what is happening:

For eighteen years your parents have been presidents, CEOs, and rulers of your life. In a few weeks, you take charge. On top of this, having a child in college might make your parents feel sad and not as young. Finish it all off with the price of college, and your parents might be feeling a little sadder, older, and broker. Meanwhile, you've never been happier and more excited in your life. But you know what? You have EVERY right to feel excited. Let them know that you appreciate what's happening in their lives. Tell them how much you love them and how much you will miss them. Make a plan about when you'll call, email and visit. Connect them with the parent group on campus, get them a book on college life, and suggest they check out the campus website. Direct them to www.HappiestKidonCampus.com. Then give them time to adjust. Just wait. Before you know it, your old bedroom will become your mom's new walk-in closet.

There will be ups and downs, excitement, anxiety, and intense anticipation—and that's all before breakfast. Some college-bound students cling to friends from high school. Some push away parents without knowing it. Some hang on to high school love. Some break it off to start fresh. Some appear so cool, nothing could rattle them (it's an act). Some are so rattled, it's hard to believe they will be able to make it (that's not an act).

One thing is clear—your feelings are irrelevant and unimportant to them. But not to me. I care. If your child makes you feel irrelevant, unimportant, and unappreciated, it's not because he or she doesn't love you anymore or isn't grateful for all you've done. It's just his or her survival skills kicking in. We tend to push away and reject the things we love the most. For many first-year college students, this is the most dramatic transition in their lifetime. There's good reason for them to be concerned. Do not cut them off and stop payment on the check (if you're helping)—they don't even know they're doing it.

> I was terrified that I wouldn't make any friends. My parents tried introducing me to strangers while helping me move in. Disaster.
>
> —Ricky, freshman

My father sang, "Na na na na. Na na na na. Hey hey hey. Good-bye" at least twice a day before I left for college. He took every chance to remind me that I was leaving. I think that was his way of coping.

—Alycia, freshman

On the other hand, you might have a child who clings to you and can't let go. You might get nostalgic and think about the fact that things will never be the same again. For a lot of you, your eighteen-year-old is a good friend. You're used to calling, texting, and sharing stories together. That can be just as hard.

If you find yourself feeling sad, having hurt feelings, being irritable, feeling extremely sensitive, or pushing your child away—this is to be expected. What happens is, subconsciously some parents make themselves less loveable so it makes it easier for your college-bound student to not miss you. Either way, they're going to miss you. And either way, you're going to miss them.

One thing I mentioned in the first part of the book and will mention again later in the book is that you no longer have to "let go." Between cell phones, email, the Internet, Facebook, video chats, and visits, you'll be in touch. Parents no longer need to let go. You just have to loosen the grip and figure out what's comfortable for them and what's comfortable for you. Yes,

My mom started freaking out over everything. She would snap at me for the dumbest things and then somehow relate it to my going away to college and what would happen when I didn't follow her advice. It was almost laughable, because she was only doing it because she was so scared of my leaving and being on my own. She was nervous about not being able to tell me what to do.

—Gena, senior

things will change, but they can change in a good way. Different is scary, but this generation of college students is more connected and will always be more connected with their parents. That's a trend that's not going away.

Make an effort over the summer to reach out to the parent organizations on campus, talk to other parents (I can connect you with other parents via my Facebook page and website), talk with friends who have been there and done that, and start planning how you'll redecorate the room once your son or daughter moves out. Use orientation and visits to campus as a time to find support and answers to the questions on your mind. Consider getting a group of friends together and checking in with each other on a regular basis (one mom told me she did this). Even if your friends' kids are going to different schools, it will still be nice to connect and share your experiences.

ATTENTION FIRST-GENERATION PARENTS

Having never gone through this experience yourself can make the months before the fall especially unsettling. When it comes to parental involvement, research shows that first-generation parents can have a dramatic impact on student success. Use this summer to soak in the information. Also, see if there are specific resources available for first-generation students by contacting the office or parent relations or the dean of students office.

WHAT YOU CAN DO TO HELP YOUR KIDS

Most students don't spend a lot of time thinking about what they will do to find their place on campus. It doesn't come up. Most will just expect it to happen. The summer before college is a time to help them start planning.

My mom and I are very close. The entire summer before I left for college my mom would have moments where she would just hug me and say how much she would miss me. This was always one of those eye-rolling moments until she would follow it up by saying, "But I'm so excited knowing the great journey you're about to go on and to see all God has for you." She always had my best interests at heart.

—Elise, freshman

Instead of grilling them with twenty questions and playing *Jeopardy!* music in the background (way too much pressure), find a comfortable time to talk. Plan a weekend road trip, go shopping together, have a manicure with a daughter, go to a ballgame (most sons prefer ballgames to manicures), just do something active that will force you to spend some time together. Whether your child is attending a four-year school or two-year community college, they all need to map out a path to help create a world of options.

Now on to the questions you might want to bring up over the summer...The summer months are a hard time to get through to them. Until they're on campus, a lot of kids won't even be thinking about putting together a plan. The time will be spent getting everything they can out of the last couple months of summer. Once you hit the three-week mark or attend summer orientation, that's when things start to get real. This is a good time to

I was most concerned with moving so far away. My mom helped by being ultimately the most supportive person in the world and road-tripping with me from our home in Texas to my college in Washington. During my road trip, my biggest worry was not having clothes, because all of mine flew out of the back of our truck. That didn't help, and neither did my mom blaming herself.

—Tracie, freshman

The most helpful thing my mom did was tell me about the struggles she had during her college years and how she got through them. I knew that I wanted to have a better college experience than she had, so I made sure that I not only got through my struggles but overcame them to have a wonderful college experience.

—Katie, recent grad

spend some time together and bring up the following five questions.

The questions below are a direct extension of chapter 5 from part 1. By discussing your child's plans, you can gauge his or her expectations, help plan, and get your child thinking about how he or she will create this new world for him or herself. When you're having a conversation, feel free to bring up any of the student quotes in this book. You can mention that I wrote it, and that might make him or her more receptive. I know you know so much more than me, but a lot of students like *The Naked Roommate* book. Having this as a companion can give you room to talk about issues that might otherwise be more awkward to approach.

When it comes to the actual wording of the five questions, please feel free to put it however works for you. These questions are more a general idea of things you might want to bring up to help before your child moves out.

FIVE QUESTIONS FOR SUMMER PREP

(Feel free to put these in your own words.)

1. **What would be your perfect first year in college (topics to discuss include friends, academics, dating, alcohol, sex/no sex, visits home, social**

life, religion, activities, and experiences outside the classroom)?

This is all about helping your child think about what he or she wants college to be beyond the first few weeks. It's about creating expectations. Without any expectations, he or she will have no idea of what he or she wants to do and no direction. Your child will just plop onto campus and wait for it all to happen. Without expectations and a plan, it's easy to do unhealthy and regrettable things you never planned on doing.

2. **How do you plan on making this happen?**

   Specifically, try to get your son or daughter thinking about the activities, organizations, and opportunities available outside the classroom that can help him or her find connections to campus life. If your child hasn't thought about this yet, be patient. Make it clear that you want him or her to get involved outside the classroom (and you should). You can use *The Naked Roommate Workbook* pages or the page from chapter 5 as a guide. If your child is open to suggestions on ways to get involved, turn to Tip #13.

3. **Who are some people on campus who can you help make this happen?**

   A good way to approach this is to have your child think of five types of people who he or she can turn to for advice and help along the way (students on campus, friends, family, professionals, spiritual leaders). These should be people who want your child to win. Again, you can also offer suggestions, but ask for permission to offer your suggestions. Your asking makes him or her feel empowered and respected in a new light.

4. **How much time are you going to give yourself to make it all happen?**

   Too many times students are in a big hurry to reach big goals and get disappointed if it all doesn't happen when they want it. Help your child set a reasonable pace. Yes, he or she should have big expectations but should also have a realistic timeline to reach them. Plant the seed that it can take a couple of years—not a couple of weeks or months—to make it happen. Otherwise he or she may be set up for disappointment.

5. **What can I (we) do to help support you to make it happen?**

   This is all about defining your role as parent, coach, or friend. Asking what you can do sends a message that you are willing to help, but more importantly, that you don't assume your child needs your help. There's nothing wrong with coaching him or her, but he or she needs to be the one to make it all happen—the majority of the responsibility is up to your child.

A Happy Way to End the Conversation

If you don't already do this, it's nice to be reminded that no matter what happens during this experience, you will always be there for your child. Telling, showing, and sending lots of care packages (students love care packages!) will help remind your child that you love him or her and will be there no matter what.

QUESTIONS AND ANSWERS

Q: My daughter refuses to talk to me about these issues. What should I do?

A: Your daughter might not be talking, but she is listening (assuming the volume on her iPod isn't drowning out your voice). You'll realize she was listening when you get that call at midnight a few weeks, a few months, or a few years into the experience. If there is a First-Year Experience course, make it mandatory that she takes it. These courses are for the students who think they know everything, but don't. Also consider enlisting the help of a student and professionals on campus. Reach out to the parent resources and explore the resources available to guide you and your daughter.

Q: My son doesn't have a worry in the world. Should this worry me?

A: Don't worry, something will come up. It might happen in the second, third, or fourth year. The cool and calm kids are the ones who usually call in the middle of the night when the world stops long enough for them to think about what's upsetting them. Make it so you are always accessible, and he will access you.

Q: My child is moody, pulling away from us, and it hurts. What can I do?

A: Give your child permission to pull away. Everyone copes differently. Always make yourself available and accessible. Lean on the parent support system to make sure there isn't anything else you can do. Make sure your child has people to turn to once he or she arrives on campus. If you hold on too tightly, there will be more pushing.

Have a question? Want to answer another parent's question?

Post your questions and answers; visit *The Happiest Kid on Campus* Parent Forum: www.HappiestKidonCampus.com.

TIP #2 SUMMER/FALL ORIENTATION

Parents, Pack Your Toiletries and Get Oriented

The Tip

Asking questions, getting essential information, and being engaged with your child's school doesn't make you a helicopter parent—it makes you a supportive parent.

The Story

When I talk to family members before the academic year begins and during new student orientation, we talk a great deal about remaining connected and engaged in the university community. Whether that is keeping up on the dates, deadlines, and logistics; the faculty lecture on campus; the concert being held; or the newest Nobel Prize winner—keeping up to date on what is happening on campus only supports their student. I also encourage them (to the dismay of my colleagues) to ask questions about when the bill is due, when move-in is, what their student needs to bring, when breaks are, when final exams are held, etc. By asking these questions they become more informed and, as my research has shown, more secure. This allows them to progress to a more functional, effective, and mature relationship with their student. I know it walks the line between "helicopter" and "support"; however, from the research I have done with our family population, it is only when our families have the "basics" down that they will be able to shift the relationship with their student.

> —College professional,
> thirteen years in higher
> education

* * *

WHAT PARENTS NEED TO KNOW

One of my favorite parent orientation moments happened when I was visiting a campus on a hot day in the summer. I was walking across campus to my event when a parent came out of one of the residence halls to ask a question. The mom thought I was on staff and explained that she needed toilet paper.

I was conflicted. I wanted to tell her, "I'm sorry ma'am, but this is a BYOTP (Bring Your

SOME "ARM-AROUND-THE-SHOULDER" ADVICE FOR PARENTS OF INCOMING STUDENTS (FROM A PROFESSIONAL WHO HAS SPOKEN TO THOUSANDS OF PARENTS AT ORIENTATION)

You're not alone. We're in this together. We take the trust you have put in this university by sending your child here very seriously, and please know that we are deeply committed to the success and well-being of our students.

We're in a partnership with you to help ensure the greatest likelihood of success for your son/daughter. Never hesitate to call, email, or get in touch if you have questions, concerns, or just want to talk.

Your relationship with your son or daughter will change, but in a good way. Just as your son/daughter today is not the same person they were four years ago, they will not be the same when they finish college. If they are, we have failed. They will change and your relationship with them will change, but it can

continued on page 175

Own Toilet Paper) weekend. We only supply toilet paper once classes start in the fall. Until then you're on your own." Instead, I bit my lip and directed her to the appropriate person on campus to get her toilet paper.

As funny as this was, the lesson couldn't have been clearer: parents need a college orientation as much as students do.

Orientation is no longer just for students—it's for getting parents oriented too. It's happening to parents of students at four-year institutions and two-year community colleges. Some parent sessions take place over the summer, and some are in the fall. Some orientations can mean an overnight stay, while others last just a few hours.

Typically, it works like this—while students are registering for classes, taking placement exams, attending ice-breakers, meeting with peer leaders, and getting essential information

continued from page 174

evolve in a very positive way if you are committed to it.

Trust that it will be OK. Trust that you've taught them well, and they'll surprise you with their decision making.

—Ryan Lombardi, Ohio University, Associate VP for Student Affairs and Dean of Students Chair of NASPA's Parent and Family Relations KC

Author's note: To date, no one has ever abused his cell number.

Parent orientation offers the ability for parents to get a feel for the "lay of the land" and the culture of the college or university. For many, orientation will be the first opportunity to visit campus. Since most parents have come to campus to help their son or daughter move in, take the opportunity to attend parent orientation in order to develop your own understanding of the college or university. Eat in the dining halls, visit the student union, attend a welcome session with the dean or president.

—Elizabeth Daly, Director of Orientation and Parent Programs, Northwestern University

My dad asked all of the important questions before I left for school—with him asking questions, it made it easier for me to think of questions I wanted to ask too, and it also made me realize that once I got to school, I could always find the answers to my own questions if I was willing to stay on the phone on hold long enough!

—Kasey, junior

from campus leaders, the parents are meeting with campus officials, mingling, learning, touring, and getting essential information. For the most part, it's a good time.

Parent orientation is your green light to have substantive conversations with people on campus and not get categorized as *that* parent. You can connect with the dean of students, the director of counseling services, the residence life director, the vice president of student affairs, campus safety, the student activities director, coaches, academic advisers, financial aid counselors, and campus clergy.

If you have questions, bring them with you. Before you attend orientation, flip through the rest of this book, browse the various topics, and see if they bring about some specific questions.

If you have to travel to an orientation, consider driving. It will trap your son or daughter in the car with you for a long period of time. If you're traveling cross-country, don't be in such a hurry to get home. This is quality time. Stretch it.

You can also help your child prepare for his or her orientation. A lot of incoming students have a glazed, stunned look on their faces during orientation—I call it "orientation game face." Setting foot on the campus with a bunch of strangers can be overwhelming. This is where those five questions from the previous tip can be extremely useful. If you know what your child wants to take away from orientation and your student knows what he wants to take away, you can help him find answers (just in case he freezes up). Asking about the date of the activity/organizational fair, inquiring about leadership opportunities, and finding out who students can contact to get involved in groups on campus is not being a helicopter parent—it's being informed and involved.

If your son or daughter has a particular concern or medical issue, orientation is a good time to meet with a professional on campus or a specialist in the community. If you have a child who has recovered from an eating

ENCOURAGE CONNECTIONS WITH ORIENTATION LEADERS

Orientation leaders are students who volunteer and help with orientation. They are typically student leaders who can help connect your child to campus during and after orientation. Suggest your child become Facebook friends with his or her orientation leader. If questions come up, a student who stays in touch with an OL can get information in a hurry. An orientation leader is someone who wants your child to win.

disorder or is dealing with a particular mental health situation, you can connect him or her to a therapist on campus in the health center or in the local community. If you help make the connection over the summer, when your child arrives on campus, he or she will already know familiar faces.

The following is an excerpt from a letter sent to parents following orientation from Ron Martel, the Vice President of Student Affairs at Johnson & Wales University (in Providence, RI). Ron is a dad and a strong advocate of connecting parents to the college experience.

THE ADVENTURE CONTINUES!

You and your child's college years will pass quickly, but I sincerely hope that you remain an active partner in their continued growth and development. Although the essence of your relationship should and will change, this is an opportunity for both of you to use this time to move to a new stage of development in your relationship. Revisit your communication patterns; how you impart advice and your role as a facilitator versus the deciding factor in their life. They are moving from adolescence to young adulthood and will flex their independence, as this is a time of great anticipation and excitement for them. Be prepared to experience fluctuations in their demeanor and behavior as they face uncertainty and change, given academic pressures, social development, and new relationships that may require impactful and difficult decisions.

Be prepared for your child's (and your own) conflicting emotions as the day of departure approaches, remembering that we brought them to this point in their lives and will be there to share in the joy and anxiety of them moving to their next stage of their personal development.

Discuss academic and financial expectations ahead of time. Encourage your student to set realistic goals and openly include them in the financial plan that will support their college education.

Discuss (not lecture) their use of alcohol and lifestyle choices they will have to make, remembering they are now the chief executive officers of their lives. It is time to be a coach rather than a rescuer, encouraging them to utilize University academic and personal support services to bring resolution to the issues they may face.

Keep them abreast of what is happening at home, and by all means continue to involve them in any and all major changes with your home and family. As much as you may find them at times to be less than interested, they do want to remain connected.

Continue to be there as an anchor for them! Listen with an open mind and be supportive.

Stay in touch with them through personalized means: cards, letters, emails, and care packages (we all love them!).

And always remember, as parents we owe our children two things in life—a firm and solid footing on which to build their lives and secondly the opportunity to let them soar!

I look forward to the year ahead as we join in supporting your child's academic and personal success.

Warm regards,

Ronald L. Martel,
Vice President for Student Affairs

As the summer rolls along, keep an eye out for special programs for incoming students occurring before classes begin. Some schools offer incoming student retreats, volunteer projects, day trips (to baseball games, museums, and rope courses), or camps that introduce students to college life before classes begin. These are optional, but they should be mandatory. I often participate in these events. They are *so* important. This is a perfect opportunity for students to get over this fear of the unknown and connect with people who will be familiar faces come the start of the year. A lot of these events cost money. If cost is an issue, contact one of the program coordinators and explain your situation. There may be unadvertised funds set aside to help students who don't have the resources. The cost of missing out is far more than the price of participating.

Finally, the MOST important paragraph of this tip (note the bold). If at any time during orientation you notice that you're the only adult in a room filled with hundreds of students, **get out of the room (a worthy use of bold)**. If you happen to see a few other parents in that room, most likely they are professionals or other parents who **need to leave the room**. Even if your kid wants you to stick around during the academic advising session, tell your student you'll meet up with him or her later. Every time I do orientation programs I see lingering parents who think they blend into the crowd. You don't. We see you. Even if you are wearing the same shirt and pants as your daughter (yes, this happens too).

On a serious note, I always think to myself, if this parent and kid are attached at the hip now, what's it going to be like later? If a child is that uncomfortable that he or she needs Mom or Dad to be in a room, that's a sign that college might not be the next best step. And if it's the mom or dad who's forcing the issue, that's a parent who needs to take a step back and look around and see that it's time to let go—I mean, loosen the grip (remember, there's no such thing as letting go).

QUESTIONS AND ANSWERS

Q: My daughter is so anxious at every turn; what can we do?

A: This is normal. The first time on campus meeting hundreds of new people can be totally overwhelming. Be patient with her. Walk her to the counseling services and introduce her to someone who can be a resource. Walk her to the residence life office and have her meet the director. Walk her to the gym and check out the activities happening in the rec center. Also consider having her speak to a therapist close to campus or a therapist near home. The more she knows and the more people she can meet who want her to win, the less that will be unknown.

Q: My son is going to miss orientation; what can we do?

A: Have him contact the orientation office. There might be alternative programs available. There could be a program in the fall for students who miss. Make sure he plans on attending welcome week activities or an activity and organization fair, and connects with the people running the organizations online.

Q: My child is a transfer student. Should she attend orientation?

A: Absolutely! Transfer students sometimes have their own orientation programs. I'm a fan of transfer students also attending any programs for first-year students that don't involve testing and placement. Also, your child should plan on attending all welcome week and other new student events. Transfer students have this idea that there is something different about them. The thing that's different about them is that they tend to be more mature, and that's a good thing. Plant the seed that she should go to absolutely everything. And you should plan on going to all parents' events too.

Q: What food plan should my son choose?

A: There are two answers. The first is to have your son reach out and ask an orientation leader, an RA, or a family friend who has lived on campus. Orientation is a time to find people who can answer specific questions. The second is to choose one that won't leave him hungry. Generally, a bigger plan is better. Just make sure you can change the plan during the duration of the contract if he ends up not using it enough.

Have a question? Want to answer another parent's question?

Post your questions and answers; visit *The Happiest Kid on Campus* Parent Forum: www.HappiestKidonCampus.com.

TIP #3 SHOPPING, PACKING, AND SHIPPING

A Moving Experience

The Tip

One car full is enough—two cars full means that you've overpacked.

The Story

As a freshman, I overpacked. Mostly it was because my dad would keep throwing more stuff in for me to pack, school supplies in particular. I think I had three boxes of highlighters, six packs of Post-its, eight notebooks, a thousand staples, three ethernet cables, a few fans, a paper shredder (which my mom refused to let me bring back with me), a few packages of printer paper, one of those lap desks—wow—so much now that I'm writing about and thinking about it. Last year we were barely able to pack everything in two cars. This year we took one car and it all fit. This time around (my sophomore year), my mom would sneakily take stuff off my packing pile when my dad wasn't looking or around. It was a funny experience.

—Josh, sophomore, University of Delaware

The summer before my first semester, my mother kept putting off going shopping for things for my dorm. What's worse is that whenever I found something I liked, she'd find a reason not to. It was a little bothersome, but I know she was only trying to hold on a little longer. It was even kind of cute.

—Caitlin, freshman

* * *

Shopping, packing, and shipping can be an emotional experience for everyone involved. Most parents tend to cry when the bill arrives at the end of the month. Most students cry when lifting the heaviest boxes, meeting their roommates for the first time, or seeing their lack of closet space.

They say that how a parent helps a student pack is how a parent will support a student in college (who "they" are, I'm not sure). A parent who does all the shopping and packing is assumed to be too involved. A parent who ignores all the shopping and packing is assumed to not be involved enough. A parent who helps a student shop and pack and sits on a suitcase in order to help get it closed is a parent who is involved just enough.

Some students want to pack everything now. Some do it a little bit at a time over the summer. Others

Shopping-wise, get kids their own credit card hooked to an account at home. That way you can deposit money for the kid to spend accordingly. It helps.

—Emily, sophomore

(Author's note: And it's a way to be building credit; see Tip #17 for more)

do it the night before. Parents tend to have their own timetable. Deciding when to do it, how to do it, and what to bring are some of those student-parent clashes that bubble up from time to time.

Shopping and packing mean the undeniable reality that

college and change are coming—there's no denying what's happening once you squeeze the extra-long twin sheets and shower shoes into an overstuffed duffel bag. Some parents and students freak out. Some bury their feelings. Some embrace it.

However you cope, big fights over nothing tend to bubble to the surface in the midst of change. It's as if child and parent are on opposite sides of a magnet, repelling each other. One line of thinking is that when we love something so much, the only way to distance ourselves is to destroy it, degrade it, and push it away. The more we fight and push away the things we love, the less we will miss them. Under no circumstance should you judge the level your child loves you during this process. In fact, the worse your child treats you, the more he or she probably loves you.

If he or she got into college, your child is smart enough to figure out this shopping, packing, and shipping part of the experience. This is a good time to start reminding your son that he is in charge. If he forgets something, he can always get it at school. If your daughter packs too much, she can sell it on craigslist. One carload should be enough.

Should your son or daughter be open to your wisdom and advice, here are some suggestions to help guide you during this process.

The best strategy is not to pack for the next few years—but only the next few months. Anything can be bought or shipped later. There are stores near campus where your child can go to buy stuff (a shocking concept). If a student doesn't have local transportation, he or she can bus it, taxi it, or ask a friend with a car for a ride. Sometimes schools have shopping trips and bus students to the mall. If there are no stores near campus, online stores can deliver everything. From school supplies to Ramen noodles, most of it can be overnighted to your student's door for less than five dollars (check out Amazon.com Prime). Literally, you can order something at noon and it will arrive the next day. That's not something parents could have done ten years ago. And still, a student will come home at some point and can pick up more stuff and stuff the stuff in a suitcase.

> Just a general tip—if you're going to a school on the quarter system, you can wait until right after all the semester schools start to get your stuff from places like Target and Walmart. As soon as the semester schools start, everything goes on sale by at least 50 percent and you'll save a lot of money.
>
> —Lesley, senior

Before going on a spending spree and checking off everything on the "going to college list" from a retailer's "back-to-college" checklist, check out what the school suggests you bring. Bringing a mattress won't work if they don't allow you to BYOM (Bring Your Own Mattress). Buying a toaster won't make anything toasty if toasters aren't allowed. Buying an air conditioner and mini fridge won't keep anything cool if the rules restrict cooling equipment. Use your school's packing guide. If something isn't on the list, check with the campus housing officials to make sure it's within the rules and regulations.

WHEN BUYING BIG STUFF

If it's too big to fit in an a car, consider buying it online, getting it shipped, or buying it over the phone and picking it up once you get to campus. Most big stuff can be shipped from retailers for less than it costs to buy it and ship it (plus, you can save on tax). Also, check to see how early you can have stuff shipped to the residence halls.

WHEN BUYING COMPUTERS

Inquire to see if the school supplies computers or iPods to incoming students. Investigate what kinds of discounts are available and the preferred vendors. Some schools have unbeatable deals with manufacturers. Also, it's important to know what kind of technical support is available through campus—buying a computer through the school may include computer support. Also worth mentioning—some schools have rental programs. When buying software, search the keywords "Academic Software Discounts" and you'll find huge discounts (75 percent or more) on major software. It's unbelievable.

THAT'S ONE EXPENSIVE BOOK

According to the College Board, the national average cost of books and supplies at four-year private colleges in 2008–09 was $1,077.

WHEN BUYING BOOKS

Now students can shop for books online and have them waiting to be picked up in the campus bookstore. There are also websites not affiliated with the campus bookstore that offer huge discounts and free shipping. There are also rental programs for books. When buying new or used books, remind your child to make sure it's the latest edition. Great deals can be found on outdated editions—returning a big book back to the manufacturer is expensive.

WHEN IT COMES TO EXPENSIVE STUFF

Computers, mp3 players, and video games look alike. Make sure your child engraves his or her first and last name on such equipment and keeps it out of sight. Then, if someone down the hall mysteriously has a new laptop when your child's went missing a few days earlier, having something engraved in a secret place will solve the crime. Check with your insurance agent to see what coverage, if any, is extended if your child's stuff gets stolen or ruined.

DISCOURAGE BRINGING ANYTHING THAT'S IRREPLACEABLE

At college, things get stolen, misplaced, or lost all the time. If there's a big event where your daughter wants to wear something special, have her pick it up when she visits home and return it the next time she comes home. Most of the time, if it's not something she can replace, she's better off not bringing it to campus.

WHEN IT COMES TO PACKING

Overpacking is a common rookie mistake. To avoid over-packing, suggest the three-box/duffel bag strategy. This revolutionary packing strategy takes into account that packing can be emotional. Here's how it works—your student gets several boxes or duffel bags (duffels are easy to transport) and then creates three different areas to pack.

1. **WHAT I NEED NOW BAG(S):** Everything that is unquestionably necessary is packed and loaded for transport.

2. **WHAT I MIGHT NEED NOW BAG(S):** Everything that might be needed in the near future is packed in a box and set aside for easy transport

3. **WHAT I NEED LATER BAG(S):** Everything that is not needed now is kept in another area for packing and transporting later.

Leaving things behind doesn't mean not having access—it just means accessing them when you need them. That's why it's emotionally pleasing.

My biggest tip would be to learn the rules about bringing things into your residence before you start shopping. My university had a general rule that you couldn't bring in anything larger than a desk chair, and every year we had to stop people from trying to drag in couches, mattresses, etc.

—Nicole, grad student

WHEN IT COMES TO SHIPPING

You don't need to haul everything yourself, jam it into the car, or strap it to the roof. Check with the school to see if there are services that will pick up the boxes, duffels, and bags from your home and deliver them directly to your student's door. The cost can be less than shipping it yourself. The only catch—unless you're attending a larger school, the services might not be available. If something weighs more than one hundred pounds and you're flying, it might not fly. Some airlines will not allow you to pack items that are more than one hundred pounds. Plus, even if they do allow it on board, you'll end up paying way too much.

The best approach is to go to your local UPS, Fed Ex, or other shipping store and see what kind of deals they have. There are often back-to-school shipping specials. Sometimes they will pack it and ship it for less than it costs for you to buy the materials and pack it yourself. Also, check out flat-rate shipping with the U.S. Postal Service. Flat-rate boxes are a great deal. See Move-In Day (Tip #5) for more information about what happens once you arrive on campus.

FOR COUPONS AND DEALS, FOLLOW ME ON TWITTER AND FACEBOOK

Check out back-to-school deals, shipping offers, and other discounts I come across by visiting my website, *The Happiest Kid on Campus* Facebook page, and by following the Twitter feeds @HappiestKid and @NakedRoommate. If you come across a deal, send me a note and I'll spread the word to other followers. You can always find me at Harlan@HelpMeHarlan.com.

QUESTIONS AND ANSWERS

Q: What are some of the things I should advise my child to bring?

A: Before turning this question over to current students on campus or recent grads, I'll mention shower shoes (i.e., flip-flops). If the floors in communal bathrooms could talk, they would just scream. No one needs to walk on that barefoot. No one!

HAVE MORE SUGGESTIONS?

Send them my way, and I'll do my best to include them in the next edition of the book! Visit www.HappiestKidonCampus.com and start a discussion topic.

And now, answers straight from current and former students:

- Two words: mattress pad. The mattresses in the rooms can be awful.
- Microwaveable dishes. I bought the cutest plates and bowls for my dorm room only to discover they aren't microwaveable.
- Cough drops and cold medicine. I totally forgot those, and I just got some sort of virus.
- Fabric to hang on my walls, a cozy alternative to posters.
- A compact collapsible shelf for my closet (bought a big one and had to return it because it took up three-quarters of my closet).

- A first-aid kit full of back heating pads, Band-Aids, thermometer, and medicines.
- A desk lamp. Especially if you are going to have a roommate (better than overhead lights).
- 3M Command adhesive strips and hooks!
- Dorm chairs suck, so having your own desk chair is nice.
- Good walking shoes and a good backpack.
- Lots of toothpaste, deodorant, and soap—enough so you never run out.
- Ramen noodles are a staple.
- Sheet clips for those unruly beds up against walls that won't keep the sheets on. It's upsetting.
- A toaster is a good idea [if it's not against the rules]. I like toast.
- Snack foods are good. I still don't have snacks. It's upsetting.
- An area rug—the floors are usually either cold or disgusting (or both).
- A fan. It gets really hot in those dorms without air conditioning.
- Warehouse club supply of ibuprofen and acetaminophen.
- Earplugs for noisy roomies, eye cover to keep out the light.
- Cheetos and peanut butter—the ultimate snack!
- Febreeze for funky smells is a must.
- Extra lightbulbs for lamps.

- Wait until the first day of class, get the syllabus, and buy the things you need to read immediately (like for tomorrow) from the bookstore. Order everything else online cheaply.
- A laundry basket with wheels—it was a lifesaver (no dragging laundry down stairs—especially when you wait till you have a mountain of laundry to do it).
- Plastic storage containers where the drawers slide out are awesome. I didn't have any freshman year and suffered from many clothing avalanches.
- Two extra toothbrushes—one for bathroom cleaning and one just in case you drop it on the disgusting communal bathroom floor.
- Clear Scotch tape works wonders for everything.
- One of those wind/white noise machines.
- My own bar fridge to store food and drinks that wouldn't fit in the shared fridge.
- A sleep mask (so you can successfully sleep any time of day or night!).
- A basic tool kit (or at least a screwdriver).
- Extra-long sheets (yes, you need the extra-long ones).

Have a question? Want to answer another parent's question?

Post your questions and answers; visit *The Happiest Kid on Campus* Parent Forum: www.HappiestKidonCampus.com.

TIP #4 COMMUNITY COLLEGE

Helping Them Connect with the Community

The Tip

The rumors about community college can be incredibly untrue. The people who I went to school with were hardworking and smart—and the professors in my classes have all been incredible.

The Story

I initially decided to go to a community college because my grades in high school were not good enough to get into a top-tier university, which is something that I've strived for my whole life. Not getting into my first choice university was tough for me, and my father had just recently taken a large pay cut at his job. Because of that, I felt that sticking close to home and going to community college was a good option. Initially, I heard rumors that community college was like high school all over again—and I was scared—but it's not like high school at all. The professors were outstanding. Unlike professors at a research institute, teachers were always available. I developed great relationships with them—relationships that I still value today. I ended up learning more there in two years than I did my entire four years in high school. I took a variety of classes in so many different areas. I was a member of the music club, the criminal justice club, the business leadership club, and many others. As far as transferring goes, the process was incredibly simple. The advisers at my community college told me exactly what I needed to take that would transfer. When I transferred to a big ten university, I had already completed sixty hours of coursework toward the 120-hour requirement for the bachelor's degree. Also, I had only paid a small fraction of what a university would have cost. My parents were so proud of me, and they were so happy that I chose a cheaper route to get my education.

—Kevin M., senior at University of Illinois

* * *

Community colleges can be a perfect fit for so many students. In fact, more high school graduates than ever are attending community colleges:

Just under 11.5 million students, or 39.6 percent of all young adults ages eighteen to twenty-four, were enrolled in either a two- or four-year college in October 2008 (the most recent date for which comprehensive nationwide data are available). Enrollments have been rising over many decades at both two- and four-year colleges, but the most recent annual spike has taken place entirely at two-year colleges. In October 2007, some 3.1 million young adults, or 10.9 percent of all eighteen- to twenty-four-year-olds, were enrolled in a community college. A year later, that figure had risen to

3.4 million students, or 11.8 percent of all eighteen- to twenty-four-year-olds. By contrast, enrollments at four-year colleges were essentially flat from 2007 to 2008.

—Source: Pew Research Center
(http://pewsocialtrends.org/pubs/747/
college-enrollment-hits-all-time-high-fueled-by-community-college-surge)

I know that there are some parents who don't have the best impression of the community college experience. But things have changed over the years—there are some community colleges that rival four-year institutions. In fact, I've met many high level college professionals working at four-year institutions who feel that many of their students would be better suited to spend a year in community college before coming to campus.

Once you become more familiar with the people and resources on campus, you'll be surprised to discover the opportunities, values, and education offered. Students attending community colleges can get involved in clubs, activities, and organizations and take on leadership roles. Because classes are a fraction of the cost, there's more room to take more courses and discover new interests. Most instructors are trained as educators (as opposed to researchers who must teach) and want to help your student win. There are academic support services, smaller classes, developmental courses, sprawling student activities, advising, career services, counseling, and health services. Community colleges also have relationships with top-tier schools and institutions that make transferring and earning a degree at a four-year school nearly seamless.

Parents of community college students are now more involved in their student's college experience too. If anything, as a parent of a student who is most likely living at home, having so much access to your child means that you will know even more than the parents of students at four-year schools. And that means you need to know how to support your student and who to reach out to should you need help along the way. Parents of students attending community college need to plug into the flow of information to stay informed. Let's look at some of the key things you need to know.

PARENTS—STICK TOGETHER

A Blog Entry from Vicki Atkinson,
Director of New Student Programs and Retention at Harper Community College

Thank you to the five-hundred-plus parents who attended Parent Orientation this summer. The feedback we received was both affirming and helpful. As we approach midterm (hard to believe), you may be seeing signs that your student might need a little help. **What should you look for?**

1. **Any change in your student's schedule?** By now, the routine should be fully apparent and you should have a good idea of how your student's Monday schedule is different from a Tuesday schedule—and so on. Are you noticing more time spent at home? Online? At work? Out with friends? It's okay to inquire—"It seems like you have more free time...how are things going at school?"

2. **Any change in your student's "wellness patterns" (eating or sleeping)?** If so, you might want to inquire. Harper takes your student's overall wellness very seriously—we have a comprehensive Health and Psych Services office on campus and tons of resources are available...not least of which is information about where or how to obtain flu shots. (Have you had yours? Just asking...)

COMMUNITY COLLEGE CAN BE TOO SAFE

For the majority of students who commute (some community colleges have housing), not having to take on all the challenges that come with leaving home and adjusting to so many new issues can make focusing on grades and getting involved much easier. That said, there are some drawbacks. The biggest one is that community college can be too easy of a transition.

What I mean is that it's just way too easy for a student to be way too comfortable. It can be like a fifth year in high school. A student can go to class with friends from high school, have the same part-time job, hang out with the same boyfriend or girlfriend, see mom and dad, and never leave his or her comfort zone. It's so easy and so comfortable that it doesn't force a student to develop all those other skills that come with being forced to get comfortable with the uncomfortable.

College should be uncomfortable at times. Never being uncomfortable means never having to look at ourselves in the mirror (in our thong) and confront our insecurities. Residential colleges force students to step outside of their comfort zone. And really, if all goes as planned at community college, your child will be at that four-year school in a couple of years and faced with all the same temptations.

A student will get what he or she puts into it—no one will force them to get involved and grow at the student's community college. But you can plant the idea and help them define a path. Whether it's playing in the band, participating in student government, taking on a leadership role, playing a team sport, performing in a play, singing in choir, or writing for the newspaper—getting involved will force students to step outside of their comfort zone, and it will enable them to find a new group of friends outside of their high school relationships. But without educated parents who can help a student get involved, it's easy to go to community college and live a safe life that resembles just another year in high school.

LIVING AT HOME

The fact that they are living at home will also make this more difficult. I do understand that you might need your son or daughter to help with younger siblings, run errands, and be there for you at home. But if there's one thing you can do for them, make it required that they get involved in at least one activity outside the classroom. Make it as important as taking classes and helping at home. If they can do this, so many good things can happen. They will meet people with similar interests outside of their high school circle of friends, they will form relationships with advisers and staff, they will get to

My son (now a successful physician) still says he learned more at his community college (where he earned two associate degrees) than at his highly selective university. In his med school class, four members had begun in a community college. I also happen to be a university professor who once worked at a large community college. The students at the community college frequently came back to tell me that their transfer destinations were much less rigorous. I think sometimes community colleges (good ones, of course) do a better job with freshman /sophomore courses than some universities.

—PK Weston, Professor, Point Park University

know themselves better, and they will know how to do the same thing at a four-year school.

As a parent who will see your child on a regular basis, you need to make a shift. This is a new time for them, and for you. Plan on your relationship changing. Give your son or daughter room to grow and change. Yes, living under your roof means living by your rules, but that can also mean creating new rules and changing the boundaries from high school to enable him or her to take on new challenges and grow. Before you know it, two years will be pass and it will be time for a four-year college experience. A community college student who knows how to find his or her place will already have a plan and a path in place to make a smooth transition to life at a four-year institution.

I loved my community college experience—I played trombone in the jazz band. I'm still in touch with my academic adviser!

—Eric Stoller, Academic Adviser, Oregon State University

THINGS YOU NEED TO KNOW

- Help them put together a plan for community college (see Tip #1)
- Attend orientation events for parents (assuming they're offered)
- Get plugged in to the campus website and resources for parents
- Understand that FERPA and HIPAA laws will mean you will not have access to your eighteen-year-old's records without consent
- Encourage your son or daughter to get involved with at least one activity or organization outside the classroom
- If they must work, encourage them to work on campus or find a job that can help them figure out their next move beyond college
- Treat your child as if he or she is attending a four-year school (give him or her space)
- Respect your child's boundaries (make it clear that there are new boundaries now)
- Give them room to stumble and fall
- Talk about curfews (they will need later ones)
- Avoid micromanaging grades and homework
- Direct them to the resources to help them when they need it
- Connect to the online resources for parents of college students

QUESTIONS AND ANSWERS

Q: What are some things I need to do over the summer months as a parent of a community college student?

A: For this answer, I'd like to share a family checklist offered to you by Janita Patrick, Achieving the Dream Director (Tallahassee Community College). This list is distributed to parents several months before classes begin:

FAMILY CHECKLIST

If you and your family are from out of town, you may want to:

· Visit housing options
· Establish a local bank account for your student

Things to do between now and the beginning of the semester:

· Review the catalog and student handbook to increase your knowledge of our policies and regulations.
· Check to confirm all documents have been received. Provide the appropriate format (original/copy) for any documents missing.
· If appropriate, contact the Financial Aid Office to confirm all documents have been received. Provide the appropriate format (original/copy) for any documents missing.
· Pay tuition and fees, and discuss personal finances with your student.
· Have your student learn their Student ID number.
· Talk with your student about various social issues he or she may face.
· Talk with your student about their fears, concerns, and expectations related to coming to college. Share yours with them.
· Talk with your student about the academic, career, and social support services available on campus and how he or she might use them.
· Sign lease/contract for student's new residence, pay deposit and any additional fees.
· Contact local utility, cable/satellite, and phone companies to establish connection dates at the student's new residence (if applicable).
· If your student is moving out of town, have him or her make hotel reservations if he or she will be staying overnight or longer prior to moving into a new residence.
· If your student will be living away from home, check your homeowners' policy to see if it covers belongings for the place your student will be living (residence hall, apartment, house, etc.).

- If your student is currently covered under your health and/or automobile insurance policy, find out if he or she will still be covered. Make sure your student has the insurance information (policy number, company name, and company phone number).
- You should each establish an emergency contact.
- Register the vehicle(s) your student will use with the campus.

Have a question? Want to answer another parent's question?

Post your questions and answers; visit *The Happiest Kid on Campus* Parent Forum: www.HappiestKidonCampus.com.

TIP #5 MOVE-IN DAY

How to Embarrass Them Just Enough

The Tip

Please no messages on the back window of the car on move-in day.

The Story

All I know is when I got here to Michigan State, there was a red van parked outside of the dorm with "PRECIOUS PEANUT IS MOVING TO MSU!!!" written on the back window. I thanked God that very minute that I didn't have those parents! Needless to say, I have always wanted to find out who this Precious Peanut character is.

—Mackenzie W., Michigan State University

* * *

It's a fantastic day for moving! The car is packed. Everyone is calm, cool, and unemotional. The weather is a perfect 72 degrees, sunny, with 10 percent humidity. It couldn't be a better, more perfect day. Today will be the most relaxing, low-key, and easiest day in college move-in history! Ahhhhh, such a nice thought...

Be there if you can. It's a stressful day, and it's helpful to have someone there to help unload the stress, even if we act like we hate it.

—Mark, senior

This is an exciting time for a new college student. They don't need you flipping out about where to park and how you plan to move everything up three flights of stairs. Don't stress too much.

—Amanda, junior

BACK TO REALITY

It can be hot, humid, and sweaty; the elevator might be broken; moods can be swinging; stress runs high; and parents are the target of it all. It's so unfair on so many levels—parents work so hard for these precious moments in life, but most students don't want to be seen with you during them. And if you're helping with the costs of college, it's like paying for the party and not getting to eat the appetizers. It's not fair. Your move-in-day emotions are important, but not a top priority. The happy sentiments are welcome, but the sad ones are best kept boxed up and in the car until that final good-bye. Once the wheels hit the pavement, feel free to rip it open and let the tears flow.

CHANGE YOUR GRIP

Some parents are thrilled for their kids to move out. Other parents are dreading it, in denial, and barely able to cope. In the past, moving day

Some campuses have amazing move-ins. They get tons of volunteers to grab boxes from your car and take them to the named room, and all you have to do is unpack and decorate. Other campuses have very organized yet not as helpful move-ins, where everything is directed but you take up all of your own stuff and then unpack.

—Meghan, recent college grad

marked the moment in time when a parent was supposed to let go. But if you've read the first half of this book, you'll know that things have changed. You no longer have to "let go." You can just change your grip—loosen it up a bit. Let your child know you're there if he or she needs you, but give all the room your child needs to find his or her own space and create a new life in college.

In addition to not having to let go, another thing that should help you make the emotional transition easier to handle is that between cell phones, Facebook, email, video chats, visits home, and visits to campus, you'll see a lot of your child. When you break it down, college is only about thirty-two weeks of classes. And some of those weeks include visits home, holiday breaks, or family visits to campus. So maybe you'll get to see your kid twenty-six weeks out of the year. Yes, the relationship will change, but it can change for the better. There are still many more summers together. And then he or she can move back in for another five years while searching for a job and saving enough money to buy the perfect condo (just kidding). Remember, it's not letting go—just changing the grip. I hope this is a comforting thought.

MOVING INTO YOUR NEW ROLE (WELCOME TO "MOM & POP'S MOVING COMPANY")

When you do loosen the grip, you will not have as much control over your child. Some parents don't do well with this. Some hold on to whatever they can. As it applies to moving, this can mean controlling their child's stuff or their child's roommate's stuff. When moving a child into a room, it's helpful to remember that it's his and his roommate's space (if he's living with someone). Pretend you're working for "Mom & Pop's Moving Service" (but you do not get moving shirts to wear during the move—embarrassing). During the move, let your child run the show. He or she is the boss. And just like a moving service, if you break it, you buy it. They set the pace. Unpacking, arranging, and rearranging other people's stuff should only be done with your child's permission (yes, you should ask for permission). Just the act of asking permission sets an entirely different tone. And when you ask, make

> Every parent needs to understand that on move-in day, they should be the submissive party. While they may be paying for it, it is still your space. It might be their natural instinct to move things around, try to start unpacking your suitcase, or comment about what posters you brought to hang on your wall, but it is important for them to understand that this is their kid's time to be independent with their living space. It is awesome when they are helpful, but unless they are careful they could end up becoming a nuisance and make move-in day that much more stressful.
>
> —Amy L., sophomore, Marymount Manhattan

sure you say "please," or you will have to ask again (just kidding about the "please").

There are a lot of parents who have a hard time asking a son or daughter for permission to do something that's going to make life easier for them. Especially parents who have been taking care of their child's needs for the past eighteen years. The mind-set is "of course my child wants my help!" It almost seems like a parent thinks he or she has a right to participate in this rite of passage. Some parents might even go as far as thinking, "I'm paying. I can do whatever I want." But paying doesn't mean controlling what drawer the underwear goes into. You might be helping with costs, but he or she has ownership over this experience.

I went without my parents, because I knew it'd be frustrating. If you think you won't handle the stress well (I am the baby of the family, that means lots of crying—and I am more patient than my parents with inevitably annoying tasks such as moving), and if it's possible, you don't need to come along. My parents drove to campus to pick up the car, drop off my fridge, and go out to dinner later on during move-in day. That was perfect; they got to see where I live and feel like they weren't completely abandoning me. I even had fun moving in by myself.

—Katie, freshman

YE HAVE FAITH, THEY CAN AND WILL MAKE IT

I hear from a lot of parents who are extremely worried that their child won't be able to survive on his or her own. Some of you have freely admitted that you have been doing everything and anything for your child. And now you don't know if he or she is equipped to handle the transition. You worry that your daughter will live out of a box, never wash clothes, and starve. I can guarantee you that she will eat, her clothes will not be as clean, and she might live out of a box (until the box breaks from sitting on it or using it as a table for eating). But this is your child's choice. Some will make better choices than others, some will be cleaner than others, but they will all survive. It will surprise you.

THINGS YOU'LL WANT TO KNOW ABOUT MOVE-IN DAY

Move-in day might seem straightforward—you move all the stuff in and then you get out—but there is an art to the madness. For example, getting there first thing in the morning might seem like a fantastic idea, but this will put you in the middle of all the chaos. If your son or daughter is worried about selecting a bed near the window, you can always get there early, check out the room, unload some stuff you can carry, and then unload the rest of the stuff later. You can also ask the residence life staff about the best time to come back and unload. If you time it right, you might be able to find an available cart and staff to help you out. The following are some move-in secrets to help you help your child have a seamless move-in day.

1. How to Say Good-bye

I can't take credit for this one. This is from a professional who has been presenting to parents for twenty-plus years during college orientation.

You say good-bye the following way—even if you're sad, your job is to make sure your student is left on campus with dignity. A kiss and a hug good-bye, and then you turn away. If you leave overemotional, your student will be more worried about you than about how to take advantage of their first day on campus.

—Bill Leipold, Associate VP, Rutgers University

One more thing I'd like to add—I've heard from several parents who chose not to participate in their child's move-in, because they couldn't handle being there. If you're not sure that you can handle the move, consider staying at home and visiting a few weeks later, once everything is set up. Having you sobbing around every corner isn't going to help. It's just going to make the floors wet (and that can be dangerous when moving heavy boxes).

> It is great to have help moving in, but keep it at that. There is no need to go around the whole floor looking at other rooms and feeling that you need to meet every new face you see.
>
> —Isaac, junior

2. How Long You Should Stick Around

Unless there is a parent event on campus—move 'em in, then move it out. Plan on staying long enough to get your son's stuff into his room and to go shopping to stock the room with food (a kid needs to eat). He will unpack his room and figure it all out. He doesn't need you there (unless he tells you he wants you to stay).

3. Let Them Set It Up (At Their Own Pace)

I was presenting at a parent session, and a mother was complaining that her son refused to set up his room to her liking. He was obsessed with getting his stereo system working just right. She couldn't handle that his room was not put together before

> **WHAT NOT TO DO**
>
> On move-in day two girls came to me saying, "We're having a roommate conflict." I responded, "What's your conflict?" They answered, "Our parents are fighting about how the room is being set up. We want you to get rid of them so we can move on with our lives."
>
> —Residence life professional, twenty-plus years on the job

she left. What she didn't recognize was that this was his room. He wanted music because he liked music. That's what made him the most comfortable.

A lot of parents want everything to be perfect because leaving a child in a room that's perfect is comforting for him or her. How about this—leave the room imperfect, and have your child email a picture or take a video to show you how perfect it is when you get home. Or you can see it the next time you visit.

4. Know the Rules, Regulations, and Logistics

Make sure you know the rules and regulations and understand the logistics. You don't want to load it all, drive it all there, and unload it all only to have this happen to you. A student might be excited to take that awesome waterbed only to find out that waterbeds are not allowed. And that aquarium—that won't work either if it exceeds the maximum allowable size. Every school has rules for living in the halls. Make sure your child knows them. Things that can start fires, damage the buildings, or take up huge amounts of electricity are questionable.

Four families pulled up in front of the residence hall with a full-length moving van. While it was four families, there was still no way the full-size armoire, full-size refrigerator, or the king-size bed were going to fit into these residence hall rooms. The dad of one of the students tried to convince me otherwise, and ended up not only moving the items upstairs, but right back down again. Not a fun moment for him!

> —Julie Payne Kirchmeier, PhD, Southern Illinois University, Director of University Housing

5. Let Them Do the Fixing

When problems or issues arise, have your child take care of it and be his or her own self-advocate.

Let your student do the talking. You can be nearby to lend support (or a check), but let them check in at their residence hall themselves, let them figure out where to get their books, etc. If a problem comes up (say, they can't get their Internet set up or their key isn't working), let them figure it out on their own. They'll thank you for it later, after you've driven away and they have to figure out where the dining center is—they'll have the confidence to ask, since they've been doing it all day anyway!

—Amanda Mesirow, Residence Life Coordinator,
University of Northern Iowa

QUESTIONS AND ANSWERS

Q: What are some additional things that parents should keep in mind during move-in day?

A: There are a few more things that didn't make it into this tip that are worth including. Instead of me sharing this information with you, I'll let Kassie, Meagan, Jeriann, Kelsey, and Jamie guide you.

There is this girl in the building next to mine; she moved in the same day as everybody else. Only her mom stayed there with her for two weeks! I think that parents need to help their children adapt to their new independent lifestyle by making their child live on their own when they need to.

—Kassie, freshman

*Know where you are and aren't allowed to park.
Restrictions are generally lifted for move-in week, but
if you go on a day when no one else is there, you are
more likely to get a ticket. Also, find out if there is an
elevator or stairs. If the former, it is easier to pack in
boxes and use a dolly. If the latter, pack in smaller
bags that are easier to carry up the stairs. Also, take
an extra person to help if possible. It takes so much less
time to move in.*

—Meagan, sophomore

*Bring a toolbox with stuff like a hammer and nails,
stick tack, a level, and tape. You'll end up being the
cool parent who saved the day.*

—Jeriann, freshman

*Don't do it all; don't do nothing. Ask for a job and
let your student determine your level of involvement.
That way you don't arrange their room in a totally
unwanted way, but they're also not stuck carrying all
the heavy things themselves.*

—Kelsey, sophomore

*Understand that it sucks and it is stressful, but once
we get our stuff in the dorm and get some food in our
stomachs, we are seriously ready for you to go home!*

—Jamie, sophomore

Have a question? Want to answer another parent's question?

Post your questions and answers; visit *The Happiest Kid on Campus* Parent Forum: www.HappiestKidonCampus.com.

TIP #6 CALLING, TEXTING, AND CHATTING

Why You'll Soon Learn to Text...

The Tip

Limit your calls and texting to twice a week. If the kid wants to talk to you more, they will; otherwise it's just overbearing.

The Story

Even though I'm capable of taking care of myself, my mom still texts or calls me every day. And often it not only is bothersome, but it adds more stress with all the questions—especially during major crunch times like finals. Having to deal with studying and the constant questions and calls of concern and wondering just add up to a whole lot of stress that isn't necessary. And no, I haven't told my mom how much this interferes with my life—partially because I fear that conversation would upset her, and because she is paying for all of this. I'd rather she just remain happy and bother me while she's paying for me being here. I'm sure someday it will come up.

—Brandon, freshman, Oakland University

* * *

The Tip

Know that sometimes we can't talk, because we're busy working—not drinking, partying, or sleeping.

The Story

My mother has yet to "cut the cord!" She calls me an average of five times a day, and sometimes in ten-minute or shorter intervals! I go to school ten hours away from home, and I think she takes it harder than I do. One day during my freshman year, I had about eight hours of homework to finish and my mom called me seven times in three hours—just to tell me something funny the cat did, or tell me who she had talked to that day. I then called my dad to tell him about it, and I asked him if he would please tell her nicely to not call me as much each day, especially if I had so much work to do. She didn't talk to me for four days.

> **THE #1 BEST WAY TO GET IN TOUCH**
>
> Learn to text. Period. Exclamation mark. Exclamation mark. If that means getting a new phone, get one with a keyboard. Please do it. I know you want to hear your child's voice, but texting is the most unobtrusive way to get a response (unless he or she is in class, sleeping, or busy). You can always talk later, but texting is your best bet for a quick response. Just make sure to check your cell phone texting plan.

—Kari, freshman, Oklahoma State University

* * *

If you can't get through this tip because you're too busy calling, texting, or chatting with your child, that's too much.

In the history of time, students and parents have

I'm an only child and was expecting my parents to be complete wrecks when I left for college, but my mom always waits for me to call, because she doesn't want to be *that* parent. My dad will occasionally leave a voice mail here but follows what my mom does.

—Brianna, freshman

One of my friends still talks to her parents every day on the phone, and often they Skype. If she doesn't answer, they get very worried and freak out. We are sophomores in college and this is still going on.

—Tori, sophomore

never had such immediate, unlimited, and cheap access to one another. A parent can call a child from anywhere at any time and find out what he or she is doing. You can email, text, instant message, video chat, write on a wall, or Tweet—and then you can eat lunch and do it all over again before dinner.

Likewise, your child can call you from anywhere at any time. He or she can share all the good news, and more frequently, the bad news. It can come by email, text message, instant message, video chat, Facebook message, or Tweet—and then your son or daughter can go to class and do it all again before dinner.

Everyone is literally a push of a button away. You are in the palm of their hands—they are in the palm of your hands—it's like everyone is in the palm of each other's hands. It's almost like holding hands. Gone are the days of letting go. This is the time when you have to change your grip.

And this brings up big questions:

- Who should do the calling?
- How often should you call? How often should they call?
- When is the best time? What is the worst time?
- Should you expect boys to call more or less frequently than girls?
- Is it better to call, send an email, text, use Facebook, or video chat?
- How can you be involved enough to support them emotionally, but not be so involved that you keep them from engaging in life on campus?
- And when is it right to call or intervene on their behalf? Should you ever intervene?

THE ANSWER: It's really up to you and your child.

I'm not trying to avoid answering the questions. There isn't just one answer. You are the ones setting the precedent. Some of you will get it wrong, and others of you will get it right. The best approach is to listen to your instincts and listen to your child.

> Follow your child's lead. Most kids don't want to be contacted every day. They will call if they have something to tell you. If they don't call you ever, then call once a week. Emails and texts are often easier to respond to than phone calls.
>
> —Colleen, freshman

The general rule is that if you feel like it's too much calling, texting, and video chatting—it's too much. If your son or daughter feels like it's too much, then it's definitely too much. If a third party tells you it's too much—it's probably too much. And if you have to convince yourself it's not too much—it's definitely too much.

IT'S TOO MUCH CALLING IF...

As an objective third party, I can tell you that these things are too much:

A morning wake-up call every single day is too much (and yes, this happens more than you would imagine). You might think you're doing it to help your daughter get up in the morning, but I know you're really doing it to help yourself get up in the morning. If your daughter answers, you know she's up and in her bed. But if she doesn't answer, that's trouble. But your daughter will always pick up a text—even if she's not in her bed (I'm not saying whose bed she's in). Calling every morning isn't going to help anyone become an independent adult. It's just going to irritate her roommate and send a message to her that Mom and Dad don't trust her to get up in the morning.

Calling an instructor to share that your child is sick with a cold or the flu is too much. You might think you're doing your son a favor, but you're not. All it takes is an email or a call from him to communicate with a professor. When your son is in the professional world and he's sick, will you call his boss? No boss or instructor wants to hear from Mom or Dad. Unless he can't speak or is in the hospital, there's no reason to call. And even if he can't speak, he can type and send an email. Calling for a student isn't going to make a student a self-advocate or self-reliant—just dependent on you.

Calling every night at 11:00 p.m. to make sure your daughter is at home studying and not hanging out too late is too much

(this happens a lot). I can promise you that your daughter will tell you whatever you want to hear, because telling you the truth isn't what you want to hear. And that's just setting her up to not tell you the truth. This is not how you engage her in honest and trusting dialogue.

Calling the moment you need technical support, directions, or help locating something that's lost at home is too much. Expecting your child to stop everything and give you answers in the moment is an unrealistic expectation. If you need immediate help, call the company's technical support number (like the rest of us).

TALK ABOUT PHONE CALLS, TEXTING, AND VIDEO CHATTING SOONER RATHER THAN LATER

Talk about expectations before anyone is irritated, annoyed, or too afraid to be honest. A lot of parents don't want to talk expectations, because they don't want to be restricted. It's giving up control. Just acknowledging this means giving your child permission to place restrictions on you and the level of communication. If you're a parent who finds the idea of checking with your child ridiculous because you're paying for college, and therefore *you* make the rules, then know that paying doesn't mean he or she owes you a daily call. Just have a conversation and discuss what your child thinks is reasonable and their preferred mode of contact (phone, email, text, etc).

Don't call every day, don't try to solve every problem; let your child grow and flourish while you stand off to the sides. Calling every single day twice a day is going to get old real fast. Make rules about when to call ("I'll call every other night at seven"). If your child has a problem, believe me, they'll call.

—Becka, junior

Give your child permission to tell you that you're calling, texting, or wanting too much. Let your child tell you, "Mom, Dad, it's too much." Too many times students are afraid to tell you it's too much. All you'll get are short, annoying, and bad conversations. If he or she knows your feelings will not be hurt and that you won't be disappointed, your child can be honest. How much is too much is a personal question. Perhaps, if you're worried about your child's safety, he or she can send you a text that says, "I'm alive!" instead of calling.

WARNING FROM MY LOVING AND WISE MOTHER

My mom suggests that you do not set up a plan to call at the same time every week. If your student doesn't call at that same time you will get scared—very scared. College students forget, get busy, and lose track of time. Arrange different times to connect and hope they remember.

As important as it is to give your child permission to be honest with you, give yourself permission to not always be available. I'm not saying you need to disconnect the phone or screen calls. I'm just saying that you can call him or her back later. You don't have to always pick up the phone or text back; that's what voice mail is for. In fact, your life should be busy enough that you can't always be available. Not being there 24/7 is not a bad thing. In fact, it's a good thing. So many students are having a hard time independently thinking through problems and life situations; there are some students who will not make a move without getting the okay from a parent. That needs to end. Thirty years ago it didn't happen, because that's how it had to be—today it's a little trickier.

THE TRICKY PART FOR PARENTS

The first year can bring on a flood of emotions for new college students. Because so many parents are so connected with their children, it's easy for a child's emotions to spill into a parent's life. When mom or dad gets the call, it's hard to know what your son and daughter wants you to say or do. I hope this helps:

1. Sometimes They Just Want to Vent

They will moan, groan, and look for an ear to listen. Given that a parent is only as happy as the unhappiest kid, listening to an unhappy eighteen-year-old is not fun. It's hard for you. The knee-jerk reaction is to want to fix it. You will want

Sometimes parents forget that when we call home, we want to hear a welcoming voice. No matter what kind of mood you're in, if your college student calls you, at least act excited to talk to them. Give advice, but don't lecture. As long as the decisions we are making aren't harmful, you need to let us make our decisions for ourselves.

—Brett, sophomore

to make it stop. You might want to offer advice. Before offering advice, ask her if she wants advice. Sometimes she will want advice, and sometimes she won't. But you need to check with her. Having read this book, it will be far easier to listen to her vent without offering advice. Once you accept the challenges that are part of the normal college experience, it's much easier to listen, because you know what's normal. Once you give her permission to struggle with roommates, relationships, academics, finances, and her social life, it will be easier to listen and not offer advice. The problem isn't that she's done something wrong—it's that this is a normal and natural experience.

2. Technology Means Being Able to Share Problems as They Unfold in Real Time

Literally, you'll get the text, email, or call as things are going down. Before getting involved, panicking, or wanting to intervene, know that most problems resolve themselves. Give it twenty-four or forty-eight hours before you lose sleep over a problem. If you know that college is naturally uncomfortable, you can give your child room to be uncomfortable and not feel the need to fix the problem before going to sleep. Fixing it is the student's job.

3. When You Have an Idea That Can Help, Don't Share It Right Away

In fact, let that be the cue to ask your son, "How can *you* fix it?" Try not to intervene unless it's an emergency that requires action. Give him names, numbers, and the tools needed to make the calls and fix the problem. It's all about helping him become an advocate for himself. And if he doesn't fix the problem the first time, let him attempt to fix it again and again, and, yes, again. By the time he fixes it, he will love that he was able to take care of himself. And that's such a good feeling.

BEWARE OF THE FIFTH WALL OF TECHNOLOGY

Never before has it been easier for a student to physically be on campus but emotionally be in a totally different world. Cell phones, the Internet, video games, and technology have made it easier than ever for your child to wall herself away from the rest of campus. A lot of new students will hide from the world around them and take refuge among friends, family, and significant others. And often parents are some of the biggest enablers. Walling themselves away from the rest of the world will not help them be happy. It will land them at another school or back at home.

> We as students need our space since we "work" in college all the time. We need our privacy. It's ok to be contacted, as long as we're not being contacted 24/7. We're not a fast-food joint/convenience store, you know.
>
> —Maria, freshman

Every minute a child is talking to you is another minute she is not talking to someone on campus. Yes, you can listen, but help her find other people on campus to engage who can listen. Also, limit the amount of time you can be available for her. This is where giving yourself permission to not be available 24/7 is helpful. If you can help her find people who can listen and give her answers, you will always know that she will be supported.

That said, it's very hard for a parent to not be there. When you are there, encourage her to be a self-advocate after the venting is over. Should it ever get to be too much—feel free to reach out to a professional on campus who can help you figure out the best way to empower, encourage, and support your child.

ESSENTIALS FOR CALLING, TEXTING, AND CHATTING

Because there are now so many ways to communicate, there are also so many more ways to miscommunicate. The list below can serve as essential reminders when calling, texting, or chatting online.

> If we send you a schedule of our classes, do your best to not call during class times. If you do, make sure it is for something important, and give us a chance to call you back on a break. My parents live in a different time zone, and we kind of schedule phone calls around when we have five or ten minutes to talk. Emails and texting are great if parents are willing to embrace technology that much.
>
> —Rebecca, senior

- When your son doesn't answer, he might be in class or busy studying. Sure he might be drinking, doing drugs, or having sex, but that's not likely. Don't assume the worst, because chances are it's not happening. Besides, a student who is doing all the things you don't want him to do can still text.

- Most students will not tell you when you're calling or contacting them too much. If they

> When we say we're busy, it probably means we have an all-nighter coming up. It doesn't mean we're partying. Believe us.
>
> —Recent grad

do tell, most parents have a hard time acknowledging it. Decide how often you'll talk and who should do the calling. Set up a minimum and go from there.

- Your son might not call you as much as your daughter. At least that's what a lot of parents have told me. Boys will call, just not when you expect them to call. Usually it happens in the middle of the night when everything is quiet.

- Video chatting, Skyping, or iChatting is a great way to get to see your child's face and his or her room. Try not to comment on how messy things are, or it will be your last chat (but you can comment on scantily clothed strangers walking around in the background).

- Learn how to text. Texting is the fastest way to get in touch with your child. Sending an email can take as long as sending snail mail. (Email is so 2001.)

- Facebook mail is a fast way to connect too. Sometimes you have a better chance of reaching your child with a Facebook message (see Tip #7 for more) than an email.

> My dad would always text in all caps. He didn't realize that meant he was yelling at me.
>
> —Lee, junior

- Each student and parent has a unique take on how often is too often or not often enough to communicate. If you're coaching your student, listening to your child, and encouraging her to get involved in life on campus, your interaction can be helpful. That

> My parents will call and ask me if I've done my homework. Seriously? Of course, Mom and Dad. I ALWAYS do my homework, and I ALWAYS go to classes too. That is my answer to all their questions.
>
> —Marc, sophomore

said, if she needs to call you before she blows her nose, that's not learning to be independent.

- If you want to call in the middle of the night to see if your child has done her homework or to see if she is going out—don't. If she hasn't done what you want her to do, she will lie. Then she will get good at lying to you. If you have no reason to worry about her studies, then try not to.

QUESTIONS AND ANSWERS

Q: What are some other things I need to keep in mind?

A: This topic could be its own book. One of the major themes is that innocent and loving communication can send the wrong message. The following advice is from experts on campus:

Don't be offended if they're not calling you every single day; it probably means you did a good job raising them to be independent. Ask your student what they need from you. Sometimes they're looking for advice, and sometimes they are just venting and want some-one to listen.

—Nicole, recent grad

I prefer a call in the early evening. Usually during the day I'm busy. Also, at the end of the day I can tell my parents everything about annoying roommates, crazy classes, and all the other good stuff.

—Marcos, freshman

I think that parents really need to recognize that sometimes all we can do to get in touch is send a text. I'm a biology major, and I am in class on aver-age eight hours more per week than my non-science major friends. Oftentimes, when my parents think I'm lazing around or partying it up, I'm at a tutoring appointment, in a three-hour lab, or at a mandatory review session. I've gotten numerous phone calls from family members when I'm in class at some odd hour of the night. An easy way to avoid this is to email, snail-mail, or fax your parents and/or family a copy of your schedule—even Facebook has an application to post it to your profile. This way you have an excuse for not picking up every time they call while you're in class.

—Iris, freshman

Being in constant communication may show your child that you are nervous for them and not confident in their adaptation during this time. This kind of behavior may lead to insecurity in your child. But on the other hand, give them little reminders to let them know that you're always there.

—Heather, freshman

Have a question? Want to answer another parent's question?

Post your questions and answers; visit *The Happiest Kid on Campus* Parent Forum: www.HappiestKidonCampus.com.

TIP #7 FACEBOOK

The Rules and Regulations for Parents

The Tip

Don't be insulted if your child doesn't want to be your Facebook friend.

The Story

Parents get really insulted and sometimes hurt when their child doesn't accept their friend request. They also get suspicious. What they need to understand is that it is not about hurting parents, or keeping things from them. It is about having boundaries. Most people act differently around their friends than they do their parents. Most parents act differently around their friends than they do their kids. There are those rare individuals who would be totally cool with having their parents come to hang out with their friends, but I cannot say that I am one of those people. And that is what it is like to have a parent as your Facebook friend. It is just a big no-no when it comes to privacy and personal space. Plus, some parents get creepy with it. They will ask you why you stayed up until 3:00 a.m. on Thursday night eating Easy Mac and watching *Law & Order* on Hulu instead of studying for class, reading a work of literature, or being asleep. Who needs that kind of attention paid to random status updates?

—Amy L., sophomore, Marymount
Manhattan College

* * *

If you're not familiar with Facebook, please flip to chapter 4 (page 105) and review (I'll play some music and have a snack while you look it over). That should give you a quick overview.

Welcome back.

While chapter 4 is all about how *you* can use Facebook to connect with the campus community, resources, and other parents, this tip is about how students use Facebook and whether or not you should be your child's Facebook friend.

Parents who are unfamiliar with Facebook might have the wrong idea about it. You might think it's a waste of time (it can be), that it makes students stupid (it doesn't), that it can put a student at risk (privacy settings can help with that), or that some students have been expelled or arrested because of posting incriminating pictures and status updates (this is true, and students who do this deserve to get in trouble).

What you don't hear about as frequently is how

I am friends with both my mother and grandmother on Facebook. We have no rules per se, but we have unspoken agreements as to their not judging my college-themed photographs by remembering when they were my age, and I cannot protest against, or de-tag for that matter, the embarrassing family photos that surface from time to time.

—Sally, junior

Facebook has helped countless students get comfortable with the uncomfortable, create connections, and find support. It's an amazing tool. I love it. I use it on a daily basis. It's part of my personal and professional life (in fact, a good portion of this book was written by using Facebook as a research tool).

WHY FACEBOOK WAS CREATED

The idea behind Facebook was to take the freshman student directory (a book often referred to as "The Facebook") and bring it to life online. Basically, Facebook was designed for students to connect with other students. In fact, the original platform was restricted so that only students could become registered users. While I can't verify this, I'm sure when Mark Zuckerberg and his friends launched Facebook at Harvard in 2004, it wasn't about helping students connect—it was to see who's hot and who's not. It's the ultimate hook-up tool for students. The poking feature (the digital form of a wink) is a giveaway.

> **ATTENTION MOTHERS**
> Mothers, do not POKE your sons. That is flirting.
> —Hilary, mom of college student

In less than a year, more than one million college students were logging on to Facebook on a regular basis. Then, in 2006, the platform was opened up to the world. Now Facebook boasts that there are 350 million active users all around the world, and it's the number-one social networking site (bigger than MySpace). And it's free.

Once a student is a registered member, he or she can find friends (the type of friends you might meet in person and not realize you're already friends), send Facebook messages (just like email), share status updates (the latest events in your life), write on friends' walls (posting notes for all to see), send instant messages (live chatting), get invited to attend events or invite friends to attend your events (great for participating in clubs and organizations), post pictures (never post anything you don't want your grandma or future employer to see), share videos, join special interest groups, share blog entries, and find interesting people, products, and services.

Facebook is more than just a way to waste time and procrastinate (although it can be great for wasting time and procrastinating). It's a powerful way for students to:

- Connect with other students on campus
- Connect with other incoming students
- Connect with current and future roommates
- Connect with student leaders on campus
- Connect with top-level campus officials (deans, VPs, presidents)
- Connect with support groups and students across the country
- Connect with mentors and professionals as they explore career options
- Connect with members of groups and organizations on campus
- Connect with classmates to share notes and information

- Connect with instructors to ask questions and share information
- Connect with residence life staff
- Connect with friends from home
- Connect with family members across the country
- Connect with parents

In a few keystrokes a student can connect with friends, family, students, instructors, and professionals around the world. It's *that* powerful. A student with a question about life in a residence hall can reach out to an RA or student living in the halls. A student who wants to join a club or organization can look it up on Facebook and connect with current members and leaders. A student who has a particular passion, interest, or concern can search for a Facebook group and connect with other students on campus and around the globe. And a student who dreams of being a White House intern can just search "White House Intern Association" on Facebook and find students who have been recent interns and ask questions. It's amazing the connections that are available! And yes, it's great for flirting, dating, and having imaginary relationships (this would fall under the category of "Facebook creeping").

If there's ever a question that comes up during your child's college experience, there's always someone out there on Facebook who can help. Of course, I'm on Facebook and I will always be happy to be your friend and your child's friend (but I won't tell you anything about your son or daughter if he or she restricts your privacy settings and gives me full access). Here's how you can find me:

www.Facebook.com/HarlanCohen

www.Facebook.com/TNRfanpage

www.Facebook.com/HappiestKidonCampus

THE BIG QUESTION: SHOULD YOU BE FRIENDS WITH YOUR SON OR DAUGHTER ON FACEBOOK?

If you're already your kid's Facebook friend, you know it can be complicated at times. Being a friend to your child means seeing, hearing, and knowing more than you might want to see, hear, or know. When it comes to sending a request, it's not like there's an option to be your child's "Facebook parent." The only option is to be a "friend." Again, not a Facebook parent. So before you consider sending that friend request to your son or daughter, make sure you know what you're getting into. The question is: should you or shouldn't you send that friend request?

The Answer

Some of you can't handle it. And I'm not being sarcastic.

Being your child's Facebook friend means having access to his thoughts, feelings, friends, pictures, experiences, fears, moods, and ideas. It means seeing and hearing what his friends are saying, feeling, and doing. Being friends is a personal decision that involves a large degree of trust.

I've warned my dad about adding me on Facebook. I said I'll accept his friend request as long as he doesn't tell me what I can and cannot post on my page. I swear often, I have pictures of me partying and smoking hookah, and I'm not going to edit my profile. If he doesn't want to see those things, then he should delete me as a friend. I'm not doing anything illegal, but my friends and I can get pretty graphic with our language and stories, and it's his choice if he wants to see that or not. Plus, I'm not living in his house anymore under his rules, and by being a legal adult, he can't tell me otherwise.

—Jessie, sophomore

Facebook is the equivalent of hanging out at the mall with his friends. While you have every right to go to the mall, few teenage sons and daughters want their mom and dad to hang out with them and chat with their friends. Being your child's Facebook friend is not a parent's right—it's a privilege. A lot of parents get offended when they find out a son or daughter doesn't want to be a Facebook friend. Before you take it personally, understand that not all parents are as cool as you. Some parents abuse their Facebook privileges.

THE FOUR TYPES OF FACEBOOK PARENTS

There are generally four different kinds of Facebook parents:

1. The "Gotcha" Parent
2. The "I Didn't Mean to Embarrass You" Parent
3. The "What's My Password?" Parent
4. The "Just Want to Keep Up with My Kid" Parent

1. The "Gotcha" Parent

I employ a nondiscriminatory rule. I refuse to allow any family member, aside from my two sisters, to be my friend on Facebook. They can email me or, ugh, even text me now anyway. They don't need to have any more access to my personal life than they already do as family.

—Michael, sophomore

The "Gotcha" parent is trouble. The Gotcha parent wants to be a son or daughter's Facebook friend for one reason: to catch and monitor. If this is the situation, your child probably doesn't want to be your Facebook friend, because she knows it's trouble. Besides, no one wants Mom or Dad watching her every move. Having access to a child's Facebook profile means you know too much and may want to ask questions. You will want to react. You might be compelled to write on a wall, write on a friend's wall, offer parental advice, or request to be one of your child's friends' Facebook friends (that's taboo). You might even demand she remove something you find inappropriate. As a Gotcha parent, you'll always be sniffing around and looking for ways to catch her. And that will get you de-friended.

Being a Facebook friend is my mom's way of "staying connected" when really she uses it to check up on me and then call and scold me on the things I do. It's invasive. Facebook is meant for friends.

—Tia, freshman

If your child doesn't want to be your Facebook friend, ask her why. Maybe you can be a friend and she can set her privacy settings. Privacy settings offer your child control over what you and other people can view. A user can restrict who views pictures, who can read status updates, who can write on the user's wall, and who can see

I had to put my mom on a limited profile on my Facebook, because I couldn't stand her knowing so much about me. If I had a bad day and posted a depressing status, she'd call me, and then my dad would call me and they'd all freak out and try to tell me I was suicidal. I couldn't take it, so I just let her see enough information that she thinks she knows what's going on.

—Katherine, junior

Sometimes I wish my mom didn't have Facebook. She freaks out over things that are posted on my wall, which I have no control over. She'll actually send me an e-mail to ask me to remove things others have written. It's just annoying to have to hold my friends accountable to my mother's standards. She'll also flip out if anything I post is "inappropriate" (according to her). One of the biggest fights we ever had was because of something I put on Facebook which involved an inside joke between me and several of my friends, but which my mother deemed "inappropriate." And now my grandmother is on Facebook, so I have to be twice as careful.

—Kristi, freshman

other features. There are just some things a parent doesn't need to see or know.

2. The "I Didn't Mean to Embarrass You" Parent

You don't mean to do it (at least most of you), but you just can't help yourself. You see a post and you want to comment. You hear about good news and want to share your excitement. You're concerned and want to express your love. You are one of the sweetest and most loving parents—you just don't know the rules and regulations. There are boundaries. Step over the line, and you will be banned from this community. Posting old pictures of your child in his awkward phase is never cool. Publicly reprimanding your child on his Facebook wall for everyone to see is never cool. Posting pictures of yourself in a bikini from a recent trip and then using it as your profile picture is never cool (even if you look great in a bikini). It's easy to embarrass your child without knowing it.

3. The "What's My Password?" Parent

This is the technologically deficient parent who signs up for Facebook and doesn't know what he or she is doing. You can either be the least intrusive parent because you don't know how to get the "good" information. Or you can be the most intrusive parent because don't know what you're doing and are always calling, emailing, and texting your kid trying to figure out how to make this thing work. You are the same parent who signs up and then loses your password and can't sign in. Or you sign up and start accidentally "poking" your child and all of his or her friends (never poke your child's friends). If you do sign up, I'll do my best to connect you with other parents and students who can help answer your Facebook question. This way you won't have to bug your kid and accidentally poke anyone.

My mom was always commenting on my status about how much she loved me and was trying to give me advice in her comments. For example, one time I wrote that I was going to a party at a guy's house. She commented, "Isn't that the guy you like? Make sure you are safe and have protection. Make sure you don't drink and drive, and don't take drugs, love mom" I deleted the comment and then deleted my mom.

—Samantha, freshman

Do not request to be friends with your kid's RA. RAs are there for them, not for you. Besides, we already have to deal with our own parents. We can't deal with you too.

—Group of RAs from Florida

4. The "Just Want To Keep Up With My Kid" Parent

This is the ideal parent to have on Facebook. The JWTKUWMK parent is on Facebook because it's a good way to stay in touch. You understand that most things that are posted on Facebook are not for you. Unless something is illegal or screams of trouble, you will let it go. In fact, you probably won't even see most of it, because you are too busy living your own life.

You see Facebook as one of the fastest ways to share information in a way that can make it easy for your child to keep up with you and life at home. If there's a big snow—you can take a picture and post it. If there's an interesting article from the local paper, you can post it in your status update. Facebook is a wonderful way to keep up with your child. When the JWTKUWMK parent sees something that is a red flag, Mom or Dad won't post a note on the wall or make a public declaration, they'll just send a friendly note pointing out that some

I am friends with both of my parents, almost all of my grandparents, and tons of other family members on Facebook. I am really bad about sending pictures home and letting my mom know what I am up to, so she actually got a Facebook account to keep up with me. I don't have any rules for my parents or anyone in my family to be friends with me. In fact, I have a rule for myself. If I am considering putting something on Facebook that I wouldn't want my parents or grandparents to see then I probably shouldn't be putting it up in the first place. Besides, it's great having my parents on Facebook. Not only do they get updates about me, but I get to see all the pictures my mom posts of my little sisters and the things they are doing. And it lets my dad, who is deployed overseas, see what we are up to, too.

—Sam, senior

people might get the wrong impression—it's not a demand, it's just helpful information. Aunts, uncles, cousins, grand-parents, and other family members also fall into the JWTKUWMK parent category.

FOR MORE RULES AND REGULATIONS, SEE Q & A AT THE END OF THIS TIP

THE UGLY SIDE OF FACEBOOK

Yes, it can get ugly. While Facebook can be an amazing resource to help find connections, it can be also be a place where people can be rude or mean, spread rumors, and get information they have no business seeing or knowing. A student can restrict privacy settings, avoid being tagged (i.e., identified) in inappropriate photos, and not accept friend requests from strangers, but that sometimes still isn't enough. Here are some things that will be helpful for you to know about the ugly side of Facebook.

There Can Be A Lot of Rejection

The social pressures of Facebook can add to the already stressful transition. Students wonder why they aren't getting friend requests or why someone is taking so long to respond to a request. Once you have friends, it's easy to see who is doing what with whom or without you. It also can appear that everyone is having a better time than you. Then there's getting "un-friended" or "de-friended." Some students don't like being on Facebook. Social networks mean the social jockeying is a 24/7 event. There's no escaping it. Bad news and rumors can spread as fast as good news and the truth.

Facebook and the Fifth Wall of Technology

Facebook is a fantastic resource if it can lead to face-to-face connections. The problem: too many students use it to replace real conversations. It's also too easy to physically be on campus and emotionally be connected to (and immersed in the lives of) friends and family from home. Students can literally walk through campus with their heads buried in their cell phones and miss out on meeting real people on campus because they are stuck in Facebook. If a student is spending too much time talking to old friends, there will be no time for making new ones.

Facebook Headlines Can Be Deceptive

Once you get on Facebook you'll notice something called the news feed. The news feed shares status updates, photos, and other information from friends within your network. A student who is not having the best time in college might read headlines of friends' experiences happening on other college campuses. The problem is that most students tend to share the best news—the bad news doesn't make headlines. If your child is having a hard time transitioning to college, all these headlines make her feel that much worse about herself. Remind her that headlines are mostly the good stuff—few students share just how hard things can be (that is, unless it's final exams).

It's Easy to Jump to Conclusions

It's never been easier for student and parents to judge roommates, future friends, boyfriends, girlfriends, and random strangers. A quick scan of their Facebook profiles, and you think that what you see is what you'll get.

This couldn't be more wrong. The most interesting people in life are some of the most different people. Wait to judge people until you meet them, and urge your student to do the same.

Also, status updates can be tricky; often students post song lyrics as their status updates, and parents misinterpret and freak out (google a status update before calling in hysterics). Sometimes students will post photos to be "funny" that will be totally out of context for you, or they will share status updates that are inside jokes. Avoid jumping to conclusions. If you're worried that something your child posted could get him expelled or arrested, send a note sharing that you know it's probably an inside joke, but that someone might get the wrong impression and he might want to take it down (it's not telling him what to do, just letting him know how things look from another set of eyes).

A Student Can Get Arrested, Expelled, or Rejected

If your child has any ambition (let's assume this is

> I typically ask parents at the very top of the parent session to "raise your right hand, and repeat after me: I, (state your name), promise (pause) to never look at (pause) my student's roommate's Facebook page."
>
> —Joseph A. Oravecz, PhD, Associate Vice President for Student Affairs

true), a student should never post pictures or be in pictures exhibiting questionable behavior (tell him or her to remove tags—tags are name tags people can post on pictures). Part of the screening process for most applicants for campus jobs and leadership positions include looking up a student's Facebook profile. Students who want to go on to become RAs, lead an organization, participate in student athletics, or take on any leadership role need to be vigilant. Pictures of an underage student drinking, smoking pot, getting naked, or simulating sex aren't funny. Even appearing in pictures in a room with other people who are drinking and smoking pot are dangerous. It's easy for students to feel safe, but a trusted friend can easily copy and paste a photo your child posts and share it with the world. Students get arrested and expelled because of pictures, status updates, or inclusion in incriminating photos.

POLICE OFFICERS SET UP FACEBOOK ACCOUNT TO CATCH UNDERAGE DRINKING

SUMMARY: A twenty-year-old college student shared pictures of himself drinking beer with buddies. He then accepted a friend request from someone who was actually an undercover officer. Want to guess what happened next? He was arrested as a result of the pictures he posted.

—Source: *The Chronicle of Higher Education*
(http://chronicle.com/blogPost/Police-Officers-Set-Up/9103)

Facebook and Safety Concerns

There are some people who don't need to read your son's status updates and browse his pictures. There's nothing wrong with having rules when getting friend requests. If your child doesn't want to reject a request, he can accept the Facebook request, set privacy settings to restrict that person's access, and then de-friend (you can de-friend someone at any time) that person later. He should NEVER give anyone the benefit of the doubt. If he is accepting unfamiliar friends, urge him to restrict what people can see via his privacy settings. When it comes to cell phone numbers, there's no reason to include a cell phone number on a Facebook profile. People who want his number should ask for it. When it comes to posting pictures, frame it like this—if he wouldn't want someone looking through a personal photo album with him at home, there's no reason to give strangers access to his personal photos. When it comes to specific information about comings and goings, it's a good idea to limit information that can let a stranger pinpoint his minute-by-minute whereabouts. One last thing—once it's out there, it's out there forever.

> **THE INTERNET IS FOREVER**
>
> Whether it's a picture on Facebook, a sexy photo text message, or a video that reveals too much, once it's out there, it's out there forever, and there is NO getting it back.

QUESTIONS AND ANSWERS

Q: When is it appropriate to say something and intervene based on something a parent has seen or read on Facebook?

A: I'm going to defer to a parent for this one:

As a parent I do have access to my daughter's profile. I try to use it as a place to encourage her. I have had discussions about how FB is public and anyone can see it, including future employers. If I saw something alarming like "I want to die," I would respond, but life does have its up and downs, so I would expect to see something on her pages besides the idea that everything is perfect.

—Elizabeth, mom of college student

Q: My son has posted something inappropriate; what should I do?

A: The biggest mistake is coming at him like a bulldog. You can't make demands. Just ask questions: Do you think that's appropriate? What if the coach saw that? Are you comfortable with that being out there? Then it's not you telling him something—it's just you being helpful.

Q: What are some other rules that parents should follow if they want to be a son or daughter's Facebook friend?

A: To answer this question, I asked my Facebook friends

what a parent should never do if a parent wants to be his or her child's Facebook friend. This question evoked some fiery responses from college students. After filtering through the replies, here are twelve things to keep in mind if you want to be your child's Facebook friend (and yes, privileges can be revoked at any time):

- Rule 1: Do not comment on every single status update with, "How are you? What are you doing? I haven't heard from you in a few days."
- Rule 2: If you have something parental to say, send a message—no wall posts, please.
- Rule 3: Parents = limited profile access.
- Rule 4: Do not "friend" your child's teacher.
- Rule 5: You might not be allowed to comment on your son's wall or on any of his comments.
- Rule 6: Do not comment on my pictures.
- Rule 7: Do not try to use my Facebook status and comments to "give me guidance."
- Rule 8: Do not send friend requests to all of my friends.
- Rule 9: No one other than me needs to know you're my friend.
- Rule 10: No posting family photos of me looking awkward or partially clothed as a baby.
- Rule 11: Only the child is allowed to post pictures in a bikini (not moms).

- Rule 12: No comments about the time I post status updates. I make my own bedtime.

Have a question? Want to answer another parent's question?

Post your questions and answers; visit *The Happiest Kid on Campus* Parent Forum: www.HappiestKidonCampus.com.

TIP #8 RESIDENTIAL LIVING

The Staff, the Rules, and the Amenities

The Tip

Encourage your son or daughter to reach out to the RA (resident assistant). RAs can save them from disaster.

The Story

I was stressing over an exam that was going to make or break my grade in my biology class. My RA found me a bio major on my floor who tutored me, and we ended up finding more people who were stressed about the exam and formed a study group. I felt so prepared, and my suitemate even bought me my favorite candy to eat as I walked to the exam to de-stress. I passed the exam with a C+. I wouldn't have been able to do it without my RA's help with networking, or without the support of my new family. My RA has been so helpful in so many ways. He made a Facebook group for my hall so we also got a way to get to know each other through "Facebook creeping." He also made a spreadsheet with our names and rooms, our majors, where we are from, and an interesting fact about us, and emailed it to everyone.

—Erika M., freshman, Virginia Tech

***

A NOTE FROM THE PRESIDENT OF ACUHO-I

As a housing professional for more than 25 years, the president of the Association of College and University Housing Officers–International, and—more importantly—the parent of a college freshman, I understand—and work hard to ensure—that student housing means much more than a place to sleep and store belongings. Housing systems around the country are dedicated to fostering a quality living and learning environment. This includes creating a place where students can grow both personally and academically and learn the art of cooperation, practice civility, enhance communication skills, experience diversity, and develop a connection to their university. A campus housing staff is never going to replace a family as a support unit, but these trained and caring professionals are going to act with the students' safety and best interests at heart.

—Michael Schultz, President,
Association of College and University Housing International, 2009–10
Director of University Housing,
Southern Illinois University–Edwardsville

What do you call a place where hundreds of eighteen- to twenty-four-year-olds are put into a complex of buildings and parents are told to stay away? No, not a juvenile detention facility. It's a residence hall, and it's a once-in-a-lifetime experience that some students love so much they experience it four or five times. Some love it so much they go on to get graduate degrees (and PhDs) and spend their lives running them.

There is so much to love about residence life. Yes, a residence hall is a place to put stuff and sleep, but it's so much more. If you look on the office of residence life website of your child's campus, you'll find words like *community*, *learning*, *engagement*, and *involvement* describing the residential living experience.

One of my favorite memories of dorm life without a doubt is from my sophomore year. The people in my hall and myself were all pretty close that year and had a lot of good times. One night we were all hungry, so two others and I decided to make chicken curry and rice for everyone (about fifteen people or so). We pooled our resources and cooked in the dorm kitchen, and the smell went everywhere. It was great; we all just stayed in that kitchen perched on counters cooking and eating together. It was great—you can't get that type of experience anywhere else, and if you live in the dorm even just one year, you'll have plenty of them.

—Gena, senior

As you dig a little deeper in the websites, you'll find descriptions of the residence halls, amenities, costs, rules, regulations, dining services, ways for students to get involved, special events, frequently asked questions, essentials for moving, the leadership structure (including contact information), menus, and other essential and non-essential information. Your child will see what to bring, what not to bring, alcohol policies, student conduct/judicial procedures, parental notification policies, the roommate selection process, information about changing rooms, and information regarding the housing contract and all that it entails. There is so much information available—in fact, it's too much information, but know it's there for you. And it's there for your son or daughter.

THE PERKS OF RESIDENTIAL LIVING

Know that the residence halls are a great place to call home. There's a reason so many institutions require first-year students to live in the residence halls. It's hard for a

I am a student assistant for residential programs. Do not fill out their housing applications, pick their favorite kind of music, and hobbies! Typically when parents do fill out that information, the students are roomed with someone they are not particularly compatible with. Also, they have no idea how to fill it out when the time to renew comes around.

—Rebecca, senior

Living in a residence hall has been an awesome experience. My hall has been extremely close with one another for the most part. On the weekends the ten or twelve of us who are closest pile into the biggest room and watch a movie and joke around.

—Ross, freshman

Our formal training is on helping college students succeed. You have to trust that you are good parents. It's a partnership between parents and student affairs professionals (or housing and residence life professionals) to intervene for student support and success.

—Catherine Bickel, EdD, Associate Director of Housing and Residence Life, Ball State University

student to *not* be engaged in college life when a student lives in the center of the action. Besides the amenities (we're talking granite counters, hardwood floors, top appliances, balconies, pools, gyms, movie rooms, tanning beds, etc.), there's the location, and the ability to make friends, get support, and get help by walking down the hall. There can be counseling, classrooms, computer labs, tutoring services, and hundreds of trained professionals waiting to support and encourage your child. It's the ultimate safety net.

When it comes to safety and support, as someone who has met and worked with thousands of residence life professionals (students and full-time professionals), I can tell you with confidence that the overwhelming majority of students and professionals working in residence life are passionate, articulate, and supportive leaders on campus who want your son or daughter to be happy, safe, and successful.

RAs are trained to help students get comfortable with the uncomfortable. They can connect your child to resources, support services, people, and places on campus to help him or her have the best experience. Having a good RA is like having a concierge service down the hall. In addition to connecting your child to the people and places on campus, RAs are charged with helping to keep communities safe and comfortable. A student who follows the rules should have a great relationship with an RA.

If your residential student has a problem, the RA is the first place to stop. If the RA on the floor doesn't have the answers or isn't responsive (not all RAs are fantastic), your child can

When I was an RA, I befriended a very quiet student with low self-confidence. I quickly noticed his shyness, so I intentionally put the time in to get to know him. Over the course of the year, he became much more outgoing, acting as a voice for my floor. He really began to blossom. I even encouraged him to speak to the girls in the opposite wing of our residence hall, which netted him a couple good friends. He then decided to apply to be an RA. I suggested that the RA position would be perfect for opening more doors and improving his self-confidence and networking skills. It eventually paid off, as he has become a very outgoing, upbeat person. He recently started a basketball league for the Purdue RAs. This required speaking to the head of residence life and communicating with RAs from each residence hall. As an RA and a friend, I like to think I influenced him in positive ways.

—Aaron, resident assistant

If a parent has a son or daughter who has a problem within the residence hall, the best advice is to encourage the student to speak to the person he/she is having a problem with. If that does not work, the student should discuss the situation with the Resident Assistant (RA). If the problem is serious or requires immediate attention, the parent should encourage the student to speak to a professional staff member; this is usually facilitated through the residence hall office. While professional staff is more than willing to speak with parents, it is most helpful for us to hear about situations from the student so that we can ask specific questions and provide help on a personal level.

—Sara Carvell, Resident Life Manager, Purdue University

turn to another RA on a friend's floor or to the resident director and the resident director's supervisors.

Yes, not 100 percent of the staff is responsive and nurturing, but most will be. I'll get more into navigating the organizational structure in a little bit and how to help your child work through it if a situation comes up.

Opportunities Are Down the Hall (Literally)

In the early part of the year, the leaders of campus groups and organizations swarm the first-year halls looking to recruit new students to participate in clubs and organizations. There are also always events, programs, and activities held on a regular basis (don't let your child ever tell you there's nothing to do but drink). There are also opportunities to take on leadership roles while getting involved within the halls. RHA (residence hall association) is a popular group on campus that offers instant connections. RHA meets regularly and has an executive board and boards within each residence hall that makes decisions to impact residents and campus.

Living and Learning in the Comfort of Their Homes

Another development in recent years in the world of residence halls has been the rise of living and learning communities. Living and learning communities are places where students live and learn together inside and outside the classroom. Sometimes faculty even live on campus with their family.

I became an RA at first because it seemed like a fun way to get reduced housing cost and a monthly check, but now I see that it's so much more than that. I've really been able to make a difference in my residents' lives. Having an almost entirely freshman floor has been a very rewarding and challenging experience. I've really enjoyed watching them as students and as people, and I'm even friends with some of them. I think being an RA is well worth the time, stress, and personal effort I've had to put in. I care about every single one of my residents (even the ones I've had to write up). In what other job do you get paid to care about forty amazing, unique people?

—Sarah, resident assistant

ROOMMATE PROBLEMS?

Your child's college campus might have professional mediation available to help roommates learn how to get along. Have him or her contact the residence life office to see if mediation resources are available.

There are a variety of living and learning communities. Some are academic-focused, some are interest-driven, and some vary in the level of involvement of the faculty. But the premise is that these communities can make a large campus smaller and connect students to professors and other students with shared interests. Given that so many students have a hard time taking risks (see chapter 5), this is a great way to get a shy student to get involved and create a world of options.

In fact, if you're reading this before your child has picked a school, the type of living arrangements available is something to factor into the college selection process. If you didn't notice the living and learning options in the housing packet, ask about it during orientation, or have your child send a note to the office of residence life and explore options. You never know—the institution your student is attending might be starting a new pilot living and learning community this year. It's a trend that's on the rise.

> Nationwide, about two hundred colleges have developed more than six hundred living-learning residential programs in an attempt to further engage students outside the classroom and allow them to live on campus with others who have similar interests. In some cases, faculty and academic advisers have offices in the same residence hall.
>
> —Source: *USA Today* (http://www.usatoday.com/news/education/2009-04-25-dorms-professors_N.htm)

The Floorplans

When it comes to rooms in the dorms, there are singles, doubles, triples, and quads. There can be suite-style living with a common living area, kitchen, and bathroom or rooms with shared bathrooms on the floor. Some halls are managed by the institution, and others are managed by third parties.

(WARNING: You might not want to know this next part.) Many dorms are coed—this can mean coed floors, and yes, there are even schools with coed rooms. Some residence

I moved into the residence halls because I wanted the "full college experience." The best part was having a group of friends on my floor who would all hang out and have movie nights. There was always someone to hang out with.

—Brittany, junior

PERKS OF RESIDENTIAL CAMPUS LIVING

· Great location (making it easy to walk to and from class)
· Convenience
· The costs
· The support staff (student RAs, hall directors, directors of residential living)
· Safety (campus security, secure buildings, and rules)
· Counseling services (some residence halls have counseling services in the buildings, meaning help is down the hall)
· Classrooms in residence halls (on some campuses)
· Living and learning communities (students live with people who have the same major, making it easier to make connections)
· No landlords, and in some cases, no monthly bills or utilities to deal with
· Meals are a few steps away—no cooking!

halls still have quiet hours, and some do restrict visitors. But restrictions are far less restrictive than they were thirty years ago.

Again, this is where you have to trust your son or daughter and trust that you did your job. If safety is of concern, see Tip #22 and investigate the safety history on campus. Before you freak out, check out the building's security procedures. Chances are, you'll be surprised and relieved.

FINAL THOUGHTS TO HELP THEM HAVE THE HAPPIEST EXPERIENCE IN THE HALLS

1. Help Them Work Through the System (If Necessary)

If your child has a problem, he is going to need to work

through the system. The first place to start is with the person who is causing the problem. The next step is to contact the resident assistant. If that resident assistant isn't responsive to a problem, then locate the organizational chart online and find answers. Typically, each residence hall has an assistant residence hall director and a director. If neither of these people can help, it's time to move ahead to the residence hall leadership. There is the assistant director for housing and residential life and then the director of residence life. From there you get into the next higher level of campus leaders. You have the dean of students, associate vice president of student development, and VP of student development. While the president of the institution might want to know what's happening, the vice presidents are usually more hands-on and closer to the students. Jumping to the top without working through the system should be avoided unless there's a safety issue.

Make sure your student documents everything along the way. He or she can even contact the media if the situation isn't resolved. Most residential life professionals respond and want to help. But if there's trouble, let this be a time for your child to become his or her own self-advocate and work through the layers of beauracracy. Working through the system and resolving a situation is a great life lesson.

2. If You Feel the Need to Intervene

There are situations in which you need to intervene. And when you do, you're going to be enraged. If there

From an RA's perspective: You don't need to tell us every detail about your son/daughter—clean slates are better. However if it is a serious concern (e.g., medical), make sure the RA does know. As a general rule, don't assume everything your kid tells you about professors, RA's, security, or deans. None of them are out to get your child. If they say a professor grades against them, take it with a grain of salt and don't get all up in arms about it. Encourage your child to talk to someone whom they think is being unfair to them; that is usually the only way it will get worked out.

—Adam, resident assistant

is a problem and if your child asks for your help, try your best not to start by picking up the phone and firing away. Residence life professionals hate this. Picking up the phone and getting yelled at isn't going to provoke anything but firing back. And threatening lawsuits doesn't get things moving either. This is a tactic that is used on a regular basis and gets no one moving. The best calls from parents are those in which a parent calls to try to understand the whole story. Assuming your child authorizes you to know what's happening, FERPA (see chapter 1, page 24) won't prevent you from hearing it. A lot of times, you'll be surprised to hear the entire story. So many students will complain to you and never let the people who can resolve the situation know what's happening—ask questions, don't aim and fire.

3. Know the Policies, Rules, and Regulations

Make sure your child is aware of the policies for alcohol and drug use. I'm talking about what happens if your son gets written up for having alcohol or drugs and how that can affect his future. He needs to know what kind of judicial process happens once he violates the rules and regulations. Getting thrown off campus can put a mark on his record that could stay with him and become a problem in future background checks or when he tries to enroll at a new institution.

4. Safety in the Halls

Residence halls are generally safe. The idea of coed floors and the images of college tragedies might make you want to grab your daughter and run as you move her into the residence halls. Recent campus violence has made college campuses that much more vigilant. Joking threats are not seen as funny. Besides the extreme vigilance, residence halls are secure buildings with 24/7 surveillance—student workers are walking halls, doing rounds, and watching over students. And if a student needs help, oftentimes help finds the student before the student needs it. Check out Tip #22 and do some background checks on campus safety. But when it comes to living in a secure, safe, and monitored environment, the halls are the place to call home. If your

I once had a parent ask me if I could go to her son's room and discreetly "smell for garlic." The mother was concerned that her son ate a lot of garlic and his roommate wouldn't want to live with him because when he sweats he smelled like garlic. It was one of the weirdest things I've had to do in my career so far.

—Name withheld, Director of Housing

child ever feels unsafe, the professional staff needs to be notified ASAP so they can take the appropriate actions.

5. The Perfect Meal Plan

There is no such thing as a perfect meal plan—just too many or too few meals. No parent wants a child to go hungry. So as a general rule, I recommend going with the bigger meal plan for the first half of the year. Have your child check with an RA or a student who has been living on campus for more guidance on specifics. Keep in mind that whomever they're consulting might have a different routine. (Someone who goes home every Thursday after class isn't going to need the same plan as someone who stays on campus seven days a week. Someone who has late classes and doesn't eat breakfast will need fewer meals. Someone who works late at night might need to have a late-night dining option outside of the dining hall.) When investigating meal plans, make sure your child knows how, when, and if you can change the plan. Again, my general rule is that more is better. Better to cut back on a meal plan the second half of the year than to not have enough to eat. Besides, there can be ways to avoid wasting unused meals. A lot of times extra funds on meal plans can be used to shop in the campus convenience store. Again, each school has its own way of doing business.

QUESTIONS AND ANSWERS

Q: When is it appropriate for a parent to call residence life professionals?

A: It's appropriate when you need help and advice. Professionals don't mind a parent who has questions and concerns. What professionals don't like is finger pointing, casting blame, and irate parents who threaten lawsuits without knowing both sides of the story. If you need to call because your child is uncomfortable and not finding answers, call to get the rest of the story (your child might need to sign a waiver). You can also call with the sole purpose of finding the names and numbers of people your child can contact for help to get the situation resolved.

Q: What is the notification policy when it comes to alcohol violations?

A: Policies vary from campus to campus. Some schools notify parents on a first violation, on a second violation, or not at all.

Q: Does my child really need extra-long twin sheets?

A: Yes. If the campus guide says you need it, then you need it. If not, you'll have a kid who has extra-short sheets on an extra-long mattress. When you do get the sheets, opt for an extra set. It will be an extra-long time between washes, so this will help. Make sure your child checks out the FAQs on the campus website for more information about furnishings and what to bring and what not to bring. Every school has different information.

Q: What is the best residence hall for new students?

A: Not all residence halls are created equal. Some are nicer than others. Some have better food than others. Some have more first-year students living at them than others. Your child should do research. If possible, encourage him or her to live in a residence hall with as many first-year students as possible. Forget the amenities; the population is what matters most. I would also recommend investigating living and learning communities. As for timing, the general rule is that the sooner you get your housing application in, the better your chances of getting your top choice. If your child doesn't get his or her first choice, it's not the worst thing in the world (although it might seem like it at first). Some students might enjoy not living with first-year students. The upperclassmen residence halls tend to be a little quieter (not a bad thing). For the student who leaves for college with a plan in place and a map in mind, where he or she lives will not be as big a problem, because there will always be something to do and places to go.

Have a question? Want to answer another parent's question?

Post your questions and answers; visit *The Happiest Kid on Campus* Parent Forum: www.HappiestKidonCampus.com.

TIP #9 ROOMMATES

From Heaven, Hell, and Everywhere in Between

The Tip

Don't expect your daughter's roommate to make sure she puts on her face cream and does her homework.

The Story

From the moment I met my roommate's parents, I was worried. They introduced themselves and then proceeded to speak about all of their daughter's issues and woes. More or less, they expected *me* to look after her all year. It fell on me to make sure she did her homework, put on her face cream, even put on a raincoat when it was drizzling. You can only imagine how she was when alcohol was involved. After countless nights spent listening to her vomit and hoisting her into her lofted bed when she was too drunk to walk, I finally filed for a room change.

P.S. My roommate also left our door open, and my iPod Touch was stolen. So I suggest students carry their valuables with them and always keep a close eye on them.

—Iris, freshman, St. Lawrence College

* * *

According to the Higher Education Research Institute, 47.9 percent of students reported having problems getting along with a roommate. So it's reasonable to assume that half of all students will have a challenge living with their roommates. What's interesting is that the divorce rate is almost the same rate as roommates not getting along—perhaps, if we can fix the roommate problem, we can fix the divorce rate. If husbands and wives could learn to be better roommates...Okay, back on topic...

FACEBOOK PAGES CONCERN PARENTS OF COLLEGE FRESHMEN

As housing officials at colleges around the country send out roommate assignments to freshmen this summer, a growing number of schools say they're getting more requests for changes—from parents who don't like the roommates' Facebook profiles.

—Source: *USA Today*
(http://www.usatoday.com/news/nation/2007-08-07-facebook-housing_N.htm)

YOUR CHILD'S PERFECT ROOMMATE

A lot of parents tend to be even more anxious about roommates than their kids. And it makes sense. For your entire life you've told your children not to talk to strangers, and then you send them off to a strange place and tell them to live with strangers. Other than prison (and I hope that

> Do not pick my roommate for me—back off and don't worry. I will sometimes be disgruntled with my roommate. This is normal. I will sometimes call you and rant about my disgruntlement. You yourself do not live with my roommate, so you should be supportive but not the decision maker.
>
> —Kelsey, sophomore

never happens), this is the only time in life your child will live with a stranger in a small, confined space. And for most of them, this is the first time they have lived with anyone. The idea of having to share a room with a small or big person can be anxiety-provoking. But I'm going to help you to make it completely comfortable for you and your child.

What is the best roommate? That's the big question.

There are so many different kinds of "best roommates." The best roommate by parents' standards is a roommate who reflects the values, ethics, and lifestyle choices that are in alignment with you and your child's lifestyle. In other words, you don't want your child to live with a drunk and high roommate who sleeps around (assuming your lifestyle isn't drinking, getting high, and sleeping around). You want your son or daughter to live with someone who is going to cause the least amount of drama and be the best possible influence. No one wants a roommate from hell.

> I never expected my roommate to walk into the room in the early morning hours, drop his pants, and pee on my bed and me. He felt bad the next morning, and I'm not just talking about the bruises he received as a result of my rude awakening.
>
> —Chad, recent grad

That said, having a roommate from hell builds character and helps students find new friendships down the hall because they've been forced to leave their own room. Other than living with a dangerous roommate (a rare occurrence), most roommate situations can be great ones. In fact, a roommate who forces your child to step outside his or her comfort zone can be the very best roommate (it just takes a few years of time and distance for your child to realize how important the relationship was). Given the right attitude, almost any roommate can be a great roommate to have.

WAIT A SECOND; IS *YOUR* KID THE ROOMMATE FROM HELL?

Most incoming students have grown up never having had a roommate—never having lived with someone before means not knowing how to live with someone. Even if your child went to a prep school and lived on campus, she will most likely end up living with someone who has never had a roommate before. Most students and parents tend to be so focused on what the person living with your child will do wrong—few roommates (and parents) focus on what it means to be the best roommate. If your daughter ends up with a roommate from hell, the roommate from hell will most likely see your daughter as a roommate from hell too. Which one of the roommates truly is the devil can be found in the details. Sometimes both roommates can be responsible.

At the end of the day or night, we have no control over someone else's behavior or actions. We only have control over our own behavior and the actions we can take along the way. A student who walks into a roommate situation understanding what it takes to be a good roommate will have a much better chance of finding a comfortable living situation—even with a roommate from hell.

One thing your child needs to know is that when people live together in a room the size of a large walk-in closet, uncomfortable moments are going to happen. That's just part of the "living together" experience. Not having uncomfortable moments is unnatural. The most adoring spouses, the very best of friends, and the closest family members all have uncomfortable moments when spending time together. With the right rules in place and mutual respect, uncomfortable moments can be gifts that lead to honest conversations and help form the foundation of lasting relationships.

BEST ADVICE FROM STUDENTS FOR PARENTS ABOUT ROOMMATES

You don't have to be best friends; you just have to live with them.

—Kelsey, junior

Don't rush into being best buddies too quickly. Just take it slow, and if the BFF (best friends forever) roomie thing doesn't quite work out, there are plenty of other options out there for BFFs.

—Karen, junior

Don't keep your feelings a secret. It's hard to be honest, because you don't want to piss them off, but keeping it quiet makes it worse in the long run.

—Dan, junior

Always let your roommate know you care about her college experience too. Ask if you can help make anything better for her while also giving her space. Let her know you're open to suggestions; you should be.

—Katherine, sophomore

BEING THE PERFECT ROOMMATE

Here are three things you can share with your child to help him or her be the ideal roommate. By following these guidelines, a roommate situation can work. All it takes is putting this into practice and everyone wanting to make it work.

Roommate Rule #1: A Roommate Does Not Have to Be a Friend

Too many roommates walk into a roommate situation expecting a new college roommate to become a new best friend. They think anything less than a friendship is unacceptable. Yes, the roommate relationship can grow into a friendship, but it doesn't have to be a friendship from the start. The only requirement of roommates is to respect the other person's space and stuff. The moment a roommate expects more is the moment he or she is set up for a big disappointment.

I know this might not fit the utopian roommate fantasy you and your child dream about for college, but this is the reality of roommate life. Roommates who expect nothing more than a roommate relationship are set up for happy cohabitation. A lifetime friendship and best man or bridesmaid is an added bonus.

THE UNIVERSAL REJECTION TRUTH OF ROOMMATES

(See chapter 5, page 137 for more on the URT.)

The URT of Roommates says that millions of roommates will become close friends, but millions will not. The truth is that not all roommates want to be new friends. Creating realistic expectations means giving a roommate

---

Roommate Rule #2: Roommates Who Want to Get Along Will Find a Way to Get Along

It's all in the attitude that a roommate brings to a new situation. A lot of roommates walk into a roommate relationship already having decided it will not work. Deciding it will not work means the relationship is doomed before it starts. People who want to get along will make an effort to do so. Wanting to get along means making an effort to treat other people the way they like to be treated. It means working to be the best possible living partner and being open to suggestions.

This takes a deliberate effort. We can either choose to get along or choose not to get along. The catch—everyone living together has to want to get along or it won't work.

The challenge is that an increasing number of roommates (and parents) come into this relationship with serious reservations. The reason? Never before has it been easier and more efficient to judge a roommate without ever meeting that roommate. The moment your child finds out who his or her roommate will be, it's off to Facebook (and MySpace) to look up the new roommate. Then it's time to analyze the profile, pictures, interests, sexual orientation, race, religion—the list goes on and on. Sometimes the pictures or information in the profile may create a bad or wrong impression. Roommates who have never met might decide it won't work before ever meeting.

This is *not* coming to campus wanting to get along; it's the complete opposite. A Facebook profile is not the same as living with a roommate. Parents need to accept this, and students need to accept this. Encourage your child to enter the relationship on a positive note and decide that he or she will do whatever it takes to get along. This can include setting up ground rules (see #3).

Roommate Rule #3: Talk about the Problem Sooner Rather Than Later

Most roommates walk into the roommate relationship willing to do anything to avoid a conflict. Everyone is so afraid of confrontations that they don't know how to have conversations. They bury their feelings until the roommate honeymoon ends and the buried feelings erupt in a fit of anger. If roommates could set up the dynamics so that they could have conversations instead of confrontations, they could talk about their problems when the problems surfaced. Here's how to do it:

THE ROOMMATE HONEYMOON

Like a newlywed couple, roommates in the early stages of a relationship will do whatever it takes to get along. Everyone wants to get along. It's easy to let the little thing go for the sake of living in bliss:

· You want to borrow my favorite clothes? Sure, no problem.

· You want your girlfriend to spend the night? Sure, no problem.

· You want to eat my food? Sure, no problem.

· You want to be a sloppy pig? Sure no problem.

· You want to borrow money without paying me back? Sure, no problem.

· You want to use my computer and watch porn? Sure, no problem.

· Your parents are visiting every weekend? Sure, no problem.

· You want people to hang out in our room? Sure, no problem.

· You want to have sex in the room while I sleep? Sure, no problem.

But once the honeymoon ends and roommates no longer want to get along, that's when all the niceties go out the window and all hell breaks loose. But roommates who understand the roommate relationship and live by the roommate rules will learn to live happily ever after.

Institute the "Uncomfortable Rule"

The Uncomfortable Rule is an agreement that helps roommates get comfortable with the uncomfortable. The way it works? All roommates agree that if anything makes anyone in the room uncomfortable, the problem must be discussed within twenty-four to forty-eight hours. If no one brings up the problem, then it can be assumed that there are no problems. When an uncomfortable problem is brought up, a roommate can't attack—it's merely a conversation.

For the Uncomfortable Rule to work, both roommates have to come into the room with reasonable expectations, the desire to get along, and a willingness to have conversations—not confrontations. Establishing the Uncomfortable Rule means creating a world where roommates can talk about problems when they come up. It helps them get comfortable with the uncomfortable. Knowing that problems can be solved with a conversation instead of confrontation means regularly having open and honest conversations.

IF THE THREE RULES DON'T WORK, GET A THIRD PARTY TO HELP RESOLVE THE PROBLEM

The undeniable fact is that some roommates walk into a roommate situation with:

1. Unrealistic expectations
2. An unwillingness to get along
3. An inability to have a conversation for fear of a confrontation.

Your child might be one of them (but hopefully not). Thankfully, there are residence life professionals on staff to help your child get along with his or her roommate.

The problem is that most of the time the most qualified people aren't aware there is a problem, because most students don't approach them. Most of the time it's a parent calling, because Mom or Dad is so fed up with a lack of action. And most of the time the people in charge ask for the student to come in and explain the matter.

The residence life staff is trained to help with roommate conflicts. If an RA isn't able to work through the problem, there will be other staff who can help intervene. Helping roommates get along is a top priority. In fact, there are even mediation services with highly trained counselors to help students work through the issues and find common ground.

PUTTING THE RULES INTO ACTION

Once a student enters a living situation with the expectation that a roomie isn't going to be a best friend, roommates can be free to be honest. But the only way to be honest is if the

> This Uncomfortable Rule can work for any kind of relationship when you're in a new environment. For example: coworkers do not need to be best friends, they just need to work together. Coworkers who want to get along will always find a way to get along. Coworkers who make it comfortable to talk about the uncomfortable can build honest relationships and improve their skills and abilities.

roommates agree to follow the rules and not keep secrets. Yes, easier said than done. Here are some hypothetical situations to see this played out (feel free to share these with your son or daughter):

HYPOTHETICAL SITUATION #1: Your daughter's roommate has a significant other over the first weekend of school. Your daughter is asked to leave the room. This is something that makes her uncomfortable. She does it because she doesn't want to be difficult—plus the roommate's significant other is already in town.

Reaction #1 (the student who does not apply the rules): Your daughter is so upset that she calls friends, family, and anyone who will listen to her complaining about her inconsiderate, slutty, and selfish roommate. She talks to everyone but her roommate. Because she never expresses her discomfort to the person causing the discomfort, the "selfish" roommate continues to invite her boyfriend over. Each time, your daughter gets more and more irritated but never expresses herself, and the roommate thinks everything is fine. After several weeks of having her guest over, your daughter unloads, because she's totally fed up. She thinks she's living with the roommate from hell—and your child's roommate thinks your daughter is the roommate from hell. Everyone is living together in hell.

Reaction #2 (the student who does apply the rules): After the roommate's significant other leaves, your daughter has a conversation with her roommate on the Monday after the boyfriend's departure. It's calm and casual. She says, "I know we're supposed to be honest when something makes us uncomfortable—I don't mind you having a guest, but I don't feel comfortable having to leave the room for the weekend." The solution could be giving your daughter more notice, limiting the numbers of weekends together, having alone time earlier in the day, spending the night in someone else's room (and that person can sleep in her bed), getting a hotel, crashing at a friend's, or moving out because the roommate is unwilling to budge. But bringing it up the first time means the situation is addressed sooner rather than later. It doesn't have to be a confrontation—just a conversation.

There's always a chance the roommate will find it unreasonable that she can't have her boyfriend spend the night, but that's something that can be discussed. She also might understand and apologize.

HYPOTHETICAL SITUATION #2: Your son's roommates enjoy entertaining in the room. They like to have friends over to drink and party in the room. Your son has early classes and doesn't like the idea of so many people doing illegal things in his room. He doesn't want to be difficult, but this is causing him a lot of aggravation.

Reaction #1 (the student who does not apply the rules): Your son is so upset that he calls friends, family, and anyone who will listen to his complaining about his inconsiderate, drunk, partying roommates. He talks to everyone but his roommates about the problem. Because he never expresses himself, the "partying" roommates continue to invite friends over. He gives subtle hints about how it's hard for him to study with all the noise but never talks about it outright with them. He even sends an instant message to one of his roommates saying, "I need to study tonight!!!" but again, he doesn't talk face-to-face and express what's making him uncomfortable. After several weeks of the roommates having guests over, your son unloads, because he's totally fed up. He thinks he's living with the roommates from hell—and your son's roommates think he is the real roommate from hell.

Reaction #2 (the student who does apply the rules): The day after the first gathering of drunken friends, your son has a conversation with his two roommates. It's calm and casual. He says, "I know we're supposed to be honest when something makes us uncomfortable—I wasn't comfortable having people in our room drinking. Besides having a hard time studying, I'm afraid I could get written up for breaking the rules." The solution could be hanging out somewhere else, hanging out without alcohol when he's in the room, partying in someone else's room, or moving out because the roommate is unwilling to budge. But the situation is addressed sooner rather than later, and it's not a confrontation—just a conversation. Sure, there's a chance the roommates might not like him as much, but being liked isn't the goal of having roommates. It's just to get along. This is another reason why it's so important for your son to have options. If he doesn't get along with his roommate, then he will have other people to hang out with. By talking about what makes him uncomfortable and giving his roommates permission to not be his best friend, he brings up the problem before it's a habit. All this said, your son might have to give a little too.

IF THERE IS A PROBLEM

In order for roommate relationships to work, both roommates need to follow the rules mentioned above. When one roommate doesn't follow the rules, there will be problems. Sometimes these problems can be resolved over time. Other times it takes professional intervention. Sometimes they can't be resolved. There are situations in which one roommate has unreasonable expectations or is unwilling to get along. If the problem can't be resolved, someone will have to move. No, it's not fair for your child to move, but if the roommate from hell won't budge, that's when someone has to move. When you get that email or call that trouble is looming, keep the following in mind:

1. Listen (ask if you can offer advice).

2. Know there are two sides to every roommate story.

3. Give it twenty-four hours to resolve itself.

4. Make sure your child is following the three roommate rules.

   A. Is he/she giving the roommate permission to just be a roommate?
   B. Does your son/daughter want to get along?
   C. Has your child discussed the situation with the roommate sooner rather than later? Is the Uncomfortable Rule in place?

5. Encourage your student to turn to the residence life staff for assistance.

6. Explore mediation services (there are sometimes professional mediators on campus for this very reason).

7. If there is no resolution, encourage your child to go to the supervisor of the RA.

> The most hurtful thing my parents did was placing the problems that I had with my first roommates on my shoulders. What was I doing wrong, what could I do more of, how I could make the situation better? Don't always assume it's your child who is causing the problems. Be unbiased during the conversations, and look at both sides of the picture. Sometimes your child is to blame, sometimes they aren't. Criticize constructively and carefully.
>
> —Becka, junior

8. If you are at a loss or if you feel there is a safety issue, feel free to contact the residence life staff. Avoid pointing fingers or casting blame. The best calls are those where parents are looking to help a child navigate the system. By explaining the problem, you can create awareness and get your child information on how he or she can navigate the system.

> Four moves in one year. My parents saved me freshman year. One of my roommates would sleep with different men every night while I was in the room. Sometimes I would wake up in the middle of the night to my roommate screwing a dude in the shower. It was insulting (not that they had sex in the shower, but that they had the nerve to do it while I was in the bedroom), distracting, and just uncomfortable. My parents did everything they could that year to contact hall directors and housing staff to get me out of that situation. Sometimes a student's words don't suffice, but Mom and Dad can always save the day!
>
> —Alexandra, senior

ADDITIONAL ROOMMATE RULES FOR PARENTS

Having roommate isn't only a balancing act for students, but trusting that the person sharing a room with your child will be responsible, respectful, and make life easier for him or her is a challenge for parents as well. You want someone in that room who is going to make life better and easier for your child. The following are some suggestions to help protect your child, win over his or her roommate, and do whatever it takes to help create the best situation without intervening:

1. Exchange cell phone numbers with your child's roommate in case of an emergency. Only call or allow a

roommate to call you if it's an emergency. Abuse this and all calling privileges will be revoked. (Talk to your son or daughter about this before asking for digits.)

> My parents came to visit for freshman family weekend. They walked into my dorm and immediately started criticizing me for how messy my room was, how I had organized everything, and how I stored my food. They proceeded to reorganize all of my and my roommate's stuff, and we couldn't find anything in our room for a week.
>
> —Colleen, freshman

2. Invite your child's roommate to dinner when visiting. It's nice for you to get a sense of the roommate

> Parents should know not to ask their kid's roommates embarrassing questions.
>
> —Victoria, junior

through your own eyes—and it's nice to give someone a meal who appreciates it.

3. Never criticize your child's roommate—you're not the roommate's mom or dad. This will help no one. And it's not your place.

4. Let your child vent and trust that they will work it out.

5. Always call before visiting—no one likes surprise guests.

6. Never touch someone else's stuff. If you want to clean, ask the roommate. Don't just assume everyone loves your motherly or fatherly touch (not that many fathers clean without warning).

7. Never try to resolve a conflict by visiting, calling, or acting as a mediator with your child's roommate; it's

One of the toughest challenges of the first year for my only child was learning to live with two roommates with different lifestyles from her. They differed in how they approached their academic work and study time. Having grown up in the shadow of a large university, my daughter had witnessed firsthand some of the pitfalls of the first year and had made a conscious decision to avoid the party scene. This was not the case for many students within her residence hall, and early in her first semester, one of them landed in the hospital with alcohol poisoning. **Lesson learned**: Although there was some "drama" during the first year (and it's easy to be caught up in it, especially for moms), the roommates learned to work through many differences and remain close friends (although not roommates) as sophomores.

—Denise L. Rode,
Director of Orientation and First-Year Experience at Northern Illinois University and a member of the adjunct faculty in college student development at DePaul University in Chicago

not your place. You're far from impartial, plus there are often professionals on campus who can do this.

8. When sending a care package, include extra food for the roommate. Chances are the roommate will eat it anyway. This way it's not stealing. Besides, it's nice to get a care package from anyone.

9. Meet the residence life staff when you move your child in. If there is a medical issue, make sure the support staff knows. If your child has special needs, it's important the people closest to him or her know.

10. Make sure your child shares vital information with the roommate. If your child has food allergies,

special needs, or a life-threatening condition, a roommate should know. It's not so the roommate can take care of the problem, but if your child should have an emergency, this stuff is helpful for paramedics and other caregivers to know.

11. Embrace diversity—living with a gay roommate will not turn your child gay. And living with a heterosexual roommate will not turn your gay child into a heterosexual.

12. Having a roommate who drinks is not going to turn your kid into a drunk. In fact, it can be a deterrent. Once your child sees how disgusting it is to always be so drunk (vomiting, sleeping around, missing classes, etc.), he or she will be even more comfortable not drinking.

13. Avoid early morning calls—that's just not cool. Ask the earliest and latest times that you should call. If your child has a roommate who goes to sleep late and starts classes late, it's rude to call in the morning.

14. When talking to your child in the room, know that your conversations can't always be so open and free-flowing. When a roommate is listening, it means not always being able to be honest. Try to schedule calls

During my freshman year, the parents of one of the girls who lived next door to me in the dorms drove four and a half hours in an attempt to solve their daughter's issues with her roommate. They stormed into the room, sat her daughter and her roommate down (against their will), and told this girl that they felt that it was best for their daughter if she moved out of the room. When they stormed out, they glared at everyone in their path, including me. I found out that the crazy parents' daughter ended up being asked to leave, not her roommate. I guess that came back to bite her and her parents.

—Isaac, junior

or have conversations at a time when your child can talk freely.

QUESTIONS AND ANSWERS

Q: My son is rooming with someone who drinks. Should I be worried?

A: A student who doesn't drink isn't going to start drinking because he lives with a roommate who drinks. A student who doesn't drink and wants to drink will find a way to drink. If anything, a student who is sober who lives with a drinking roommate sees how disgusting it can be to drink. There's nothing like seeing your roommate come home and vomit to reinforce a lifestyle choice. Now, you might be thinking that it's horrible for your son to be in this situation, but trust me, the vomit can be cleaned, and a roommate who can be honest with another roommate can prevent this from happening again. Or at least make it clear that this isn't cool.

Q: My daughter sleepwalks—should her roommate be warned?

A: Students who sleepwalk, talk in their sleep, and do other unusual things while sleeping (knitting in one's sleep would be considered unusual) should tell the roommate about this before moving in. They should also instruct the roommate what to do and what not to do. It's also important to contact the residence life professionals; perhaps special arrangements will need to be made.

Q: Our son wants to move into a single. We can afford it, but we're worried—is he just hiding from an uncomfortable situation?

A: Yes, he might be hiding from the situation. Discuss the rules listed in this chapter. Get him *The Naked Roommate* book. Also, have him get in touch with a professional on campus. If he still wants to move into a single, it's a personal decision. Just make sure he gets involved and engaged in life inside the classroom.

Q: My daughter wants to change rooms. How long should I tell her to wait?

A: Unless safety is an issue, there's no rush to change rooms. Most institutions have rules that make it impossible for a student to change rooms unless there is a serious situation happening. If your daughter is having a hard time with her roommate, encourage her to shift expectations, work to get along, and reach out to the residence life staff. And if she is having a hard time getting help, feel free to find the right person for her to contact.

Q: My son is living with his best friend and thinks it's a good idea. Any advice?

A: My advice is that living with a best friend is never

the best idea. Sure, it can work, but there's never anything to gain other than something he already has. Plus, living with a good friend means missing out on living with someone different. Even the worst roommates can turn into some of the best learning experiences. And with a friend down the hall, there's always a place to escape. Don't just take it from me...

To parents with kids thinking about rooming with their friends freshman year, please take Harlan's advice and don't do it! I read the book The Naked Roommate *before going to college and pretty much ignored that section of the book, because I thought I knew better. I didn't. You probably don't either, and you don't want to get yourself into a situation like mine, because I have now lost a friend and will be moving to a different room next semester. Do yourself a favor, and don't move in with a friend!*

—Caitlin, freshman

Have a question? Want to answer another parent's question?

Post your questions and answers; visit *The Happiest Kid on Campus* Parent Forum: www.HappiestKidonCampus.com.

TIP #10 THE FIRST FEW MONTHS

Being There as They Find Their Place (or Feel Out of Place)

The Tip

Sometimes we are just as surprised as you are at how hard our emotions can hit us. When they hit, listening and being there for us can make all the difference.

The Story

The most challenging thing I faced my first week of school was just being away from my family and my usual life. My parents dropped me off on campus on a Friday. I was surprised that I was able to hold my emotions in until that Sunday night. That Sunday night I was just so overwhelmed. I went to my car that night in the parking lot, called my mom, and started gushing so many tears! I just couldn't stop that. I cried for almost twenty minutes; it was so horrible. Finally, I pulled myself together a bit and started walking back to my dorm, but I started crying again and took off, because I didn't want anyone to see me like that. I had to stay outside another thirty minutes to get myself completely together. It got better over time. It was just hard for me at first. Though this really sounds simple, my parents helped me through the sadness by just being there for me and being happy to see me when I came down to visit them.

—Marcos, sophomore attending college in Texas

* * *

Let me start off this tip by reminding you that college is 90 percent amazing and 10 percent difficult. I haven't shared this with you in a while, but it's worth mentioning again. I want to mention it because this tip can be a little bit heavier than the rest of them.

For a lot of students, the 10 percent difficult takes place during the first few months of college. Let's just say that a student is on campus two hundred days a year; that's a total of one thousand days (if on the five-year plan). Applying the 10 percent rule means one hundred tough days and nine hundred amazing ones (not so bad).

This tip is focused on the tough ones. And really, these are the days you have a better chance of hearing from your child (oh, lucky you).

The first few months of college are the equivalent of springtime weather in the Great Plains. In Kansas the most beautiful morning can turn into a tumultuous afternoon and back into the most beautiful evening

The toughest adjustment for students is their parents not being there to help them make decisions. Today's parents make sure that their children are getting the most of their experiences, and with their parents not around they sometimes make mistakes, but they learn and re-learn. Parents need to allow them opportunities to learn, just like we had when we were in college.

—Dr. Ed Dadez, VP for Continuing Education and Student Services, Saint Leo University (think Dorothy in *The Wizard of Oz*). In order for college students to make it through the storm, they need to come to campus with an idea of where they can get firmly rooted.

Some students have an easy time with this whole transition; others stumble at times. And some fall. When you get the text, email, or call, the knee-jerk reaction for some of you might be to stop and solve all your child's problems; others will turn the ringer off and go back to sleep. But there's a better approach than ignoring or fixing. That's what this book has been about.

> I'm an only child and was expecting my parents to be complete wrecks when I left for college, but my mom always waits for me to call, because she doesn't want to be *that* parent. My dad will occasionally leave a voice mail here, but follows what my mom does.
>
> —Brianna, freshman

The first few months are game time! This is when your ridiculous knowledge of the college experience coupled with your calming nature to be patient and understanding will come into play. While all the *other* parents (those who have not read this book) are freaking out, trying to fix the problems, you can calmly help your child get comfortable with the uncomfortable, exercise patience, map out a path, identify people who can help, and take steps to become a self-reliant adult in college (and beyond).

THE SNOW GLOBE FACTOR

Imagine a snow globe. Envision your child's college campus inside the dome. Now imagine taking that snow globe and shaking the hell out of it. The frenzy that results inside represents everyone scrambling to find friends, to find their classes, and just to find their place on campus. This is what the first few weeks (or even months) of college life are all about.

The best way to be prepared is to know what your child will be facing during those months so that you can be ready to help him or her. I've put together a quick three-month forecast to give you a sense of what might be coming. Please keep in mind, like your local weather forecast, this is only a rough forecast based on data in my research radar.

THE TIMELINE
Month One

It's a pure adrenaline rush. For most incoming students it's a time of new independence, new friends, new situations, and a very different lifestyle. The first few weeks of school are filled with lots of new things. It's night after night of new friends, new situations, and new experiences. There's always something happening. Groups and organizations are busy recruiting new members to join. Welcome week activities are in full swing. Everyone has yet to take their place in the social-role ladder. Classes have barely started. Everyone is a straight-A student. Money from the summer is abundant. Clothing still fits (no freshman fifteen). For those living on campus, the roommate honeymoon is going strong. For commuters, connections are still forming. For those who don't catch the wave of euphoria and excitement, the good times never start. Homesickness hits—it's a surprise longing for friends, family, and significant others. Life on campus is nothing like it looks like in the movies or in the brochures. With all the new situations and new experiences, emotions run hot and cold like the showers in the residence halls. Everyone is trying to get comfortable in his or her new role. Everyone wants to find a sense of belonging. Some people will do whatever it takes (use your imagination). There's an incessant need to feel appreciated, included, and desired, but this takes time, work, and patience. As students try to find their place, they face the Universal Rejection Truth of the First-Year Experience—the truth that says not everyone will always appreciate, include, and desire them. The more uncomfortable a student is during this transition, the harder it is to take the risks needed to find his or her place. The student who has mapped out his or her path and exercises patience will be able to handle the emotional storm that's part of the first month. Those who haven't will get lost in the storm.

Month Two

The new factor fades and life takes on normal routines. Classes are in full swing and work is piling up. A surprise B can throw that straight-A student. A surprise C, D, or F can throw any student. The

The first week of school was incredibly difficult. So much so that in that first week I had even considered transferring after the first semester. I would call my parents crying almost every day. I thought I had made a huge mistake moving from a large metropolitan city to an incredibly small town. It wasn't until I made friends and joined different clubs and activities that I truly felt happy. I am now completely passionate about my school and all it has to offer. I even became an ambassador to help other people discover what Humboldt has to offer.

—Natalie, Humboldt State College

seed of fear is planted. Friends from the first week turn out to be not all that friendly. That "fresh start" and new social standing achieved in the first month starts to revert back into what it felt like in high school. Cliques form. If you're in, you're good (assuming you like the people in your clique). If you're out, it can be very lonely and deflating. The students having a hard time rarely admit to one another that they are having problems. Everyone is under the false impression that everyone else is having the best time ever. The roommate honeymoon starts to fade. Emotions bubble to the surface. Roommates no longer care about getting along, because they have enough friends outside the room. The menu is now in its second or third rotation. Homesickness starts spreading. If a student hasn't found a place, this is when he or she starts to get uncomfortable. Looking around at campus, it appears that everyone has found something or someone—everyone but your child. Some take refuge by hiding behind the Fifth Wall of technology and leaning on comfortable relationships from high school. Weekend visits can become common. Then thoughts of transferring begin to surface. Life in college is not what he or she expected it to be; it's not like it appeared in the brochures.

> My first day of college, I felt like I was going to throw up. I was nervous. My palms were sweaty, and I did not want to go to class. I just felt like college couldn't really have been happening yet. It was like I just got out of middle school!
>
> —Brooke, sophomore

Month Three

School is in full stride. The students who have found their place are living the good life. For the rest of them, life can be less than blissful. Midterms have come and gone. Some friendships have come and gone too. The roommate honeymoon is over. A student who hasn't found connections feels disconnected and disillusioned. The hope of finding quality connections is fading. Students start questioning what they did wrong and why this is not how they imagined. Instead of getting involved and being patient, they become detached and impatient. They forget that finding their place doesn't take a few weeks or a few months—it's a few semesters. Conversations with high school friends on other campuses make transferring seem like the best option. They want to get involved, but not having gotten involved, they feel like they missed the ride (see Tip #13 for more on how to coach your child to get involved). Long-distance relationships can become strained. New relationships seem as far out of reach as home.

The most helpful thing my parent has said during my college years has been to remind me not to expect everything to be easy. "There will always be an issue, no matter what, so learn to deal with them and not let it control you." My mom said this to me when I called her one day and was complaining about all the things that I had to do and things that were going wrong. She basically told me nicely to shut up and stop whining instead of sympathizing with me. I'm glad she did, because I realized that there wasn't anything really horrible or life-threatening going on that I couldn't fix, and it kind of made me feel thankful that nothing more serious was really happening.

—Shayna, senior

Thanksgiving break is fast approaching and students need time to regroup. This will be a good time for them to find space and clarity (more on this in Tip #12). Sometimes things look very different after having been home and returning to campus. Instead of getting comfortable with the uncomfortable, they are just uncomfortable, impatient, and too beat up by the transition to remember just how talented, wonderful, and amazing they are—that's where you step in.

WHEN THE PHONE RINGS OR THE TEXT OR VIDEO CHAT ARRIVES AND IT'S TROUBLE

There will be good calls the first months and then there will be the *other* kind of calls. The good ones will leave you with a big smile and brighten up your days. The other ones will test you. Knowing all that you know about college life and appreciating that this first-year experience can be the best and the worst all before breakfast should

> A lot of times if I have had a rough day at class, I need someone to vent to, but I don't know who to go to at school, so I will call my parents. I really like when they will just listen to me even if they don't tell me anything other than "just relax, things will be fine," and it makes me feel better already. Listen to your students if they call.
>
> —Erica Jean, freshman

help make the difficult calls much more predictable and easier on the ears. Still, even the most informed parents can get a little rattled at times. The following is a list of reminders to keep in mind when trouble comes calling:

1. **BE THERE:** Sometimes all they want is someone

to listen. Most of them don't want their parents to fix it. They just want to feel connected to someone who knows them and be reminded that they are loved.

2. **INSTITUTE THE TWENTY-FOUR-HOUR RULE:** I know this has been mentioned before, but it's worth including again. Most problems will be resolved themselves within twenty-four hours.

Before you get wrapped up in fixing a situation (and it's easy to do this), look at your watch and give it twenty-four hours, or even forty-eight hours. Just make sure you ask your child if the problem is still a problem, because most kids won't tell you when the problem has been resolved. While you're busy coming up with the solutions, they've moved on to the next new problem.

THE TWENTY-FOUR-HOUR RULE

A student will call or write home more often when things have been going poorly, but will call their friends when things are going well. This can lead to a skewed view of how the student is actually handling the transition. Administrators often recommend taking twenty-four hours to see whether a situation diffuses before a parent needs to get involved. Acting immediately discourages the student from learning to problem solve on their own and instead teaches them to look outside themselves for the "right" answer.

—Elizabeth Daly,
Director of Orientation and Parent
Programs, Northwestern University

3. **HELP THEM FIND THEIR OWN ANSWERS:**
I'm sure you're tired of this one too. So instead of me saying it and annoying you, I'll let someone else say it.

When offering advice, if need be, ask, "What do you think you should do?" and give them something to think about.

—Lenora, junior

4. **HELP THEM IDENTIFY PEOPLE WHO CAN FIND ANSWERS**: When there is a problem and they green-light your advice, tap in to that knowledge base you've accumulated in part 1, and point them in the direction of the people who can answer these questions and help. Coach them to make the moves.

5. **LEAN ON YOUR OWN PARENT SUPPORT SYSTEM:** When a child is struggling, it's hard for you to be happy. Find a support system for yourself and utilize it. Don't keep it in. Most parents are dealing with these same issues.

6. **FEEL FREE TO CALL AND ASK, "IS THIS NORMAL?":** If you're not sure if something is right, contact the parent programs contact or a professional on campus and ask the contact, "Is this normal? Who can help?" This is not being *that* parent. This is being a helpful, loving parent.

7. **FEEL FREE TO CALL AND ASK, "CAN YOU CHECK IN ON MY CHILD?":** If there is a situation where your child is exhibiting behavior that has you concerned, let the people living close to your son or daughter know that you're concerned and let them

help. If FERPA is an issue, make it clear that you're not looking to *get* information, but that you just want to share helpful information that will enable someone to do his or her job better and support your child.

8. **AVOID GETTING STUCK BEHIND THE FIFTH WALL OF TECHNOLOGY**: I explained the Fifth Wall of technology in the talking, texting, and chatting tips (see Tip #6), but it's worth including here too. Helping means being there to listen and guide (if a student is looking for guidance), but it also means setting limits. If your son or daughter is always reaching out and expecting you to fix it all, that's not going to get anything fixed. Don't get trapped.

9. **AVOID CASTING BLAME:** A lot of parents want to put all the responsibility on their children or everyone else. A parent doesn't want to be at fault. Instead of blaming your child or everyone else, focus on finding an answer. When you avoid placing blame on one another, you begin to move forward.

10. **PATIENCE, PATIENCE, PATIENCE:** Remind your child to be patient. The only way you can do this is if you are patient. Too many parents want it all to be just right. But this isn't something that gets fixed fast. Besides, you aren't the one who is responsible for doing the fixing.

11. **SEND SOMETHING IN THE MAIL:** No, not a bill. Students love care packages (you've seen a lot of quotes from students urging care packages).

Something baked or bought can be a surprise treasure. Notes work well too.

One more thing I need to share with you. Whatever is happening in your child's life, care packages make everything better. I know I mentioned it in Tip #1, but college students *love* care packages—no, they are obsessed. I can't even count how many times students mentioned the pure joy of getting a care package in the mail. If you want to increase the number of happy calls and contacts, increase the flow of care packages you send to your child. You will quickly discover that there is a direct correlation between cookies sent and happy calls home.

MAKING NEW FRIENDS AND KEEPING OLD ONES

Everyone wants and needs friends. For many students, making friends in high school was a process that took years. For some students, their closest friends are the same friends from elementary school or earlier. Coming to college can mean starting from scratch. A lot of students don't know how to make friends. Unless they've moved around, most have never had to up to this point in their lives.

When it comes to making friends, it's all about finding

the right people in the right places. And the way to find the right people is to get involved in campus activities and organizations with the right people and to be extremely patient along the way. Getting involved and making friends takes time. And that's a problem for a lot of students, because they are extremely impatient. They want it now! Impatient students tend to get uncomfortable when things don't go as planned. And this is when they forget that they live in a world of options and start to get desperate. This is when they compromise their values and associate with the wrong kind of people.

As you'll read in Tip #13, getting involved can present many unique challenges. The most helpful thing you can do as a person in your child's corner is remind him or her to be patient and encourage him or her to continue to get involved. Too many times students see that everyone else on campus appears to have friends and feel like they're missing out. Or they read about friends from high school having the best time on other campuses and feel like something is wrong with them because they aren't forming friendships as quickly.

Friends take time to grow. They forget that not making friends fast isn't a reflection of their being likable or not likable, it's a sign that making friends takes time. It's a sign that making friends means putting themselves in places and situations where friendships can grow (in the classroom, by participating in group projects, clubs, organizations, Greek life, volunteer work, etc). A student who leaves with a plan and patience can take the steps needed to surround him or herself with the right kind of people and create a world of options.

One last piece of information on friends: the type of people your child hangs out with will not always become the type of person your child will become. Yes, it happens, but there's an exception to this rule. A student who lives in a world of options can have friends who are different and not feel the pressure to abandon his or her core values. For example, if your son hangs out with people who drink a lot, but also has a group of friends who don't drink, he will always have the power to say no. As long as your son has other friends who make lifestyle choices in alignment with his choices, being around people who are different won't mean turning your son into an addict. The students who get in trouble end up with only one group of friends who do the wrong things.

My most challenging college experience was missing friends back home. Though I was having a blast at college and making lots of new and wonderful friends, I could not create carbon copies of the people I had grown so accustomed to back at home. What helped this was realizing that my true friends will always be there, and that I didn't have to replace them—I had the amazing opportunity to make more room for more incredible people in my life who I got to meet in college.

—Heather, freshman

A few words about old friends from high school—yes, high school friendships will change, but the strong and healthy relationships will only change for the better. Bonds formed during the high school years don't break with distance or change; they only grow stronger. And now, with Facebook and social networking, it's easier than ever to stay in touch. That brings up one of the big pitfalls—the Fifth Wall of technology. Because it's so easy to be in touch, it's very easy to spend too much time connecting to friends from home and not connecting with new friends on campus. The suggestion I make in *The Naked Roommate* and during speaking events is for students to cut their talk time with friends from high school in half. This is especially important for the student leaving for school in August with friends who aren't leaving for school until September. The friends from home can pull a kid back home. It can take having a conversation with a good friend. If this makes your child uncomfortable, *The Naked Roommate* has an entire tip on the Fifth Wall of technology that spells this out in clear terms. Using the book and my words can be an easy way to discuss the situation: "I read that we should talk half as much once we go to school— that makes me so sad. I'm going to miss you." Everyone can blame me.

FIRST-YEAR SEMINAR COURSES

One of the most important developments in recent years has been the creation of first-year-experience classes. They might have a name like Freshman Seminar or University 101. These courses are often optional, but the trend is moving toward making them required.

Not a lot of parents know the value of these courses. These classes are designed to help students get comfortable with the uncomfortable and engage in life on campus (commuters and first-generation students should make this a required course). These classes introduce students to instructors, academic issues, lifestyle choices, rules, regulations, peers, events on campus, and mentors (upperclassmen who sit in on classes). They are places for students to reflect on their own experiences through journaling, engage in thought-provoking conversations with other students, and get extra credit for attending events on and around campus. In fact, *The Naked Roommate* book is frequently incorporated as a text in many of these classes. In addition to these courses helping incoming students gain access to essential information, a student who is having a hard time transitioning can be more easily identified and helped. These courses put your child in touch with the most passionate and knowledgeable professionals on campus.

The First-Year Experience movement is strong and growing stronger. There is even an annual conference facilitated by the National Resource Center for the First-Year Experience and Students in Transition. The conference is focused on helping and supporting students in transition. The next trend coming is the sophomore-year experience (you've heard of the sophomore slump?). The need to support students and continue to help them thrive is spilling over beyond the first year. While some students might drag their feet and think this class isn't for them, it's the students who kick and scream who secretly delight in the value (although they might never admit it to you).

If you find that your son or daughter is reluctant to take one of these first-year-experience classes, this is a time to push a little harder. I don't think I've encouraged you to do a lot of pushing in this book. This issue is one of those times to give a little nudge. While it might be an optional class, I can't see a better or more valuable way for a first-year student to spend their time than in a room with other first-year students and leaders on campus who are passionate about helping your child to be successful.

After my daughter dropped organic chemistry, she filled the gap with a first-year seminar/college success course late in her freshman year (informing me that most of the freshmen football players were also in the class). As one who oversees the coordination of these courses on my own campus, I had not been able to convince my student of the value of such courses in her first semester. She begrudgingly admitted after the course was finished that she learned a few things. **Lesson learned**: Students may initially ignore our advice but may see the value at a later point when they are ready.

—Denise L. Rode,
Director of Orientation and First-Year Experience at Northern Illinois University and a member of the adjunct faculty in college student development at DePaul University in Chicago

QUESTIONS AND ANSWERS

Q: My daughter has been on campus for a few months and never seems to have a care in the world. Is this normal?

A: Some students have an easy time with this transition. They work through problems on their own and choose not to talk to you about it. Then there are those who keep it a secret because they don't want to burden you. Make sure you make it clear that sharing challenges or sharing a rough day will not upset or burden you. Also, make sure your child has access to the people who can help if she needs to reach out. But don't worry—assuming she is doing it right, something will come up.

Q: We're having a hard time drawing the line between being helpful and being too helpful. For example, my daughter was sick and had to buy medicine. She called us from the aisle to ask us which one to buy. We were reluctant to answer, but she didn't know what to get herself. We struggle with the times we should fix things and the times we should let her fix it herself. Any suggestions?

A: When your child calls you with these types of questions, direct them to a resource who has the answers. In this situation, there had to be a pharmacist at the drugstore who could answer the question. There are also people in the health services office. You can always offer an answer and then mention, "In the future, here's who you can call or talk to." A sick child might not be thinking clearly. At the very least, you can get her in the habit of thinking about the right people to ask before calling you.

Q: Our son is having a very hard time on campus. How do we know the difference between normal growing pains and dangerous behavior? He seems paralyzed and unable to take the steps to find his place.

A: If you have even the slightest concern that your child might be having a harder time than what's normal, or suffering from depression or some other issues, connect your child with care in the community. Visit for a weekend and spend some time together. Seeing him in his natural environment is helpful. If possible, make the visit on a day when classes are in session. It will give you a sense of the buzz on campus and offer an opportunity for you to connect your son to resources that might not be accessible on the weekends (doctors, therapists, etc). Also, reach out to the residence life professionals and ask for advice. Also, turn to the support staff and parent contacts to see if there are other steps and resources available.

Have a question? Want to answer another parent's question?

Post your questions and answers; visit *The Happiest Kid on Campus* Parent Forum: www.HappiestKidonCampus.com.

The Tip

The best thing a parent can say when you feel homesick is to tell you a day that you will get to see your family again. This helps because whenever you feel homesick you just keep remembering that you will see them all soon. Telling them to "imagine that I'm there with my arms around you" doesn't.

The Story

I was very nervous about going to school, because the only time I had been away from home for a long period of time was a two-week sleepover camp. The whole time I was miserable and homesick. This experience led me to believe that I would be homesick every day while at school. I was very surprised to find that school felt like home for the majority of the time. However, every Sunday morning I would feel homesick. This is because Sunday is normally the day that my family and I would be together for the whole day. During these Sundays I would get really upset and call home, and sometimes that made it worse, or sometimes it made it better. My friends knew I felt this way, and they would usually plan something for us to do on Sundays, like see a movie or go shopping. This definitely helped me take my mind off of it. Another thing that helped was when my parents would remind me of when I would see them again. I am now a sophomore, and I don't get homesick anymore. Although thinking about my return home and doing activities helped, I think time is the best way to fight homesickness.

—Sarah B., sophomore, University of Delaware

* * *

Dear Harlan,

I am a freshman in college. I got here eight weeks ago. I wanted to leave home very badly; I had spent eighteen years in a city that I just needed to leave. Weirdly enough, I hate college. I am a very likable person and had an awesome group of friends back home. Here, I love my roommate but don't really have any other close friends. I know I'm supposed to "give it time," but I don't think I can. I just want to be back home with my best friend and boyfriend and my close friends from home. I'd rather be back in high school than here. What gives? When will it get better?

Freshman Blues

Dear Freshman,

Good news. It gets better NOW! Well, maybe not right now.

No one tells you this, but what you're feeling is normal. According to the Higher Education Research Institute at UCLA, 65.1 percent of new students get homesick. When you're in an uncomfortable place—which college can be (new bed, new address, new friends)—the knee-jerk reaction is to run toward things that are comfortable. With cell phones, email, and instant messaging, it's easy to be in one place physically and another emotionally. That's a problem.

Here's what you need to do: Get comfortable with the uncomfortable. Turn to the people who can point you in the right direction—counselors, resident assistants, upperclassmen, and professors. Walk into rooms on your own and meet people. Do the things you loved to do in high school. Find new things to do that look interesting. Even if this year is awful, you'll learn so much about yourself. And be sure to avoid getting trapped behind the Fifth Wall of technology—too much use of cell phones, instant messaging, Facebook, the Internet, and video games can wall you off from the rest of campus and keep you from finding connections. Until you're in the same place in mind and body, you're going to get pulled in too many directions—and when you're pulled in so many directions, you won't be able to get it together.

According to the Higher Education Research Institute, 65.1 percent of college students reported feeling some sort of homesickness. That's a lot of homesick students. This number is big, and it's gotten bigger over the past several years. Forget the flu—homesickness the first year in college is an epidemic. If your kid isn't getting homesick, he or she is in the minority.

Knowing that homesickness is normal should help you be better prepared when your child calls or expresses feelings of homesickness. Instead of being shocked, panicking, or trying to convince your child that he or she isn't really homesick, you can listen and think, "My son loves home so much it's making him sick. Oh, isn't that wonderful." Or "My daughter loves home so much it's making her sick. Oh, isn't that wonderful." No, it's not *really* wonderful, but knowing it's normal can help you be a better listener and cure the sickness.

What is homesickness? If you take it literally it would be someone who is sick when home. It really should be called *awaysickness* or *dormsickness*. It's not really a sickness. It's more of a longing. How about *homelonging*? I see homesickness as longing for those comfortable feelings you get at home when you're around familiar friends, family, and people you love and trust. It's the feeling of curling up in a cozy bed with your favorite pillow on a cold winter's night (people in Florida won't know this feeling).

As a New College Parent you are more accessible when your child is homesick than the previous generation of parents. It's much easier to reach out to you (and aggravate you) than ever before. Because you will hear more about it and see more of it, there are three challenges you will face if your child feels homesick:

- Being able to listen to it (not fun).
- Being able to help fix it.
- Being able to identify when it's more than just a passing sickness.

CHALLENGE #1— LISTENING TO IT

Most parents do not want to listen to their child being miserable. The idea that your child is spending thousands of dollars and is homesick can make it seem like a big waste of money. And really, what's so hard about it? I mean, college is the good life, right? Students should be running around kicking their heels and jumping up and down with glee, not moaning about a professor who asks them to read a book!

> When I was homesick and having a hard time adjusting the first two days, my dad just seemed really unsympathetic. I know he cares about me and loves me, but at the time I felt like he didn't really care.
>
> —Kassie, freshman

The idea that a child is sad, lonely, and upset can really bother some parents. In fact, it can be so irritating that a parent will refuse to accept it. But fighting the fact that your daughter is homesick is just going to make her feel more isolated and alone. It's also going to make it so she avoids being honest about her feelings in the future.

The moment you can accept that homesickness is just part of the college experience is when you will become a better listener. Homesickness isn't a reflection of something you've done wrong or something your child has done wrong—it's a reflection of all the changes. It is a reflection of the transition from being a young adult who relies on Mom or Dad to fix it all to becoming a young adult who must create his or her own new life.

On the other side of the spectrum are the parents who want to do anything to fix homesickness. The most common reaction is to have their child come home. Parents want to "home it away." As you'll read in the advice from students, this is not the best approach. It might make you feel better to see your child at home, but it will just end up with their going back to school longing for what they've left behind. If you want to see your homesick child, consider going to campus and spending a day (if it's close enough) and having dinner together.

Homesickness can be a good thing. It's a wake-up call that helps a student see that he needs to make things happen (as opposed to a wake-up call from you in the morning). Allowing your child the time and space to feel it all and work through it all will make all the difference. Helping him work through it means listening and asking him what he thinks might help.

TO HAVE A CAR ON CAMPUS OR NOT

Most campuses do not allow cars on campus for first-year students. This is not a bad thing. It forces students to engage in life on campus. Getting in the car and going home or to visit with a significant other doesn't help students find connections on campus.

If your child took the time to put together a plan in the beginning of the year, you can use that as a guide. If he doesn't want to talk about a solution, know that just listening and being there for him is helpful. As time passes, classes will take up more of his time. And that will mean less time to think about how much he misses home. Time, listening, and encouraging him to get involved are the best cures for homesickness (see Tip #13 for suggestions on ways to get involved).

CHALLENGE #2—WHAT TO DO (OR NOT DO) TO HELP FIX IT

If a student is homesick, then it would make sense that the cure would be at home. But giving a homesick kid more home is like giving someone on a diet chocolate cake and a pint of ice cream. I'm not saying that home isn't going to make a kid happy, but like someone on a diet after eating a cake, once your child leaves home, he or she will be just as unhappy and longing for that feeling. So the cure isn't at home.

The way to help your child get over "*homelonging*" is to encourage her to create a place on campus where she feels at home. And that takes time. Most of the time homesickness won't last too deep into the second half of the year. Something will happen to cure her. It could be a resident assistant who offers support, a class, a professor, an organizational meeting, a leadership position, a new boyfriend, a sorority, an upcoming alternative spring break, an event on campus—there will be something that happens that will give her a sense of belonging. It can take months of participating in a group activity for her to start to feel some of those deeper connections that she longs for.

> The best thing a parent can do before the student even arrives on campus is to agree that the student may not come home that first month. The first month is always the hardest, and if they do it early on, they'll be coming home constantly. My mother imposed a rule that I wasn't allowed to come home for a visit before Thanksgiving break. Harsh at first, but it taught me to toughen up and make the best of things.
>
> —Becca, junior

What are some other suggestions that have helped students to find the common cure to homesickness? The following advice comes from formerly and currently homesick students on today's college campuses:

- The worst thing to do is to drive to school and come and get us or let us drive home. I have found that by not going home the first month, I adjusted much better, and the homesickness is not happening as often as it is with my friends who went home after their second week.
- The best thing a parent can do is encourage us to go out and get involved in campus life and not get caught up in coming home all the time.
- The worst thing you can do is let us come home every weekend. It just adds to the drama and does not allow us to adjust to our new life. The best thing to do is help us to look at this as a new adventure and to take advantage of meeting new people and trying new things.
- The worst thing to tell us is to suck it up. Followed by something about how you do not like hearing us complain.
- The best thing to do is to pack us some of our favorite (but not too expensive) things to go with us so that we're more familiar with our surroundings.
- The worst thing is to tell us to stop whining.
- The best thing to do is to encourage me to keep trying to succeed and reach my goals, to take initiative and make my life what I want it to be.
- The worst thing to do is to tell us, "Call when you have something to say that's worth hearing."

- The best thing to do is to send us care packages, money, or random cards. We love care packages and surprises in the mail.
- The worst thing to do is to talk about how everyone keeps asking about us, how everyone misses us, and how we should come home (when we clearly can't).
- The worst thing is to not answer emails, phone calls, or texts.
- The best thing is to limit our coming home to once or twice a month—to save on gas and to push us to be independent.
- The worst thing to do is to call every day and visit too often.
- The best thing to do is occasionally take us out to lunch (if you live close enough).
- The worst thing is to tell us how we should've stayed closer to home and talk about how everyone misses us. A guilt trip is not the way to go.
- The best thing to do is to listen and encourage us; sometimes a listening ear is all that we need.

CHALLENGE #3—KNOWING WHEN IT'S MORE THAN JUST A PASSING CASE OF HOMESICKNESS

The scariest part of having a homesick child and being too far away to see your child is not knowing when normal homesickness has become something more serious. If you suspect something is beyond normal, get in touch with the professionals on campus who can help guide you and watch your child more closely. Become familiar with the symptoms of depression (see Tip #23), and make sure your child has access to hotlines and resources (again, see Tip #23). Also, make sure your child's roommate or friends have access in case of an emergency. Also, contact the professional staff in the residence hall (if living in the halls), a counselor in health services, and the parent support resources on campus.

If you're concerned, also visit campus. Make the visit during the week so you can find the right people to check in with on campus. It's also nice to be able to see how your child interacts with others on campus.

QUESTIONS AND ANSWERS
(The following Q & A was originally printed in the *Boston Herald* to help parents address their students' homesickness.)

Q. What signs should parents look for that normal homesickness has turned into something dangerous?

A. Any of the common signs of depression: not being able to sleep, sleeping too much, skipping classes, not eating, eating too much, not doing things a student loves to do, expressing thoughts about hurting oneself, changes in behavior, drinking to get drunk, etc. If a parent, roommate, or friend suspects a student is in trouble, that person should reach out to the residence life staff and mental health experts on campus.

Q. I-chats, Facebook, and Twitter—do they help ease homesickness, or make it harder for college students to cut the cord?

A. Everything in moderation. It's easier than ever for students to be physically on campus and emotionally in a totally different place. Facebook, texting, and chatting can keep a student too dependent on parents, friends, and significant others. I always suggest that students cut in half the time they communicate with people they know from home. Use that extra time to connect with new people on campus. If a student is depressed, Mom or Dad should direct the student to talk to experts on campus. It's these experts who can help a student put together a plan of action and use the resources, support services, activities, and organizations unique to the campus to make connections.

Q. What about the hometown boyfriend [or girlfriend] away at another college? Friend or foe on the homesick-enhancement meter?

A. Long-distance relationships are fine if a student can have a life on campus too. The problem is that too many students get uncomfortable and use this relationship as a crutch. Having a long-distance relationship can be a great place to channel all of a student's anxious energy—the result is that a student makes no new connections on campus. On the other hand, a student who can have a long-distance relationship and create new relationships can have an amazing college experience.

Have a question? Want to answer another parent's question?

Post your questions and answers; visit *The Happiest Kid on Campus* Parent Forum: www.HappiestKidonCampus.com.

TIP #12 VISITING

Seeing It All, Hearing It All, and Smelling It All

The Tip
Just in case you didn't think about it, turning our bed-room into a storage room doesn't make coming home all that inviting.

The Story
I came home for Thanksgiving break and found that my mom had moved all of the Christmas decorations into my room after I left so that she wouldn't have to go all the way to the attic. When I asked where I was going to be sleeping, she offered the couch. We finally came to an agreement to downgrade my bed to a futon and I would sleep in my room still. The side effect has been that I don't go home as often, and when I do, I don't stay for too long. On the plus side, though, it's made growing up slightly easier knowing that after college I can't crash with the parents.

—Joseph, senior, Point Park University

* * *

Dear Harlan,

This note is in regard to "Going Home," the college student who wrote to you unsure how to handle going back home for college break. I must say that I think you glossed over a critical issue in your reply—namely, the parents' point of view.

We always look forward to our daughter's visits (she's now twenty-two and moved out at seventeen), but within three days we are ready for her to leave. It seems she has not grasped the fact that OUR lives are also different since she moved away. She has no concept of how to be a good guest. Even though we give her a bed, dresser, and closet to use while she's here, she dumps her stuff anywhere, comes and goes at all hours, takes over the bathroom, leaves dirty clothes and wet towels on the floor, calls about a dozen friends, gives out our number (which then rings at all hours), invites them over to hang out, smokes (we don't), and plays loud music for hours on end. We have spoken to her about it, but each time it is the same. We feel used and unappreciated.

Once a child moves out, returning adult children are GUESTS, and they need to be as respectful of their parents and their parents' home as they would if they were visiting the parents of one of their friends. Thanks.

A Mom in Pittsburgh

Dear Mom in Pittsburgh,

One thing is clear—your daughter is a sloppy guest. I never felt like a guest when I went home. Home is the one place where I'm not a guest. Isn't that what feeling "at home" means? I'm not saying she's entitled to be a pig, but she is entitled to feel like she's not a guest.

She doesn't listen very well, and you don't communicate very well (at least to her). She's probably just doing what she's been doing over the years. How's she supposed to know all the roles changed the moment she moved out? I can't imagine she knows that you feel used and unappreciated.

I'll remind other college kids to be mindful of the transition regarding their parents. You can explain to your daughter that things need to change—that is, if she can hear you over the loud music, ringing phone, and your hacking cough from all the smoke.

SO CLOSE YOU CAN TOUCH THEM

Finally you get to see your kid! Forget the video chats, phone calls, and text messages. The long-awaited visit is here!

Whether the visit is on your turf or on theirs, a visit is a chance to see them, hear them, and smell them (yes, some of them might smell a little bit). Being in the same room means being able to pick up on all the nuances that can't be communicated from a distance. You can see that big smile, watch those little telling mannerisms, and see all the new tattoos and piercings (assuming they are visible). Seeing it gives you the real story.

Whether your child is having the time of his life or the worst time ever, the visit is a telling experience. Whatever you find, a visit can help you see if your child needs some additional help and support. If there's a problem that needs to be addressed, the visit is the time to do it. No matter who is doing the visiting or where the visiting is happening—if your child is having a tough time in college, sometimes all it takes is a little love

> Please don't surprise us. We might have already had plans, and we don't want to make you feel bad.
>
> —Amanda, freshman

> If you ask your child if it's okay to visit at a certain time, chances are, if they're free, they'll say yes!
>
> —Elizabeth, junior

and attention to help him or her get back on the right path.

There are many different kinds of college visits. There are parents' weekends (aka family weekends), Thanksgiving break, winter break, surprise visits, and random other visits. This tip covers most of them.

Oh, one thing the students all told me to tell you before I get any deeper into this tip—*do not surprise them with a visit*. They don't like this.

PARENTS' WEEKEND (AKA FAMILY WEEKEND)

Some schools call it parents' weekend, but a lot of them call it family weekend. Family weekend allows all the moms, dads, step-parents, and partners to feel included.

This special weekend takes place roughly eight to ten weeks into the school year (with some exceptions). And the timing couldn't be better. If you remember all the way back to Tip #10, there's a lot going on two months into the school year. Visiting at this point will help you see what your daughter has created for herself. You can see her room, her friends, and the people who have become her new family.

If your child discourages you from coming to parents' weekend, that's one of the best reasons to go. Even if you can only drop in for an afternoon, be present. It's a special kind of weekend.

We schedule Parents' Weekend within six to eight weeks of the beginning of the school year, because it gives students time to put their roots down, get acclimated to the academic rigor of college, make new friends, and get involved. Students are happy to see their parents by then, and parents have a concrete time when they can look forward to seeing their student again.

—Beth Saul, Assistant Dean of Student Affairs, Director of Fraternity and Sorority Leadership Development and Parent Programs, University of Southern California

When you visit campus, students like to do three things with you—shopping, eating, and sleeping.

They like shopping (and you paying). They also like groceries, clothes, stuff for their rooms, and anything else you can buy. They will take cash too. They enjoy eating meals with you (when you pay), preferably at a place where they can't eat when paying on their own. Once they're done shopping and eating, they like to sleep. Don't be offended if your child sleeps; college kids sleep a lot (but do be offended and concerned if your son sleeps during dinner at a nice restaurant he can't afford).

While you're shopping and eating you'll have a chance to spend some quality time together. If you plan it right, you'll have time to hang out with him between the shopping, eating, and sleeping to see the set, cast, and crew behind the drama you've been hearing about over the past few months.

Before the family weekend festivities begin, you should check the parents' area of the campus website and view the schedule of events (there's probably little chance your child will look for you.). Surprisingly, the schedule will include more than eating, shopping, and sleeping. You'll discover receptions, panel discussions with faculty, dinners on campus, museum tours, campus tours, speakers, entertainers, plays, musical performances, and presentations by deans, instructors, and college presidents. Make sure you check out the festivities months ahead of time. Sometimes you will need to make reservations or buy a ticket ahead of time for an event. Again, this isn't something your child will tell you. So if you get there and they say you need a ticket, you've been warned. Attending some of these events can help you feel connected to campus and other parents (some might be familiar faces from orientation programs). And yet another bonus—you get to see your child interact with new friends in his or her own environment.

Things to Keep in Mind and Do during Parents' or Family Weekends

Lodging

If you're spending the weekend, hotels can fill up a year in advance (yes, you read that correctly). Consider getting a bigger room or a suite if booking a hotel. The reason for a bigger room? Your child may want to crash with you. It's nice to get away from campus for the night.

> My parents got me a GPS navigation for the car. I'm horrible with directions. That little voice has saved me multiple times.
>
> —Amy, sophomore

Take a Walking Tour

Ask your daughter to see a day in her life (make this required before shopping). Start in the residence hall and walk to her classrooms. If she is involved in a sport, check out the facilities. If she is involved in the campus newspaper, check out the newsroom. Go to the places where she spends her time. If she doesn't know where classes are by this time in the year, that's not a good sign.

Invite Friends, Girlfriends, Boyfriends, Roommates to Dinner

Meals are a golden opportunity to see the people your child spends time with. Not only can you give a hungry kid a decent meal, but you'll also get to see their interactions and get a sense of the people with whom your child is surrounding him or herself.

Talk to Them before Making Plans

When it comes to activities, don't assume you'll be hanging out with your child all day and night. Don't be insulted if your son wants to go out with friends after you go to bed. That's a sign there's something happening in his world—and that's a good thing.

Avoid Early Activities

When getting together in the morning, don't expect it to happen too early. No student wants to get up early. This can be a great time for you to go off on your own and get your own flavor for the town.

Check the Online Schedule

I mentioned this early, but it's worth repeating. Visit the parents' weekend/family weekend area on the campus website and check out the schedule. Your child will be surprised to know there is a schedule.

> I have seen moms at the bars with their daughters, dressed just like their daughters, talking to guys their daughters' age about things that probably a daughter, not a mom, should be talking about. I guess it's "cougar" syndrome mixed with trying to be your kid's BFF. I don't really get it.
>
> —Shayna, senior

Go for a Drive

Find interesting places to explore within an hour's drive. Going for a short drive and getting your child off campus can give you a chance to be together. Something active can take the focus off of college and give you a chance to talk.

My mom once came down for a moms' weekend and guilted me into going for a drive that Saturday to visit a nearby town where she'd lived, thus resulting in my missing an intramural championship game that day and letting down the rest of my team.

—Paul, recent grad

Avoid Hooking Up with Other Students (Yes, This is Real)

You'd be surprised that some single moms will look at a campus visit as a time to pull out that Mrs. Robinson (we now call Mrs. Robinson a cougar) scenario. Dads have been known to prowl campus too (they don't call them Mr. Robinsons, just dirty older men). Do not mess around with the students—please.

Make Sure They Aren't Busy

I know it's hard to believe that a fifteen-hour-a-week class schedule can keep a kid busy over the weekend, but it happens. If your child is involved outside the classroom, the weekend can be busy with events and activities. It could be homecoming one weekend, fraternity or sorority rush the next weekend, a huge fund-raiser the next weekend, and an intramural playoff game the following weekend. Then there can be midterms, papers, and final exams to compete with. Check to see what works for your child's schedule before assuming he or she needs to work around yours. Give him or her time to plan and coordinate (cleaning his or her room can take a good week or two).

> **ATTENTION: DIVORCED PARENTS AND FAMILIES**
>
> If you can't get along with your ex, don't go to campus together. And do not make your student choose. Make two parents' weekends. You can trade off which set of parents visits during the official campus parents' weekend. This works the same for all breaks. Creating your own parents' weekend can be special and wonderful.

THE THANKSGIVING VISIT

Thanksgiving break is a very exciting time for parents.

Having your child home again is just about the most wonderful thing that could happen (that and actually cooking the turkey to perfection). There are so many things to do and so much catching up. There are meals to share, rooms to clean, lightbulbs to change, computer issues to resolve, things to buy, stuff to rearrange, relatives to see, family outings to go on—there are so many things to do as a family and so little time to do it.

College students get excited about Thanksgiving too. For them, it's a time to sleep, eat, hang out with friends, and see a boyfriend or girlfriend. Oh, and if there's time to visit and shop with parents, that's a bonus too.

I think that parents just need to listen to their college student and be aware that when they come home for vacations, things are going to be different. As we go through our classes at school, we evolve into who we will be in the future. I know that the first vacation I was back, my parents could tell a difference. I felt that they weren't really prepared for that. I was much more mature when I came home for Thanksgiving than I was when I left in August. They seemed shocked about that.

—Emily, freshman

One thing that makes me ready to come home is the good ol' home cookin'. During breaks, I always know that when I get home, there will be one of my favorite home-cooked meals waiting for me from either my mom or dad.

—Jennifer, sophomore

My advice for parents is to let their kids rest; we've just come off of a three-and-a-half-month "job," and we need time to relax, so don't get on our case about jobs or volunteering, please!

—Rachel, junior

Notice the difference? What I'm trying to say is that

first-year college students home for break might have different expectations than their parents. This is especially true of students whose break is their first visit home.

Being back home is like being transported to another world. The last time your child was home he or she was a kid. So much has changed. The boy is a man and the girl is a woman. The life your daughter left behind is now part of her past. Coming back home can be like being a deer in the headlights. So try not to run her over by having too many expectations. She might actually need a break.

Coming home is also like visiting a new country, but a country with far fewer freedoms. One of the biggest struggles a college student faces is living under your rules. I mean, your rules can suck at times (that's not me talking; that's me talking like your child is thinking. I love your rules). Being on your turf

The most surprising, craziest, and wackiest thing I've ever seen a parent do has been to come to campus to do their son's laundry. I see moms in the laundry room all the time.

—Sal, freshman

means following your rules; there's no arguing with this. But asking her how you can change the rules to reflect how things have changed in her life sends a powerful message. It's the difference between telling her and asking her. Asking her what she thinks is a reasonable time to come home seems reasonable. By putting it this way it's not about your controlling her, but acknowledging that she

is no longer that same high school kid who left home.

That said, there are some parents who refuse to change and will once again rule with an iron fist. Parents who refuse to acknowledge these changes will find themselves with kids who plan short and infrequent visits home. So your child now has options. Whereas before the only options were moving to a neighbor's house or filing a petition in the courts to become a legal adult at age sixteen, she now has a life where she is in charge of

If your child is bringing home a significant other from school, expect to share all of your time together. For the first visit home I would discourage this. There will be plenty of visits for guests down the line. In fact, winter break is a great time for this, because there's more time to share.

My mother doesn't require a curfew, but she is overbearing and completely neurotic. I went to a college three hours away for freedom, and being back home is driving me up the wall. Parents, don't hound your kids. My mother is guilting me into doing everything she hasn't done for herself the past three months of first semester. I am going nuts.

—Lauren

her own actions. She also has a place to stay (and yes, you might be paying for it).

When your rules and your child's rules clash, make sure your child understands the reason behind your thinking, or she will jump to the conclusion that you don't trust her. Explain what's happening to avoid misunderstandings. For example, a curfew isn't about a parent's lack of trust; it's about a parent's lack of sleep. Parents don't sleep when they know their kids are out late at night. Your child sleeping in your home means you know when she's out. So when you explain the rules, explain the reasons behind them. She doesn't have to love them, just respect them. Perhaps there can be a compromise.

Another area where kids and parents clash is when budgeting time at home; specifically, spending time with boyfriends and girlfriends. Parents don't like sharing or competing. Before break, ask your child about her plans and where you fit in. It's not reasonable to expect 100 percent of her time. One thing that can help is to include a significant other in the plans (but not all plans).

SOME THINGS THAT MIGHT SURPRISE YOU

· Expect your child to see his or her high school friends in a different light. A lot of students will now see their old friends as stupid, immature, or just different. They will not understand how they were friends with such people.

· Know that the visits will get better. The first visit home can be strained, awkward, and uncomfortable. Give your son time to get comfortable. If you've turned his room into a coin collection room, expect more time.

· If you've made changes to your child's room, explain this before she gets home. Don't expect your child to come home a lot if she needs to sleep on a yoga mat because you've turned her room into a yoga studio.

· Avoid overscheduling him. He'll be like a deer in the headlights— you don't want to run him over with too many plans.

· Don't take her sleeping personally. I've mentioned this several times, but I've heard from a lot of parents who don't like this.

· Appreciate that this is a break for him (he might just want to have a break).

Just because we came home for a weekend doesn't mean we are going to stay at home all weekend; we'll actually just drop off laundry and then go out with old friends for three days.

—Ryan, freshman

WARNING!

Do not allow your child to drive home late at night from campus just because you want an extra night with him or her. Students fall asleep on the road driving to and from home. Tell your child to make the drive in the morning. Make it non-negotiable.

OTHER VISITS
Winter Break

Finally a break when there's time to hang out, sleep, see everyone, and work (by this point in the year, your child's bank account could be suffering). Some winter breaks can last as long as four or five weeks. If possible, between the sleeping, eating, working, and hanging out, plan a family trip and spend some time doing something together.

Revisit that conversation from the summer, the one

where you talked about expectations—what's gone right, what's gone wrong, what your child's plans are for the second half of the year. Having the first half of the school year in the past means having an opportunity to take pause and figure out what went well and what went wrong. It's also a time to plan for what's next.

Other Parent and Family Weekends

There can be some groups and organizations that plan their own parent and family weekend. If your child joins a fraternity or sorority, plan on going to the Greek parents' weekend. You'll want to take advantage of opportunities to meet the other parents and participate in the organization's special events.

I'M NOT GOING BACK!

There are some students who will come home from break and not want to go back to school. And as a parent, it's going to put you in a tough spot. Is it quitting? Is it normal to not want to go back? Should you push them to make it work? Turn to Tip #25: Transferring to read more.

I've had the best winter break job for the past four or five years. I'm the head counselor of a park district winter camp. There are usually only like twenty to thirty kids, grades 1–6, and the best part is that the counselors and I are all friends. We get to just chill, make some random crafts, eat, and then once a week go on a field trip...I get paid to go to cool places with my friends! How great is that? Don't get me wrong—we pay attention to the kids, I promise, but yeah, it's great!

—Heather, junior

Sports Weekends

Athletic weekends are a cool time to come down and hang out on campus. It's amazing to be part of the energy of a football weekend. Even the worst teams have great football weekend. If you're not into football, go to a basketball game, hockey game, baseball game, soccer game, softball game, lacrosse game, tennis match, volleyball game, or any other kind of sporting event. Live college sports are awesome. Going for an event can mean coming into town in the morning, grabbing a bite, and then heading back home—you don't even need to spend the night. If you're going on a drive, you can always stay in a bigger city close to campus and make it a couples' getaway.

The biggest challenges I had been anticipating before coming to college were making friends and getting places (how to get there, whether or not to, where I'd be most comfortable/less at risk to get into trouble). My parents fixed that on my first day of orientation. They took my car. Now I can't get anywhere, so there's no need to worry about all of that.

—Lindsey, freshman

THE FREQUENTLY VISITING STUDENT

Some students come home frequently. Some of these visits are to see a boyfriend or girlfriend, some are for a doctor's appointment, some are for work, and some are to sit around without having to walk across campus to eat a meal and worry about a drunken person peeing on your floor in the middle of the night.

But unless there is a family emergency, home should be college. There are very few legitimate reasons your child should come home frequently.

Yes, coming home to see a boyfriend or girlfriend, go to work, or do laundry might seem like fantastic reason for you to see your child, but all this will do is keep him from being on campus. Instead of encouraging him to come home, encourage him to see his significant other significantly less, encourage him to get a job closer to campus, and encourage him to do laundry in the residence halls (who knows, maybe he can get a job working in the residence hall and find a new girlfriend while doing laundry).

A student who is constantly going home is constantly not on campus. And constantly not being on campus makes it virtually impossible to make a new campus a new home.

When your child says, "There's nothing happening on campus," whip out Tip #13 and go through the list of ways to get involved. Students who are involved find plenty to do on the weekends.

One way to help keep a student on campus is to not allow her to bring her car to campus. (If first-year students aren't restricted from having cars, you can always have

SHOULD THEY HAVE A CAR ON CAMPUS?

If your child goes to a school close enough to drive himself there, force him to leave the car home for at least a semester, if not the first year. Most schools don't allow freshman residential students to have a car for a reason—it's important for them to stay in their new community on the "off hours" and weekends. Think twice about fighting for your child to have a car for convenience reasons. The truth is that Johnny won't die if he has to not see his high school friends or get a part-time job on campus.

—Jeff Wakeman,
Director of Campus Activities
and Student Leadership,
William Paterson University

I love that my parents are not hounding me with "Be home at midnight." It's a hard transition backward to being under someone's watch all the time.

—Jeriann, junior

them keep the car at home the first few months.) A student who can't come home will have no choice but to stay on campus.

Frequent visits home might be nice for Mom and Dad to see a kid, but it's not going to help make college feel like home.

> I love my roommate, but her mom visits just about every weekend. She never calls. Then she bursts in and tells her that my side of the room is a mess, takes over the room, and then starts cleaning.
>
> —Amy, freshman

THE FREQUENTLY VISITING PARENT

SIGNS YOU'RE VISITING TOO FREQUENTLY

· If you visit so often you earn a nickname from your child's friends, that's too often.

· If you have a "usual" at a campus bar, that's too often.

· If you know the soup of the day by heart, that's too often.

An afternoon visit can be a huge boost. Sharing a meal with a parent who lives close to campus is a real treat. Being there when your child really needs you can be loving and supportive. But it's easy to get carried away and think he or she needs you to be there more than you need to be. It's a hazard of knowing so much.

No one can tell you to stop visiting (other than your child, although campus safety can politely ask you to leave campus). Parents need to self-regulate. Unless your child has a medical condition that requires your help (a broken leg, mental health issues, etc.), visiting too often might be a sign that you don't have much going on in your own life. For example, coming to campus with food on a regular basis might satiate your hunger to see your child, but it's not going to help him or her find new friends. Coming to campus to bring things for his or her room might seem loving, but UPS delivers too. Oh, and buying a new home and moving closer to campus counts as visiting too frequently (yes, this happens).

> The most frustrating thing my parents did was beg me to come home every weekend. Not exactly helpful.
>
> —John, freshman

> I knew a parent who traveled six hours to see their child every weekend of his first year of college. Even if the child seems accepting, it can have a negative impact on their growing process. He spent less time with his friends, his girlfriend, and even doing homework. It's so important to learn at this stage in life to be independent, both emotionally and financially.
>
> —Name and school withheld

As for ways to help pass the time and help you focus on something other than missing your child, take the same advice you are giving to him and get involved in the community, volunteer, get active, get involved spiritually, and take time to be selfish and spend time with *you*—really, you deserve it.

Whether the visit takes place at home or on campus or at a Denny's between home and campus, the visit is about making sure your child is happy and healthy. Plan quality visits and you'll be able to gauge what's *really* happening. Being there and seeing it, hearing it, and smelling it will reveal the whole story.

QUESTIONS AND ANSWERS

Q: Regarding visits home, how often is too often?

A: I don't feel comfortable giving a number. It can vary from student to student and campus to campus. Every weekend is too much. Every other weekend is also too much. Once every six to eight weeks is reasonable unless there's a good reason to come home. If a student wants to always come home, then there's no reason to go away to school. Again, this is a personal issue that can vary based on you and your child—have an honest discussion.

Q: How do you limit visits and still be a supportive parent?

A: The same way you set any other limits as a parent. You can explain that you love your child and that coming home isn't part of the college experience. You can refer her to this book or my other books. You can get someone she trusts to tell her for you. But set limits. One way to make it harder for her to come home is to not give her a car. Then coming home won't be an option.

Q: Everyone on my son's campus goes home for the weekend. Forcing him to stay on campus would mean being all alone. Besides the safety issues, there really isn't anything to do. What should we do?

A: There are some schools that are suitcase schools. These are the types of schools where students go home on Thursday afternoon and return late Sunday night. The best way to combat this is to encourage involvement during the week. A student who is so involved during the week will be forced to get involved on the weekend. That said, there are some schools that are ghost towns on the weekend. If this is the case and your son doesn't want to pack a suitcase, consider having him go home with a new friend over the weekend or visit other campuses. He can also start some weekend events and try to change the culture over time. Anything is better than coming home every single weekend.

Have a question? Want to answer another parent's question?

Post your questions and answers; visit *The Happiest Kid on Campus* Parent Forum: www.HappiestKidonCampus.com.

TIP #13 STUDENT INVOLVEMENT

Exploring the College Buffet of Opportunity

The Tip

Encouraging your student to get involved in the right organization can change the wrong type of behavior.

The Story

As a sophomore and during most of my junior year, I spent most of my free time getting drunk at parties. The second semester of my junior year I joined my first official student organization. I joined the HELP (Health Enhancement Led by Peers) program, the peer education group on the campus of the University of South Dakota. My roommate at the time was a member, and I had heard about the group at orientation in my freshman year but really wasn't interested then. Little did I know how much the HELP program would change my life! Not only did I join the group and love it so much, but I went on to become the president the following year, then graduate assistant, and finally the adviser. Not only did joining the HELP program help me to change my life by cutting down on my drinking, but it helped me decide what I really wanted to do with my life. I had decided in about sixth grade that I was going to be a speech-language pathologist. After joining HELP, I decided this wasn't where my heart was anymore. So after my first semester in the graduate program for speech therapy, I changed my master's degree program to alcohol and drug-abuse prevention. Now I am an internationally certified prevention specialist. I absolutely love what I do.

—B. Jensen, MA, ICPS,
University of South Dakota, class of '04, '07

* * *

FROM THE NAKED ROOMMATE FORUMS:

www.TheNakedRoommate.com

QUESTION: I have been at college for a little over two months now, and I am still not completely settled in. I am kind of drifting between different groups of friends, which I know isn't really a bad thing. I have a group of friends from my floor, and my boyfriend is pledging a fraternity, so I end up going to parties there pretty often. I just feel so adrift. I feel like I don't have one specific niche that I feel really at home in on campus. I see my boyfriend and how tight he is with his fraternity brothers, and I really want that kind of camaraderie. What should I do?

RESPONSE: Relax. It's only been two months. Finding your niche is what college is all about. You're not supposed to be settled until you're ready to graduate. What did you do in high school? Were you part of any clubs? Find the corresponding organizations at your college and go to a meeting. From what you've written, you hang out with your boyfriend and in your dorm exclusively. Ask your dorm friends what they do and ask to tag along. If you've already decided on a field of study, go hang out with professors, grad students, and fellow undergrads (I'm assuming you're an undergrad). But again, it's only been TWO months. That may seem like a long time, but it really isn't compared to the four (give or take) years you'll spend in total.

—From "Theater Undergrad, Class of 2010"

THE "GET INVOLVED" CHOIR

There's this chorus of voices that will tell your child to "Get Involved." If your child happens to join chorus, he or she might hear it in three-part harmony.

Generally, it's parents, college life professionals, older siblings, recent grads, and me singing the "get involved" song. Everyone wants first-year students to get involved, because getting involved means feeling connected to campus.

College is an all-you-can-do buffet of opportunities. There are academic clubs, honor societies, student government, cultural organizations, leadership groups, volunteer opportunities, special interest clubs, the performing arts, student publications, spiritual organizations, Greek life, internships, study abroad programs, alternative spring breaks, part-time jobs, and many other ways to get involved. In addition to helping students find their place in college, they can discover an interest that can lead to a career, and they can help them make campus smaller and much more manageable. If you look at a campus like a large city, student groups and organizations are these smaller communities (or neighborhoods) of people who share common interests.

MEET THE ADVISERS

All clubs and organizations have faculty or staff advisers. What a great way to know your professors outside of the classroom. You will find they want the group to succeed and will be a great resource for you. Then, when it's time to apply for an internship or job, these folks will be great resources for you with recommendations or contacts.

—Ed Wirthwein,
Assistant Director, Elliott Union
University of Central Missouri

A student can hang out in the neighborhood and will find a sense of community. It all starts with getting involved.

Yet with all these opportunities available, a lot of students don't get involved. For some parents this can be extremely frustrating. It can help to know that there are three main reasons why students have a hard time getting involved:

1. They don't know they should get involved
2. They are discouraged from getting involved
3. They are too uncomfortable to get involved

1. They Don't Know They Should Get Involved

In high school it's all about getting into college. There's so little focus during the search process on what students will do once they arrive on their college campus. They don't think about getting involved until they're there. And sometimes it doesn't happen until their second, third, or fourth year. The focus during the search process is all about potential majors and picking the best school. But the best school might not be the best fit if a student can't get involved on campus. A student who gets involved will discover his or her *real* passion. It takes getting involved to figure out what they *really* want to do with their lives. After you have read this book, your child will have thought about, researched, and mapped out a path to get involved. Assuming you encourage him or her to get involved. Which leads to...

2. They Are Discouraged (By Parents, Friends, and Others)

You'd be surprised—many parents see the college experience only as a place for students to achieve academic excellence and earn a degree. Getting involved outside the classroom is looked upon as a waste of time.

But this couldn't be further from the truth. This entire First-Year Experience movement, the rise of living and learning communities, experiential learning, and the time and resources spent focus on getting students involved on campus. The more a student is engaged in campus activities, the greater the likelihood of that student succeeding and graduating.

Being involved starts with being present physically and emotionally. It starts with summer programs and spills into the beginning of the year. A student who is surrounded by people who have similar interests and goals will find a circle of friends just by showing up every day. Parents can have a dramatic impact on helping students see the value in life outside the classroom by

WARNING: GOOGLE YOUR CHILD'S NAME

When a student is applying for leadership positions on campus, the selection committee will google students and look up profiles on Facebook, MySpace, LinkedIn, and other social networks. Have your child do a search or do one for him or her and see what comes up.

WARNING: BEWARE OF JEALOUS FRIENDS

Some of your students will have friends at home who are jealous or threatened by their success. Cell phones and social networking have made it easier than ever for these friends who are not in college to send negative and discouraging messages to your achieving son or daughter. A student who is involved will be surrounded by successful people who will drown out the people sending the wrong messages.

encouraging them to pick out activities and organizations that will enable them to engage in life on campus.

3. They Are Too Uncomfortable to Get Involved

Getting involved can be uncomfortable—it means meeting new people, approaching strangers, and being potentially judged. The students who do get involved easily are either invited to get involved or make a conscientious effort to get involved.

The problem is that if no one invites your child to tag along or get involved, it can be awkward and uncomfortable for that student to do what it takes to find his or her place. It can mean asking strangers for information. It can mean walking into rooms filled with people who already know one another (feeling like an outsider). It can mean attending meetings, events, and auditions with upperclassmen present (intimidating). Even eating in the cafeteria and finding a seat can be a challenge. Most students don't want to eat alone, but they don't want to sit with strangers.

This constant fear of doing what it takes to get involved is pervasive—incoming students sometimes skip orientation programs, avoid going to sporting events, don't take part in floor events, and eat in their rooms, because they don't want to do such things alone. They just wait and play it safe, hoping they'll get invited to participate. And then, sometimes, the invitation comes from the wrong people doing the wrong thing. Students living in a world with very few options might take up these offers. And that is not what you want to have happen.

When the Uncomfortable Pops Up

If your child has a hard time getting involved, it helps to have some suggestions in your back pocket (assuming you have the green light to share some advice). The following suggestions can help your child have an easier time getting comfortable with the uncomfortable when getting involved on campus.

1. **ENCOURAGE THEM TO PLANT THE SEED EARLY:** Make sure she knows that you want her to get involved in at least one or two activities or organizations from day one. This should be done over the summer. If you're reading this into the first year, start encouraging her now.

2. **TALK UP THE ACTIVITIES FAIR TO THEM:** Every school has an activities and organizations fair. It's a time when groups and organizations set up booths and recruit students to attend meetings and events. Anyone involved in orientation or student activities will be able to help your child find the date, time, and location.

   STUDENT ACTIVITIES BOARD

   Student activities board members plan campus events (speakers, bands, films, novelties, etc.), attend conferences, produce events, promote events, and work with large budgets and professionals.

3. **ENCOURAGE THEM TO REACH OUT TO THE RIGHT PEOPLE:** The right people are student

leaders, and asking questions before the school year begins will start relationships that can be continued face-to-face on campus.

4. **HIGHLIGHT FIRST-YEAR-FRIENDLY GROUPS:** Spiritual, cultural, athletic, Greek, and volunteer groups tend to be welcoming and accepting of new members. Try to point your child to places where having success is easier and more accessible.

5. **ENCOURAGE THEM TO GET INVOLVED IN THE NEIGHBORHOOD:** There are some living situations that enable students to get involved more easily. The residence halls are one of these places. Living and learning communities are even better.

6. **REMIND THEM, "YOU AREN'T SUPPOSED TO KNOW PEOPLE":** A lot of students won't get involved, because they feel like they don't know people. But the only way to know people is to embrace the fact that you're not supposed to know

FACTS AND STATISTICS

According to the Higher Education Research Institute (2008 survey results), a record number of incoming college students are politically engaged, with 85.9 percent reporting that they frequently or occasionally discussed politics in the last year.

LIVING, LEARNING, AND MAKING FRIENDS

My freshman year I was in this learning community program where we lived in a Small House (a dorm for about thirty or so residents) and all had two classes together. So I saw the people that I lived with on a regular basis, and we all got to know each other pretty well—some of us became good friends. So I got lucky there because of the program.

people. Everyone who is anyone knows this. The sooner your child can accept that he isn't supposed to know people, the sooner he can walk into rooms and start meeting people.

7. **REMIND THEM TO GET OUT OF THEIR ROOMS:** Students have to get out and into other rooms with other people. Sure, your child might get invited to get involved by a new roommate or friendly RA, but don't count on it. She needs to get out of her room and into other rooms for life to happen.

> For me, my college experience has been defined by the Free Hugs Campaign. I have made my own mark by walking around campus holding a sign above my head that says "FREE HUGS." It's really been life-changing, meeting and hugging so many people. Sometimes things go bad, but the good moments far outweigh the bad moments. I wouldn't give it up for anything.
>
> —Dave, sophomore

> I got involved with Students for Barack Obama my freshman year of college. I became politically active for the first time in my life—I registered people to vote, volunteered at Obama activities, and even called people in other states to remind them to vote for him in the primaries.
>
> —Kasey, junior

8. **SUGGEST THAT THEY GET PAID AND GET INVOLVED AT THE SAME TIME:** Food service jobs, rec center jobs, residence life jobs, and activities jobs that pay will help a student earn Ramen noodle money (not beer money) and meet people.

9. **ENCOURAGE THEM TO TAKE CLASSES AND COOL ELECTIVES WITH GROUP DYNAMICS:** Classes help people make friends and build

relationships with instructors, teaching assistants, and classmates. A first-year experience class should be a must. Other classes like bowling, wine tasting, yoga, human sexuality, and group guitar lessons (one of my personal faves) make it easy to naturally meet people.

10. **SUGGEST THEY DO IT AGAIN AND AGAIN:** One meeting isn't enough to decide something sucks. It takes weeks of attending to get a feel for the group. It also takes weeks of attending for the people in the room to get to know one another.

11. **HELP THEM PRACTICE SAYING NO:** Students who get involved will be asked to do more than they can handle. It's a hazard of the job. It's way too easy to get overly involved. Some students need help saying no.

In the next section I've included a quick rundown of ways students can get involved. This should be helpful to read when you hear, "There's nothing going on here." You'll be able to show your child differently.

HOW CAN YOUR CHILD GET INVOLVED?
There is a buffet of opportunities available to your child.

Athletics
Athletics can be a comfortable and sweaty way for your child to make friends and avoid packing on the pounds from that new 3:00 a.m. breadstick habit. It can also be

a way to get a scholarship if he or she is really good. There are competitive sports, intramurals, club sports, and pick-up games. There are organizations for baseball, tennis, crew, equestrian interests, badminton, cheerleading, table tennis, ice hockey, martial arts/self-defense, basketball, lacrosse, rugby, paintball, cycling, roller hockey, skiing/snowboarding, soccer, Frisbee, soccer, wrestling, and all kinds of the other clubs and sports.

If your child plays NCAA, NAIA, or NJCAA sports, make sure you aren't being too involved for him or her. It's easy to be too involved given how much athletics has been a part of your life as a parent. Coaches tell me they love you on game days, but hanging out at practices can be too much. Check with your child and check with the coach. Sometimes the coach will be more honest with you, because your son or daughter doesn't want to hurt your feelings.

As a student affairs practitioner who embraces the value of student engagement in the campus community, I was disappointed and concerned when my daughter held back from getting involved in residence hall activities and the vibrant campus life at XYZ University. She auditioned and was selected for a dance team but did not seem very involved, preferring to spend most of her time studying. **Lesson learned**: My daughter was very similar to many other academically oriented first-year students I have worked with. She waited until she had experienced success in her coursework within the competitive environment at XYZ U. Only now, as a sophomore, is she beginning to take on roles in her residence hall and seek out service opportunities on campus and in the community. In developmental terms, she tested out her competence in the classroom and now is branching out to other areas.

—Denise L. Rode,
Director of Orientation and First-Year Experience at Northern Illinois University and member of the adjunct faculty in college student development at DePaul University in Chicago

Fraternities and Sororities

There are social fraternities (see Tip #14), service fraternities, professional fraternities, and honor societies. Service and professional fraternities are open to members of both genders and offer access to people with similar interests. Service fraternities are focused on community service. Professional fraternities are a great way to meet people focused on particular careers. All of these groups and organizations can connect students with upperclassmen and professionals on and around campus.

Spiritual Life

Almost every religion can be found on campus (or near it). There are groups for students who are Catholic, Muslim, Jewish, Lutheran, Baptist, Protestant, Hindu, Buddhist, agnostic, and just about every other religion. If there is no

SO YOUR KID WANTS TO BE A WALK-ON?

Here's how it works for one of the nation's winningest coaches. Bill Fennelly is head coach of Iowa State University's women's basketball team:

The Summary: Normally it starts with a call from an interested student. The coach will encourage the interested player to stop in once she arrives on campus. Once practice starts, he'll encourage her to attend and watch practice. From there, the player might work out with the team. The coaching staff will do their due diligence and find out more about the prospective player. There might be two or three out of twenty or thirty contacts that go through with it this far. Then who knows? That walk-on just might make the team.

Joining my sorority has been so important!! It's a professional sorority for girls in agriculture. It's amazing to be able to meet more people with similar interests who understand how important and vital ag is. We aren't all just farmers, and by getting more involved in the college of ag on campus, I made a ton of friends! It was a perfect fit.

—Caroline, junior

group for your religion on campus, your child can become the founding member.

There are retreats, Bible study groups, worship services, and campus events. These groups tend to be some of the most inviting, welcoming, and inclusive organizations on campus. Surprisingly, though, some of these groups can be a little intense (see Q & A at the end of this tip). Passionate people can be that way. But campus religious organizations are a great place to find students with similar values and outlooks on life.

> When I started college, I quickly got involved with Hillel—the Jewish student organization on campus. I'm not very religious, but in a strange environment it helped me to have a group of people who shared at least one common trait with me. As it turned out, I made some of my closest friends there. Two of them married each other.
>
> —Jon, recent grad

Special Interest Clubs and Organizations

There are literally hundreds of student organizations on some campuses. There can be volunteer groups, special interest groups, political groups, student government, GLBT groups, and any club or organization you can imagine. Browse the campus website and you'll find the video gaming club, juggling club, checkers club, chess club, BBQ club, improv club, etc. If your child has a special interest and there isn't a group, then he or she can start one.

Performing Arts

There may be dance groups, a capella groups, bands, choirs, spiritual singers, poetry clubs, and other

I was invited by my friend to see a video of what was going on with Joseph Kony's child soldiers in Uganda, and a group there was selling items to donate toward the cause. I now am part of the group and donate twelve dollars a month. I didn't have a clue of what was going on in Uganda before that movie.

—Jennifer, sophomore

The Butler University Marching Band and Butler University Basketball Band have had the greatest impact on me. I have made so many friends in college this way, and I had a lot of fun along the way.

—Geoff, freshman

performing arts groups. When I was in college, I was a founding member of an improv group that's still thriving on campus. Sometimes being involved can mean auditioning. If so, make sure your child does his or her homework. Nothing is worse than a student who loves singing showing up and discovering the show choir doesn't take first-year students.

Publications/Media

College media offers students an opportunity to get published, be on television, host a radio show, and have a voice in media. And it happens FAST! College media is the real deal. There are also opportunities for students to learn about production, sales, advertising, graphic design, web development, etc. Tomorrow's industry

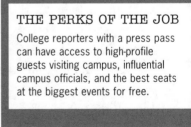

THE PERKS OF THE JOB

College reporters with a press pass can have access to high-profile guests visiting campus, influential campus officials, and the best seats at the biggest events for free.

leaders are nurturing their craft on today's campuses. My newspaper writing career began after I saw an

informational flyer posted on a wall in the campus
school of journalism. I attended a meeting, and within
a few weeks I had my first piece published. It really can
be just that easy.

Academic Organizations

Psychology, Spanish, math, prelaw, geology, accounting,
chemistry—the list of clubs goes on and on. These clubs
are another way to meet people with similar majors and
connect with instructors and grad students outside the
classroom. The best way to find out what academics organizations are available is by visiting the campus website
and then visiting the department office.

Leadership Organizations

Leadership groups and programs on campus are an
amazing way for your child to get involved, meet the
right kind of people on campus, and build life skills. If
you're thinking your child doesn't have a high enough
GPA to participate, think again. Gary Tuerack, founder
of the National Society of Leadership and Success, says,
"The society attracts new students and helps them to get
active on campus and take on leadership roles. Most honor
societies are limited to students with a certain GPA—the
top of the class. The society recognizes that potential
future leaders have varying GPAs, and so does not have
a strict GPA requirement in order to join." The society
encourages academic excellence but offers students who

might not have the grades that reflect their potential the opportunity to participate and create connections on campus and beyond.

Multicultural Organizations

If you have a cultural identity (that would include everyone), there will be a place for your student on campus. A little research might reveal the African Caribbean Society, Armenian Club, Collegiate Women of Color,

> **THE NATIONAL SOCIETY OF LEADERSHIP AND SUCCESS**
>
> **Core Philosophy:** One can achieve one's dreams with proper support and dedicated action. We help people realize their dreams and change the world in the process.
> **(www.societyleadership.org)**

Italian American Organization, Haitian Organization, International Student Organization, Organization of Latin Americans, Irish Society, Japanese Cultural Club, Korean Culture Club, National Association of the Advancement of Colored People, Slavic Students Association, or Asian Students Association. The list goes on and on. If there isn't already a group on campus, then your child can found one.

Alternative Spring Breaks

Spring break isn't all about bikinis and beer. Alternative spring breaks offer opportunities to take trips, meet new people, and give to the community. I have never met someone who didn't have the time of his or her life on an alternative spring break.

Residence Life

I touched on this earlier, but becoming a resident assistant, running for a position in the residence hall association, and working in residence life give students a sense of belonging, leadership experience, training, and often free room and board. Taking on a leadership role in residence life is a life experience. There's nothing more real than having to mentor residents in the midst of dramatic change. In addition to helping students manage change, a by-product of being a student leader means being held to a higher standard than the rest of the students on campus.

I have been a member of ASB (Alterative Spring Break) for three years. As ASB president, I've been responsible for making sure that we market ASB to the entire student body to increase participation, facilitate weekly meetings, make sure that we have an effective fund-raising plan, assign site leaders for each trip, review each trip to make sure that everything is in order, and many more activities.

—Senior, University of West Florida

This year my friends and I are going to Statesboro, Georgia, in Bulloch County to build houses for Habitat for Humanity. Our job is to work on different aspects of building houses. We might make stairs, finish the roof, put in insulation, or put up walls. It's a nice feeling to know you've helped someone.

—Junior, UNC–Asheville

Internships

Internships offer students opportunities to meet people and get a taste of their dream job (sometimes it's not so delicious). There are paid internships and non-paid internships. Some are available year-round. I've met White House interns, students who worked on naval vessels, and students who interned at veterinarian offices (not a clean or glamorous job). I interned at *The Tonight Show with Jay Leno* the summer after my senior year in college (I graduated in four and a half years). A writer there told me about his advice column in college and planted the seed that eventually grew to become my syndicated advice column.

Study Abroad

Students can make friends, earn college credit, and travel the world (oh, what a life). While you would think that price would be prohibitive, in many situations studying abroad can be comparable to the cost of college or even less expensive. A student interested in studying abroad should visit the study abroad office and investigate the details.

The most powerful experience from my university days was the two years I spent as a DON (residence assistant). Being a DON meant living with fifty-five first-year students as they transitioned into their first year of university. The connections I made with the students and my teammates had a lasting impression, as I am now working professionally in residence life.

—Kate, residence program coordinator

I ended up studying abroad for a semester in Florence, Italy, and it was the *absolute best* experience of my life. I learned so much about myself and life in general and would do it again in a heartbeat. I *highly* recommend to absolutely every college student to study abroad if they can. It is the most valuable experience and opportunity one could ever have in college.

—Colleen, senior

I'm going to London this summer for seven weeks to work in Parliament. The cost is about the same as summer school, but I have to pay for my flight.

—Sophomore, Albion College

A FEW WORDS ON GETTING COMMUTERS INVOLVED

Commuters can be pulled in a lot of directions—jobs, family responsibilities, and financial issues may make living on campus just not possible. The only way your commuter student will know to get involved is if you or someone else makes it important and he or she understands why it's important. Not taking advantage would be the equivalent of staying at a hotel and paying a resort fee and not using the resort. The resources, support services, and activities are part of the price of tuition. Direct your child to the Organization of Commuter Students and let that be the place to start. Here are some suggestions to help your commuter student be the happiest kid on campus when he or she is on the campus:

> It appears that the farther away from campus (walking distance, driving distance) he or she is, the less likely a student is to take advantage of the educational resources the institution provides. Thus, proximity to campus makes a difference in commuter students' level of engagement, with the caveat that in certain aspects of the classroom experience commuters are comparable to their campus-based counterparts.
>
> —"The Disengaged Commuter Student: Fact or Fiction?"
> George D. Kuh, Robert M. Gonyea, Megan Palmer
> National Survey of Student Engagement

SOME TIPS TO HELP YOUR COMMUTER GET INVOLVED

- Treat it like a workday. Stay on campus and study.
- Form study groups in class and get together outside the classroom.
- Take public transportation (time to study and harder to leave campus).

- Make office hours with instructors part of the routine.
- Get a job on campus (get paid to get involved).
- Make getting involved in a club as important as class.
- Instead of working out, play an intramural sport.
- Join a leadership group.
- Run for office in the student government.
- Eat on campus in the dining halls.
- Do not take classes with high school friends.
- Move near campus.

Getting involved on campus is as important as going to class. Involved students learn about themselves and the people around them. Internships and leadership positions force students to be held to higher standards. And they can be a way to explore a career or a major and see if it's the right fit.

On top of creating friends, finding a career, and learning how to create a world of options, an involved student has a fantastic resume. A student who is president of the activities board and was in charge of planning and executing events with six-figure budgets and twenty committee members under her leadership has something to offer. As you'll read about more in Tip #16 on majors, a student who gets involved leaves campus with experience that separates her from the rest of the pack. She will find success, gain invaluable skills, and leave college with direction and hopefully a passion.

QUESTIONS AND ANSWERS

Q: How much involvement is appropriate?

A: When it's more stress than fun, it's too much. When the enjoyment is gone, it's too much. I suggest starting with one or two activities or organizations the first few months (add another the second half of the year). At a minimum, he or she should get involved in at least one way. WARNING: Some students become overly involved to cope with change. Being consumed means not having time for themselves, other people, or their feelings. Everything should be in moderation.

Q: What about cults and other groups that target vulnerable students? How can we know when a group is too inclusive?

A: Yes, there are still groups out there that will prey on students who haven't found connections on campus. Here are some signs to watch out for.

BE CAUTIOUS OF GROUPS THAT USE:

· PRESSURE AND DECEPTION: They use high-pressure recruitment tactics or are not up front about their motives when they first approach you.

· TOTALITARIAN WORLDVIEW: They do not encourage critical, independent thinking. In contrast, higher education aims to enable students to think for themselves. Be aware of groups or leaders who try to control your life or who claim to possess the truth exclusively.

· ALIENATION: They want to choose your friends for you. While all religions have moral standards, watch out for groups that encourage you to sever ties with close friends and family who do not belong to their group. Such groups employ unethically manipulative techniques of persuasion and control, and they are dangerous.

- EXPLOITATION: They make unrealistic demands regarding your time and/or money. If participation in a group takes away significantly from your study time, beware. A group or leader who cares about you understands that your studies represent your future and are thus your first priority as a student.

—Source: http://www.usc.edu/programs/religious_life/about/caution.html

Q: Is hazing a ritual in any clubs or organizations outside of social fraternities and sororities?

A: Yes. Hazing can be a ritual in many organizations. Results from a recent report on hazing reported that "55% of college students involved in clubs, teams, and organizations experience hazing. Hazing occurs in, but extends beyond, varsity athletics and Greek-letter organizations and includes behaviors that are abusive, dangerous, and potentially illegal." Your child needs to know what to look for. Most students who are hazed do not know it's happening. You can always make an anonymous report by contacting the college life professionals or the local authorities. Turn to Tip #14, page 377 for a definition of hazing.

Have a question? Want to answer another parent's question?

Post your questions and answers; visit *The Happiest Kid on Campus* Parent Forum: www.HappiestKidonCampus.com.

TIP #14 GREEK LIFE

The Good, the Bad, and the Ugly of Fraternity and Sorority Life

The Tip

Whether it is Greek life, theater, or student government, it is all right for parents to throw questions at their children about their reasons for wanting to be involved, but make sure it is to help them reaffirm that it is something that makes them truly content.

The Story

I grew up in a Christian household with loving parents who encouraged me to be involved in extracurricular activities. As a home-schooled student, I was able to form a bond with my parents that benefits me to this day. I had honestly never considered joining a Greek organization, let alone becoming a founding father. All I knew was what I saw on TV and in the movies. Once I became more familiar with the fraternity and got to know the other founding members, my idea of what a fraternity could be changed. I don't think I would have taken this opportunity had it not been for the support that my family showed from the beginning of my interest in becoming a founding father to the chartering of my chapter in 2006. It was something that they didn't quite understand, because I was the first person to go Greek in my immediate or extended family, but nonetheless they supported me, because they could tell that I was passionate about it. It was an opportunity that to this day has proved to be one of the most valuable decisions that I have made, not only for a career choice (I'm now working for Pi Kappa Phi national headquarters), but also for my personal development.

—Curt Herzog,
Director of Chapter Development,
Pi Kappa Phi Fraternity

***

I should start this tip off by coming clean. I pledged two fraternities, so that makes me twice as qualified to address this topic (I depledged when I transferred). I've been fortunate enough to get to know some of the most passionate and supportive fraternity and sorority advisers and professionals at conferences over the years. I've also had the chance to work with student leaders involved in Greek life on campuses across the country. All these experiences have given me a unique perspective. I've witnessed the accomplishments, opportunities, and experiences afforded to the students who participate in Greek life. Most have been overwhelmingly impressive.

All of these good things having been said, there can

also be an ugly side to Greek life that parents need to understand. A student (or parent) who goes into the experience understanding the good and the not-so-good can make sure to avoid the bad. A parent who understands the good, the bad, and the ugly can help prevent things from getting ugly.

A QUICK OVERVIEW OF GREEK LIFE

If you're not familiar with Greek life, here's a quick overview:

"A Greek organization is a group of individuals of similar interests bonded together by common goals and aspirations. These bonds are created through rituals in which all members participate. Rituals are based on common principles such as honor, friendship, truth and knowledge, to name a few. Each group works to instill these ideals in their members through their everyday activities. It is referred to as a Greek organization because the name consists of Greek letters. These letters serve as a reminder of the values of the group. Fraternity is a name applied to all Greek organizations, but specifically men's groups, while Sorority is the name applied only to women's Greek organizations."

—Source: Case Western Reserve University
parent resources website
(http://studentaffairs.case.edu/greek/parent)

Most Greek organizations are officially recognized by the school. Being recognized means being an official campus organization. The significance of that to you and your child is that you know the organization must follow the rules and regulations set forth by the school (an organization that isn't officially recognized warrants some additional research.).

You'll find that most fraternities and sororities are part of a larger national organization. The national offices offer guidance, education, and mentoring to the members of each chapter. National organizations also have rules, regulations, and standards that must be met for chapters to remain on campus. There are some Greek organizations that have no national affiliation. This does not mean that it's a bad organization; it just means that your child needs to do more research before joining. Unfortunately, there are some local fraternities and sororities that are founded by members who want to circumvent the rules and regulations that come with being officially recognized.

> With the rise of Latina, Latino, Asian, and multicultural groups—so many of those don't have national organizations, because they are at the point in time when they're making history, creating what will someday be national organizations.
>
> —Mark Koepsell, Executive Director at Association of Fraternal Leadership & Values

Officially recognized fraternities and sororities have an adviser to guide and work with the organization. When investigating the history of an organization, the adviser is a good place for your student to start. Your child might discover that the local fraternity is so new that there isn't a national affiliation, because the group has only been around a few years. Latina, Latino, Asian, and Native American groups are some examples of newer groups without national organizations. Give it a hundred years, and these organizations will have a long, storied history—and your child will be the founding father or mother (making you a founding grandfather or grandmother).

As for living arrangements, fraternity and sorority members may live in a house together (on or off campus) or on a designated floor in a residence hall, or be independent of a physical structure. Joining an organization that has a physical structure can mean having to live in the house for a specific amount of time. If it's a choice (most of the time it's not), a first-year student is far better not living in the house during the first semester (in my opinion). Living in the residence halls means meeting friends outside the Greek community. It's one of the few times pledges have to make friends outside the Greek system (it gets harder after pledgeship ends). Not living in the Greek house means creating a world of options and finding balance.

I went to a sorority recruitment night not knowing all that much about Greek life and loved the girls. It turned out to be a great way to help me find my place. I learned leadership from all the positions in the sorority and was able to work with other groups on campus through my sorority, such as Relay for Life (an American Cancer Society Fund Raiser).

—Meghan, recent grad,
UNC–Charlotte

HOW STUDENTS GET INVOLVED IN GREEK LIFE

Students who are interested in participating in Greek life go through a process called rush (yes, they're all rushing to get in). Rush is when prospective members are introduced to the organization and its members. The process may occur during the first or second half of the year; each school has very specific rush policies.

Women often participate in a formal rush. Formal rush can mean getting dressed up, touring all the houses, meeting the members, getting interviewed (oh, the probing questions), and sharing meals together. Men's rush tends to be a lot of hanging out, eating, playing sports, and entertaining at night during very fancy parties (just kidding about the fancy parties).

Rush concludes with bids (invitations to join) being offered (or not) to potential

THE LEGACY QUESTION

A lot of parents have strong Greek ties and want their children to follow in their footsteps. It's a nice thought, but it's not always the best fit. The letters over the fraternity or sorority's door might be the same, but the people inside and what's happening inside might be very different from your experience. One chapter of a fraternity or sorority on one campus can be completely different on another. One chapter can have the highest GPA on one campus and the lowest GPA on another. As for your chapter on your campus, things change over the years. There are situations where chapters close and an entirely new membership comes into being once the chapter reopens. Even if a fraternity or sorority hasn't had a charter revoked or suspended, the culture of what you knew and what the organization has become can be dramatically different. And even if it's all the same, your child might not find it a good fit. If it's not the right fit, do your best not to push. The wrong house can turn into a house of cards.

members (a dramatic event where dreams are made and lives are shattered). The rush process can be physically and emotionally grueling. Acceptance is great; rejection can be brutal, even devastating to some students.

One way to help your child through this process is to make rush all about what he or she wants—not about who wants him or her. It's about where your child feels the most comfortable. These groups need your children more than your children need these groups. Without new members, the organizations would die.

One issue I've repeatedly seen over the past eighteen years is the legacy issue. Mother is a member of XYZ sorority and believes that her daughter should be as well, but I believe it's a personal decision. Every chapter is different on every campus. Even if your child is on the same campus where you went to school, chapters change over time. On one campus the chapter will be a perfect fit, and on another, the wrong fit. Look beyond legacy and look to what would be the best fit for your son or daughter. The fraternity and sorority experience is very personal one.

—Mark Koepsell, Executive Director at Association of Fraternal Leadership & Values

The students who go into the process having another plan in place can go into this experience with perspective. Greek life should just be one option of many that make up the college experience. Not getting in can be devastating—unless your child has other options. A student with options will move on and take away new friendships formed during the process. If it doesn't work out the first time, that just gives your child more time to get to know the members and decide what's right for him or her. There are a lot of students who go through rush and decide not to join. Either way, the rush process means meeting new people who will be familiar faces for years to come.

Once bids are accepted, the pledge period begins. Pledging can last several weeks or months. It's a time to learn the history of the organization, take part in rituals, and bond. Once the pledge period ends, it's time for initiation. Once initiated, new members become the new leaders in the organization.

TO GO GREEK OR NOT

When your child mentions to you that he or she is considering going Greek, there are three major concerns that may cross your mind: What will it cost? How much time will it take? How will this impact my child socially? When your child weighs the benefits of Greek life, there are two main concerns that rise to the surface: How will this impact me socially? How can this help me make the right kinds of friendships?

If your son or daughter decides to go Greek, there are a lot of benefits in it for them! My sorority has this cool hook-up where during your senior year you match up with an alum that was in your major, and they try to help you get a job in your field. We have study buddies and old tests to study from and all kinds of things to help put academics first. That's why we're in college, after all.

—Liz, junior (resident assistant)

Major Concerns for Parents

1. **THE COSTS:** The costs will vary from campus to campus. One-time initiation fees can range from $200 to $300. One-time pledge fees can range from $75 to $150. Annual member fees can range from $200 to $300. Living in a fraternity or sorority house is often comparable to or less expensive than living off campus and often involves a meal plan.

2. **THE TIME COMMITMENT:** Pledging can definitely take up a lot of time. Most parents are concerned that it will negatively affect their child's grades. But a student who pledges an organization filled with high achievers will get a crash course in time management and study skills. Having access to brothers or sisters who know how to study hard and balance time is invaluable. Also, study hours are almost always part of the pledge program. The time commitment will decrease once the pledge period concludes. Of course, if your child takes on leadership roles, there can be additional time commitments.

3. **THE SOCIAL COMPONENT:** Parents get concerned that being in a Greek organization will mean having too much fun. A student who comes to school wanting to make strong choices and knows he or she has social options will be able to find the right friends, select the right organization, and make the right choices. Having access to a social life doesn't mean becoming all consumed or consuming too much

alcohol. Students who want to be social will find ways to be social—Greek or not.

Major Concerns for Students

1. **THE SOCIAL COMPONENT:** Greek life provides instant opportunities to meet people inside and outside the Greek system. Greek life is not all about parties, hooking up, and drinking. Yes, it can be easier to find a party and a date, but it can also be easier to plug in to the top leadership opportunities on campus and connect with other student leaders. Beyond college, the relationships formed can lead to friendships and professional connections.

2. **FINDING FRIENDS:** Greek life helps students make friends. The challenge is finding the *right* friends. A student who goes into rush looking for people with similar values and character will find the right match. A student who goes into rush looking for anyone who will take them and who wants to party will find that too. Each fraternity and sorority has a different energy and vibe. It's not about getting into the best fraternity or sorority; it's about finding the one that fits your child's personality and needs.

I am a fraternity adviser—I walk with the young men I advise as they wrestle with their ethical and moral dilemmas in the areas they personally face where they are growing into their own sense of who they are.

—Dr. Charles "Doc" Eberle, Fraternity Advisor (forty-six years on the job), Counseling and Student Development, Eastern Illinois University

SO YOUR SON OR DAUGHTER IS THINKING OF JOINING A FRATERNITY OR SORORITY?

Fraternities and sororities can provide a wonderful experience for your child. Frequently, fraternity and sorority members are among the leaders on campus. It's also a way to get involved on campus and make lifelong friends (twenty years after graduating, I just took a trip with five members and their families). Understand that the culture of each individual fraternity or sorority may be vastly different. To make an informed decision, there are questions your student should ask during this decision-making process to make sure this it the right fit:

· Does the chapter have an active adviser?

· What is the grade point average of the organization over the past five years?

· Has the chapter won any local or national awards recently?

· What are the number of service hours and money raised for charity the previous year?

· What are the costs for joining and maintaining membership?

continued on page 373

That can be hard to figure out in a few weeks of rush, especially when answering interview questions like, "Do you have any pets at home? What's your dog's name?" Sometimes it can take pledging to realize if it's the right or wrong fit. Going into the process with this mind-set makes the process more about what your child wants than who wants him or her. And that's how your child can find the best kinds of friends.

THE GOOD, THE BAD, THE UGLY

The Good

Greek life can be an awesome, overwhelmingly positive, and life-changing experience on so many levels. It's a fast way to make great friends, have a social life, become a leader on campus, and find mentors who want students to win.

The opportunities to assume leadership roles are everywhere—they are inside and outside the organization. Within the organization there are executive board positions, rush chair, social chair, philanthropy chair (for fundraising), and other leadership roles that pop up throughout the year.

Outside of the organization, members can participate in the Pan-Hellenic Council, Interfraternity Council, and other Greek governing boards. Greek members and leaders are often required to work with other students and

continued from page 372

· Does the chapter have a history of academic or social violations?

· What does your student hope to get out of this experience?

· Why does your student think this fraternity or sorority is the right fit for him or her?

· Is there a campus staff member who is assigned to work with fraternities and sororities? If there is no staff member who is assigned to work with fraternities and sororities, that is a BIG red flag.

—Thomas B. (Tom) Jelke, PhD, Chairman of the Association of Fraternity Advisors Foundation; Member of the National Board of Directors of Sigma Phi Epsilon Fraternity; CEO of t.jelke solutions, a consulting firm for Colleges/ Universities, Fraternal Organizations, and Non-Profits.

professionals on campus while planning and organizing campuswide events (homecoming, acting/singing/dancing competitions, athletic events, community service projects, fund-raisers, etc). These roles can involve negotiating contracts, organizing people, and working with leaders on campus and in the community.

Academically, Greeks are often the highest achievers on campus. Yes, Greek life can take up time, but being surrounded by highly successful students can help your child learn how to effectively manage his or her time in no time. Greek life provides a way to engage in campus life that can create lifelong friendships and a professional network. Many sororities don't look at sisterhood as an experience exclusive to the college years. Some consider this a lifetime commitment that carries over into their adult lives.

If your child decides to go Greek, the best way to approach fraternity and sorority life is to remember that it's just one way to get involved and can lead to finding several social circles of friends. The idea is to use the fraternity or sorority as a springboard to meet other people from different groups and organizations inside and outside the Greek system. Over time, a student can establish several different circles of friends, plug in to endless opportunities, and develop the ability to make strong choices because he or she is living in a world of options.

The Not-So-Good

While Greek life can be a fast way for your child to make lifelong friends, have a busy social life, and develop leadership skills, it can also provide an opportunity to make the wrong friends, have an unhealthy social life, and become a follower. As easy as it is to take risks and become a campus leader, it's just as easy to stay in the background, avoid taking risks, and hide inside the Greek bubble.

Some students just sit back, relax, and enjoy the ride. It's easy to become complacent when so much is provided for you. You have friends, dates, a social life, and people to study with. Some students wall themselves off from the rest of the world and hide inside their fraternity or sorority. They avoid leadership roles, do just enough to get by, and are the ones who perpetuate all the negative stereotypes.

The student who has no life outside of the Greek world can also become vulnerable and get caught up in the group think. It's hard to think for yourself and assert yourself when your only friends are the people you live with and associate with 24/7.

Some students let their Greek letters define their identity instead of being the ones to define the

Although a fraternity or sorority may have had problems in the past, it doesn't mean that they're having the same problems now. The dynamic will change every two or four years as new leaders emerge.

—Marc West, Baldwin-Wallace College, Director of student life and involvement, Greek life, new student orientation programs

meaning of their Greek letters. It's possible to get caught up in a cookie-cutter mentality. Individuals with unique personalities enter the system. The pledge period kneads them into homogenous dough. Then they are cut into the shape and form of the organization. They look the same, dress the same, and think the same. Straying from the groupthink means being rejected from the group. That's what it means to let an organization define the individual instead of an individual defining his or her role in the organization. A student who is aware of the risks can make sure Greek life is only one part of his life, maintain his individuality, and still reap the benefits of the group association (friends, opportunities, a social life, a network beyond college).

The Ugly

1. More than half of college students involved in clubs, teams, and organizations experience hazing.
2. Nearly half (47 percent) of students have experienced hazing prior to coming to college.
3. Alcohol consumption, humiliation, isolation, sleep-deprivation, and sex acts are hazing practices that are common across student groups.

Every year I get emails and notes from students who are being hazed on a college campus. Hazing still happens on campus. It can happen in Greek organizations, on athletic teams, and even in performing arts circles (I was surprised to hear this one).

Every parent and student needs to know what hazing means. Most college websites have information on how to report hazing. I've included this definition and the hazing hotline in *The Naked Roommate* (888-NOT-HAZE, or 888-668-4293).

DEFINITION OF HAZING

The term *hazing* means any conduct or method of initiation into any student organization, whether on public or private property, which willfully or recklessly endangers the physical or mental health of any student or other person. Such conduct shall include whipping; beating; branding; forced calisthenics; exposure to weather; forced consumption of any food, liquor, beverage, drug, or other substance; or any other brutal treatment or forced physical activity which is likely to adversely affect the physical health or safety of any such student or other person, or that subjects such student or other person to extreme mental stress, including extended deprivation of sleep or rest or extended isolations.

—Source: Harvard University Extension School

The need to be included, appreciated, and desired can cause students to allow themselves to be subjected to rituals that are unhealthy and dangerous. It's very easy to forgive hazing activities like sleep deprivation, long runs through campus, and eating special soup made by the brothers, but it's never right.

Members of the organizations often disguise these types of actions as tradition and rites of passage. A lot of times members don't realize they're participating in criminal behavior. But the truth is, hazing or even having knowledge of hazing and not reporting it can be a crime. This is because it can be deadly and should NEVER be tolerated.

In 2005 there was a hazing incident at the University of Texas in Austin that resulted in the death of a student. As part of the legal settlement, fraternity members participated in a video that is worth sharing with your student. Information about the incident and the video link are included below. The link can also be found on my website and on my Facebook fan page.

On December 10, 2005, Phanta "Jack" Phoummarath, an eighteen-year-old pledge of Lambda Phi Epsilon, was found dead after the fraternity's initiation party. Jack's blood alcohol level was well above the legal limit at the time of his death following the fraternity's practice of getting pledges drunk at the initiation party. Prior to the party, said to be the end of the initiation process, the pledges had endured months of physical and psychological hazing.

Hazing is illegal in the state of Texas and is also prohibited by the *Rules and Regulations of the Board of Regents of The University of Texas System*. As a result of their actions,

> I honestly can't stand watching my pledges being hazed. I'm the nice sister who is very easy on the girls and always telling them on the phone how well they're doing and encouraging them. In my chapter there was no physical hazing, but the emotional strain we put on people is enough to make anyone feel demoralized and hate themselves. It's terrible! It didn't bother me when I was pledging, because I didn't take it too seriously, but I can't stand watching others go through it.
>
> —Vicky, junior

Lambda Phi Epsilon's status as a registered student organization was suspended by the university until 2011. Three active members of the fraternity were indicted on criminal charges under Texas hazing laws. As part of their legal settlement, fraternity members participated in the production of an educational anti-hazing video, which can be found at *http://inmemoryofjack.com*.

Call If You Suspect a Problem

When I was pledging (for the second time), a parent called the national chapter of the fraternity and notified our adviser that Hell Week was coming. Hell Week is the name given to the final week of pledgeship. Sleep deprivation, humiliation, and psychological tests are often part of Hell Week (many of these rituals fall under the definition of hazing). When the national office heard about the pending "Hell Week" they immediately intervened. Hell Week was forbidden by the national organization. The week never happened, because that parent called the national headquarters and notified the dean of students. Many of my pledge brothers were disappointed, but I couldn't have been happier.

If you ever suspect something is happening that is dangerous or unhealthy in your child's fraternity or sorority, contact the national office, contact the Greek adviser's office, contact the dean of students, and call the hazing hotline and make some noise (888 -NOT-HAZE, or

888-668-4293). Urge your child to do the same. You can offer an anonymous tip. You can contact me (Harlan@ HelpMeHarlan.com) and I'll contact the powers that be. I've done it many times. If your student tells you he or she can't talk to you because it's the final week of pledge-ship, that's probably a sign something is up. If you think something is wrong, there's a good chance it's wrong. Unfortunately, smart students get so wrapped up in the process that they are too isolated to see the dangers.

Perhaps, given the changing role of the New College Parents, students and parents will slowly put an end to hazing. There are so many valuable and fantastic components of Greek life that the risk of hazing shouldn't be the deciding factor. If your child encounters a hazing culture, there are people, places, and resources to stop it. Then your son or daughter can reap the best benefits of Greek life.

WANT MORE INFORMATION ABOUT HAZING?

Visit www.HazingPrevention.org to find links to state laws, resources, and vital information.

A HAPPY GREEK ENDING

To end on a happy note—I'm a big fan of Greek life. The negative parts of Greek life aren't exclusive to Greeks. People engage in dangerous behaviors in places that don't have Greek letters hanging over the door too. It's not the system's fault; it's the fault of a few students who make poor choices. In general, Greek life can be an extremely good life for a lot of students. The rewards and opportunities are immeasurable and, as I see it, far outweigh the risks. A student who comes to school with a plan that Greek life will be one part of his or her world in college will find a rewarding experience that can continue for the rest of his or her life.

QUESTIONS AND ANSWERS

Q: Does everyone who participates in rush get a bid?

A: It depends on the campus and the number of students rushing. There are situations in which students get bids, but not from their first choice (that can be hard). Then there are situations in which a student does not get a bid from any organization.

Q: How do you avoid hazing?

A: Make sure your child is aware of what hazing is and how to address it if it comes up. Also, make sure you know what hazing is and what to do if it comes up. Vigilant and anonymous parents can help.

Q: How much of a time commitment is rushing, pledging, and being a member?

A: The pledge period tends to be the most time-consuming part, but if it's a quality organization, much of your child's time will be spent volunteering, participating in campus events, taking on leadership roles, participating in educational programs, and studying. Being a pledge can be a crash course in time management.

Q: My son is considering a fraternity without a national chapter. How can we know it's a safe environment?

A: This is where you have to do more research. Have your son talk to the Greek adviser on campus and contact past members. Just like any experience, the best way to find out information is to talk to those who have been there. Also, contact the office of student life. While local groups might not be affiliated, members who violate the student code of conduct can face repercussions, and you can find out the organization's track record.

Q: Are there minimum GPAs required to be part of Greek life?

A: Yes, there are usually minimum GPAs required to participate in Greek life. (There are also minimum GPAs required to be a student on campus.)

Q: What if a pledge realizes it's not the right fit? Is it hard to de-pledge?

A: Once someone is a member, they can always de-pledge or unaffiliate. The hardest part about de-pledging is dealing with the members of the organization once someone de-pledges—it can be uncomfortable. If a student has another group of friends to turn to, it makes the process easier. As for the contractual or financial obligations, if someone is living in the house and has signed a contract, there could be financial implications.

Have a question? Want to answer another parent's question?

Post your questions and answers; visit *The Happiest Kid on Campus* Parent Forum: www.HappiestKidonCampus.com.

TIP #15 ACADEMIC EXCELLENCE

Passing Classes, Pleading with Professors, and Accessing Academic Advisers (But Not in that Order)

The Tip

If we're coming to you for help, being disappointed won't help us. Supporting us and encouraging us to fix the problem is most helpful.

The Story

This past semester I wasn't doing terribly in my classes, but I wasn't doing great either. I was close to losing my academic scholarship that paid full room and board. I thought there was nothing I could do to get the 3.25 GPA I needed. I started to freak out and just be stressed about it, and I was not helping my situation at all. I relayed what might happen to my parents, and even though they said they would be disappointed because I would have messed up a great opportunity, my mom said that no matter what happened they would always love me and be proud of me. Even though I had heard this millions of times, it calmed me down. I went on to buckle down the last two weeks, talked to some professors, and I ended up keeping my scholarship. In this situation my parents helped me mentally, and it calmed my nerves. I knew that whether I lost the scholarship or not, my family would still love me, and all my friends would still be my friends.

—Matt P., sophomore, Arkansas Tech University

* * *

POP QUIZ (FOR MOMS AND POPS)

Welcome to the academic tip. Yes, college is about earning a degree. Once your child can get comfortable with the uncomfortable outside of the classroom, he or she should be able to do some good work inside the classroom. In this tip we'll look at how parents can support academic success, discourage academic mediocrity, and help avoid academic disaster. We'll also look at good professors and not-so-good professors. We'll then finish up with a look at the invaluable and often underappreciated college adviser.

Since this is an academic section, it's only appropriate to open up with a few questions and answers (this will replace the Q & A at the end of the chapter). Please keep your eyes on your own book.

> **Q: What do you get when you put one hundred students who have earned straight A's for their entire academic careers in a classroom together for sixteen weeks?**

A: A lot of students who will be surprised, humbled, and

uncomfortable because for the first time in their lives, they will not all get straight A's.

Q: What do you get when you put one hundred students who have done "just enough to get by" their entire academic careers in a classroom together for sixteen weeks?

A: A lot of students who will continue to do just enough to get by and avoid getting put on academic probation.

Q: What do you get when you put thousands of first-year students into classrooms where attendance is optional and no one calls home if they skip classes?

A: A lot of angry parents and a lot of students returning home to old bedrooms and parents' couches.

Q: What can a parent do to help a student succeed inside the classroom?

A: Here are five things that can help:

1. Discuss Expectations Early (Yours and Theirs)

Before school begins, it's important to have a conversation with your child about what you expect from him academically. Instead of coming up with a GPA as a benchmark, consider having him share what he has in mind as a goal. Even then, you might want to hold off on offering a number. Instead emphasize actions. Things like expecting him to go to every single class, do the required work, and make his best effort are reasonable expectations that will result in good grades. If his grades are in the toilet, then you might need to establish a GPA. Before sharing your expectations, understand that the first year can be challenging on many levels. A student who has a rough start can go on to have a powerful finish. Some might struggle at first.

As for determining a target grade point average, you can go with the institution's academic standards or set up your own. You can also ask your son to find out the minimum GPA for a particular major. Some institutions require students to apply to be accepted to a particular program or major. Regardless of the major, each institution has a minimum GPA students must meet to be eligible. If the GPA isn't met, a student is put on academic probation. If the student can't meet the minimum GPA while on probation, it's good-bye college.

> My first semester freshman year, I got an F in a calculus class. My parents told me I was a failure to them even though now my GPA is around 3.4.
>
> —Amanda, junior

ACADEMIC FACTS

- 70 percent of surveyed freshmen "frequently" or "occasionally" skipped class. (HERI)

- Approximately one in five first-year students report that they frequently came to class without completing readings or assignments. (NSSE)

- Freshmen spend an average of 13.2 hours a week preparing for class. (NSSE)

- 90.8 percent of students surveyed "frequently" or "occasionally" studied with other students. (HERI)

When setting expectations, appreciate that some high schools prepare students better than others. Your student might have been getting great grades, but isn't at the same level as other students. Also, some professors are very stingy when it comes to handing out A's. As for attaching threats to your expectations (if you don't get this particular grade, you're paying us back), students who are threatened will be scared. And a scared student is less likely to reach out to you for help. Just something to keep in mind.

> My dad constantly asks me about my grades. He's really proud of me when I tell him I've done well on a test, but he also gets mad when I tell him that it looks like I'm going to get a B in a class. He tells me I should be putting more effort into my studying and spending less time having fun. It really bothers me, because I know a B is a perfectly good grade if I've worked hard in the class.
>
> —Katherine, junior

2. Encourage Them to Get Help before They Need It

My mantra to students is "Get help before you need it." Following this practice means embracing that first D or F on a quiz or paper and seeing it as a great gift. *Yes, the first time is a gift* (as opposed to the second, third, or fourth). The reason it's a gift is because it's a sign that a student needs help. If your child seeks out help right away, before it becomes a serious problem, she can avert disaster.

Instead of threatening her if she struggles, turn to the resources available. Encourage her to talk to the instructor during office hours, to get tutoring (often free), to form study groups, to use the writing center, and to ask upperclassmen for help. A student who can get help when she needs it will be in a position to get to know an instructor better (helpful when trying to get that extra point for the higher final grade), know the resources on campus, and understand how to manage difficulties before they turn into a real academic crisis.

I was a little nervous to approach my organic chemistry professor, because of his strong "tell it like it is" personality in class. When I approached him for extra help, I was almost expecting him to question why I didn't understand the material. Instead, it was as if he appreciated that I wanted to learn and did whatever he could to help me. On multiple occasions he'd literally spend hours answering my questions, never stopping until I understood the material. That's something I never expected.

—Senior, Southern Utah University

3. Make It Okay for Them to Make Mistakes without Making Them Feel Stupid

Students hide bad grades for two main reasons:

1. They don't want to look stupid in the eyes of a professor.
2. They don't want to disappoint you.

Remind your child that all students stumble at times. A student's job is not to know everything. An instructor's job is to help a student learn. Therefore, getting help isn't being stupid; it's doing the job of a student. It's also allowing a professor to do his or her job. Instructors

I was proudest when he called to say that he had gone to the campus writing center to get some help with a paper. It was a great moment, because seeking out help there was not MY idea!

—Mom of freshman son

respect students who make the effort to do well before they are in a crisis. In fact, by getting help at the first sign of trouble, a student who can be build a relationship early with an instructor is going to be in a much better position to get that extra point that can be the difference between a B or a C or a B and an A. And a

little bonus tip within the tip—if your child is ever trying to battle for an extra point and the instructor says, "If I give this point to you, I'll have to give one to everyone. It wouldn't be fair otherwise." The answer is, "I couldn't agree with you more. And if everyone cared as much as I did and all those people were here talking to you, that would be fair. But I'm the only who cares. I hope that counts for something."

DROPPING AND ADDING COURSES

If a student is dropping a course, make sure it's done by the deadline and that it won't affect his or her transcript. Sometimes dropping a course might seem like the best idea, but it can be costly in terms of money and even graduation.

4. Define the Job Requirements (i.e., Attend Class and Study)

Going to class is the equivalent of showing up for work. Studying is the equivalent of doing the work on the job.

With just five or six classes a week, it seems that going to class and doing the work would be easy. But still, 70 percent of students frequently or occasionally miss class (HERI). Here's one way to help your child see the importance of going to class. Break down the costs of blowing off a class. For example: If a credit hour is $500 and a class consists of three credit hours, the total cost of the class would be $1500. If there are sixteen weeks of classes in a term and the class meets twice a week, that's thirty-two classes. So for each class a student misses, it's $42.85 of wasted tuition. Factor in the other costs of being on campus, and that's a lot of wasted money. I'm not suggesting you have your child reimburse you for each missed class (if you do, I wouldn't cash the check and expect it to clear), but putting it in these terms can help your student see the value. I suspect students paying for their own education tend to be more aware of the value of each class.

> **INVALUABLE WORDS OF WISDOM**
>
> Want them to get your son or daughter in and out on time? They need to see an academic adviser once a semester.
>
> —Judy Salinger,
> Executive Director of
> Undergraduate Student Services,
> University of Central Florida

5. Consult an Academic Adviser Once a Semester

The academic adviser is the head coach of your child's academic career. A good academic adviser will get to know your child, ask questions to gauge his or her interests, help him or her take the right courses, find the best instructors, discover a major, and figure out the best way to navigate the system in order to graduate on time. Considering that only about a third of students graduate in four years, students need the help of their academic adviser. If a student is struggling, having a trusted adviser can be a lifesaver. When a student is struggling with questions about dropping classes, taking a class pass/fail, or auditing a course, the academic adviser is the go-to person. Also worth mentioning, if your child is attending a public institution, new regulations and policies that can affect students are constantly being mandated by the state. A good academic adviser can make sure your child is taking the appropriate courses and credit hours as mandated by the state (and institution) to stay on track to graduate on time and keep financial aid packages intact. Most students have no idea of changes taking place unless they are in contact with their advisers. Sometimes a student needs to be the one to make appointments. Advisers don't always hunt students down and force them to meet with them. I'll share more with you about academic advising in the later part of this section.

> I was taking Latin, and I got behind. Once you get behind in any language, it is almost impossible to get caught back up. It snowballed, and before I knew it I had a D in the class with a few weeks to go. After much deliberation, I decided to withdraw. I felt horrible knowing a W would be on my transcript, but decided it was better than the F I would have probably gotten.
>
> —Jake, freshman

Only about one-third of students will graduate in four years.

Telling my parents the truth about my lower-than-imagined grades was the hardest thing to do. My fear of their reaction to my grades prevented me from being honest with them and actually receiving helpful advice from them. After everything was resolved, they told me that as an adult my education was my responsibility and all that they could do was encourage and point me in the right direction. Their reaction wasn't so bad after all.

—Dipavo, junior

If Your Child Is Failing or Faltering

Some parents are surprised by first semester or first quarter grades. Others are just happy their kids aren't back at home. If you're not so thrilled with your child's grades, try not to automatically assume that she is partying and wasting time and money. There can be a lot of legitimate reasons why he or she may be struggling. For example:

- Not all high school grads are prepared to do college work. A student who barely got into college might be in classes with people who were at the top of their class. New professors, new classes, and all the other changes outside the classroom can make life in the classroom a surprising challenge. A student's memory of inflated high school grades can be deflating when he or she is faced with the new academic rigors of college life.

- Taking undesirable classes can cause undesirable grades. In the first year of college, students may be required to take courses that aren't always a student's strength. Couple that with the huge life changes and an imperfect start to college life, and some subpar grades are not unreasonable.

- Mental health issues, depression, addiction, and sickness can affect grades. So many changes outside the classroom can be challenging.

A student's first year is not indicative of the rest of her college career. In fact, it's those classes and instructors that challenge your child that can serve as a wake-up call. A lot of times it's hard to know how to manage time until it's too late. A lot of parents expect results immediately or feel like their child is wasting money and time if she doesn't meet their expectations, but it can take a couple of semesters for her to figure it out. There are few things more rewarding than allowing a student to struggle and then watching her get it together and make the dean's list in her junior and senior year.

A Few Words about Academic Probation

Sometimes a student has a bad semester. While you might be cool and calm, the institution can step in and put your child on academic probation. Once on probation, he has a certain amount of time to improve his grades or he will be disqualified or expelled. No, not good.

Sometimes the best way that students learn is through failure or unfortunate outcomes. Obviously, no parent wants to see their child face difficulties, but if I recall back to my own University experience, it was getting that one F on my transcript (because I was too afraid to go see the prof to get clarification on the assignment) that made me the most successful with follow-through (in all aspects of my life) afterwards. I wear that F like a badge of honor, and it makes me a more effective counselor to students.

—Beth, college professional
(nineteen years on the job)

While a lot of parents may consider pulling a student who is struggling from campus (if they are paying), they should also think about allowing the institution to step in. Student affairs professionals and staff do not want students to fail and leave without earning a degree. In fact, in recent years the time, money, and resources spent to help at-risk students figure out how to stay in college and earn a degree has dramatically increased.

> When I was on academic probation for a semester, my father threatened to come to the campus and make an example out of me. I know that was his way of getting my butt in gear, but he would not even listen to me explain circumstances under which that probation came about.
>
> —Danasha, senior

One part of retention strategies is to identify the high-risk students and help them connect to the people, places, and resources on campus that can help. Schools recognize that students who are struggling can be helped. A student who can be saved is a student who can stay enrolled. And a student who is enrolled helps the bottom line (one of the perks of retention). Retention is a win-win situation for everyone involved.

For students on academic probation, there are academic

support programs designed to help them improve in the classroom, learn new study skills, and work closely with instructors. Support programs can also involve one-on-one mentoring, time management assistance, and comprehensive advising.

Sure, it might seem expensive to allow a student who is struggling to continue on campus, but think of the opportunity—if your child can identify what went wrong and learn how to fix it, that's an invaluable life skill. Learning to do that will be as much of an accomplishment as making the dean's list. Struggling

I've been on academic probation and then gotten my grades back up. I not only got myself off of probation, but onto the dean's list. I did three things that helped: 1. I got perfect attendance and sat in the front row of every one of my classes. 2. I emailed professors and TAs even if I just had the smallest question about the syllabus, or any assignment. This helped them to get to know my name and face. 3. I cut back on social events, really giving myself more time to relax and meditate about what I was trying to do. It helped me stay centered (and the lack of hangover on Sunday morning wasn't too bad for studying either).

—Desiree, junior

I was put on academic probation last year and got back in; I have a B average now. I got in with a tutor at school (free, by the way). They kicked my butt in gear.

—Jimmy, junior

academically and then learning how to get back on top might be the best thing that ever happened to your child.

A Few Words about Time Management

Students who are used to going to class five days a week light up with delight when they see a Monday schedule with one class at 10:00 a.m., a Tuesday with two classes at 8:00 a.m.

and 11:00 a.m., a Wednesday with one 3:30 p.m. class, and a Thursday with an 8:00 a.m. and 11:00 a.m. class. And Friday (cue gleeful music), a Friday with no classes! This means a three-day weekend with one class on Monday, and that's practically a four-day weekend. Could this be true? Could it be real? Is this *really* what college is about?

They don't realize just how fast all that "free" time can disappear. Between studying, working, volunteering, taking on leadership roles, dating, band practice, athletic practice, pledging a fraternity or a sorority, communicating with Mom and Dad, spending time online, playing video games, working out, going out at night, praying, playing, and sleeping, that 168 hours in the week goes very quickly. It's deceptive. Until they're at school, it's hard to appreciate what it means to have to learn how to manage time.

Rather than going through the ins and outs of time management, the best plan for your child is to get a planner (old-fashioned or digital). The next step is to make a list of the names and resources available on campus to help him with time management. If he is taking a first-year experience course, the course should include time devoted to helping him manage his time. Additional resources available can include his academic adviser, orientation staff leaders, residence life

> High school seniors do not want to talk about time management or selecting appropriate classes when they're focused on the prom, or on taking their last senior finals, or whatever. In most cases, it's pointless to push. They're not "there" until they get there.
>
> —Judith Termini, Director, First-Year Experience, Gallaudet University

staff, counselors, professors, and upperclassmen. If he can get in a workshop or group focusing on time management, he will learn to set long-term goals, intermediate goals, and short-term goals. He will also learn how to balance the physical, intellectual, social, career, emotional, and spiritual demands. Help is available, but getting help means taking the time to address time management if it's a problem.

For parents who are worried about a student getting overly involved too soon, try not to worry until there's a good reason to worry. I look at college like a restaurant at 3:00 p.m. versus a restaurant during the 7:00 p.m. dinner rush. At 3:00 p.m everything is so slow. There's no rhythm. At the dinner rush everything is in motion. A student who's busy and in motion tends to do a better job than a student who has one class and an entire day with nothing planned. Having a lot going on will not only keep him busy, but it will also put him in contact with more people who can help him learn the tricks of time management.

A FEW WORDS ABOUT STUDENTS WITH DISABILITIES

STUDENTS PROTECTED UNDER SECTION 504 OF THE U.S. DEPARTMENT OF EDUCATION'S REHABILITATION ACT

Section 504 covers qualified students with disabilities who attend schools receiving federal financial assistance. To be protected under Section 504, a student must be determined to: (1) have a physical or mental impairment that substantially limits one or more major life activities; or (2) have a record of such an impairment; or (3) be regarded as having such an impairment. Section 504 requires that school districts provide a free appropriate public education (FAPE) to qualified students in their jurisdictions who have a physical or mental impairment that substantially limits one or more major life activities.

Today there are more students attending college with documented disabilities than at any other time in the history of higher education. Parents of students who have previously diagnosed disabilities should have their students check in with the office of student disabilities. Students will need to show the proper documentation to be eligible for the benefits. Once registered, a student can find academic support, group support, and academic accommodations. Instructors will often make arrangements to allow students more time to finish exams, a different room to take an exam, and extended timelines on assignments. Students with disabilities are some of the most supported students on campus, so make sure your child knows about all of the support available, and encourage him or her to seek it out.

There is a tendency among some parents of deaf and hard-of-hearing students to be overprotective, and that's understandable. Throughout the K–12 years, students with any disability usually have Individual Education Plans every year, and parents are required to participate in the planning process. When students reach the age of eighteen, they're considered adults, and parents are no longer part of the process. So we have to address aspects of this change with new parents, and some have a harder time letting go than others.

—Judith Termini,
Director of First-Year Experience,
Gallaudet University

A lot of parents will discover during the course of the college experience that their child has a disability that has gone undiagnosed or surfaces during the college years. This is when so many issues can surface (depression, anxiety disorders, attention deficit disorder, etc.). All of these can be categorized as disability with the right documentation. The most helpful thing parents can do is support their child and connect her to the appropriate resources on campus. The worst thing parents can do is ignore or deny the situation. Make sure your child gets proper documentation so that special arrangements can be made. If you're struggling, make sure you get support.

I've had a nonverbal learning disability since sixth grade. I've been getting help ever since. Disability services have helped me with everything under the academic umbrella. I have a private tutor on campus—it's really helped. Parents need to be patient. There's nothing wrong with your child! They just learn differently. There's nothing worse than being told that there is something wrong with you.

—Lauren, freshman

A student with a newly diagnosed mental health issue, illness, or physical impairment may be eligible for special accommodations. She can also be connected to students and professionals to support her as she is treated and learns to thrive on campus.

For more information on mental health issues, turn to Tip #23.

A Few Words about Cheating

Cheating happens all the time. Instructors hate it and will bust students for it. The consequences are serious—it can leave a permanent mark on a student's record and even get him or her expelled.

The problem is that cheating is so easy and so accessible now. Cheating has gone high-tech. It involves cell phones, Bluetooth, texting, and access to computers with exams.

But it's not just that cheating has gotten easier—there is also a more surprising reason that students cheat, and it involves you. The fact is, when a student gets caught cheating, the most common reason they give is: "I didn't want to disappoint my parents with a bad grade."

PROFESSORS USE TECHNOLOGY TO FIGHT STUDENT CHEATING

"Several new software companies are giving instructors even more fire-power to fight cheating. Turnitin.com, SafeAssign, and a few other new companies have built up databases of millions of school papers, books, articles, and Web pages that they compare against homework. Millions of students around the world now turn in their homework electronically to the companies so that the programs can highlight parts that match other sources. Teachers sign on to the companies' sites to look at the results and decide how much similarity is too much."

— Source: *U.S.News & World Report*
(http://www.usnews.com/articles/education/2008/10/03/
professors-use-technology-to-fight-student-cheating.html)

You must make it clear to your child that cheating is more disappointing than a bad grade. A good way to start this conversation is to mention to your student that just like technology has made cheating easier, it has also made it easier to get caught cheating. Professors now use technology to see if submitted papers have been plagiarized. Students studying in a group and using the same information can also be implicated for cheating. Students who use old papers can be implicated for cheating. Students who buy papers online can end up turning in papers that have already been turned in. That's bad—very bad. Considering how widespread cheating has become, it's a good idea to make sure your child understands in the most explicit terms that there would be nothing more disappointing to you than cheating—nothing. Do this, and if he cheats and gets caught, he can't point the finger at you and say, "I didn't want to disappoint you."

The Bottom Line about Academic Success

Students who want to be successful need to go class and get help before they need it. It's really that simple. When students aren't going to class and aren't getting the help they need, it's a symptom that something is wrong. Sometimes it's something that can easily be corrected, but other times it's a much bigger issue. Before giving the heave-ho or assuming your child is just lazy, partying too much, or feeling entitled, find out what's happening. You might discover there's a lot of work she needs to do outside the classroom in order to be able to focus and achieve inside the classroom. Helping her find these answers sooner rather than later will enable her to not only become the happiest kid on campus but also the happiest adult throughout the rest of her life.

PROFESSORS: THE GOOD AND THE BAD

They are called professors, instructors, and teaching assistants. These are the people who have the power to grade. Most are passionate professionals with a love for teaching and learning. Some have lost that loving feeling or never had it. There are two kinds of professors in the college world.

1. Professors Who Love Students

These are the best professors. These are the ones who are passionate about sharing knowledge, mentoring students, and building relationships. Some are effusive when it comes to sharing their feelings for their students; others secretly love working with students but put on a tough façade that needs cracking. A student who can bust through will find a softie who wants students to learn. Most instructors have a love for teaching. Some even have a love for parents too.

On the first day of class, Mississippi State University professor Tom Carskadon snaps a picture of each student (with the student's permission). He does this to help him remember names and faces. He then takes the photos home to practice. By the second day of class, he already remembers everyone's name. "It lets them know they are important and can't be anonymous. It creates a friendly atmosphere," says Professor Carskadon. At the end of the semester, when most of campus has packed up and left for the holidays, he stays an extra day or two to put together a special gift. This is when he takes out the photos from the first day of class and writes a personal letter to each student's parents. He talks about the course and

the student and shares some kind of "upbeat message."
He'll then take the photo, letter, and a favorite reading
from class and send it to the student's parents. He does
it because he cares. "It has an impact and it doesn't cost
that much," he concludes, "They love it, they absolutely
love it."

2. Professors Who Once Loved (or Never Loved) Students

These can also be the best professors, but you don't want
too many of them. These are the ones who never loved
their job but ended up teaching for whatever reason. There
are also those who once had a love for teaching but then
got burnt out along the way (those are the saddest ones).
Being in the classroom with one of these instructors is the
equivalent of working in an office with a miserable boss
who isn't interested in anything anyone has to say and
only does things his way. But because of that, these can be
some of the best professors, because they inspire students
in other valuable ways.

The Bottom Line

Whichever type of instructor your child ends up with, he
can make it a rich learning experience. The instructors
who love teaching will inspire hunger for more knowledge.
Those who have lost that loving feeling will inspire
avoidance of bad professors and teach students to make
the most of a bad situation. It will teach them to talk to

upperclassmen, department heads, and advisers when scheduling classes. If your child still isn't getting what he needs to achieve the grades he desires, he can ask the instructor for help. If the instructor refuses to help, it becomes a lesson in finding other people to help work through the system. If the professor continues to be horrible, your child can document the interactions while trying to get help and share the information with the dean of the department or with the campus newspaper. Having a paper (or email) trail will help document it all.

Of course, no one wants a crappy professor, but there are crappy people in life. Most students want to be taught and want it to be easy, especially given the prices they are paying. Paying to be treated poorly is different from being paid and treated poorly. The best *and* worst professors can

TEACHING ASSISTANTS

You might hear your student talking about teaching assistants. Some are good. Some are bad. Some are grad students. Some are undergrads. Some speak English as a first language. Some don't. TAs tend to have a larger role in introductory courses. Sometimes a passionate and knowledgeable TA who is plugged in to campus can be a better resource than a professor who has lost the love for teaching new students.

inspire students to learn in different ways. There will be a point in life when your child will have a miserable boss or coworker. Learning how to manage a soulless, cold professor will yield life skills. Having a parent who can appreciate this and help guide him through it will make it much more tolerable. Some of the worst instructors can provide the most valuable life lessons.

Why Students Must Make an Effort to Know Their Professors on Some Campuses

Unlike high school, interacting with college instructors can mean making an effort. As an experienced professor explained it to me, the architecture of some college campuses makes it possible for students and teachers to never cross each other's path.

For example, a professor can arrive on campus, park her car, and then walk into her office without passing through the student-populated areas. When it's time to teach class, the instructor can exit the administrative part of the building, walk a few hundred feet through campus, and enter the classroom through a back door leading to the front of the classroom.

Meanwhile, students can walk from their residence halls across campus, enter the building through the front doors, and walk into the classroom through a different door in the back of the room. No one usually sits in the first couple of rows, leaving a physical space between student and teacher. When class is dismissed, the students exit through their doors and the instructor exits through that same door she entered through. Everyone goes back to his or her respective places without ever physically crossing paths. If a student has a question, she doesn't need to talk to

I practically failed the final, which accounted for 50 percent of our total grade. I went to the professor and, well, cried. I'm not sure how it worked, but I ended up getting a B. And yes, I do realize that this was not the best way to resolve the situation.

—Erin, recent graduate

a professor. It's possible to just send an email or Facebook message. Even on a smaller campus, there can be minimal face-to-face interaction in introductory classes. Students can go an entire semester without ever having a meaningful conversation with an instructor.

So if they want to really connect with their professors, students need to make an effort. Making an effort can mean asking a question one-on-one after class, visiting during office hours to discuss a grade, or asking about a professional club or organization. A student who is struggling is presented with the perfect opportunity to get to know an instructor. Keeping all this in mind, when your child tells you, "I got a D on my first quiz," you can enthusiastically answer, "Fantastic! Now you have a reason to hang out with your professor." Bad grades provide the perfect opportunity to get to know an instructor better.

Without a bad grade or complication in the classroom, a lot of students don't interact with instructors. A student who has a lot of trouble can get to know a professor a lot better when they work together to try to solve the

> **OFFICE HOURS**
>
> Instructors are required to keep office hours. This is dedicated time when they make themselves available to help students. Most students rarely take advantage of office hours.

problem. After a couple months of struggling and getting help, a instructor can get to know your child so well he'll extend an invitation to have dinner with his family or ask if she minds babysitting his young children. It happens all the time. And so many times it starts with a stumble in the classroom.

Parents Who Contact Instructors

There might be a situation when you want an explanation or feel the need to intervene. You might want to reach out and talk to your child's instructor. You might want to unload. You want to cast blame. I promise you, however, that if you do it, you will not help your child. Instructors don't like or want to hear from parents—especially college-level instructors who served in the armed forces. Veterans are bewildered that a parent would do such a thing. The idea of a mother or father calling on behalf of a student makes instructors fear for this generation. If a student has issues, that student needs to discuss it with the instructor. Mom and Dad shouldn't fight their battles. That's not how a kid builds character. Sure, a mom and dad can do the coaching from the sidelines, but never the calling. This also means no emailing or attempting to become Facebook friends with your child's instructors (that's completely over the top). Getting in touch with an instructor is the equivalent of calling your child's boss. While some employers will

WANT TO ACCESS YOUR KID'S GRADES?

In order to see your child's grades, you may need your son or daughter to authorize you. **FERPA** *(Family Educational Rights and Privacy Act)* means that your eighteen-year-old's grades are confidential. For more on FERPA, turn to page 24.

send a letter to parents upon a student's request (can you believe this is happening?), it's doesn't make it reasonable or acceptable. Besides overreaching, FERPA laws can mean the instructors won't be able to share information with you that will explain the rest of the story. It's just a bad idea any way you look at it.

Additional Professor Advice

- If your child is sick, it's a good idea for her to contact the instructor. She should also get a note from her doctor. Documentation always helps just in case an instructor thinks your child is trying to pull a fast one.

  I got sick this year and missed a lot of school, and one of my classes had an attendance policy that didn't allow you to miss more than a week. I had to miss more than that, and as a consequence I failed that class, because I got points off of my final for every day after seven that I missed. And on top of that, I had tons and tons of makeup work to do in the meantime that ended up amounting to nothing because of the final.

  —Jen, freshman

- The best time to approach an instructor for the first time is *not* in a state of panic or in desperate need of a fixing a final grade.

- If your child needs to miss class for religious reasons, check with an academic adviser and the instructor before classes begin (or before registering for classes).

- Professors hate texting in class. So avoid texting your child during class times. You don't want to be the reason for that bad grade.

One big problem I have is that many religious holidays fall during the year, and during the holidays I'm not allowed to go to school or work or do anything secular. So I'm forced to miss school, and that has been a setback—especially in language classes. I even had to withdraw from one.

—Vicky, sophomore

The best college experience is one with a mix of professors. What matters the very most are the instructors who are in the department of your child's major. These are the people who shape the curriculum, create the energy, and play the most prominent role in their lives. But to find the best major, and the best professors, a student needs to get the best guidance. The next section explores the academic adviser and how a good adviser can have profound impact on the academic experience.

THE ACADEMIC ADVISER: YOUR CHILD'S ACADEMIC COACH AND SUPERHERO

What does an academic adviser do? An academic adviser can help your son or daughter select the right classes, get into the best classes, choose the right major for all the right reasons, take the courses required to get a degree, change majors, and stay on track to graduate as soon as possible. Advisers can also be mentors, motivators, and people in your child's corner, rooting a student on to victory. Yet very few students fully take advantage of academic advisers.

When a student has an urgent need for advising, that's usually when advisers are slammed working with other students (the ratio can be 600 to 1). Typically the beginning and end of the semesters are the craziest times (scheduling classes, dropping classes, changing classes, etc). The busiest times are not always the best times to build a relationship. It's hard to fully engage with an adviser when there are three panicked students standing outside his or her door.

Encourage your child to build a relationship with his adviser before or after the crunch. Should there ever be an academic question or concern, suggest your child see the academic adviser. The majority of advisers are passionate professionals, but as in all situations some can be better than others.

ADVISER or ADVISOR?

The two spellings are interchangeable. Whether you spell it with an *e* or an *o*, advisers want to help your child get an A (coincidentally the first letter of both spellings).

The good news is that students and parents have access to class catalogs and crucial information. A student should know the number of credit hours it takes to earn a degree and the requirements needed within a major to be awarded a degree. If a student needs 120 credit hours to graduate, he

QUICK TIP ON SCHEDULING CLASSES

should know what classes are required. *Never* depend solely on an adviser. Always have your child double-check to make sure he is on track. Given your access to the Internet, there's nothing wrong with your doing a little research, too, to make sure he's on track.

In addition to making sure your child gets in and out of school on time, the most important thing an adviser can do is listen and guide. Some advisers will talk first and listen later. That's not a good adviser. If your child doesn't find the right fit, encourage him to find another adviser who is willing to listen and eager to help.

What else can a parent do to help throughout the advising process? The following list has been put together by Cynthia Jenkins, PhD, assistant vice president for student affairs at the University of Texas at Dallas.

FIVE THINGS PARENTS SHOULD DO TO SUPPORT THEIR STUDENTS DURING THE ADVISING PROCESS

By Cynthia Jenkins, PhD,
Assistant Vice President for Student Affairs, the University of Texas at Dallas

1. REFLECT on your student's high school career. What courses did they like and not like? What courses did they do well in and what courses were they challenged by or did they need extra help with? How did your student study best? Alone? With friends? What extracurricular activities did your student enjoy? What got them really excited about school?

2. ENCOURAGE exploration of new areas. High school is limited in the disciplines it offers, while colleges often require students to take classes in areas that are completely new to them. This may open your student's eyes to a whole new area of interest! Participation in campus clubs and organizations can also lead students to discover their passion. Expecting your student to clearly define his or her career path at the age of eighteen may simply be unrealistic.

3. RECOGNIZE that majors and careers do not share a direct linear relationship. Majoring in a certain discipline and taking a particular career path are much less related today than they were twenty years ago. The passion a student has for her major will drive the connections she makes and the opportunities that are presented for a future career doing what she enjoys.

4. ACCEPT change. The national rate at which students change their major from the beginning of the freshman year to the beginning of their junior year of college is close to 70 percent! Changing direction is the norm, and it reflects that students often discover something new and exciting to pursue only after they begin their college experience.

5. SUPPORT your student's choice. Their success will come with studying something that they are truly interested in and for which they have a passion. The ultimate value lies in the college degree itself, as it alone can create a world of options. Regardless of the career your child pursues, having a degree will create endless opportunities.

QUESTIONS AND ANSWERS (SEE PAGE 385)

Have a question? Want to answer another parent's question?

Post your questions and answers; visit *The Happiest Kid on Campus* Parent Forum: www.HappiestKidonCampus.com.

TIP #16 MAJOR DECISIONS

Picking Their Majors for Them (Well, Not Really)

The Tip

Even if you know what's best for us, we need time to figure it out for ourselves.

The Story

I was awarded an internship through my major, psychology, and was offered to spend six to eight weeks of my summer at a facility halfway across the country. While this opportunity should have been a no-brainer, I had a hard time making a decision. It was the dream internship—paid, free housing, free meals, and they even paid for travel. However, I already had my summer planned out, working at the golf course during the day and spending the nights with my friends and boyfriend. Did I mention this summer was the summer of my twenty-first birthday? For two weeks I went back and forth in my head, writing pros and cons lists, and talking to my friends and family about what to do. This decision ate at me day and night. I didn't want to miss out on the "fun" of summer, but also on what I would miss out at this opportunity of a lifetime.

What really helped the most was knowing that my parents and sister were 100 percent behind me no matter my choice. It relieved all the pressure and helped me see the situation clearly. The only pressure I felt was the pressure I put on myself. Thankfully, I took that risk and took the internship! I had one of the best experiences in my life and will now pursue a career doing what I was observing and working on for those six weeks. My parents knew I would have an incredible experience and knew that I would go the whole time, but they knew I had to find that answer by myself and in my own time.

—Caitlyn P., senior, Augustana College

＊＊＊

THE MAJOR QUESTION

What your child wants to do for a living is the "major" question. So you want her to be dancer, but she has a dream of becoming an accountant? You want him to be a poetry major, but he has this passion for political science and a hunger to go to law school? You want her to get a master's degree in English lit and work for a nonprofit, but she wants to attend med school and become a cardiovascular surgeon?

When I asked my parents what they thought about my switching majors, they just let me know they supported whatever decision I made. It helped to know that I could talk to them openly about something that would impact my entire experience and career beyond college. I'm really glad that they supported my changing majors, because I love my new major and now actually want to go to classes.

—Courtney, junior

I know, I know, your

child wants to play it safe, and you're telling him to chase his dreams. What's a parent to do?

Okay, maybe I have the roles reversed. But then again, maybe not. A lot of students are scared about their future. With more students working to pay their own way through college, reducing debt and making money is very important to them, more important than in over forty years.

According to the Higher Education Research Institute's 2009 data, 56.6 percent of students reported picking a college because it was "very important" to attend a school where graduates got good jobs. "Being well-off financially was a top goal for students last year and is even higher this year, at 78.1 percent, the highest we have seen since 1966," says John H. Pryor, lead author of the report and director of CIRP. He further explains that given that more students are taking on debt to finance college, it's a natural progression to want to make money and repay loans.

For parents who want their kids to be secure, this can be reassuring. For parents who want them to choose a passion first and a career second, this can be alarming. A student might be able to pay down debt in the next ten to fifteen years, but once the debt is repaid, the passionless job is still there. They need your help to not be scared to dream big!

There is a place where practical can intersect with passion. The ideal major is a focus that can keep them engaged and keep them current with their bills. I talked a lot about this with an educator with thirty-five years on the job. He encourages students to chase their dreams, but he will also explain the realities. A student who is earning twenty-five thousand dollars a year won't be able to have the same lifestyle he had at home (unless he returns to live at home). Then again, there's always the chance that a passionate student with an entrepreneurial zest can turn a lower-paying job into a highly paid position. It happens all the time.

Who's hiring? Here are the **top jobs for the class of 2009 according to the** Fall 2009 *Salary Survey*, National Association of Colleges and Employers.

Job Function	Starting Salary Offer
Teaching	$35,496
Management Trainee	$41,353
Financial/Treasury Analysis	$52,043
Consulting	$56,472
Sales	$41,577
Accounting (Public)	$49,437
Accounting (Private)	$45,859
Software Design & Development	$63,798
Registered Nursing	$45,229
Project Engineering	$58,570

HOW I FOUND MY PATH (AN UNUSUAL ONE)

I left for college without a major. I knew that I enjoyed television, and I had a good time giving speeches when running for student council positions in high school (I never did win—not one election). Not knowing what I wanted to do, I chose telecommunications as my major. My oldest brother was a telecom major, so it was a placeholder while I figured out what I really wanted to do.

My career path emerged in a hallway of an academic building. I saw a help wanted ad for someone to write editorials for the *Indiana Daily Student*, the campus paper. I didn't know anyone at the newspaper, but I was intrigued. I went to the meeting by myself (remember the "Go Alone" mantra in Tip #13).

A few weeks later, I wrote my first editorial. I offered an analysis about deer hunting. Having neither held a gun nor ever gone hunting, I had something to say about the extended hunting season needed to curb the record deer population. My suggestion was to shoot the deer with contraception instead of bullets (that takes good aim). The editorial caused a stir.

I continued writing and hanging out in the newsroom. One day a columnist didn't show up and I was asked to write. That's when I became a regular columnist with a circulation of over twenty thousand and a readership of over forty thousand. (The opportunities presented to students are jaw dropping.)

As a columnist, I wrote slice-of-life pieces. One of my favorites spotlighted the unfair pricing of the submarine sandwiches in the library cafeteria. I discovered that the veggie sub was more expensive than the cold-cut sub, but yet, the cold-cut sub had all the same veggies plus cold cuts. Naturally, the cold-cut sub should have been more expensive. After ordering a cold-cut sub without cold cuts and being charged for the more expensive veggie sub, I was outraged. I saw this as an example of big-school bureaucracy gone bad. After I exposed this injustice, prices were later changed to reflect the contents of the sandwiches.

As my column grew in popularity, my love for writing did too. It was the second semester of my junior year when I talked to the academic adviser to find out what it would take to change my major to journalism. I was told that if I took a class over the summer, I could change my major and graduate in four and a half years. This meant an extra semester in college. After getting the details, I brought up the idea to my parents. I explained what this would mean, and thankfully, they didn't resist. They encouraged me.

The summer before my final semester in college I had another life-changing moment. It came during an internship at *The Tonight Show with Jay Leno*. I got the internship by interviewing for it (I didn't know anyone influential). While interning, I met a writer who had written an advice column in college. I thought this was a cool idea and went back to campus and started writing my "Help Me, Harlan!" advice column.

Two months after it launched, I went home for Thanksgiving break and told my parents, "I want to be a syndicated advice columnist." I saw myself as the answer for newspapers trying to reach younger readers. I had a professor who was syndicated and a newspaper adviser who mentored me. I thought my parents would think I was crazy. But my dad took half a second to respond with, "If anyone can do it, I know it's you." My mom was just as encouraging. Honestly, if my mom and dad had told me, "No, the odds are that you will fail. We don't want to see you fail. Do something else," I probably would have done something else. Or tried for a little bit and given up.

TEN TOP-PAID BACHELOR'S DEGRESS

Major	Average Salary Offer
Petroleum engineering	$86,220
Chemical engineering	$65,142
Mining and mineral engineering (including geological)	$64,552
Computer science	$61,205
Computer engineering	$60,879
Electrical/electronics and communications engineering	$59,074
Mechanical engineering	$58,392
Industrial/manufacturing engineering	$57,734
Aerospace/aeronautical/astronautical engineering	$57,231
Information sciences and systems	$54,038

Source: Winter 2010 Salary Survey, National Association of Colleges and Employers. Data represent offers to bachelor's degree candidates where ten or more offers were reported.

Two years after starting my advice column in my college newspaper, my column was running in the *New York Daily*

News on the same page as Ann Landers (little did readers know I was working three days a week in the insurance business). That's when I was offered my first book deal, which led to speaking events, which led to more books. Nine years later, I was offered a contract from King Features Syndicate.

Fifteen years later, I'm even more passionate and excited about the adventure to come. I love what I do. I can admit, the journey has been long, difficult, and challenging beyond anything I could imagine. I've needed my mom, dad, brothers, and wife on my team. That's the intangible that has made all the difference.

FASTEST GROWING OCCUPATIONS, 2008–2018

Occupation	Education or Training
Biomedical engineers	Bachelor's degree
Network systems and data communications analysts	Bachelor's degree
Financial examiners	Bachelor's degree
Medical scientists, except epidemiologists	Doctoral degree
Physician assistants	Master's degree
Biochemists and biophysicists	Doctoral degree
Athletic trainers	Bachelor's degree
Dental hygienists	Associate degree
Veterinary technologists and technicians	Associate degree
Computer software engineers, applications	Bachelor's degree
Physical therapist assistants	Associate degree
Veterinarians	First professional degree
Environmental engineers	Bachelor's degree

FASTEST GROWING OCCUPATIONS, 2008–2018

Occupation	Education or Training
Computer software engineers, systems software	Bachelor's degree
Survey researchers	Bachelor's degree
Physical therapists	Master's degree
Personal financial advisers	Bachelor's degree
Environmental engineering technicians	Associate degree
Occupational therapist assistants	Associate degree

Source: Employment Projections Program,
U.S. Department of Labor, U.S. Bureau of Labor Statistics

YOUR CHILD'S MAJOR

Some students have known what they wanted to be since they learned to talk. Others thought they knew what they wanted to be until they took organic chemistry. Then there are those students who have no clue what they want to be or do in life. Given that today's students are expected to live six years longer than their parents (Men 72.3 / Females 79.1) they have more time to figure it out than you did (I know, not the happiest thought, but true nonetheless).

The good news is that students want to hear what you have to say. The bad news is they are going to do whatever they want, whether you want them to do it or not. I suppose that's better than doing what you tell them to do and being miserable just to make you happy.

The rest of this tip will offer insight into ways you can

help your child discover his or her passion and find a major. The discovering-passion part can get a little tricky. Some students change their major more often than they change their bedding. Before giving you some suggestions on what you can to do help, I'd like to share a professional's look at this process of choosing a major:

YOUR STUDENT'S MAJOR AND ACADEMIC SUCCESS IN COLLEGE

By Cynthia Jenkins, PhD,
Assistant Vice President for Student Affairs, the University of Texas at Dallas

When I was the director of academic advising, I would greet students and parents at every Freshman Orientation with the message that those who were beginning their college career as undeclared or "undecided" were the wisest students of all. I knew I had a bit of a hard sell, as the idea of not declaring a major can carry a negative stigma, as if somehow it indicates that the student isn't very serious about college. But in most cases, nothing could be further from the truth. Many students simply don't want to limit their options—they have interests in a wide variety of areas and they're concerned that selecting one closes the doors on all the others. Students who acknowledge they aren't ready to commit to a particular course of study (and the parents who support them) will reap the rewards of getting comfortable with this often uncomfortable beginning.

Let's take a closer look at what should go into choosing a college major. Consider this: you are 18 years old, you just graduated from high school, where you had little to no choice as to what classes you took or which subjects you studied, and now you must decide what you are going to do for the rest of your life. Sound a bit unreasonable? I think so. But this is the expectation conveyed by pressuring students to select a major at the beginning of their college career. And the data confirms that it's not working. Across the U.S., around 70% of college students change their major at least once by the start of their junior year. Clearly, for most students, their first choice isn't the right one. But this is understandable when you consider what really influences students' decisions as to their path of study: experiences with a wide variety of classes and with the college experiences itself.

Most universities have a core curriculum or a set of general education courses required of every student in the first two years, regardless of his or her major. They also require a certain number of elective courses—classes that students are free to choose from any area—in each degree plan as well. The value of these courses is that they expose students to many disciplines that they haven't necessarily studied before, and enable them to learn the material from professors who are experts in the field (something which can make a big difference in how engaged a student will be with a subject). Students often discover a whole new world of possibilities in areas they didn't even know existed by taking classes that are unrelated to what they think they want to major in.

Campus involvement can also open a student's eyes to things she's good at and the kind of work she enjoys. Involvement in student government can result in a political science major and the goal of going to law school. Serving as treasurer of a fraternity or sorority can result in an accounting major, and doing community service at a local hospital or school can result in the desire to go to medical school or pursue an education degree. The new world of college offers so many unique experiences and opportunities that students have never had before, that involvement in extracurricular activities often illuminates his or her true passion. And that's the key to choosing a major.

We can't underestimate the importance of students finding what it is that turns them on. Their excitement about what they're studying will motivate them to go to class, learn more, and successfully progress to graduation. It will prompt them to build relationships with professors, seek out internships, and discover how to turn their major into a career. But get ready—what your student decides to major in may be something you didn't see coming.

One of the most important things you can do is support your student while he is exploring options, testing the waters in different fields, and discovering new things about himself. And when he finds his calling, let him answer it with your full support. I've had too many students distraught in my office because of failed grades resulting from pursuing their parents' major instead of their own. College courses are too hard and require too much effort for a student to truly do well if she doesn't like it. We sometimes need to remind ourselves that our goal is for our children to be independent, productive, and happy members of society, and the greatest chance of this happening is if they can work at something they love. Their passion and success in the major of their choosing will pave the way to a prosperous career and make you proud.

HOW TO HELP THEM FIND A MAJOR

Some schools require students to declare a major when they arrive on campus. Others require students to apply to a particular college or program during the admission process in high school, meaning a student who is admitted can already have a major. Declaring a major is important because your child's major will determine the classes he or she takes. It can also help if your child wants to participate in a living and learning community.

If your child is unsure of a major, it's not a big deal. A student's class schedule consists of mostly general education courses the first couple of years. Therefore, declaring a major isn't as vital. There are even some living and learning communities for undeclared majors.

By the third year (junior year), a student should have declared a major and a minor (a minor is a second area of concentration, but with fewer required classes). Most schools allow students to double major or have more than one minor. So if your child is conflicted, double majoring or having multiple minors can be an option. This just means being required to take more courses to be able to earn a degree (and possibly delay graduation).

Figuring out what to major in can be a stressful process. Students think of a major as the rest of their lives, but it shouldn't be this way. It's not "till death do you part." A major is just a general direction. Choosing one (or two) should be an adventure.

When students ask me about pursuing a particular career, my first reaction is, "Someone has to do it. Why not you?" And with that, I suggest they get a part-time job or an internship, find a relevant organization on campus, start a blog, talk to professionals doing what they want to do, and take action. Wanting it is one thing. Getting the information needed to make it happen, getting in touch with the right people who can help make it happen, and then making it happen is another.

So many students have a hard time taking the steps needed to find an interest and discover a passion. They don't know how to figure it out. Opportunities to discover their interest are everywhere in college. Students just need encouragement and someone who knows where to direct them to find them. Some ideas:

1. **GO TO THE CAREER CENTER**: The college career center is a hub of information, resources, opportunities, and mentors. Students can take self assessment tests to help understand their skills, interests, values, and ideal work environment. They can meet with advisers and discover relevant classes,

campus clubs, organizations, and campus jobs that can help provide experiential learning. They can connect with mentors and alumni to learn about internships, part-time jobs, career fairs, and recruitment opportunities. According to the National Association of College Employers, career fairs are the number-one method by which companies look for interns. Campus recruitment is number two.

2. **TAKE CLASSES "JUST FOR THE FUN OF IT"**: There are required courses and then there are electives. The electives can be the ideal opportunity to explore an area of interest just for the fun of it. Sometimes students can take an extra class for no extra costs. These classes can even be taken pass/fail. There are some unusual, amazing, and wonderful classes accessible to students. Even a guitar class can be life-changing. I took a guitar class with the extra credit I had available and was taught guitar by a gifted grad student in the school of music.

3. **GET PART-TIME JOBS AND INTERNSHIPS**: One of the most valuable things students can do for themselves is to get a part-time job or an internship. This is the ultimate in experiential learning. Students can intern in places most people can't get jobs. I've met students who worked in D.C., on oil rigs, aircraft carriers, movie sets, and at NASA. Not only will an internship give a student a real-life view of a job (oh, the joys of being a veterinarian assistant

and cleaning up a mess), but it will also increase his or her chances of landing a job. Employers love to hire interns.

4. **GET INVOLVED IN RELEVANT CLUBS AND ORGANIZATIONS**: Professional clubs and organizations can give students an opportunity to connect with like-minded students, campus professionals advising the groups, and often professionals in the community. They also expose students to leadership positions and a network of members on other campuses in similar organizations. Experiential learning is one of the most powerful ways for students to engage and find an interest.

> The most helpful thing my parent has said: "Pick a major that you know you will be good at and enjoy for the rest of your life. Don't pick a major because you think it will make you money. Your major will most likely lead to a career in that field, so make sure it is something you enjoy."
>
> —Amanda, junior, Rutgers University

5. **FIND PEOPLE DOING WHAT THEY WANT TO DO**: Never before has it been easier for students to get in touch with powerful people doing the things they love to do. The industry leaders are an email, Tweet, or Facebook message away from them. Most successful people like talking with a passionate, driven student. It works like this—a student says she's writing a paper for class and reaches out to do an interview on what it takes to get to the top. After the initial contact she schedules an interview. Following the interview, she asks if it's

okay to stay in touch as she continues her studies. A year later she reaches out to ask about an internship. The next year she gets an internship. Then, when it's time to graduate, she has a job. The other situation is that a student hears about the entire journey and realizes it's not the right fit. So she either finds a mentor or finds valuable information to make an informed decision.

The best way for your child to find a major is not to sit around waiting for it to find him or her. A student needs to be active and involved. It's picking classes that sound interesting. It's going to clubs and organizational meetings that are intriguing. It's getting a part-time job or an internship. It's taking advantage of the resources available on campus and doing, doing, doing.

A LITTLE STRUGGLING IS GOOD FOR THE SOUL

Parents don't want their children to struggle. As a result, some parents see certain degrees as a waste of money. I don't need to mention them, but typically they have something to do with art and being liberal.

The risk is that a student will graduate with an expensive liberal arts degree and not get a job. Some parents want practical—not passion. I understand. College is too expensive to get a degree that isn't going to result in a job.

But from my vantage point, I don't think any college degree is a waste of time or money. If a student has trouble finding a job, he or she can always go back to school for a graduate degree or get a job in a related field. The degree means always having options.

What I truly see as a waste of time is what a student does or doesn't do while finding a major and earning that degree. If she wants to pick a major but not take advantage of the college career center, part-time jobs, internships, mentors, alumni networks, career services, relevant activities and organizations, that is something I would consider a waste of time. These are the things that help build the potential for landing a great job and discovering her ideal career path.

If your daughter has to work during college to help pay the bills, instead of getting a minimum-wage job she can barely stand, she should find a job in a related field on campus or in the community. If there are no campus jobs, then summer jobs and internships should be related to her interests. If there are not relevant jobs at home, then she can stay with a relative over the summer and find relevant opportunities in another city. When she's back on campus, she can get involved in professional organizations and relevant student organizations that will help her figure out what she loves to do, and more importantly, what she doesn't love to do.

Also, it is important to know that having a major that isn't on the list of top jobs doesn't mean your child should plan on being unemployed in the future. New jobs are always being created in the workforce. Jobs like a social media manager (think Facebook), business continuity planner (people responsible for developing business plans in case of cyber attacks), distance learning coordinator (people who coordinate online learning), wind farm engineer (green jobs), and video game designer are all jobs that didn't exist ten years ago.

I know, you might think being a video game designer is an absurd career choice, but the starting salary can range from $50,000 to $80,000-plus. And beyond designing games, the skills needed to design video games can be used in other fields. A student who starts off designing video games can evolve into a medical training software designer. Given the pace of technology and how quickly careers are evolving, a student who has passion, skills, and mentors can be successful in ways parents can't even comprehend.

Or take a student who wants to be a sports broadcaster. Parents might say, "Not a chance. I know you like sports, but come on. Between the odds of failure, the competition, and the lifestyles, it's a bad career choice. Then there are the big media companies to deal with. We don't like it one bit."

I hear what you're saying, but things have changed. Ten years ago that aspiring broadcasting student would need to work his way through the system and depend on everyone else to give him his big break. It's different now. Here's one plan: He works at the campus radio and TV station and does play-by-play whenever possible. In the meantime, he starts a YouTube channel and creates a one-minute daily sports report from his dorm room. He gets a piece of green construction paper from the student union office and tapes it to his wall. He has a friend (a graphics major) design a cool graphic and then uses his laptop computer with a camera to shoot video that makes him appear to be on a set. He can even create boxes over his shoulder with graphics. Not only can he write, shoot, and broadcast this from his dorm room, he can monetize it by running ads. It will cost him nothing more than his time, and he can make money. He can start his junior year and broadcast five days a week. In two years he'll have three hundred broadcasts and a following. Then he can get a job or keep doing what he's doing. Technology and the ability for one person to reach billions of people have changed the world.

> The most helpful thing my parents have said is, "Either get a job that is your hobby and don't expect to get paid much, or get a job that pays a lot to support your hobby." I have been lucky to finally be able to find a job that can hopefully do both.
>
> —Chris, senior

Again, students with passion, desire, and strong mentors have to change the world and avoid the struggle that parents want them to avoid. Sure, some students will struggle. It's a part of life. But struggling early in life makes it so much easier to understand what it means to struggle and how to overcome adversity should it pop up again. If there's ever a time to struggle in life, it's when a student is in his teens and twenties.

A MESSAGE FROM PATRICK COMBS

Author of *Major In Success: Make College Easier, Fire Up Your Dreams, and Get a Great Job* (Ten Speed Press). Founder of Good Thinking Co., www.goodthink.com.

What are some of the best ways to help a student succeed? I recently had the opportunity to answer that question for a room full of college instructors who were all involved in a special career guidance program where they mentored and counseled students.

My answer was simple: Keep your fears, doubts and limiting beliefs to yourself. If a student tells you his or her dream and it stirs in you visions of failure or starvation, zip your lip and encourage them to go for it!…Students don't need more reasons to be afraid of the real world. They need more reasons to believe in themselves. Students don't need more naysayers in their lives. They need more champions of their hopes. And students don't need more fear. They need more votes of confidence…Might some students fail if we send them off whistling to the tune of their heart's desire? Only if you believe in failure, which I don't. There is no such thing as failure, there is only feedback. Plus, the world takes perfect and great care of those who are marching confidently in the direction of their dreams. Of course it doesn't always give us the exact job we want at the exact time we want it. And of course the real world serves up rejection. But the dream-doers know that the world does rise up to meet all consistent and persistent dreamers with an extraordinary life. If we desire to serve students into greater success, we must be for them champions of hope, not fear.

WHEN THEIR MAJOR CHANGES

Choosing a major is like going to a buffet and saying that you are going to eat chicken for the next four years. It's okay to explore. Don't worry about them changing a major—a lot of students change their major after they take exploratory courses.

—Eric Stoller, Academic Adviser,
Oregon State University

Even if you have a child who knows what he wants to do, there's a good chance that it will change. Most students will change majors. The reason isn't to torture you. It's because experiences change their minds. The more he lives life and gets involved, the better chance his major will change. When the phone rings and he is crying because he doesn't want to disappoint you, remember this part of the book. The idea that he is having an experience that is stirring his passion should be what you want. And yes, I understand that no parent wants a child to struggle, but his struggle will be his journey. And a student who is driven, works hard, and surrounds himself with people who want him to win will find huge success.

A degree isn't a job. It's a direction. A student can

Another tough challenge was deciding on a major. To ease this, I met with the dean of the program I am most interested in. Our meeting was extremely helpful and informative. Needless to say, it gave me a great goal, an additional motivation, and I plan on declaring very soon!

—Heather, freshman

double-major or have a minor creating more options. The goal shouldn't be finding a job, just a general direction. Once there's a general direction, he needs to do something. Waiting around to graduate to find a job is too late. This is where getting involved changes lives. Again, internships, part-time jobs, and campus experiences will help him figure it out.

WHEN YOU THINK IT'S A WASTE

Some parents will never like their child's major (just like you'll never like a boyfriend or girlfriend). There are some mothers and fathers who think majoring in music is a waste (especially a parent who downloads music for free). Some parents think that art history is a horrible choice (although you might get free museum tickets). Some moms and dads can't be convinced that sixteenth-century European literature is going to make a child employable (just wait until he goes on *Jeopardy!* and the category of the final *Jeopardy!* is sixteenth-century European literature). I understand your concerns. They are legitimate.

But negating your child's passion and dreams will not get him to listen. Asking him open-ended questions and explaining what concerns you will. If he still won't change his mind, suggest a double major or minor in something that can help him be employable, just in case it doesn't work out for him as planned.

Here are some things to keep in mind when your child wants to dream big and defy the odds, and you are concerned he is making the wrong choice or not thinking through the decision completely:

- Encourage him to show you that he's serious. This means reaching out to professionals who are doing what he wants to do. Finding professors and mentors on campus. And mapping out a path that will take him to where he wants to go.
- Explain the financial repercussions. Help him realize that struggling for a few years will mean not living the lifestyle he is accustomed to living. Also, break down the finances. Have him budget what it will mean to pay rent, pay student loans, and work in his chosen field. It might mean five more years with a roommate. Make sure he knows what you are willing to do and not do.
- Encourage him to get an internship or a part-time job to experience the position. The idea of being a veterinarian

might be better than a summer working as a part-time assistant and cleaning up mess after mess.

- Make sure the school is the best school for his major. If he is set on being an engineer at a small liberal arts college, it might not be the best fit. Again, this is why having an internship or part-time job can be helpful in getting him to understand the job before transferring to another campus.

Before shutting him down, give him a chance to experience the things that you already know. The worst thing that will happen is that he will prove to you just how badly he wants it and how far he is willing to go. Your dislike of a major can motivate him to take action and prove to himself that he really wants to do this.

THE MAJOR BOTTOM LINE

A student who says he wants to be a rock star can be a rock star. But to get a parent's support, he needs to connect with successful musicians and find out how a student goes from kid on campus to rock star. He needs to talk to some club owners who have hosted some big bands and find out how a band gets an audience. He needs to talk to agents of successful bands and find out how they found representation. He needs to identify the top bands with a social networking following and see how they mapped their path to greatness. Then he needs to talk to a band that was big in college but fizzled. He needs to figure out what went wrong and how he can map a path that will take him to the top. While he's doing his research, he'll discover that he needs to find a way to make enough money to pay the bills while paving this career path to rock stardom.

Once he does this, his parents will know that he's serious about becoming a rock star and can be confident he understands the journey ahead of him. Whether or not the kid becomes a rock star is not important, because anyone willing to do all this can do absolutely anything with his life.

All students can be rock stars in their chosen fields. It just takes the desire, ability, and a fan base of parents who believe.

QUESTIONS AND ANSWERS

Q: How does a student declare a major?

A: Typically, a student fills out a declaration of major form in the department. She is then assigned an academic adviser with the department. There can be several majors available in each department. Sometimes she can create her own major. In order to be accepted into a specific program, she may have to apply and go through an admission. Every major has a minimum GPA and required prerequisite courses.

Q: What does it mean to double major?

A: It means declaring two majors, which means taking a lot of classes. For each major there are required courses. A double major can be extremely busy.

Q: How does one declare a minor?

A: At some schools you can declare a minor after completing the required coursework. Others have students declare a minor and then take the required coursework. An academic adviser can offer the best direction.

Q: Can a student major in the arts and have a minor in the sciences?

A: Most schools will allow a student to mix and match. If you're not crazy about your child's artistic major, then encourage a minor or double major.

Q: Is it easy to change majors?

A: Switching majors can be more complicated than just having a desire to change majors. Some majors require a minimum GPA or an application to be accepted into a particular program. Some programs only have room for so many people. Sometimes changing majors can mean having to delay graduation. For more information, have your child contact the academic adviser in the school of her chosen major.

Have a question? Want to answer another parent's question?

Post your questions and answers; visit *The Happiest Kid on Campus* Parent Forum: www.HappiestKidonCampus.com.

The Tip
Even if you can't afford college, help support us while we find a way to pay for it.

The Story
My most challenging, emotional, and unexpected college experience was getting the money to go to college. I come from a family who lives paycheck to paycheck. My mom pretty much gave up the idea that I was going to college. So I decided to find any way to get the money to go to college. I found a one-thousand-dollar grant for freshmen and a two-thousand-dollar need-based grant. My uncle cosigned a three-thousand-dollar loan through Sallie Mae. My biological dad gave me some money. My mom and step-dad give me whatever they can, which I totally understand because they are broke. Half my paycheck goes right to the school to pay off the remainder. It was just really hard and heartbreaking that my family would give up so easily like that. A dumb option that I didn't take advantage

of were scholarships. I've already started applying for next year. I've had to learn the hard way, but at least I've learned!

—Katie, freshman, Kansas State University

✳ ✳ ✳

THE BIG MONEY PICTURE

Saying good-bye to your son or daughter can be emotional—but paying the tuition bill can make even the strongest parent break down!

Money concerns are on the top of most people's minds. And this has been a challenging time for a lot of families preparing for college. More so than in almost forty years, today's first-year college students report having concerns about their ability to finance college.

- 78.1 percent of students say being well-off financially is a top goal (the highest seen since 1966)
- 41.6 percent report that cost was a "very important" factor in choosing which college to attend
- 33.7 percent of students enrolled in college are not attending their first-choice school because of financial reasons (as reported in 2006)
- 66 percent of students received some kind of financial aid (reported in 2008)
- 49.3 percent of students intend on getting a job to help pay for college

- 44.7 percent of students reported that an offer of financial aid was important in their college choice

—Source: Heri's The American Freshman: National Norms for Fall 2009

This tip is about helping your child find money to pay for college, managing his or her finances in college and beyond, and making money while in college. But first a few words about setting expectations early.

SO WHAT DO YOU GET OUT OF THIS?

Whether they are contributing 1 percent or 100 percent of the costs, all parents want a return on their investment. Some want a sweatshirt with a school logo (that will cost you another seventy-five dollars; please transfer the money). Some just want their child to graduate in four years and not move back home. Some want the satisfaction of knowing that they've given their child the gift to do anything and be anything.

Others have particular demands. It might be a high GPA, a particular major, a daily phone call, choosing a roommate, veto power over a boyfriend or girlfriend, control over a student's social life, or final say in big life decisions.

Money means having control. And considering that parents now have more contact with their kids at school, this means being able to exert more power and control. If a student doesn't live up to expectations, it's very easy to threaten to stop helping financially—it will scare them.

But here are a couple of things to keep in mind:

1. Students who feel threatened are more likely to lie to their parents. Students will keep secrets because sharing the truth might mean going home.

2. Students who feel threatened are more likely to make choices to please their parents instead of making choices to please themselves. There's no reason to be an independent thinker when there's no option to be independent.

The "growing up" parts of college (i.e., the difficult 10 percent BS) can be the parts of college life that fall below your expectations and seem like a waste of money. The first year can be ugly and clunky at times, but in reality, these are some of the most valuable times on campus. Yes, a student needs to know a parent's expectations, but you might want to give your child room to learn to become an independent thinker and grow up. It might seem like a waste of money at times, but it will pay big dividends.

> **WARNING**
>
> There might be a day when your child calls home or visits and is in a bad place. He won't love class, she won't love her friends, he might even cry. At first your heart will bleed, and then you'll hang up the phone and be pissed because you'll realize, "I'm paying too much money to listen to this miserable BS. Suck it up!" There might even be a few expletives exchanged with your spouse. Then you'll talk about how this is an expensive lesson and it would be much cheaper to have him cry at home. Better to keep this stuff to yourself than share it with your kid. It will pass.

A REALITY CHECK

Here's the truth: The majority of students will not graduate in four years (most will take five or six). Millions of dollars in unclaimed scholarships will never be claimed. The federal and state government and the institution may attempt to help students pay the bills in college by offering loans, grants, and scholarships, but the individual is in charge of finding the money to pay for college and paying it back.

I didn't realize how lucky I was to have my parents supporting my education until I saw students who hadn't talked to their parents in months or in some cases even years. My parents paid for my out-of-state tuition, and to see students who had no relationship with their parents and were working multiple jobs in order to afford school, it was eye-opening. I was very lucky to have parents who supported me so much that they let their baby move hours away and focus solely on being a student.

—Kate Elizabeth, recent grad

You might know all of this already, but your child might not. This is the reality—he needs to understand that when picking his dream major and attending his dream school, the dream might have a monthly payment. This doesn't mean limiting his career choices, it just means educating him.

Some financial questions he should know the answer to before he heads to school (it's never too late to know this):

1. How much does this college cost over four years? Then five years?
2. What's the average debt load for a student in this particular field of study?
3. What's the average salary for an entry-level position in this particular field?

4. If taking loans, what will be the monthly payment to repay loans?

5. When do payments start?

I found a scholarship through my parent's employer. I found (after working in higher education) that there are many employers that offer scholarships and few students apply because both the parents and students don't know about them.

—Dick, recent grad

THE REALITIES

By Larry Dietz,
Vice-Chancellor for Student Affairs, Southern Illinois University–Carbondale

REALITY #1: Students graduate in four years—this has never been the case overall in the history of American higher education. It always takes closer to five years as students switch majors, courses are not available, financial challenges force some students to go part-time or stop out, etc.

REALITY #2: Students should also be encouraged to apply for scholarships offered through service organizations, professional organizations, church groups, etc. Sometimes students will complain that it takes time to fill out an application or write an essay to support the application. That is correct. One way to look at this time spent, however, is if it takes an hour to fill out a scholarship application (which it usually does not) and it results in a scholarship of $100, where else can a person without a college education make $100 per hour in doing any work? The bottom line is that it is worth every minute financially and personally.

REALITY #3: At one time the overall philosophy was that society benefits from an educated citizenry, so society should pay the lion's share of the cost through scholarship and grant programs. The philosophy has shifted now to one that asserts that the individual benefits more than society, so more of the costs for a higher education should be borne by the student. Thus, there is more emphasis on self-help in the form of loans and work than in previous decades. Thus, the student who is now assuming a larger debt burden should be a wise consumer and consider the cost/benefit of studying particular disciplines based on job prospects and anticipated earnings so that the loans they are assuming can be paid back upon graduation. Of course, in this process the students should pursue areas of interest that match their aptitude but still need to ask good consumer questions.

Parents shouldn't offer an opinion on any bill they themselves are not paying, i.e., Greek organization dues or picking classes if the parent is not paying tuition.

—Linde, recent grad

The least helpful thing a parent can do is say a student needs to fill out scholarship and loan applications and not give an ounce of help. It is especially a pain when your parent loses certain papers and then blames you for not being organized. There aren't many eighteen-year-olds who know what a W-2 is and why it is important. Parents really need to work side by side with their students when it comes to loans, especially government loans.

—John, freshman

I am on a full-ride scholarship to Hobart and William Smith College with a guaranteed seat at SUNY Upstate Medical School, no MCAT's. The tuition is approximately forty thousand dollars a year for four years, and the medical school seat is priceless. I had to start showing my intentions in the medical field starting at the end of my junior year to get the scholarship. I also received high grades all through high school.

—Adam, freshman

Students need to understand how much it's going to cost and how long it will take to pay it back. That idyllic private school might be their first choice, but paying off the loans for the next thirty years might not.

Make It a Family Affair

Forget going to the movies; instead, go online and make it a FAFSA night! (Yes, sounds like the perfect evening!)

Whether college is affordable or a financial stretch, working through the finances together is a golden opportunity to help your child understand the financial implications of life beyond high school. Understanding the costs of each credit hour and how much each class is worth in terms of dollar amounts can put more value on skipping classes. Understanding interest rates and how loans are paid back can have an impact on career choices. Understanding how to get grants and scholarships can help students work harder to get better grades and go after scholarships.

Once they understand the money, they can appreciate that an extra semester can mean an extra ten or twenty thousand dollars of debt. If they're unsure about their major, doing things now to figure it out can save them a lot of money. Students should understand that grants can be awarded, but they can also be taken away, and sometimes students must repay them (drug convictions can result in ineligibility of federal financial aid). Being included in the process will give them ownership and a deeper appreciation.

> Parents and students need to discuss college costs, complete the FAFSA together, and review scholarships and loan options together. So many students are unaware of the cost of tuition or how much student debt they are accumulating. Each extra semester toward a college degree beyond four years is more than just tuition expense. It is student loan debt, interest, lost salary, and lack of retirement benefits. There is a lot to think about for an eighteen-year-old in the transition to college. Parents and families need to set the teaching example, not just do the job for our students.
>
> —Debra Sanborn,
> Student Affairs Administrator
> Facilitator of first-year seminar and
> leadership development courses,
> Iowa State University

Poof! More Money is Out There

I'll assume you've already had the pleasure of filling out your FAFSA applications and CSS/Financial Aid Profile (if necessary). You've been to numerous meetings about aid and know that there are two general categories of aid—gift aid and self-help.

Gift aid is in the forms of grants and scholarships. Self-help aid would be things like Perkins loans, subsidized Stafford loans, and work-study programs.

One mistake students (and parents) make is thinking the first financial aid package offered is the final offer. Always try for a sweeter deal. There could be federal, institutional, scholarship, or state money out there.

One student shared a story with me about how he ended up attending his first-choice school by accident. When he called to let his first choice know that he wouldn't be attending the school, the adviser asked him why. He explained that the other school had offered him a much better aid package. The adviser asked the student to forward the offer from the other school to him. What happened next stunned the student—the adviser matched the package dollar for dollar. The student wasn't even looking for help and got it.

The bottom line: give your school a chance to give you more money. Encourage your child to smile big and ask for more. It might just happen. Here are some ways to make it happen:

- Once you receive your financial aid package, write a letter to the person who sent your financial aid package and ask for "professional judgment." Specify exactly why you feel the decision should be changed. If your income has changed or you've incurred unexpected expenses, share the numbers and back it up with financials. Real numbers help them use their formulas.
- Send your letter as soon as possible. Financial aid can be first come, first awarded.

• Have your child meet with a financial aid adviser and build a relationship. Simply asking for more money can mean getting more money. There could be scholarships or extra funds that become available throughout the admission process.

• Have your student ask about scholarships specific to the college or university. There might be money that isn't advertised out there.

• Ask about special grants or new programs that will soon be available. The government is constantly starting and stopping new programs.

• Encourage your child to find more money. Make applying for scholarships a part-time job. If a student spends five hours a week applying for scholarships and picks up a few hundred dollars here and there, it can add up fast.

I just found out today something that would interest education majors. If you get a job in a low-income school and work there for a set amount of time, they will cancel any loans you might have for school, undergraduate, or graduate. It's called the TEACH grant.

—Darrell, junior

Take Advantage of Free Financial Expertise

When you or your student has a question, the answer is one person away. The

I'm on the board of a state foster care association, and we give scholarships to foster children and the foster family's children.

—Ronda, board member

I always did well in high school and graduated as a valedictorian, so I did receive a good bit of scholarship money from my college (about $20,000 a year). Even with this and federal loans, the bill came to about $5,000 a year. So my parents encouraged me to apply for outside scholarships. I got two that came to $4,000 a year. This was very encouraging, because that meant that there was only $1,000 left, and I paid that by cashing in savings bonds that I had gotten as gifts from people throughout my life. Without my parent's encouragement, I would have had to pay $5,000 up front, but it was only $1,000 instead.

—Susan, freshman

experts in the financial aid office know the answers and are usually happy to help. These people know the most efficient ways to get the most money for school. They can suggest lesser-known scholarships, highlight relevant grants that might not be familiar to you, and make sure your student meets deadlines, understands terms, and sees the big picture. Having a trusting relationship with a caring adviser can mean saving thousands of dollars. Even if college is affordable, financial aid professionals might be able to help make it even more affordable. One thing I discovered during my research is that they thrive on getting students who don't think they can afford college to make it happen.

Pat Watkins, EdD (aka Dr. Pat), is one of those people. He's the director of financial aid at Eckerd College. He began his career in financial aid in 1974 and has worked in private and public universities, private colleges, and community colleges. He says, "I've seen it all and I'm still here." Here are some of his suggestions for parents:

FINANCIAL AID IS A FAMILY AFFAIR: While the student is the beneficiary, parental information will be required. Both the student and parent will need to find out what applications are required, what programs are available, and what deadlines are approaching. Don't leave it up to the student. It probably won't get done. Most schools and scholarship programs have deadlines. You want to maximize your chances for receiving funding.

APPLY: Don't select yourself out by thinking that you make too much money. It does not cost anything to apply for financial aid. The FAFSA is free. While it is difficult to receive federal grants, you may qualify for scholarships and grants from schools or from state agencies.

DON'T PAY FOR A FINANCIAL AID CONSULTANT: Most consultants will guarantee that you can apply for five forms of financial aid. These are the Federal Pell Grant, the Federal SEOG, Federal Perkins Loans, Federal Work Study, and Federal Stafford Loans. They cannot guarantee that you will receive more money by using their service. Many times people don't complete the forms accurately, which only delays their application. If you need help in completing the FAFSA, call the financial aid office. Or attend a College Goal Sunday event where financial aid professionals provide help free of charge. And remember to apply at www.fafsa.ed.gov. If you just google FAFSA, you may be directed to a fee-charging site, such as www.fafsa.com. The first word in FAFSA is FREE. Don't pay anyone to do your FAFSA.

DON'T WAIT: In the fall is the time to look for scholarships. If you wait until the spring, many of the deadlines have already passed. There are some very good free scholarship sites. Don't pay for a scholarship search. Save your money.

When Talking to a Financial Aid Adviser, Ask the Right Questions

The goal for you and your child during his or her first year of college is to understand the big picture. Each year, your child should try to get more free money and the lowest possible rates for loans (if necessary). Good questions can yield valuable information and big financial rewards. An interest point here or there can mean tens of thousands of dollars later. Some questions to bring up during the early stages of planning:

1. What's the average debt for graduating students?
2. Will my first year's financial aid package be representative of each of my child's remaining years in school?
3. Is the first year loaded with gift awards and the rest made up of loans and self-help assistance?

4. How do additional scholarships impact my award?
5. Can tuition be paid on a monthly basis? If so, is there a service fee?
6. Are there part-time jobs on campus or just work-study jobs available?
7. What are some scholarships unique to this campus that I can pursue?
8. What are the deadlines? How can I be made aware as they approach?
9. What's the best way to appeal decisions and try to get more money?
10. What can I do to get more money next year?

HELPING THEM MANAGE THEIR OWN MONEY

Beyond books and tuition, college students have to learn to manage their own money. For most students this will be the first time they've had to manage weekly, monthly, and annual expenses. College is when students learn about bouncing checks, working to pay bills, and selling plasma to buy pizza.

> My parents have done a great job helping me keep up with my finances, especially my first year in college. They made me sit down and write out a budget before I ever even went to school, and this was helpful because I realized that I couldn't just spend without a plan.
>
> —Sterling, senior

To start off the personal finance section of this tip, I want to share some advice from a pro who helps students and young professionals make strong financial choices. Peter Bialagus is a licensed financial adviser, speaker, and author of *Getting Loaded: A Complete Personal Finance Guide for Students and Young Professionals.* Keep the following in mind when preparing your child to manage his or her finances in college:

FIVE TIPS FROM A FINANCIAL EXPERT

By Peter Bialagus

Be careful of the "this is the time of your life" speech. Remember last Thanksgiving when Uncle Ted said to your daughter, "Enjoy it while it lasts"? And Aunt Bettie said, "Oh, to be young again"? And Grandpa Joe said, "This is the time of your life"? Well, when you put those ideas into a student's head, you're literally encouraging them to spend like there is no tomorrow. So watch the jokes about living for today. You might be kidding, but they're not laughing. They're swiping their credit card.

Know thy monthly payment. I speak at over sixty colleges per year. After every speech at least one student approaches me and tells me the total amount they have in student loan debt. Regardless of the tally, my response is always the same: "I don't care." What I *do* care about are the monthly payments and whether or not that student's career choice can support those monthly payments. Ask your student to visit the financial aid office and ask this question *every* semester: "If I were to drop out at the end of this semester, what would my monthly payments be?" They should be comfortable with that before they go any further.

Tell your child to check their credit report. Employers are now checking credit reports in addition to resumes. Your child can look at their report for free at www.annualcreditreport.com. If they see a mistake on their report, there are instructions right on the website on how to get that mistake fixed. By the way, parents, you should check out this website as well!

View college as an "investment" and not as an "experience." Unless you have recently won the lottery twice, college is pretty expensive. While college is a wonderful experience, it's simply too expensive to view solely as an experience where one can switch majors several times, drop classes on a whim, and not consider the total return for four years of higher education. Today college can only be viewed as an investment, and whatever you and your child put in, you need to be sure you can get back in raw dollars. So form a four-year strategy, even if your child has already begun college. Perhaps a few summer classes at a local community college will shave down the cost. Or something online. Whatever your student chooses, make it an investment plan.

Make financial education a priority. The recent financial crisis only proves that everyone needs to take control of their own financial lives. The fat cats of Wall Street did a lot of the damage, but they've done that before, and they'll do it again. The only way to truly protect yourself is to educate yourself. So buy your child a book, send them to a seminar, bribe them to watch a financial education video. They may not get excited right away. (Wait, who am I kidding? They *won't* get excited right away.) But your job is just to plant that seed and keep throwing water on it. Their passion for finance will eventually grow.

For more information, visit www.peterbspeaks.com.

Creating a Budget

How much will your child need—a week? A month? A year? Budgeting makes sense, but it doesn't make sense for you to do it for her. Have her figure it out. If she isn't certain, have her make a rough sketch of her needs using the cat-egories below. If she is uncertain about week-by-week expenses, have her reach out to a student on campus who has been there and done it. (Late-night meals, T-shirts, meals out, a weekend outing can burn through cash.) If she can't figure it out, then have her log her expenses the first few weeks.

> My mom told me, "You'll face times of plenty and times when your funds are scarce. Learn how to live on twenty dollars for a week before your next paycheck, but get through it by remembering it's not forever. It's just the life and times of a college student."
>
> —Gena, senior

There are five areas that can help break down the budget. Billable costs like tuition, fees, and room and board should be calculated separately from the indirect costs such as phone, books, T-shirts, pizza, and beverages (nothing alcoholic).

BASIC COST COMPONENTS FOR BUDGETING

1. Tuition and Fees
   Varies based on your academic program and number of credit hours.
2. Room and Board
   Varies based on institution and dining options
3. Books and Supplies
   National average at four-year public colleges in 2009–10 is $1,122.

Where a student lives on campus can influence how often she can eat in a dining hall, which will mean buying more groceries or ordering food in. A student attending school in New York City's Manhattan will spend more on food than a kid living in the Manhattan, Kansas. A student who lives an hour away from home will spend far less coming home than a student who lives eight hours away from home. If your child can't seem to put together a budget ahead of time, then have her log expenses for the first two months and talk about it over parents' weekend.

PART-TIME JOBS, WORK-STUDY, AND SELLING BODILY FLUIDS (AND HAIR)

There are part-time jobs, work-study jobs (part of financial aid), and selling bodily fluids. All these can be helpful ways to help pay for college and manage the everyday expenses.

I'm a student at Indiana State University, and I work in the athletic department. It is a great job because I get paid to go to the games that I was already going to attend. It also gives me several connections in the sports management field, which is the field I want to go into after graduation.

—Courtney, junior

Work-study jobs are part of the financial aid package. These jobs are used to help pay for books, fees, and other expenses that pop up during the year. Students seeking part-time jobs on campus might not be eligible to work certain jobs because they are work-study positions. Some of the best jobs put students in departments with faculty and staff. Other great jobs include sitting at information desks in low-traffic areas and doing nothing. Students can literally get paid to study.

Part-time jobs can be a great excuse to get involved on campus and explore interests. I'm always a fan of encouraging students to get a job that will help get them more than a paycheck. A student who wants to go into restaurant management can get a job in food services. A student who is interested in finance can get a part-time job at a local bank. A student who wants to go to medical school can work in a hospital. All these jobs will either help students realize this is what they love or hate. A summer working in a hospital carrying dirty linens to the washing machines can be telling.

> I work at the campus mail and copy center. I have to admit that I love this job so much! It gives you a change of pace and allows you to meet/interact with a lot of people on campus like teachers, students, even people from the main offices on campus. I always get a sense of excitement when I have to go to work, because I absolutely enjoy the people I work with and the people I can encounter.
>
> —Terron, junior

One of my favorite campus jobs is resident assistant. Often it means free room, free board, and a stipend. Students are only required to be on call for a certain number of hours. They can usually get another part-time job if necessary. In addition to all the life experiences, it's leadership at the core.

There are some clubs and organizations that actually pay members. Some elected officials can earn money. There are also jobs working in campus departments as research assistants or administrative support. Being in an office means seeing, hearing, and getting to know the most influential people on campus. There are also social jobs that can put a student in the center of activity. Then there are jobs that can allow students to sit at a desk all day and read a book and get paid doing the things they would be doing anyway.

Selling Bodily Fluids (and/or Hair)

Students can often find advertisements for medical testing or medical studies on college and university bulletin boards, in campus newspapers, and on craigslist. They want blood, plasma, sperm, eggs, even hair. Students can donate plasma a couple times a week, get some

WHAT STUDENTS GET PAID FOR FLUIDS AND PARTS

- Hair goes for as high as $2,500+ (visit www.hairtraider.com)
- Plasma for about $20–$50 (limit twice a week)
- Female's eggs for $3,000 to $8,000 (higher if a student has high SATs), but know the risks!
- Sperm sells for less than $100. (Demand has gone down given advance technology for men with low sperm counts. Single women and lesbians are still interested.)

cash, and maybe even get a cookie. There are students who use this money for food, books, and extra cash. This probably isn't something you'd ever think about, but it's something that's out there. Some of the benefits include food (I mentioned cookies), testing for sexually transmitted diseases and infections, and cash.

Given that so many students are strapped for cash, it's no surprise that donations are up. But students don't often look at the fine print when it comes to signing authorizations and wavers when they participate in medical testing and research. The risk in participating in medical research is that it may not be a legitimate program or the risks are too great. Every clinical trial in the United States must be approved and monitored by an Institutional Review Board (IRB) to make sure the risks are as low as possible and are worth any potential benefits. An IRB is an independent committee of physicians, statisticians, community advocates, and others who ensure that a clinical trial is ethical and that the rights of study participants are protected. All institutions that conduct or support biomedical research involving people must, by federal regulation, have an IRB that initially approves and periodically reviews the research. If your child is interested in undergoing a medical test (some of these can be low-risk experiences), have him or her visit "Understanding Clinical Trials" (http:// clinicaltrials.gov/ct2/info/understand) to ensure that what they are doing is safe, legal, and well thought out.

A FEW WORDS ABOUT CHECKING ACCOUNTS

The local bank might offer a free toaster (don't assume students can have those in the residence halls), but that might not work so well during the summer months. Not that students don't enjoy toast in July; I'm talking about the ATM fees and not having access to the bank over the summer months. Signing up with a local bank upon arrival on campus might make sense at the time, but unless there's a branch at home, managing finances during the summer, transferring money, and dealing with ATM fees can be a hassle. Plus, that free account might not be free if a student isn't actively using the account. Here are some things for your child to keep in mind when opening a local checking account near campus:

> Have your child open a student checking account at a bank with locations in both their college town and hometown. This way if you need to get money to them quickly, you can deposit it directly into their account instead of mailing or wiring the funds. I recommend the bank also be a nationwide bank so that when your child graduates and moves to another city, for graduate school or a job, they don't have to open another account. Having the same account for a longer period of time will help their credit history, especially if they need to take out a loan from that bank.
>
> —Janita M. Patrick, Tallahassee Community College

- Watch ATM fees
- Make sure there is online banking (most have this)
- Make sure there are no fees
- Get overdraft protection (a must!)
- Get checks with carbons
- Find a bank that has a local branch and branch at home
- Watch out for debit cards (see next section)
- Consider having a parent on the account (makes it easier to take money from your kid—only kidding)

A FEW WORDS ABOUT DEBIT CARDS

You might hate credit cards, but those debit cards are more dangerous. They can be more confusing and harder to manage than credit cards. And because it's just a checking account, a student doesn't build much credit. Some vendors will "hold" money as a deposit (for example, when pumping gas), which ties up funds, making it unavailable to pay other bills (like that pizza from 3:00 a.m. the other night). And considering most students don't have thousands of dollars in their accounts, it's very easy to get overdrawn. Debit cards with a little Visa or MasterCard symbol can be used like a credit card, but the money comes right out of checking.

Suggest that when they use their debit card they write everything down that they spend. I use the one that you are supposed to write checks in. I just write every transaction in there to keep track of how much I spend. Then I make sure it's correct by looking at my banking with the online statements. Some of the transactions take awhile to go through with most banks, but once they do, you can make sure the math is correct.

—Stephanie, sophomore

Have two accounts: one that is attached to your debit card, and one that holds a bit of extra money that will be your overdraft protection, so that just in case you do overdraw, you will either have the amount to pay the fee, or if you're lucky your bank will automatically draw from the extra account.

—Blair, freshman

Change your debit card number at least once a year to reduce the likelihood of any stored information being used successfully. I have routinely seen my debit card charged for cancelled subscriptions after the end.

—Jason, college grad

If a student signs up for a service that has a monthly charge or uses a debit card for online transactions, it's hard to keep track of what funds are coming out and when they're coming out. This is another reason why those little debit cards can be hard to manage.

A FEW WORDS ABOUT CREDIT CARDS

You might not know this, but new credit card laws have made it illegal for credit card companies to distribute candy, T-shirts, and miniature footballs for signing on the dotted line. Credit card companies are still looking to sign up college students, but the rules have changed.

A lot of parents hear the word credit card and think, "Not my child!" But there's something to be said about

CREDUCATE THEM

Credit cards used properly can help build credit and help you educate a student about what it means to use and not abuse credit. Ten years ago a parent couldn't log on to an account and monitor purchases— now you have access. In fact, you can even set it up to get alerts about purchases and payment due dates. Some suggestions:

1. Set a low limit. Make the limit as low as $500.
2. Use the card to pay for essentials.
3. Use the card only for emergencies (discuss what constitutes an emergency).
4. YOU can be the one to pay the balance every month.
5. Have the bill sent directly to you (or have access via the web).
6. Set payments using an automatic payment system (online).
7. Explain how paying the minimum means paying the maximum amount of interest.
8. Make sure they understand what a FICO score is and how late fees and missed payments will haunt them.
9. Make an agreement that they will have ONE card. More than one is when they get into trouble.

a student who uses a credit card responsibly, sets a low

limit, and uses it to pay for things a parent is paying for. Meaning, if you're going to buy textbooks, instead of using your card, he should use his own. You can still pay the bill (lucky you), and your child can build credit. Later, when it comes time for buying a car, renting an apartment, or applying for a mortgage, your child will be grateful that you helped him establish a credit history. A checking account, paying rent, and having a credit card help. I know how a lot of parents feel about credit cards, but it helps to use a credit card to make purchases online and have in case of an emergency (no, going to Cancun for spring break is not an emergency). Sure, debit cards can work, but having money taken out of a checking account can be confusing and trouble if in the wrong hands. Credit cards are not the enemy—it's college students who don't understand the rules, pay bills late, only pay the minimum, and get a bad FICO score because they didn't understand the risks. The consumer has to be educated.

THE MONEY MESSAGE

Whether you're paying for all of it or paying for a small portion of it, paying for college can be emotional for everyone. A student who can learn how to manage money without allowing it to cause her stress will learn a lesson that will carry over into the rest of her life. But for that to happen, parents need to lead by example and connect students to the resources and information to guide them.

When it comes to managing their own personal finances, some students don't really want to manage their money. That's fine. Give them time. All students face a day when the well runs dry and they're out of plasma, hair, and fluids to pay the bills. This is when you'll get a call or text asking you for more money (the nerve, to text you!). When it happens, ask your child to send you over her budget and spreadsheet. That can be the day the money lesson begins.

QUESTIONS AND ANSWERS

Q: How soon do your recommend a student get a job on campus?

A: Some students need to take a job immediately. Work-study jobs might need to be started immediately (jobs can get filled). If the part-time job is low stress and flexible, it can be started right away. Jobs like working information desks and working in campus departments tend to be flexible and low stress.

Q: How does a student qualify for Federal Work-Study jobs?

A: A student needs to fill out the FAFSA and check the appropriate box for Federal Work-Study. When a student is awarded a financial aid package, there will be a notification if he or she has qualified for the program.

Q: Can a student choose a work-study job?

A: Students can be assigned a job, but can usually choose a job from a list of on-campus positions. Students can then interview for the job. The best advice for your child is to find out as much information as possible once he or she is approved. There is always a chance that all the jobs will be taken before your child acts.

Q: Where are some of the best places to get scholarships?

A: Check with the financial aid office for local scholarships. Check with a parent's employer, spiritual organizations, and service organizations to see what kind of scholarships are available. Also, visit www.FastWeb.com and www.SchoolSoup.com. Have your child make applying a part-time job. A few hours a day can yield big money.

Have a question? Want to answer another parent's question?

Post your questions and answers; visit *The Happiest Kid on Campus* Parent Forum: www.HappiestKidonCampus.com.

The Tip

Forbidding a college student to date someone will just mean they'll keep it a secret from you. It's out of your control.

The Story

From personal experience, I know that hiding one's significant other from parents is a very difficult and stressful thing to do. While on break, discreetly making phone calls and text messages or covering your tracks if they are nearby and you are visiting them is insane. It is best to be open about your relationships now that you are an adult. If parents are concerned about how it may affect your health, relationships with friends or family, or academics, it is best to alleviate those concerns by having a mature discussion with them. My parents found out about my girlfriend by retracing the phone calls on my phone bill, which was way over on minutes for the first few months of college. What a nasty surprise for them!

—Dipavo, junior, University of California–San Diego

* * *

Some people know me as "Help Me, Harlan!" from my advice column. (My tagline: He's like Dear Abby, just younger, hairier, and a man.) For the past fifteen years, I've been helping college students deal with their dating and relationship dilemmas. From the first crush, to the first date, to the first breakup, I've been given a front-row seat to all the action.

Not only do I help college students, but I've also become a trusted source for parents. Here's a recent letter that ran in my column from a concerned mom with a daughter in college:

Dear Harlan,

I just had a huge argument with my eighteen-year-old daughter. She recently left for college. She has always been an excellent child—no problems, no drinking, no drugs, etc. Now she has a boyfriend, whom I thought would be OK. He is not. He's not abusive, but he cancels plans without notice, and he didn't do anything for her birthday. Still, she is not interested in spending time with her family. She mopes around the house when she comes home for the weekend. She does not call anyone when she gets home. She sounds like she is enjoying college and is meeting a lot of people, but she's not the same. We used to be closer, and she was more respectful until he blew into the picture. Should we just let her run with it?

Sad Mom

Hi Sad Mom,

The problem is that you can't tell her what to do because she'll do whatever she wants at college. But still, you can lovingly explain to her that the first year in college can naturally be an uncomfortable one. Sometimes, first-year students use relationships as a safety buoy in unfamiliar waters. The risk is that they don't learn how to take care of themselves and use unhealthy relationships as a crutch. That's why it's so important to make it essential that she get involved socially, academically, and spiritually. Let her know that you respect her choices, BUT that she deserves the very best. And from what you've seen of this man, he's not the best. Tell her you hope she will demand the respect she deserves. Then trust that her eighteen years of excellence will lead her to a better life on campus and him to the door leading out of her life.

So if you're looking for an objective third party who understands what students are dealing with and appreciates what parents are facing, I'm your man.

The straight truth is that while incoming students are

required to pass their SATs to get into college, there's no test to gauge their dating aptitude. If there were a test, most students would have a hard time passing. Book smarts aren't the same as dating and relationship smarts. While the most educated and brilliant students can change the world, they can't always ask someone out on a date (while totally sober). It's really quite shocking.

The search for college love or lust can be one of the most distracting, time-consuming, and emotional parts of the college experience. I can't even begin to calculate the number of hours students spend daydreaming about class-mates, scouring Facebook for flings, hanging out at parties to hook up, drinking to find a date, and then worrying about what happened the next day. Finding love or lust, hanging on to love or lust, and getting over love or lust (and a morning hangover) are some of the major reasons students skip class, drink, and oversleep. When it comes to the 10 percent difficult that occupies so much of students' time, the drama surrounding dating, relationships, and the search for happiness can be all-consuming.

They don't teach Hooking Up 101 or Dating 102 in col-lege. It's all about street smarts. Sure, accounting class is important, but a relationship is life-changing. It's how we find our lifelong companion.

So how does a student find a date and have a relationship when so many of them have little or no experience? I have an answer. The following tip is ripped from the pages of *The Naked Roommate: And 107 Other Issues You Might Run*

Into in College. This tip is one of the most often referred to by students. It answers the question and gives you and your child a sense of how dating and relationships work in college:

The Naked Roommate: And 107 Other Issues You Might Run Into in College

Chapter 8—Dating and Relationships

TIP #54 THE RULES OF COLLEGE LOVE (OR JUST LUST)

The Tip

Relax, chill, and talk to the people you want to date without getting stuck in your head.

The Story

I was way too worried about what girls thought about me and how I could get as many as possible to hook up with me. I'd either say nothing to them or say the wrong things. It took over my life. Until I relaxed, found a life in college, and stopped trying so hard, relationships eluded me. Once I relaxed, it became so much more manageable. It took me a few years to figure it out, but now I'm there and much happier.

—Junior, University of Illinois–Chicago

***

Please note: this tip can get you a date. If you put cologne or perfume on this page and rub it on you, it can be even more effective.

Some of you might plan on hooking up in college (note: a hook-up can be anything from a hug to procreation). Some of you might plan on dating in college. Some of you might plan on finding your future husband or wife. Whatever you want, here's a quick five-step plan to help you find it all—while sober.

1. *Meet people by putting yourself in as many rooms as possible.* Dating in college works like this—if you're in a room long enough you will hook up. Put yourself in classrooms, lunchrooms (cafeterias), study rooms (libraries), meeting rooms, work rooms (on the job), rec rooms (gyms), dorm rooms, party rooms, and any room where you can be part of a shared experience.

2. *Say what you feel once inside these rooms.* If saying something is too hard for you, then you need to embrace the Universal Rejection Truth of Dating and Relationships and come out of Rejection Denial. The URT of Dating and Relationships states that not everyone you desire will always desire you. Some will, but not all. It's impossible for everyone you want to want you or me (sorry). Rejection Denial is a deep, dark, dangerous place where you think that everyone you want should want you, and when someone you want doesn't want you, you think there's a huge problem—but the problem is that you can't embrace the Universal Rejection Truth—celebrate it.

3. *Train for the sport of taking risks:* Training means working to be your personal best, physically and emotionally (e.g., putting on a tight thong and being completely comfortable with what you see in the mirror). It means surrounding yourself with people who want you to be your personal best. Training can take months or years. Once trained, you can put yourself in rooms and say what you feel without letting fear stop you. This is the difference between living a life of passion as opposed to one paralyzed by fear.

4. *Take risk after risk after risk.* If the first object of your affection doesn't share your interest, don't let it throw you. Consider him or her a friend and don't let a little rejection stop you—this friend might be interested later or have another friend who could become your perfect match. Keep taking risks and give the world an opportunity to experience you and all you have to offer.

5. *Research, Recoup, and Repeat.* If a risk doesn't go as planned, find out why it didn't go as planned (yes, this can be scary—that's why you've trained). Next, take some time to get comfortable in your thong. Know that you are attractive, desirable, and live in a world of options, and then repeat. You might want to repeat with the same person or with someone new. Continue this process until you find the best choice—not your only choice. Because truly, you have endless options.

Dating in college is not usually about options; it's more about fortunate accidents. If they're in a room long enough it will happen. If they're in a room with alcohol it will happen faster (not encouraged). If they don't think about finding it, it will find them. Not knowing how it happens, when it will happen, or if it will happen again can mean hanging on to bad relationships way too long, because without other options a better relationship isn't accessible. For a single and searching student to make strong choices, he or she needs to know how it happens, why it happens, and how to make it happen again and again (while totally sober).

The crazy thing about dating in college, and finding love in life, is that we can be totally scared of taking risks and totally uncomfortable in our thongs, but still find a date, love, marriage, a family, and a life without ever being comfortable enough to be honest with a partner or ourselves. Too many times, one partner discovers that he or she has options and either cheats or breaks off the relationship. My thinking is that if college students could learn that they live in a world of options and train for the sport of taking risks, then instead of ending up with what they think are their only choices, they could end up with their best choices and best options. When you're with your first choice and know you have options, when other options pop up later in life (and they will), they will be far less tempting, because nothing can be better.

SO HOW CAN YOU HELP?

Some parents want to be involved in every relationship their child experiences. Some parents know nothing about their child's relationships. However much you know, the following suggestions can help your child live in a world of options, make strong choices, and never look back.

1. **HELP THEM COME OUT OF REJECTION DENIAL:** Remind him that thousands of people will

want him and thousands will not. Help him focus on the thousands of people who *will* want him. Let the people who aren't interested not be interested. Remind him that he has options. Never let him forget. People who know they have options never settle for anything less than the best.

2. **HELP THEM FIND THE RIGHT PEOPLE TO BE IN THEIR CORNER:** Too many students surround themselves with people who like seeing them get beaten and bruised. Help your child see that people who say negative things are not positive friends. Encourage her to find friends who want her to be successful. Friends should help her win, not call her stupid, ugly, slutty, or anything else that's destructive. Direct her to the places where she can naturally meet these people. Spiritual groups, culture-based organizations, and professional/leadership groups can be places to meet them. Also, point her in the direction of professional staff on campus who can help her win. Make sure she has people she can talk to other than you (some things you just can't tell Mom or Dad).

3. **ENCOURAGE THEM TO SPEND TIME IN LOTS OF ROOMS:** The more people your child knows on campus, the more people she will have in her corner. Having options means being able to make strong choices and being surrounded by people who want her to win. The way people meet is by hanging out

in lots of rooms and sharing new experiences. This is one more reason why every student should include in her college planning three ways she can get involved outside the classroom (assume at least one won't work out).

4. **ENCOURAGE THEM TO BE HONEST WITH THEMSELVES:** Forget being honest with you. That will come naturally if he can be honest with himself. This is a huge risk. Being honest means looking at himself in the mirror and being completely vulnerable (i.e., looking in the mirror wearing a thong). Being honest means he can say what he feels and do what he knows is the right thing to do. It's a big risk because not everyone will like him or love him when he's honest. But someone who lives in a world of options, embraces the truth, and trains for the sport of taking risks can be honest. The end result is a passionate, confident, and centered student who can demand and command respect.

5. **HELP THEM RECOUP AND REPEAT:** When she gets hurt, when things go wrong, when she faces rejection, be there to listen. Help her remember her best qualities. If she is still hurting, direct her to counseling services, peer mentors, spiritual leaders, and friends who want her to win. Once she recuperates, encourage her to put herself in more rooms with more people. Never stop reminding her that she lives in a world of options.

QUESTIONS AND ANSWERS

Given the wide range of relationship issues that come up, I wanted to use the rest of this tip for an extended question and answer session.

For this section of the tip, please imagine you're in a big room at a parent event and the topic is "College Dating: Hooking Up Parents with the Naked Truth about College Love and Lust." As your advice columnist, I'd now like to open the floor up to answer your questions about college dating and relationships.

The Hook-Up

Hi Harlan,

Can you please explain what hooking up means? My daughter talks a lot about hook-ups. Should I be worried?

(pause for nervous laughter)

Hi Worried Mom,

If she's talking about it while you're in the room, I wouldn't be too worried. Hooking up can be anything from meeting up with a group of friends, to a hug, or a kiss, or all out—yes, the stuff that worries you. When a hook-up happens and where it happens is unpredictable. College students often use the hook-up as a way to gauge if a relationship is possible. Unlike in the past, hooking up often comes before dating.

The Inexperienced Single Student

Hi Harlan,

My daughter is very impressionable and wants to please. We're afraid that she's going to leave for college and go absolutely wild. Should we be scared?

Hi Scared Parent,

Thank you for the question! Trust that she won't do anything in college that she is not already doing (that can be good or bad). If she has places to go, things to do, and meets the right people in the right places, she will find people who want to respect her and not exploit her. Being a pleaser can be a good thing—as long as she also wants to be respected.

The Long-Distance Relationship

Hi Harlan,

My son is going to be a freshman, and his girlfriend is a senior in high school. They have a strong relationship and want to make it work. We're afraid this will keep him from having the best possible college experience. Any advice?

Hi Concerned Dad,

It can work, but it's a long road. There's one thing I would tell him: he needs to have a life outside of the relationship. Being miserable while apart is not a sign of loyalty or devotion; it's a sign of a bad relationship. The big risk in having a life outside of each other means they'll both need to spend time in rooms with other people. And when people are in a room, things can happen. That's why insecure couples get jealous and into trouble. He should encourage her to have a life, and she should encourage him to have a life—if they can't have a life outside of each other, it's not going to last.

A CHEATING STORY

The five minutes of physical happiness with someone else was absolutely not worth the pain that my actions caused. In the first month of my freshman year, I met and fell in love with a junior. We had a great relationship, and things went well for nearly a year. And then little things started to go wrong—he wanted to be completely exclusive and serious, but I felt that he wasn't giving me the kind of attention that a serious relationship of that level demanded. But I didn't want to talk to him about it, because I didn't want to start any fights, so instead I cheated. When he found out, he was absolutely heartbroken, and I felt like a first-class b*tch. But we decided to try again. We stayed together for another year, but things just weren't the same, and we broke up for good last fall. Now that I look back on it, I realize that by cheating on him instead of talking to him, I ruined a beautiful relationship and lost someone I cared about very much. My advice is, don't cheat. If you're having problems in your relationship, do everything in your power to make things better, and if it still doesn't work, don't cheat and then lie about it—just break up! And then you'll be free to do whatever you want without having to be dishonest with them or hurt their feelings. In the long run, it works out better for everybody involved. Cheating doesn't just affect you and the person you cheat on—it affects your mutual friends, it affects the person that you cheated with—basically, it's a huge headache that can be avoided through honest communication.

—Name witheld, Kutztown University

The High School Honey Relationship

Hi Harlan,

My son wants to dump his high school sweetheart when he heads to college. We love her. He says he doesn't want to miss out. What do you think?

Hi Disappointed Dad,

If he doesn't want to miss out, he's in no place to be with this girlfriend. Better he not string her along and pretend to be loyal and devoted and then cheat on her and destroy any possibility of a future together. Too many times high school couples do this halfway-dating thing and end up getting torn apart. If a couple isn't committed, it will be a drama factory. My prediction—in a few months, when things settle down, he'll realize that the only thing he's missing out on is a loving, trusting relationship. Whether or not she'll be available will be the question.

The High School Couples at Same School Relationship

Hey there Harlan,

My daughter insists on going to the same school as her boyfriend. We're very worried she won't make friends and find her place. Any suggestions?

Hey there Concerned Mom,

I see the future—I see a future where your daughter is on the same campus as her new ex-boyfriend!

(pause for wild audience laughter and applause)

Sure, there's a chance this will work out, but most relationships don't last through college. Instead of fighting it, encourage her to get involved in something other than her boyfriend. She needs to have something that belongs to her other than her boyfriend. She needs to have options. This can be Greek life, an academic club or organization, intramural sports—just something to give her balance. The risk is that she will arrive on campus and make her whole life him. That's not college. She needs to have her own life. If the relationship lasts, encourage her to go abroad or get an internship away from him. The more she does on her own, the better the chances she will have a life outside of this boyfriend.

> Even if you don't approve, the boyfriend/girlfriend will probably come visit and sleep over. It's your responsibility before they move out to teach kids about protection and reinforce your beliefs so that when they're out on their own they can make better decisions. If you were a very strict parent, your child is likely to go nuts once they get to college, because they've never had this much freedom. It's up to the parents to set good boundaries so the kid is ready for school.
>
> —Tori, sophomore

The Disrespectful Relationship

Hi Harlan,

This is a tough one for me to share in front of everyone. My daughter's boyfriend treats her like garbage. He won't acknowledge her in public, but she puts up with it. What can I do?

Hi Concerned Mom,

Thank you for having the courage to bring this up. This situation is entirely too common. Girls who feel like garbage allow themselves to be treated like garbage. Try asking her this question: "If you knew there were a thousand guys who always wanted to love you, adore you, and treat you the way you deserve to be treated, would you ever put up with one who ignored you, didn't acknowledge you, and disrespected you?" When she says, "No," ask her what you can do to help her see that she lives in a world of options. Consider getting her professional help so that she can find the courage and confidence to get rid of this guy.

Oh, whatever you do, avoid calling him a loser or making the issue about him. All this does is put her on the defensive and create a distraction. This isn't about him. It's about the fact that she can't demand and command respect.

> **WHEN THEY'RE IN A BAD RELATIONSHIP...**
>
> Ask the question, "If you knew there were one thousand guys who wanted to love you, adore you, and treat you the way you deserve to be treated, would you ever put up with one who ignored you, didn't acknowledge you, and disrespected you?"

The Home Every Weekend Relationship

Hey there Harlan,

My kid comes home every weekend to see his girlfriend. He barely has any friends on campus. We don't think this is part of the college experience. Any suggestions?

Hi Frustrated Father,

We all know why he barely has friends on campus. It's hard to make friends when you're not on campus. Coming home every weekend to be with a girlfriend is not getting the most out of college. I don't know what kind of expectations you guys set up when he left for school, but considering part of college is getting involved, coming home isn't following through on his end of the college experience. I would revisit your expectations and make some changes. Once every few weeks is a lot, but it's not every weekend. In the meantime, suggest that if he's not able to stop, he might want to move to a school closer to home.

NEVER CUT THEM OFF

Abusers want Mom and Dad to cut off the kid. It's so much easier to be abusive when Mom and Dad aren't in the picture. Even if you don't support her decisions, stay close enough so she can reach out for help when she needs it.

The Abusive Relationship

Hi Harlan,

This is also very hard for me to share, but I will.

We think our daughter is in an abusive relationship.
She denies it. All the warning signs are there. She
has very few friends and not much of a life outside
of her boyfriend. He isolates her and pits us against
her. He shames her and humiliates her. He's con-
stantly breaking up with her. Just when she's done
with him, he apologizes. She is tight-lipped about
him. What should we do?

Hi Hurting Mom,

Thank you for asking this question.

This sounds abusive—emotionally and quite possibly physically. She needs to get out of this relation-

> **NEED A DOMESTIC ABUSE HOTLINE?**
>
> VISIT: The National Domestic Abuse Hotline and Website
>
> **1-800-799-SAFE (7233)**
>
> www.ndvh.org

ship ASAP, but she needs serious help to do so. Whatever is keeping her in the relationship needs to be addressed by a therapist. First, get in touch with professionals with experience in domestic abuse counseling. Start by finding someone who can coach you. Contact the director of counseling services to get a referral and ask for some advice (if they say, "Can't do it because of HIPAA," speak in generalities). Find out what resources are available on campus and in the community. Once you talk to a specialist, you can figure out what's next. It could be family counseling. It could be offering her support to end the relationship. It could be bringing her home (if she's away at school). She needs help, but being so far away can mean being limited in what you can do. One thing not to do is make this him versus you—if she chooses him, she'll be even more isolated and dependent on him. At the end of the day, this is about her self-respect and demanding what she deserves.

The Daughter Who Can't Find a Date

Hi Harlan,

Really enjoying the questions tonight! My daughter is sweet, attractive, and single. She can't seem to find a date. What's the problem? Think she might be gay?

Hi Mom,

Glad you're enjoying the event!

You might have a gay daughter or you might have a shy daughter or a very attractive daughter whom men have a hard time approaching. Guys are very scared to approach attractive women (while sober). And women are waiting to be approached. Everyone is so afraid of rejection that a lot of attractive and single people aren't connecting. Here's an idea—tell her that you will always love her no matter who she brings home (gender, race, or religion). Then encourage her to be active on campus. Sit back and watch. Soon enough you'll be standing in a wedding or commitment ceremony in some exotic locale.

The Guy Who Can't Take No for an Answer

Hi Harlan,

Lately my daughter has been bothered by a guy who can't take no for an answer. We're starting to get concerned for her safety. What should I do?

Hi Worried Mom,

She needs to be very clear. If he can't take a hint, she needs to be as clear with him as possible. It has to be, "I'm not interested. Your not listening is making me uncomfortable." If he still persists, have her talk to campus safety. Rejection isn't cruel—it's giving them a chance to date someone else who will appreciate all their best qualities. Not everyone can handle it. If he doesn't stop, that's a safety issue that needs attention.

(for more on stalking, see tip #22)

Mom Hates Kid's Significant Other

Hey Harlan,

I really dislike the girl my son is dating. She is selfish, manipulative, and completely wrong for him. I wish he could see it. What can I do to get him to see it?

Dear Mad Mom,

So how do you really feel?

(pause for nervous laughter)

Unfortunately parents don't get to pick who their children date. She might not be that horrible. Get to know her better. She might have some good qualities. Even if she's *that* horrible, making an effort to get to know her will give you a little more authority than making gross generalizations. Once you get to know her better, you can have a better-informed opinion. If you don't like her, acknowledge to him that you have no control over who he dates, but express what concerns you. Unless it's abusive, let it go and trust that he will realize that she's selfish, manipulative, and totally wrong for him.

I have time for one more question.

The Breakup

Hi Harlan,

My son just broke up with his girlfriend. He's completely heartbroken and four hours away. This is his first love, and he's incredibly depressed. We don't know if this is a normal breakup or something more serious. How can we help him?

Hi Concerned Mom,

Thanks for the question. If he's so down that you're this concerned, it's worth a visit. If you're close enough to make it for dinner, then come in for the night. Once you see him and see his room, you can gauge just how bad things are. You might also want to connect him with a counselor or therapist on campus so that he has support.

This Concludes Our Time Together

I want to thank you all for coming to this discussion this evening. I look forward to continuing this online and during future events together. Please trust that the values you've instilled in your children and the lessons you've shared over the years will guide them. Expect them to make some mistakes and get hurt along the way, but a student who is supported and understands the sport of taking risks will be able to recuperate and take more risks until he or she finds the very best option—and that will make your kid the happiest kid on campus and happy far beyond life in college.

Have a question? Want to answer another parent's question?

Post your questions and answers; visit *The Happiest Kid on Campus* Parent Forum: www.HappiestKidonCampus.com.

The Tip

Beware of letting your parents (our grandparents) offer us sex advice.

The Story

I was home visiting my eighty-three-year-old grandmother. She asked me if I was dating anyone seriously. When I told her that I had met someone who I had been dating for three months, she said, "Don't date more than four months. You're young; there are too many girls out there to settle on one. You should 'experience' them all." I didn't expect that.

—John, recent grad

* * *

WARNING: You might not want to hear this.

I don't know how to say this to you, but some of your children will have sex in college. In fact, they might already be having sex.

Then again, a lot of students won't want to have sex in college (ahhh, relief). Some will just hear other people having sex in college. This tip is about helping your child have enough information to make smart choices. When it comes to sex, a lot of college students do things they regret. Sometimes it's just an emotional wound. Other times the result is a sexual souvenir or a child before graduation. There are some things your child needs to know. This tip can help you if you're up for sharing it.

In my opinion, parents do not need to know anything their child drinks, does drugs, or has sex. Their children are adults and can make their own decisions about those things.

—Isaac, junior

I had sex for the first time at college. I was never told to make sure to go to the bathroom after sex. A few days afterward I started to have excruciating pains down there. Immediately I assumed I had caught an STI, so I was freaking out and went to the nursing station, and it turned out to be a minor urinary tract infection. Even though I was relieved that it was not an STI, I was still embarrassed about the whole situation. Had I known about going to the bathroom afterward, I would have saved myself a few days of stress and pain.

—Hannah, SUNY Oneonta

One more warning: not all college students want to hear what a parent has to say about sex. Some students think it's none of your business. Even so, sharing what you know isn't telling them what to do or what not do. This tip isn't about how you can find out what your child is or isn't doing. It's just about making sure he or she has the right information to make the choices he or she won't later regret.

A VIRGIN CELEBRATION

Here's something you won't expect me to say: there are a lot of virgins in college. There are a lot of students who are choosing to wait. It's a trend I see on campuses across the country. Most times the virgins are loud and proud. It's not a secret like it used to be. I always ask students in audiences at my events to raise their hands if they are virgins. I always want students to know it's an option.

Why are students making this choice? Like everything in college, no two reasons are the same. The stories below show some of the different takes students have on why they chose virginity.

THE MALE VIRGIN TILL MARRIAGE

I'm a virgin, and I don't plan on this changing anytime soon. This doesn't mean that I've never fooled around with a girlfriend or anything like that, because I have. I just don't want to go all the way. The biggest misconception people have about virgins is that it's a bad thing. People automatically think that a virgin is a poor, pathetic loser who's so depressed that he can't "get any" that he just sits in his room all day. Some people are just saving themselves as a gift to their future spouse. It sounds kind of corny, I know, but if you're a virgin until your wedding, you can tell your wife that you loved her before you ever met her, and you showed this by not having sex with anyone until now (meaning the wedding night).

—Freshman, Valparaiso University

THE FEMALE VIRGIN TILL MARRIAGE

I am a virgin! And in college I will stay a virgin! I wear a chastity ring on my finger, and it doesn't come off until a guy replaces it with a diamond! I made my decision to stay a virgin when I was sixteen—I wear the ring, and if people ask, I tell them what it's for…it makes a lot of people uncomfortable. Guys are just like, "Okay, I was just making small talk." But I like to get the awkwardness out of the way so there is no confusion later. I run across three types of guys' reactions. A lot think it is really cool and are impressed—they look at me like I'm on a pedestal or made of glass. Others ask if I'm going to be a nun and think they can't approach me. Others make it their mission to change my mind—be the first to get in my pants! I really respect Northwestern and the way they handle the whole thing. There are no rules about the mixing of sexes. We are respected in our decisions. I actually wrote an essay for my application here about my chastity ring and being a virgin—and I got in! So it is something talked about here, and I feel respected.

—Freshman, Northwestern University

THE VIRGIN, FOR NOW

I am still a virgin. I am not abstinent and do not plan on waiting until I am married. I do not even know if I will ever get married, but I most certainly would never marry someone I have not had sex with, because I think you don't have a complete perspective of who that person entirely is without that experience. I think that sex today is seen as "no big deal," and I believe that the youth of today do not consider the emotional and attachment aspects that go along with having sex, and I believe that for this reason many people regret losing their virginity the way they did. There are a few HUGE misconceptions about virgins my age. First of all, many people think we are abstinent, but that is not always true—some people are simply waiting for the right person and deciding to take their time and wait it out in order to assure that they do not do something they regret. Another is that we are prudes and unwilling to explore ourselves sexually. My answer to this is do not judge a book by its cover.

—Freshman, Ohio State University

But even if your child has made this choice, that doesn't get you off the hook for the sex talk! Yes, the likelihood of getting pregnant is next to nothing, but sometimes virgins can be sexually active—it's just the vaginal part that is off limits. Thus, they are just as much at risk of getting sexually transmitted infections (or STDs). Plus, the students who aren't saving themselves for marriage might just lose their virginity during the college years. So even if your daughter is a virgin now, even if she plans to be when she graduates, your child needs to have a sex talk too.

I went my entire freshman year in college holding on to my virginity. I ended up losing it the summer after my freshman year with one of my good friends from back home. We had dated on and off throughout high school, and we've always had feelings for each other, but we just didn't want to be tied down to a long-distance relationship (tangent!). Anyway, I did it with him, and I think because he was a really good friend who I could trust, I don't regret it. I don't feel any special attachment to him, which is weird, but I am glad. I was nineteen before I lost my virginity, and nowadays it is becoming rare to even wait that long. I have now had sex with six people. I'm not proud of all of them, but I don't really feel bad about any of them. So I consider myself lucky.

—Junior

THE SEX TALK...

"Son, it's time I told you. I got genital herpes my freshman year in college...And it wasn't from your mother. Yes, she's known since we met, but I wanted you to know too. Let's just say it wasn't what I expected to bring home with me for Thanksgiving break. Fair warning. It's out there..."

(awkward pause)

Kid runs out of the room to Q-tip his ears, hoping to rid himself of what just entered his head.

Talking about sex can help your child make better choices. Parents are the most powerful influences on their children. You have an opportunity to get them essential information that can help them get help before they need it. Even if they don't want to hear it, they will listen (assuming their iPods are at a low enough volume). But for you to be able to help them out, it will help to have the latest and greatest information. (And I understand that the whole idea of a sex talk might make you uncomfortable or might not be compatible with your faith. If so, you can always have the talk indirectly—share this information with your child, and tell him it's so he can pass the word along to other friends.)

For example, if you know that one in five college-age students has genital herpes, you can mention this after meeting five new friends (whisper: "I wonder which one has herpes; you know one in five has it"). If you know that chlamydia is easily transmitted and can have no symptoms, you can ask if the health center offers pap smears (because any sexually active woman needs a regular pap). As a parent, knowing that two-thirds of sexually active women are on birth control, you might want to think twice before having your child sign a HIPAA waiver—if they know you know it all, they might be less likely to get the help they need.

As you read those STI statistics, you may be wondering, "How can so many intelligent students open themselves up to so many risks?" I see it as being connected to this whole concept of living in a world of options. Too many times students have sex because they don't think they have options. When sex presents itself, it's hard to say no when you don't know if and when the opportunity will arise again. It's hard to stop in the heat of the moment and say, "Let's get tested this week and have sex next week," when you don't know if the person you're with will want to have sex next week. Not knowing there are options means being impatient and not communicating clearly.

Another reason why smart students make regrettable choices is that it's connected to the Universal Rejection Truth and the need to be accepted. Having sex with someone means being accepted (at least for a good thirty seconds). Newer students want to be accepted. The student who can give the world permission to not always appreciate him or her doesn't need to try so hard. And that means being able to go slowly and make well-thought-out decisions.

TIME FOR THAT SEX TALK

So how do you have the sex talk? There is no one best way—you should communicate the information to your child using the ways and styles you've found best to teach and communicate with him or her about anything else in your life. To help you out, though, here are some things I know do work well:

START WITH A TENSION BREAKER (A LITTLE LEVITY HELPS):

- Suggest she turn up her iPod so she doesn't have to listen to the sex talk.
- Tell him the only souvenir he should bring home is a sweatshirt or a T-shirt—no herpes, please.
- Mention that a dorm room is too small for a crib. Plus, the crying would keep her roommate up.

THEY HAVE THE POWER (WHETHER YOU LIKE IT OR NOT):

- Acknowledge to your child that he has the power to do whatever he wants, and make it clear that he lives in a world of options. This is the truth. He can have no sex or as much consensual sex as he wants. While you hope he doesn't have sex with everyone he meets, it's his personal decision. You just hope that he doesn't rush into anything, makes safe choices, and is always able to be honest with himself and his partners. By putting it in these terms, you're making it clear that he lives in a world of options and that you hope he will make the healthiest choices.

But regardless of how you do it, the important thing is that you get across the key information in this section. The information below is not a script. Rather, it's information that time and time again I've seen students lacking. Some learn it too late.

So learn the information below, and take every opportunity to pass it on to your child. Perhaps you can share some of this information as situations present themselves. Should there ever be a story about someone cheating or sleeping around (not that this ever happens), you can use it as a chance to throw in some facts and statistics. This can always make for good conversation for the ride to school.

> I bought an economy-sized box of condoms and sold them to people for five dollars apiece when people knocked on my door in the middle of the night.
>
> —Melissa, junior

WHAT TO TALK ABOUT WHEN YOU HAVE THE TALK(S)

NOTE: If you believe in promoting abstinence only, or if sex before marriage isn't compatible with your faith or culture, or if birth control is not compatible with your beliefs, please change this to fit your values.

Avoid Regrettable Sex

The way to avoid regrettable sex is to be honest and go slowly. People go too fast because they don't think the sex will be around tomorrow (that's not a good reason to have sex). If they can't be honest and open before sex, it's only going to get complicated later. If someone can't be honest, it's wrong. It someone feels pressured, it's wrong. If someone can't talk about his or her history, it's wrong. Making it right means being honest and knowing it's 100 percent right. The message—moving too fast and not being honest lead to regrets (and itching, burning, and children).

Risks and Prevention

There are emotional risks and there are physical risks of sex. Anyone who thinks having sex isn't emotional hasn't had sex, or has had unhealthy sex. Sex void of emotion always becomes emotional at some point. When it comes to the physical risks, sexually transmitted infections and diseases are everywhere on campus (see list below). Students need to know that burning, pain, discharge, trouble urinating, a late or missed period, or anything unusual needs to be addressed. Then there's the risk of pregnancy, what to do about birth control, and who to talk to if they need help and can't talk to you about it. I've also included an entire section on birth control and pregnancy scares that can also be helpful to share with your child.

COMMON COLLEGE SEX SOUVENIRS WORTH MENTIONING

Genital Herpes: According to the Centers for Disease Control and Prevention, in the United States one of every five teenagers and adults is infected with genital herpes. Women are more commonly infected than men, and it is estimated that one of every four women has herpes. Condoms can help prevent infection, but can't eliminate the risk. Once infected, the virus is always present. It's the lifetime sexual souvenir.

HPV (human papillomavirus): HPV is the virus that causes genital warts. It's one of the most common causes of sexually transmitted infection (STI) in the world. Health experts estimate there are more cases of genital HPV infection than any other STI in the United States. Genital warts are very contagious. HPV can be transmitted during oral, vaginal, or anal sex with an infected partner. It can also be transmitted by skin-to-skin contact during vaginal, anal, or (rarely) oral sex with someone who is infected (virgins beware). Like herpes, the virus is always present once a person is infected. HPV can be a precursor to cervical cancer.

Chlamydia: Referred to as the silent STD, because there can often be no symptoms, chlamydia, a curable sexually transmitted infection (STI), is the most frequently reported bacterial STI in the United States. It is estimated that there are approximately 2.8 million new cases of chlamydia in the United States each year. Chlamydia cases frequently go undiagnosed and can cause serious problems in men and women, such as penile discharge and infertility, respectively, as well as infections in newborn babies of infected mothers.

HIV/AIDS: The U.S. HIV/AIDS epidemic began in 1981 and continues to disproportionately affect minorities, men who have sex with men of all races, women, and youth. More than 1 million people in the U.S. currently are living with HIV/AIDS. Twenty-one percent of those infected with HIV are unaware of their infection. In 2006 there were approximately 53,600 new HIV infections, with the highest proportion among African Americans, despite the fact that they make up only 12 percent of the U.S. population. HIV-positive students who are unaware of their infection are serious risks that most students don't think about.

Gonorrhea: Gonorrhea, a curable sexually transmitted infection (STI), is the second most commonly reported bacterial STI in the United States, following chlamydia. In 2006, 358,366 cases of gonorrhea were reported to the Centers for Disease Control and Prevention (CDC). When examining race and ethnicity, age, and gender, the highest rates of gonorrhea were found in African Americans, 20 to 24 years of age, and women, respectively. Gonorrhea can spread into the uterus and fallopian tubes, resulting in pelvic inflammatory disease (PID). PID affects more than 1 million women in this country every year and can cause tubal (ectopic) pregnancy and infertility in as many as 10 percent of infected women.

Hepatitis B: Hepatitis B is a contagious, acute disease of the liver that may become chronic. Hepatitis B virus can be found in the blood, semen, vaginal fluids, and other body fluids of infected people. Transmission happens when infected body fluids enter another person's body.

Syphilis: This bacterial infection initially causes genital ulcers (sores). If untreated, the disease will progress to more serious stages of infection, including blindness and nerve damage. Although syphilis rates in the United States declined, the number of cases rose from 5,979 in 2000 to

9,756 in 2006. In a single year, from 2005 to 2006, the rate of syphilis jumped 12 percent.

WHERE TO GET TESTED

The campus health center will often offer STI screenings, free condoms, and counseling. They usually have inexpensive prices. If the health center doesn't offer screenings, the center will refer students to local clinics that have a relationship with the school. In addition to campus services, there are local clinics, home testing, and websites that can connect students to resources (I've posted links on my website to pass along to your students).

For more information on STIs, visit http://www.cdc.gov/std/default.htm

For state-by-state reported STDs in young people 15–24 visit: http://www.cdc.gov/std/stats/by-age/15-24-all-STDs/default.htm.

Source: http://www3.niaid.nih.gov/topics and http://www.cdc.gov/std/default.htm.

Birth Control and Pregnancy Scares

Source for birth control statistics in section: Fall 2009 American College Health Association, National College Health Assessment

When mentioning condoms, birth control, and abstinence, the following information, facts, and statistics can give you some credibility and information they might not know.

Condoms

Condoms can help reduce the risk of spreading STIs, but do not fully protect someone. Approximately 69 percent of females and 61 percent of males reported using male condoms. When it comes to birth control, condoms used correctly can have a low failure rate (around 2 percent). Condoms used incorrectly can have as high as a 17 percent failure rate (scary). Considering that alcohol is often a factor in sex, incorrect use of condoms can be common. This is one more reason to mention the risks of alcohol and sex. Most students are using contraceptive and condoms.

Birth Control

While there are shots, rings, sponges, birth control pills, and the withdrawal method, the pill is the most popular form of birth control (62.7 percent of sexually active females reported using birth control pills [monthly or extended-cycle]). While the pill can help prevent pregnancy, students need to be reminded that this doesn't protect either partner from STIs. There can be side effects and costs to consider.

Waiting, Abstaining, and Choosing Carefully

This might surprise parents, but according to the Fall 2009 American College Health Association, National College Health Assessment, 34.5 percent of college women and 33.4 percent of college men reported having no sexual partners over the past twelve months. This idea that not everyone is having sex is a powerful message that can help students wait and know they have options. The longer a couple waits to have sex, the better they can know each other's sexual history and, even better, develop a relationship built on trust and a strong emotional connection.

Pregnancy Scares

Good kids make mistakes. Every year there are stories of students who get pregnant and hide their secrets because they are too afraid of parents. Being a couple hundred miles and a few hours away from home can cause students to do unimaginable things.

Tragically, in February 2009 the following situation happened at the University of Arizona. A student got pregnant and hid the pregnancy from her friends and family.

POLICE: BABY BORN IN UA DORM FOUND IN BAG, GASPING FOR AIR

"The full-term baby delivered by a UA student in a dorm was found in a bag at the foot of her bed, gasping for air, police say in an interim complaint.

The University of Arizona sophomore was arrested on a charge of attempting to kill her newborn son..."

—*Arizona Daily Star*

I happened to meet some of the residence life staff who helped with the situation. No one knew the young woman was pregnant nor could anyone imagine this would happen.

It's a tragic reminder to make sure your child knows that there are people, places, and resources ready to help. Make sure she knows that no matter what happens, you will be there to help. Students can easily forget that when they are in trouble.

If you have any preferred places where your child should turn, pass them along. She needs to know that she is not alone.

- 14 percent of sexually active college students reported using (or reported their partner used) emergency contraception ("morning after pill") within the last twelve months (male: 11.6 percent; female: 15.0 percent).
- 3.3 percent of college students who had vaginal intercourse within the last twelve months reported experiencing an unintentional pregnancy or got someone pregnant within the last twelve months. (male: 3.1 percent; female: 3.3 percent).

IT'S ALL ABOUT CHOICES AND TRUST

At the end of the day, when sex is something that comes up and becomes available, trust that your son or daughter will make the choices that reflect the values you've instilled in him or her. If your student makes mistakes, trust that he or she will learn from them. A student who lives in a world of options and is engaged in campus life will be able to make strong choices that will make you proud.

QUESTIONS AND ANSWERS

Q: What's the best and the worst sex advice parents have given students?

A: The best advice is honest advice, but not too graphic. The worst advice is no advice. Parents are still the number-one influence on their children's lives. To help guide your sex talk, I've included the best, worst, and most embarrassing advice from parents, as reported by students.

THE BEST ADVICE FROM MY MOM OR DAD

- "No glove, no love."
- "If she sleeps with you on the first date, she's done it before (works both ways)."
- "Here's a box of condoms and some lube; don't tell me anything. I don't want to know."
- "Telling me how emotional sex can be and that no one is admitting it."
- "I'm against sex before marriage. But make sure to use a condom if you do have sex."
- "Unless you are in the hospital or jail, I don't need to know."
- "Pee after sex. It's the best way to avoid a urinary tract infection."
- "My parents told me my mom waited for marriage and my dad didn't. They were both just extremely real and honest with me about how much it meant for both of them that it was my mom's first time, and how my dad wishes that it had been his. It left a big impression on me. It's prompted me to wait."
- "That I should check out a sex shop because they sell 'a lot of weird stuff there.'"

THE WORST ADVICE FROM MY MOM OR DAD

- "Wrap it twice and wrap it tight."

- "Handing me a book and not telling me anything."
- "That I was conceived in some hotel in Pittsburgh and my sister on some river in Maine. And whenever we are remotely close to either of the areas on road trips or whatever, they always love to recount the story."
- "My mom told me the night before I left for college that I should measure the way men make love by the way that they eat. For example, if they eat fast and scarf down their food, then that's indicative of how they will treat me in the sack."

THE MOST SHOCKING/EMBARRASSING ADVICE FROM MY MOM OR DAD

- "When I was sixteen my mom told me, much to my shock, that she didn't want me to wait until marriage to have sex, because a couple's sex life can reflect other aspects of their relationship, both good and bad, and that it's something you want to figure out before you tie the knot. She also then said, 'Besides, the first time is awkward! You don't want that for your wedding night!'"
- "Even if she's on birth control, always wear a condom. That's how you were born."
- "PULL and PRAY."

Have a question? Want to answer another parent's question?

Post your questions and answers; visit *The Happiest Kid on Campus* Parent Forum: www.HappiestKidonCampus.com.

TIP #20 THE GAY TALK
When the Truth Comes Out

The Tip

Coming out to a parent is the hardest thing for a child to do. A parent should never suggest that it's his or her "fault," ask where they went wrong, or advocate the idea that their child could become heterosexual. Take it from a guy who came tap-dancing out of the womb.

The Story

Coming out is scary, terrifying even, and it renders a person extremely vulnerable. I've known I was gay since I was really young. I knew I was "different" as early as when I was five or six. Being gay is something you can't change, and coming out is such a huge step. It's perhaps the hardest thing I've ever done. Congratulate your child for their courage. Don't ask why it took so long to tell you or turn their coming out into a sort of interrogation session. The last thing a recently out teen needs to hear is a promise of hellfire and damnation. Reassure your child that you'll love them no matter what, no matter who they are or who they love. Hug them. Tell them you love them. But don't lie to them if it's not automatically acceptable to you. Let them know if you need time to take it in, but also don't

I think about it every day. How do I tell my parents? If I tell them, what will happen? I fear that my parents will disown me, hate me, but most of all stop loving me. I am afraid of breaking their hearts. I am so afraid of telling them that I cry every time I think about it. I know I will eventually tell them, but that time isn't now. I know that once I tell them, it's going to take a lot of getting used to, but I don't want to lose my parents either.

—Male, sophomore

leave them hanging for a long period of time. Get educated. Do some soul-searching. Your child is your child no matter what, and they will always be your child, gay, straight, tall, stout, purple, etc. To show some support, perhaps go out and buy a book about having gay children, go to a local PFLAG (Parents and Friends of Lesbians and Gays) meeting (www.pflag.org is a great resource), or visit the site http://www.gayfamilysupport.com.

—Rich V., junior

* * *

THEY MIGHT HAVE A SECRET

Your child might be gay, lesbian, or bisexual. If so, you might not know it. Or you might suspect it but not want to admit it or pressure her to share it until she's ready.

In either case, many of you have children who are keeping it a secret from you. I know, because they write to me looking for help. I also hear from them on campuses all over the country. They are often "out" with their friends but playing it straight when they are home. They are so afraid to tell you. The reason is that no one wants to be rejected by the people they love the most and want to be loved by the most.

How you feel about whether or not your child is gay is too personal for me to influence. All I can say is that so many children are secretly living in pain because they think their parents can't handle the truth. It might have been something you said in passing, a harmless joke about a friend or relative. It might be that you're from a small community and it would be too hard for you to tell the neighbors. It might be your spiritual beliefs and the fact that being gay or lesbian conflicts with your faith.

No matter how you feel about it, this is the best advice I can give you: if you want to be a parent who has the happiest kid on campus, give your son or daughter permission to be who they are. Let them know in the clearest terms that you will always support and love them regardless of their sexual orientation. Have the conversation when you're talking about dating. Make it clear that you will love them no matter who they bring home.

> It does not matter what your views and opinions are; you must understand: if your child comes out to you, that is the hardest thing they have ever done. I know it was for me, and I know it was for my GLBT friends who have already jumped that hurdle (and many are still mustering up the courage).
>
> —Male, sophomore

I respect that this might be incompatible with your moral or religious beliefs, and therefore this approach isn't going to work for you. But if you can't accept the idea that your child might be gay or lesbian, do appreciate that there is a community who will accept, support, and love your child. Of course, no one can replace you, but it should be comforting to know that there is more support out there for gay students than ever before. This should help you be able to sleep at night knowing that your child, whom you will always love, is safe.

IF YOU ALREADY KNOW YOUR CHILD IS GAY

This is a good time to be the parent of a gay, lesbian, or bisexual child. So much has changed over the last twenty years, even the last ten years. (It's only been since 1974 that homosexuality was removed from the *Diagnostic and Statistical Manual* [*DSM*] of the American Psychiatric Association!) Growing up gay today means getting a job, having a partner, raising a family, and being protected by the law against hate crimes and violence. There are still people who reject, judge, alienate, and have moral problems with GLBT couples, but in general the world is more accepting than ever.

> **WHAT IS TRANSGENDER?**
>
> A person who identifies with or expresses a gender identity that differs from the one which corresponds to the person's sex at birth
>
> —Source: *Merriam-Webster Dictionary*

Gay and lesbian students can find a home and communities on college campuses across the country. GLBT centers (gay/lesbian/bisexual/transgender) are a part of the campus culture. GLBT clubs and organizations and professional organizations (for undergrads and grads) have taken root. There's even a national gay fraternity. Students looking for support can also find allies on campus (trusted staff and mentors to offer GLBT students guidance and support). Beyond the college years, there are professional networks for gay and lesbian professionals.

Colleges and universities protect gay and lesbian students from harassment or harm on campus. It's serious business—students violating codes of conduct can face expulsion and criminal charges.

The GLBT movement isn't just something you'll find at public schools. It's pretty much everywhere. It's even visible on campuses with strong religious values. For example, if a student attends the University of Notre Dame and is a GLBT student, there's a place for them to find support. The **Core Council for Gay and Lesbian Students** (previously known as Standing Committee on Gay and Lesbian Student Needs) acts as a resource to the Vice President for Student Affairs in identifying the ongoing needs of gay, lesbian, and bisexual students, and assists in implementing campuswide

MISSION STATEMENT

The IU GLBT Student Support Service Office provides information, support, mentoring, and counseling to members of the IU campus and the larger community. We seek to do that through networking, collaborating, education, and outreach in an attempt to create a climate where all members of the community are encouraged to promote and defend diversity.

—Indiana University

IF YOU'RE A PARENT OF A GLBT STUDENT

Encourage your child to connect with the community and support services on campus. Even the most comfortable gay and lesbian students need community. A student who looks online and sees no student group or organization will know that it might not be as easy as he or she thought.

educational programming on gay and lesbian issues.

If you do have a child who is openly gay, encourage him or her to connect to these people, places, and resources. Even if they

> When I told my mother that I was bisexual, she started assuming I had feelings for my friends. When she would see pictures of me on Facebook with other girls, just hanging out, or hugging, she would make cruel assumptions about my intentions. It was very hurtful.
>
> —Name withheld, senior

aren't looking to be active members, it's helpful for them to know that there are people and resources on campus to help support them should a situation come up where they need to enlist the help of the community.

IF YOUR *NOT*-GAY CHILD LIVES WITH A GAY STUDENT

Parents of kids who aren't gay don't always love the idea of their child living with a gay roommate. Likewise, parents of gay students don't always like the idea of their child living with a heterosexual roommate. Heterosexual roommates who aren't tolerant can be impossible to live with. I understand why heterosexual students might have a problem at first, but once they think through it, there really isn't anything to worry about. Considering that approximately one in ten people are gay or lesbian, living with a gay or lesbian roommate can be an important lesson in embracing diversity. The problem is that being a new student means being a little uncomfortable. Anything unpredictable or new can make someone run or attack.

A parent can either elevate the situation or alleviate it.

So here is some information to comfort and guide you and your student:

- Having gay friends and gay roommates will not turn your child gay. Students don't "turn gay."
- If your child is worried about a roommate hitting on him or her, trust that it is unlikely to happen. (Homosexual students know and respect boundaries. Besides, a gay student isn't going to be interested in someone who isn't gay. If your child is concerned, suggest he use the uncomfortable rule in Tip #9 and talk about it.)
- If your child can't handle the situation, have her quietly move to another room.
- If you can't handle the situation, appreciate that it's not your situation to handle.
- Openly gay students are happy to answer questions. If your child has a concern, have him talk about it with the roommate.
- If you're unsure what advice to offer, reach out to a counselor on campus, or contact the GLBT center on campus and ask to speak with the director.

IF YOUR CHILD COMES OUT

You might have been waiting for this to happen for years. Or it might surprise and shock you. Whatever you're feeling, this is what your child wants:

1. Hug him/her (if possible).
2. Don't blame, judge, or try to fix him/her.
3. Get yourself support.

If you're having trouble, reach out to the community of parents who have been down this path. Allow yourself to go through all the emotions. Contact PFLAG (see page 504), a resource that has over five hundred chapters. Visit the website and read some of the stories from other parents. Also, check out their resources. The organization can connect you with other parents and help you answer any questions regarding specific challenges gay students face on campus.

In addition to PFLAG, parents should reach out to the GLBT resources on their child's campus to help identify campus professionals who can help. A parent who knows the resources, support services, and people on campus who can be supportive can be the best resource.

IF YOUR SON OR DAUGHTER COMES OUT TO YOU: TEN TIPS FOR PARENTS

By Doug Bauder
Coordinator of the Gay, Lesbian, Bisexual, Transgender Student Support Services, Indiana University

1. Realize you're not alone. There are lots of parents who have discovered this about their children. And it's really not about YOU—what you have done or not done. It just is.

2. Take time to listen closely to what your son/daughter is saying and to the feelings they are expressing.

3. Don't be afraid to ask questions, but try to do so without being judgmental: Tell me more about how you know this and how long? What can I do to learn more and/or be supportive of you? What do you need from me right now?

4. Seek out resources. Contact the GLBT Office at IU. Become familiar with organizations like PFLAG—Parents & Friends of Lesbians & Gays (www.pflag.org). One of their excellent brochures is entitled "Our Daughters and Sons." Take time to read it.

5. Remember that sexual orientation and gender identity is not a choice. It is a discovery.

6. Recognize that you might not be at all surprised. On the other hand you may go through a very real grieving process (shock, denial, anger, guilt, loss). Don't condemn yourself for your feelings. Find someone with whom to share them, ideally someone who will understand.

7. Be as supportive and nonjudgmental as you can possibly be. (Think about the fact that, in the long run, whatever the neighbors think really isn't as important as the genuine relationship you have with your son/daughter.)

8. Consider the truth that what your son/daughter has just done is an act of trust, and, ultimately, of love. Try to match your child's courage with your own.

9. Realize that you haven't "lost" your child. In fact, this experience could lead to a deeper and richer relationship for you and your family.

10. You are on a new journey. You may well come to recognize it as a gift.

QUESTIONS AND ANSWERS

Q: What should I do if I think my child is gay, but he hasn't come out?

A: Be patient. Make it clear that you will always love him no matter who he brings home for winter break. He'll tell you when he is ready to tell you.

Q: What do I do if my daughter tells me she's a lesbian but doesn't tell my spouse and wants me to keep it a secret?

A: It's not right for your daughter to force you to keep secrets too. Then it's a violation of your relationship with your spouse. Should this happen, enlist the help of a third party (counselor, therapist, spiritual professional) who can help you and your daughter figure out the best approach to tell the other parent.

Q: Is gay or lesbian a phase?

A: No. To label it a phase means you expect it to change. And that's not accepting your child for who he or she is. And that can be damaging.

Have a question? Want to answer another parent's question?

Post your questions and answers; visit *The Happiest Kid on Campus* Parent Forum: www.HappiestKidonCampus.com.

TIP #21 DRUGS AND ALCOHOL
Sober, Wasted, or Addicted

The Tip
Nothing speaks louder than the deafening silence of a disappointed mother or father.

The Story
It was the day of my twenty-first. The day started with a few friends and teammates having lunch and a couple of beers. A few hours later I went to tennis practice and out to dinner with friends. I had a few more drinks. An hour later I went to their apartment and drank more than I can remember. One of the friends helped me back to my dorm room, where he put me in my bed. From here on I can only share what I've been told, because I blacked out. The story is that I ended up in the bathroom puking up my dinner and apparently blood. Some people found me and called the RA, who called the resident director and security. I was then taken to the hospital, where I had my stomach pumped—twice. The next thing I remember was waking up the next morning with a terrible headache and thanking God my one class for the day had been canceled. The next day I had to talk to the director of residence life, the athletic director, the medical coordinator,

my coach, and my teammates. Then came the call that would shape the rest of my life. When my mother answered, I had already started to cry. I told her what had happened. It was a silence that seemed to never end. She didn't get mad or yell. After the silence she said, "To be honest with you, David, I am not happy with the choices you made yesterday. Had I told you not to do it, would you still have done it?" I answered, "To be honest with you, Mom, I don't know, but I might not have gone as far as I did." There wasn't much more for her to say. Knowing that I messed up and hearing the disappointment in her voice made it hit home for me. I was an adult, and I decided that would never happen again.

—David, junior

* * *

PLEASE RAISE YOUR RED PLASTIC CUPS

Have you heard? Some college students drink—some a lot, some a little, and some not at all. They drink on dry campuses (that means there's no alcohol allowed), and they drink on wet campuses (this means alcohol can flow). Oh, and some of them aren't just drinking; they are smoking pot, experimenting with drugs, and taking prescription medicines that aren't their own.

Just because we think we're adults and we're finally "on our own," we don't forget what they taught us. There were a couple of occasions when I was offered weed and even harder stuff, and even though it wasn't my ideal situation, I remembered what my parents taught me, and I'm proud to say I've never even touched a cigarette. To parents: it's scary letting your child go and not knowing what we're doing every minute of the day. But if you really feel like you did your best, we listened. Trust me.

—Kate, recent graduate school grad

And before they even get to college, some students are more experienced with drinking and drugs than you might think. The sidebar on this page shows the most recent data on drug use among twelfth graders (according to the latest information from the National Institute on Drug Abuse and Alcoholism).

You might be a parent who does not have a problem with an eighteen-year-old drinking or smoking marijuana at times. Still, most parents have a hard time swallowing the reality of drugs and alcohol. So much of high school life is about preventing use and abuse, but despite all the effort, some are smoking it, drinking it, and popping it.

And now with your being so far away, there's only so much you can do to stop it from happening. Some schools will let you know if there's an alcohol or drug violation, but that could happen as early as a first violation or as late as a third offense. And even with that, unless your

PREVALENCE OF VARIOUS DRUGS FOR TWELFTH GRADERS, 2009

ALCOHOL 66.2% used in past year/72.3% used in lifetime

MARIJUANA/HASHISH 32.8% used in past year/42% used in lifetime

COCAINE 3.4% used in past year/6% used in lifetime

CIGARETTE 20.4% used in past month/44.7% used in lifetime

CLUB DRUGS/HALLUCINOGENS 4.7% used in past year/7.4% used in lifetime

INHALANTS 3.4% used in past year/9.5% used in lifetime

LSD 1.9% used in past year/3.1% used in lifetime

—Source: National Institute on Drug Abuse

My parents are the type of people who grant me freedom but strongly encourage me to make the right choices. They are the "We Assume We've Taught You Correctly" parents.

—Brett, sophomore

child does something wrong and gets busted, it's hard to know what she's doing and who she's doing it with.

So this tip is about helping your child be smart about being stupid. There are a lot of opportunities to be stupid in college. The goal is to not have it ruin her life or haunt her later.

WHY STUDENTS DRINK AND DO DRUGS

I'm a researcher at the core. I love talking to students. One of my favorite questions is, "Why do you drink or do drugs?" Assuming someone isn't drunk or high, they usually answer with something like, "It's fun." I then ask them, "What makes it fun?" The next answer is, "I don't know, it's just fun." I don't badger them, because the truth is that this is the answer. A lot of students who drink and do drugs don't even understand why they do it. And not understanding why they do it means when they do it, it's easy to get caught up in it. I find that a student who understands the WHY behind drinking and drugs can then learn the HOW—that is, how they can get the same results without drugs or alcohol.

So if they don't know themselves, why do *I* think students drink and do drugs? The following four reasons are the major motivations I've seen draw students to drugs and alcohol:

1. It's easier to take risks
2. The people around them are doing it

3. Because they can
4. It's an addiction

1. It's Easier to Take Emotional and Social Risks

The bigger the student's buzz, the easier it is to take a risk. It's easier to talk in rooms with strangers. It's easier to talk to guys or girls. It's easier to be alone.

You know from reading this book that students aren't the greatest at taking risks while sober. Alcohol and drugs can help numb the pain of the Universal Rejection Truth of life in college. If a student is wasted and a risk doesn't go as planned, he or she can blame it on the drug or alcohol (assuming the kid is sober enough to remember). The more students consume, the less they fear being judged and accepted. Drinking makes it easier to hang out with unfamiliar people, strike up conversations, hook up, or hang out all alone.

What Can Be Done to Help?

If your child can go into the college experience knowing that college is naturally uncomfortable at times, the uncomfortable feelings won't hit him so hard. If he arrives packing patient, realistic expectations and a plan for how to make friends and get involved, unhealthy drinking and drug use won't be as much of an issue. He can have one or two drinks and stop. Over time, the risk of getting caught drinking will become more of a deterrent than the benefits of drinking itself. If he is comfortable with the uncomfortable, the benefits of the high become greatly diminished.

2. The People Around Them Are Doing it

If your child comes to school not knowing anyone and not having a plan, it's easy to connect with the wrong people. Hanging out in a room with people who are drinking and doing drugs and having no other options in terms of friends means she may eventually be tempted to drink or do drugs. It's hard to say no to new friends when you have no other friends.

Even if a student doesn't think it's peer pressure, just being in the room is pressure. That's peer pressure. What's so frustrating is that many times students think everyone is drinking and they start drinking, because they think that's just what new students do in college. While 94.3 percent of students think everyone is drinking, the reality is that, based on the American College Health Association National College Health Assessment, a third of students hadn't had a sip of alcohol in the past month. Knowing that not everyone is drinking means having the option to *not* drink too.

What Can Be Done to Help?

Students need to have several groups of friends and need to know that a lot of students are not drinking. It's just harder to find those students, because they aren't out at the bars or at parties acting stupid. A student who has more than one group of friends will always have the option to make strong choices, and if a few of these groups are related to clubs, activities, and organizations, there will be sober students in these groups. (Another way to find sober friends is to get a part-time job.)

Being involved means naturally meeting other groups of people who do

> ### FIVE WAYS TO AVOID DRINKING AND DRUGS AT PARTIES WITHOUT ANYONE NOTICING
> · Be the designated driver
> · Hold one drink or beer can all night (switch off)
> · Dance, dance, dance, and keep moving
> · Drink a beverage that looks like alcohol
> · Act a little buzzed (no one will know otherwise)

> Sometimes when I don't feel like drinking, I carry around the same cup or can all night. I like to have two empty cans so that I can change at random intervals, and people think I'm drinking because they can't tell it's the same can all night. Just so I'm not pressured. Usually it doesn't work with my friends, because they give me their cans to walk around with, but random people I meet that night never know.
>
> —Ryan, freshman

different things. Living in a world of social options means having the power to say no when something doesn't feel right. A student who has options doesn't have to play drinking games, take a hit of a joint, or get wasted to make friends. You can remind your child that most students are just having zero, one, or two drinks.

It takes time to make the right friends. In the meantime, check out the sidebar on the previous page and share with your child the five tips to avoid drinking and drugs at parties without anyone noticing.

> My parents told me to do whatever I wanted to, but to always think. For some kids this might have been the golden ticket to a lifetime of drug use, but the idea that my parents were giving me freedom in my choices made me want to stay clean. It made me want to make them proud.
>
> —Melissa, sophomore

3. Because They Can

For the first time in her life, your child will have access to whatever she wants. If she is living on campus and sleeping on campus, you will never know. She is accountable to no one other than herself (unless she gets busted). She will make adult decisions with adult consequences. Some students will experiment. Some students will be able to

I'm a 4.0 student. I'm the leader of one of the most active and respected groups on campus. I smoke marijuana and drink alcohol.

—Student from Texas

handle it, but others will get into trouble.

What Can Be Done to Help?

Students need to be smart about being stupid. This means having enough information to understand the risks to make better choices. It means if they are stupid they shouldn't be so stupid that they risk getting expelled, arrested, hospitalized, or worse. If any of these things happen, that's a sign something is out of control. This

My parents just said to be smart about drugs and alcohol, like everything else in college.

—Caissa, junior

is the time when you and the drug/alcohol educators on campus can intervene and get your child the professional help he or she needs. There's a very important distinction—students who do stupid things need to be supported. Instead of blaming them, they need help and need to know that it's safe to reach out to you to get it.

In the meantime, talk to your child about what it means to be smart about being stupid. These are the things they need to hear:

The best advice my folks ever gave me about drinking, which I think applies to things both alcoholic and not, was: never take a drink that you did not open or pour for yourself with your own two hands. Never leave your drink sitting on some random table, even if you're sitting right next to it. Always take your drink to the bathroom with you. Honestly, I have never gotten bad advice from my parents about drinking.

—Bob, junior

- **CONTROL YOUR ALCOHOL (AND DRUGS) AT ALL TIMES:** There are people who will slip date rape drugs into drinks. New students are often the target of predators. It happens at parties, at bars, in houses. Tell your child to never set a drink down and never take a drink that has been opened by someone else.

- **KNOW WHERE THE STUFF IS COMING FROM (ESPECIALLY DRUGS):** Drugs pass through many people's hands. Alcoholic punch that is made in big buckets can contain grain alcohol. A glass or two can be too much.

- **BEWARE OF DRUG INTERACTIONS:** Never mix alcohol and drugs. Students who pop pills need to know that it can be lethal. Students on prescription drugs or antidepressants need to be extra vigilant.

- **DRINKING GAMES CAN BE VERY DANGEROUS AND STUPID:** Drinking mass quantities of alcohol as part of a game can send you to the emergency room. Avoid playing and avoid having to test your limits. If you do, only do it with trusted friends. (By the way, if you see a Ping Pong table without a net, this isn't a new form of Ping Pong—it's beer pong.)

- **IF YOU'RE DOING STUPID THINGS, DO THEM WITH FRIENDS YOU TRUST:** Explain that if he blacks out, freaks out, or can't find his way home, a trusted friend will help keep him safe. Strangers might rob, hurt, or abandon him.

> My parents told me to never drink the punch. You never know what's in it.
>
> —Katie, freshman

- **EVERYONE WHO ARRIVES TOGETHER LEAVES TOGETHER:** Never give anyone the benefit of the doubt when drinking or doing drugs. Have a system to make sure that no one is left alone or left behind.

If you are going to drink, just make sure you have someone to cart you home at the end of the night, and make sure that person has your keys and cell phone and knows where the hell to bring you in the morning.

—Chrissie, junior

- **NEVER GET INTO A CAR UNLESS YOU'RE SURE THE DRIVER IS SOBER:** Remind your child that one drink is driving under the influence. According to the Fall 2009 American College Health Association National College Health Assessment, 25.6 percent of students admitted driving after having any alcohol (students reported behavior over the past thirty days). There is nothing more dangerous than getting behind the wheel after drinking. There are free cab services and campus ride programs that you can let your child know about. (Sometimes it's the sober kid who has to take

> **FACT:** More than 97,000 students between the ages of 18 and 24 are victims of alcohol-related sexual assault or date rape. NOTE: The victim of sexual assault or date rape is NEVER to be blamed, even if he or she has been drinking.

the cab, because everyone else has been drinking.)

- **IF YOU GET ARRESTED, DO NOT KEEP IT A SECRET:** Students sometimes get arrested or written up and hide it from their parents. They don't understand that pleading guilty to a crime can leave a lifetime mark on their record, leave them without a license, get them expelled, or make them ineligible for federal financial aid. Schools often offer legal services, but the counsel students get might not prevent long-term consequences that can creep up through their lives. Hiding an arrest from parents and having a felony record can be devastating.

- **NEVER GET INTO FIGHTS:** Students get drunk and get mouthy. Every year I read articles about college students who drink, get into fights (usually with people who are not from campus), and get beat up, stabbed, or shot. It's so tragic, but it happens every single year. No fighting—ever.

- **NEVER WALK HOME ALONE:** Women and men should never walk home alone. Drunk and wasted people are targets for crimes. Also, sometimes wasted people can't find their way home. Falling into a body of water, getting hit by a car, or falling asleep outside in freezing weather can happen.

- **AVOID DRUNK SEX (EVEN IF YOU'RE SOBER):** It's hard to know if it's consensual sex if one or both people have been drinking. If a partner is too drunk to say anything, it's not consensual. Also, condoms can be used improperly when a person is wasted (if they're used at all). And discussing a person's sexual history doesn't usually come up when someone is wasted.

> D.A.R.E. was enough education for me. And I guess they were right. I have no desire to do any of that garbage.
>
> —(On www.DARE.com)

- **VOMITING BLOOD = SEEK IMMEDIATE MEDICAL ATTENTION:** My college roommate vomited blood. He didn't seek help right away. Eventually we forced him to get help. It turned out he had ruptured his esophagus and was hemorrhaging. He needed emergency surgery. He survived, but only because he was forced to get help.

- **DO NOT GET PHOTOGRAPHED OR RECORDED ON VIDEO DOING ANYTHING ILLEGAL OR EMBARRASSING:** Facebook, MySpace, and cell phones have made it easier than ever for students to be photographed or recorded on video doing something illegal or embarrassing. Once caught on camera, there's no way to hide it or cover up that proud keg-stand moment.

  FACT: Unsafe Sex: 400,000 students between the ages of 18 and 24 have had unprotected sex, and more than 100,000 students between the ages of 18 and 24 report having been too intoxicated to know if they consented to having sex.

- **NEVER SELL DRUGS (NOT EVEN A LITTLE):** The moment a student sells drugs is the moment he risks getting arrested, getting expelled, and losing all federal aid. Every year students get arrested for drug deals.

- **DRINKING AND MISSING CLASS IS MORE THAN STUPID:** Being hungover and missing class is the same as being hungover and not going to work. If class is work, missing class because of drinking is stupid and won't make anyone smart.

- **WHEN IN DOUBT, CALL FOR HELP:** If your child can't tell if someone she's with is too wasted, that person needs professional medical attention. At the least, the paramedic or 911 operator will instruct your child how to determine how serious the issue is. If anyone gets mad because your child calls, that person is sick and needs help.

> **FACT:** About 25 percent of college students report academic consequences of their drinking, including missing class, falling behind, doing poorly on exams or papers, and receiving lower grades overall.

· **YOU ARE ALWAYS THERE FOR THEM:** Remind your child that you are always there for him. You might not always agree with his choices, but you will always be there to help and support him. Kids can never hear it enough.

WHAT YOUR DAUGHTERS NEED TO KNOW

· Women are generally smaller than men. Weight effects the distribution of alcohol. Therefore, a woman who drinks the same as a guy and weighs less will feel the effects faster than a guy.

· Women have a lower total body water content then men. Therefore, women achieve higher concentrations of alcohol than men. Think about two glasses of water—one is filled to the top and the other is filled with far less. Pour the same amount of alcohol in both, and the one with less water will have a higher concentration of alcohol.

· A woman's ability to metabolize alcohol can be affected by her menstrual cycle. Ovulation and just before menstruation are times of the highest BAC when drinking. Also, there's evidence that birth control pills can impact the rate alcohol is metabolized, meaning a woman on birth control may remain intoxicated longer.

· Women absorb alcohol in the bloodstream faster than men. The enzyme ADH breaks down alcohol. Women on average have 25 percent less. As a result, more alcohol enters the bloodstream.

—Source: The Bacchus Network (www.bacchusgamma.org)

4. It's an Addiction

Some students go too far. They can't recognize when innocent fun turns into dependence or an addiction. It's hard to know something is wrong when their new friends are doing the same thing. The hope is that there will be enough warning signs and people outside of their social circle to help them see that there's a problem and get them the professional help they need before long-term damage is done.

What Can be Done to Help?

If you have a history of alcohol or drug abuse, tell your child. Knowing that she may have a predisposition can mean having a higher level of awareness and making better choices. Experimenting isn't "just fun" when the stakes are so high.

Students who get arrested, fail a lot of classes, hurt themselves, hurt other people, or are hospitalized are in need of help—not blame or guilt. A lot of parents feel like a child's addiction is a parent's failure—it's not. There's new research indicating that addiction may be a brain disease. Sometimes mental health issues can surface during the college years. Drinking, drugs, or addic-

> My mom told me drinking games were a big no, that they were only acceptable if I wanted alcohol poisoning.
>
> —Jessie, freshman

tive and destructive behavior can be a byproduct of those issues. Before blaming, guilting, or talking about wasted money and opportunities, get your child treatment so that she can figure out why this happened and how it will never happen again. Getting to the source means helping your child become the happiest kid on campus.

Drug abuse symptoms include:

- Failure to fulfill major role obligations
- Legal problems
- Use in situations that are physically hazardous
- Continued use despite interpersonal problems

The term dependence (addiction) includes:

- Taking drugs in larger amounts than intended
- Inability to cut down drug use
- A great deal of activities necessary to obtain drugs
- Continued use despite knowledge of health or social problems

MOST STUDENTS WILL BE FINE

> If you don't want to drink, just flat-out say no. There's nothing wrong with that, and if people want to judge you based on if you want to drink or not, that's their problem, not yours.
>
> —Chrissie, junior

Most students will not overindulge and lose control. Most will have one or two drinks and be responsible. Some will take a puff or a toke. The smartest, brightest, and most ambitious students might experiment with drinking and drugs. Experimenting doesn't mean they are ruining their lives or destined for destruction. Some will manage it with no problem. Most of the time you will never know or hear about it.

This doesn't mean you can't talk about it and make sure your child is being safe when he's being stupid. And if you hear about it, that's when it's a problem. (A minor alcohol or drug offense could actually be a good thing, because it can be the thing that helps him figure out why he's doing it before it takes over his life.)

He can say it's not a big deal, but being *stupid* when being stupid is a sign of trouble. But always, before blaming your child or being disappointed, first find out if there's a bigger issue under the surface.

QUESTIONS AND ANSWERS

Q: What is considered binge drinking?

A: According to the National Institute on Alcohol Abuse and Alcoholism, binge drinking is defined as a pattern of alcohol consumption that brings the blood alcohol concentration (BAC) level to 0.08 percent or above. This pattern of drinking usually corresponds to five or more drinks on a single occasion for men or four or more drinks on a single occasion for women, generally within about two hours.

Q: My daughter has gotten into trouble with alcohol in high school, and I'm worried it will happen in college. What should I do?

A: See if she has a plan for making better choices when presented with alcohol. Ask her why she drinks. Ask her to come up with ideas so she can avoid getting into trouble. Help her create a world of options before arriving on campus. Also, make sure she goes through an alcohol education program. A lot of schools require students (and even parents) to go through such programs. (And for you, make sure it's a campus that will notify you on a first offense.) Also, make sure she knows about all the alcohol resources and consequences that come with drinking. You can also share the tips and stories in this book and in *The Naked Roommate*. This way it's not your voice, but the voice of other students. Peers have a dramatic impact.

Q: My son is afraid of getting caught up in the alcohol culture. What can I do to help him not feel pressured to drink?

A: All schools can be party schools. The most conservative students can party, and the most liberal students can party. But one thing all party schools have in common is that not all students are drinking. When mapping out your son's path, make sure his three ways of getting involved include groups and organizations that will give him a wide range of people to meet. Spiritual organizations, a part-time job, or a fraternity with a reputation for not partying can be options. Make sure he knows that it can take time to find the people who aren't drinking, because they tend not to make as much noise.

Q: My daughter says she doesn't have a drinking problem, but I have a strong suspicion she is in denial.

A: Contact the alcohol education counselor on campus and share your concerns. Let the professional on campus guide you through the system and connect your daughter to the resources. You can also talk with a counselor on campus. If someone tells you they can't discuss your daughter because of FERPA or HIPAA, ask general questions or ask your daughter to give you consent. It might be worth taking a trip to campus.

Q: Is prescription drug abuse on the rise?

A: Yes, it's estimated that 20 percent of people in the United States have used prescription drugs for non-medical reasons. College students are abusing drugs to get high, to improve concentration, to cram for exams, to excel in sports. It a growing problem among college students, and health educators are actively highlighting the dangers and risks.

Have a question? Want to answer another parent's question?

Post your questions and answers; visit *The Happiest Kid on Campus* Parent Forum: www.HappiestKidonCampus.com.

TIP #22 KEEPIN' 'EM SAFE

You Might Be a Little Worried (or A Lot Worried)

The Tip

There are some things you just can't prepare us for.

The Story

It was about 7:30 on a Wednesday night when I had just left a meeting at the Humane Society. I was waiting at the bus stop to hitch a ride back to campus. I usually feel safe by myself at night, but for some reason this night was different. While waiting, I noticed a young man approaching me. Although I was a little nervous, I assumed he was just another student, possibly leaving the meeting I was just at. I ignored him until he came a little closer. I glanced up and noticed he had a strange smirk on his face. I began to turn away when I quite unfortunately looked down toward his pants. He was exposing his genitals, flashing me. In utter shock and disgust I quickly turned away, exclaiming, "Oh, my God!" About a second later, the bus I had been waiting for pulled up, and the young man ran away. I dashed onto the bus and told the driver what happened. He advised that I call the police, and I did just that.

—Rich, sophomore, Point Park University

I know a lot of parents worry about their child's safety (the biggest understatement of this book). Here's something that should put you at ease: the likelihood of your child having a happy, healthy, and safe college experience is exponentially greater than the likelihood of anything bad happening.

It's the truth. I can promise you that campuses are more vigilant than ever when it comes to campus security. The shootings at Virginia Tech and Northern Illinois University have had a ripple effect that has changed procedures, alert systems, training, and the level of sensitivity to safety issues on college campuses.

Security and safety on campus is nothing to joke about, literally. A campus life professional in judicial affairs shared a story with me about a case where a student jokingly referred to a care package from his mom as a bomb. He thought it was funny until law enforcement officials knocked on his door and took him into custody. Safety has gotten that serious.

WANT EMERGENCY ALERTS?

Parents can often be included in a school's emergency alert system. Inquire with campus safety, the dean of students' office, and the orientation office.

Schools are doing everything they can to provide a safe environment. There are hotlines to call, security guards and escorts (not *that* kind) to walk students at night, and foot patrols all around campus. Cameras, guards, and police are constantly surveying students. College professionals are working 24/7 to keep campuses safe.

Keeping your child safe is everyone's top priority. A student needs to be aware of the risks and work to avoid them. This tip explores some of those risks and offers some suggestions to help your child help him or herself.

My mom is what you would call the safeguard parent. It's not that she wants to be overprotective/controlling, but she is just constantly worried about my safety. When I was moving in, she purchased me more than fifteen cans of Mace, and she texts me once a day reminding me to follow my gut and not to be embarrassed to ask campus police to trail me if I feel uncomfortable.

—Sarah, sophomore

WANT CRIME STATISTICS? YOU GOT 'EM!

Curious about crime on campus? Want to know what's happening in the residence halls? Worried about crime in the community?

Run (or walk) to a computer and type in this URL: http://ope.ed.gov/security. What you'll find is the Campus Security Data Analysis Cutting Tool. This tool is brought to you by the Office of Postsecondary Education of the U. S. Department of Education and gives you access to campus crime data. The data are drawn from the OPE Campus Security Statistics Website database—to which crime statistics are submitted annually via web-based data collection, by all postsecondary institutions that receive Title IV funding (i.e., those that participate in federal student aid programs), as required by the Jeanne Clery Disclosure of Campus Security Policy and Campus Crime Statistics

Act. This is a new resource that can give you and your child access to data regarding:

- Arrests on campus, in the residence halls, and in the community
- Disciplinary action on campus, in the residence halls, and in the community (this includes stats on illegal weapons possession, drug law violations and liquor law violations)
- Criminal offenses on campus, in the residence halls, and in the community (includes statistics on murder/non-negligent manslaughter; negligent manslaughter; sex offenses, both forcible and non-forcible; robbery; aggravated assault; burglary; motor vehicle theft; arson)

When you're browsing the latest statistics, appreciate that the figures you'll see don't reflect people who have been convicted. Some of these are just allegations. But knowing that in 2008, 128 robberies, 323 liquor law violations, and 5 sexual assaults were reported can give you information to pass along to your child. Too many times, students don't think it can happen to them until happens. Having the facts can help.

ADDITIONAL PLACES FOR PARENTS TO GET CAMPUS NEWS

- Sign up for your child's school's Twitter feed
- Become a fan of the school's Facebook fan page
- Read the campus newspapers online
- Visit the campus safety website

TAKING CARE OF THEMSELVES

Your child is the one who needs to take care of himself. You can't be there to do it. What you can do is give him the information he needs to know and help him to get the training and tools to protect himself. Mace and a whistle are helpful, but a student who minimizes risks and walks with a sense of purpose and confidence is less likely to be a victim.

Here are the best tips you can give your child, to help him keep himself safe on campus:

- Have the campus security and emergency number programmed into your phone.

> Call the safety escort service. They are 24/7 and it is their job, so they are very happy to help you.
>
> —Courtney, freshman

- Avoid walking alone, especially at night. If you need to walk alone, call security or use a campus escort program.

> I had a late class at night. It would get pretty dark. I would call my mom and we would talk until I got home. It was a good reason to talk, and it made me feel safer during my walk.
>
> —Stephanie, recent grad

- Always walk on the busiest, most well-lit, and most traveled streets. It's worth going a block out of the way to be in a populated area.

> Find people to walk with back from your class, and try to take roads where people are, even if it might be a longer walk.
>
> —Cody, freshman

- Be careful when posting Facebook status updates that give people information about your whereabouts. And never let people know you are alone. Posting, "Feeling bored, alone tonight..."

might seem innocent, but if the wrong person reads it, that message can be dangerous. Especially if a student has his residence hall address and phone number in the profile.

- Use privacy settings on Facebook and NEVER accept friend requests from strangers or people you don't know well. If you do, make sure to avoid posting personal information (no cell phone numbers or addresses).

- Lock dorm room doors and windows. NEVER lend out the key. People have been known to walk in dorm rooms uninvited.

- Be smart about being stupid, and follow the rules on page 521.

- Avoid walking on campus while wearing earphones that cover both ears. It's hard to be aware of surroundings when you can't hear.

- Take a self-defense course on campus (preferably the summer before going to school). While schools don't

Download the "Offender Locator" application on your iPhone and study offenders who live near your dorm or university.

—Jason, recent grad

Lock your dorm room door EVERY TIME you leave it and every time you go to sleep. Even if you're just going down the hall to brush your teeth—lock it. I had a friend get robbed when she was using the bathroom, and another had a creepy guy walk up and down the girls' hall, trying doors to see which were unlocked late at night.

—Beth, recent grad

If you're drinking out of a cup, keep your hand over the top the whole time. Don't let anyone else get you a drink, and if someone brings you an open can/bottle/cup, don't accept it. Don't let your drink out of your sight. Use the buddy system, and NEVER leave a friend.

—Beth, college life professional

require a self-defense exam, it should be a prerequisite required by parents.

- Do not keep violence, threats, or assaults a secret. (Make sure your child knows it's safe to turn to you for help.)
- Always follow your instincts. If something feels wrong, it's wrong. Do not worry about offending or pleasing anyone.

CREATING A SPIRIT OF SAFETY AND SECURITY

By Erin Weed,
Founder and CEO—Girls Fight Back (www.girlsfightback.com)

Even though you won't physically be there to protect your child anymore, there are things you can do to create a spirit of safety and security.

#1: Ask questions about campus security. Take note of how your inquiries are handled. Are they taken seriously or are they blown off? This alone will tell you how committed your college is to keeping you safe. (Get a full list of questions at www.securityoncampus.org.)

- Are campus police sworn officers of the state or just security guards? A good security force consists of both.
- Do the annual crime statistics include reports to the dean's office, judicial hearings, and women's rape/crisis centers?
- Are security logs open for public inspection?
- Does the school ask applicants if they have been arrested and convicted of a crime? If so, are applicants with a criminal history admitted?
- Are bathroom doors in coed dorms secured with master locks for floor residents?
- Are single-sex and substance-free dormitories available?

#2: Encourage good boundary setting. Parents usually dislike when their child says "no" to them, but it's important to encourage young people who are strong in expressing their wants or needs. As they learn it's okay to set boundaries, they will get better at it...and develop a great skill for independent living. Especially encourage your child to set boundaries for themselves when it comes to drugs and alcohol, since a vast majority of campus crime is committed while the perpetrator or victim is under the influence.

#3: Empower your child to be his/her own best protector. Too often, especially with young women, we teach them to rely on others for their safety. While at college, young people need to become self-reliant in case a bad or violent situation arises. Sign your child up for a self-defense class before he/she goes to college. You can find a Girls Fight Back course at http://girlsfightback.com, and a great program for young men is called FAST Defense (http://fastdefense.com).

TAKING CARE OF EACH OTHER

Regardless of their differences, there's an unspoken bond that connects all students. Students must take care of one another. This doesn't mean fixing each other. It means protecting each other. It means alerting the professionals on campus and in the community who can help when there is trouble.

When I think about students taking care of one another, there's a story that comes to mind. A student went to a party, drank too much, walked home alone, and was found the next day. What makes this tragic is that it was winter, and he was found outside the next day unconscious. He died of hypothermia. It was a preventable tragedy. There were opportunities for students to take care of him and stop this, but no one did.

Students need to take care of one another. This means calling the police or paramedics when someone needs help instead of looking the other way. It means anonymously calling the police on a friend who insists on driving drunk. It means your child talking to the director of counseling services when she thinks a roommate, friend, or classmate is exhibiting disturbing, self-destructive, or threatening behavior.

She likely won't do this right away—what she'll do first is complain to you. It's easy for a kid to call a parent and complain. But when you hear about it, encourage her to tell the right people to get help. That is taking care of one another. When in doubt, she should make a call (it can always be anonymous).

A FEW WORDS ABOUT SEXUAL ASSAULT

Sexual assault is something no parent wants to think about, but it's something you need to know about and your son or daughter needs to know about. Some of the statistics say that as many as one in five students will be the victims of rape or attempted rape (some people think that number is high, but the fact is that many cases go unreported).

A child can take every precaution in the world but yet still be a victim. Most of the time, rape happens with an acquaintance, not a stranger. Intelligent, responsible, and vigilant women (and men) can find themselves victims of assault. Or as one sexual assault educator told me: "Harlan, we are survivors, not victims."

Over the years, I've spoken to many survivors of sexual assault. I'm always taken aback by the intense feelings of shame and guilt they feel. Survivors are often so embarrassed and confused. It tears me up inside, because these women feel like they did something wrong when they did nothing wrong.

No one has a right to physically impose himself on anyone, but it can happen to anyone. Smart and responsible women (and men) can be sexually assaulted, and your child needs to know this. This isn't about scaring her; it's about helping her avoid the shame and guilt should the unthinkable happen. She needs to know it, hear it from you, and believe it. This is the truth.

THE SURVIVOR IS NEVER TO BLAME

No matter what someone is wearing, how much someone has been drinking, or how many drugs someone has been taking—the blame is ALWAYS with the perpetrator, NEVER with the survivor. Your child needs to know that you will never judge her or blame her. She needs to know it before anything happens. If she is ever in this unthinkable situation, your words will be there to help guide her to get help.

Make sure she knows how to access a local sexual assault hotline and resources if she ever needs them. Also, make sure she is familiar with the RAINN (Rape, Abuse, and Incest National Network) website and helpline. On the RAINN website (www.RAINN.org), survivors can find live support online (anonymous and free). The phone number is 1-800-656-HOPE.

There are three things every rape survivor should hear: "I'm sorry," "It's not your fault," and "Tell someone." Unfortunately, rape is prevalent on college campuses. Healing begins the minute the survivor tells someone (I promise). College campuses have so many resources to offer survivors, everything from twenty-four-hour staff on call in residence halls to counseling centers, health centers, and the deans in the Student Life office. You don't need to press charges, you don't need to make any choices you are not comfortable with, but telling one of those people is going to help you heal in the long run. It takes a great deal of courage and strength to survive and heal from rape, and it takes a great deal of courage and strength to tell someone you are a survivor. As Audre Lorde once said, "Your silence will not protect you." Protect yourself, protect your friends, and speak up!

— Resident life professional

WHAT IS STALKING?

While legal definitions of stalking vary from one jurisdiction to another, a good working definition of stalking is a course of conduct directed at a specific person that would cause a reasonable person to feel fear.

—Source: www.ncvc.org/src

STALKERS AND CREEPS

Some of you know the terror of stalking. Hopefully your child will never experience that terror. Being stalked can be terrifying and debilitating. And stalking can occur between romantic interests, acquaintances, or complete strangers.

Stalking has reached an entirely new level. The Internet, cell phones, and technology have given stalkers more opportunities to threaten, elicit fear, and make repeated threats. Stalkers can often easily find personal information, cell phone numbers, and addresses online. It's reported that some stalkers now use text messaging and sending devices to repeatedly send threatening messages to a target's cell phone. Some stalkers post inflammatory messages on public bulletin boards and use someone else's information to turn the person they're stalking into a target. These are all reasons why a student should NEVER have a cell phone number or home address posted on Facebook, MySpace, or other social networking profiles.

Fortunately, there are now laws in effect to protect victims. In the 1990s the first anti-stalking legislation was passed. Stalking laws exist in all fifty states. If convicted, stalkers can face felony or misdemeanor (depending on the state) charges.

THE LEGAL ELEMENTS OF STALKING

In most states, to charge and convict a defendant of stalking, several elements must be proven beyond a reasonable doubt: a course of conduct or behavior, the presence of threats, and the criminal intent to cause fear in the victim.

Course of Conduct

Almost all states require that the defendant engage in a "course of conduct"—a series of acts that, viewed collectively, present a pattern of behavior. Some states stipulate the requisite number of acts. For example, Colorado, Illinois, Michigan, and North Carolina require the stalker to commit two or more acts on different occasions.

If your child ever feels she is being threatened or is in fear of a stalker, have her contact campus police and local law enforcement. The issue can be addressed internally through the appropriate judicial procedures and externally through the courts. Your child needs to be very clear that someone's behavior is making her uncomfortable. If the behavior continues, have her enlist the help of the campus and community resources. Never keep it a secret. The professional staff on campus might need to take precautions to protect your child. Sure, the doors are secure in her residence hall, but someone looking to gain entrance can get inside a side door if they are persistent enough.

IF YOUR CHILD IS ARRESTED

I mentioned this earlier in the book, but it's important to say again here: if your child is ever arrested, written up, or in trouble, make sure he knows to let you know. Feel free to let him sit in jail overnight to learn a lesson if that's what you want, but once he's out of the holding cell, he might need a lawyer. I'm all for consequences, but I'm also for getting a student the best legal representation possible. Campus legal services might be able to offer helpful advice, but if your child ends up pleading guilty or being convicted of a crime, it can mean getting expelled, losing federal financial aid, losing his driver's license, and possibly losing his freedom. If he wants to get into a graduate program, work for a government agency, or apply for a job that requires a background check, that minor offense he never told you about because he didn't want to get in trouble with you could end up holding him back in places he never expected. So make sure he knows he can turn to you for help so that a small mistake doesn't turn into a big mistake that follows him for life.

Also, tell him to *avoid fights*! Do a Google search for college students who have been injured or murdered because of fights, and you'll find headlines from campuses across the country. It's usually a student and someone from outside the community who gets into a confrontation after a drunken exchange. These are some of the most dangerous and unpredictable situations. A lot of students don't think fighting is serious, but anyone who assaults another person can be arrested and convicted. Brilliant people with the best grades and brightest futures get arrested and in serious trouble from fighting. It's not a badge of honor; it's careless and dangerous. As a parent, this is definitely something worth mentioning and discussing with your child.

Remind him that if he ever does something he regrets, you will always be there to help. You might disagree with what he's done, you might be incredibly disappointed, but you will always be there to help and guide him.

A HAPPY REMINDER

There are roughly 16 million students enrolled in college in the United States alone. The chance of your child having a life-threatening emergency is remote. College campuses are some of the safest and most secure places in the country. Many are gated with security guards at all entrances. All are patrolled by car and foot on a regular basis. Cell phones mean that every student has the ability to call 911 wherever and whenever he or she feels the need. Campus security and the local police are down the street. Trained professionals are down the hall.

If you have specific concerns, contact the head of campus security, contact other parents, or talk to the dean of students. Whatever your concerns, there are people who share your concerns and are working to protect your children and assure that they are protected, safe, and secure.

But remember that the most important person who can protect your son or daughter is your son or daughter. Giving them the information, tools, and resources to take care of themselves is the most loving thing a parent can do.

QUESTIONS AND ANSWERS

Q: Are coed dorms safe?

A: A strange thing happens when men and women live in the same building—a lot of the men become very protective of the women in their community. Sure, there are some men who have their issues, but in general, women living in coed residence halls tend to feel safe and secure. Plus, while all residence halls have secure doors, what's also comforting is that many residence halls have security at the doors, monitoring who comes and who goes.

Q: How can a student avoid walking alone at night?

A: Most campuses have programs that provide free escort services (just a reminder: not the kind that dress in leather and G-strings) for students. Sometimes escorts and rides are provided by campus security. Other programs enlist students to escort other students at night. Some students might be reluctant to call an escort or get a ride in the shuttle. Encourage them to try it out. Most likely they will be surprised how easy and convenient it can be.

Q: How are students alerted when there is an emergency?

A: Most schools have emergency alert systems in place that send messages to students (and parents) in case of an emergency. Students (and parents) are invited to sign up. Some schools may offer safety awareness alerts that notify students of campus area crimes. For example, here's what the University of Chicago offers students:

Safety Awareness Alerts briefly describe what happened, when, and where; descriptions of the offender are given if the victim's report is sufficiently detailed to aid in identification of a specific suspect. Safety Awareness Alerts do not identify the victim by name, exact address, or university affiliation, nor do they report domestic crimes or crimes where the victim knows the offender.

Emergency Notification System (cAlert): The Emergency Notification System, called cAlert, enables authorized university officials to reach members of the university community through mechanisms other than regular University email and telephones. The new system can transmit short notifications by email to any outside email address, by text message to a cell phone, or by voice message to an off-campus telephone. This system allows the University to contact individuals in case of emergency, a University closing, or some other event that requires rapid, wide-scale notification of the community.

—Source: http://www.uchicago.edu/safety/faq.shtml

Have a question? Want to answer another parent's question?

Post your questions and answers; visit *The Happiest Kid on Campus* Parent Forum: www.HappiestKidonCampus.com.

TIP #23 KEEPIN' 'EM HEALTHY

From Counseling to Cough Syrup

The Tip

Depression doesn't mean there is something terribly, horribly wrong with your child. It just means they need help and your support.

The Story

It all started after I contracted mono about two years ago. It seemed like I never recovered. I had a bad semester (1.9 GPA). It put me in the tank a bit. I never smiled, I wasn't living. I was a shell of who I was before, I had no energy. I stopped loving music. My parents hated seeing that and did anything they could to make me better. My mom said that she thought I might be depressed. I took a screening that Baylor provided. The results said I was probably depressed. After the screening I was called into the university counseling center. At Baylor we get twelve free visits a year, and extra visits are pretty cheap. I was then set up with a psychologist, who set me up with the staff psychiatrist. The psychiatrist did some tests, and I was diagnosed with major depression. My parents were extremely supportive of my going to a psychiatrist. They viewed it as a medical condition, not some sort of punishment or freak disease, or something wrong with me. There was no stigma. They were the ones who suggested I go in for screening. That really *REALLY* helped. I'm still in school. I now take meds every day, surround myself with great friends, and have the best support group I could ever want, my parents.

—Geoff, junior, Baylor University

* * *

College is supposed to be 90 percent amazing and 10 percent difficult. When the 10 percent difficult takes up 100 percent of your child's time, the problem might be more than her not being prepared for what's ahead, being a little homesick, or having a hard time competing at a new academic level. Sometimes there can be bigger issues under the surface. Some students arrive on campus managing mental health issues and other illnesses. Others discover new medical issues during their college experience.

The worst thing they can do is panic and show up at the school to take care of you. You are an adult, and telling your parents that you are sick does not give them license to drive six hours to come give you Tylenol. We can do that ourselves.

—Sterling, sophomore

Being aware that this reality exists and accepting the possibility can help detect and manage these conditions. In this tip we'll explore mental health disorders, addiction, and what happens when your child gets sick.

COMMON COLDS, MONO, AND MEDICINES

There are three rules for helping a sick child:

1. Don't panic
2. Don't come to campus (unless it's serious)
3. Don't call the school or instructors (not your job)

It was the tail end of Parents' Weekend. After a full weekend of showing my family around campus and sleeping very little, I woke Sunday morning in my family's hotel room with a fever, my pillow covered in snot. I felt like my head was enclosed within a hazy bubble and could barely stand up without getting dizzy. I was sick—sicker than I had been in a while, and my family was due at the airport in less than two hours. After a quick team meeting and a phone call to Southwest Airlines, my mom decided to stay with me while my dad and sister headed home for school and work. I lived in my mom's hotel room for the next three days. She brought me soup and my textbooks from my dorm. I took long baths in a real bathroom and slept in a queen-sized bed. When I was feeling up to it, my mom walked with me to class so I wouldn't get too far behind, kissing me good-bye at the door to the lecture hall. Even though I was feverish and congested, it was almost like being in elementary school all over again. But it didn't last. I got better, and soon it was time for her to leave. As she kissed me good-bye before she got in the shuttle that would take her to the airport, she said, "I'm just glad I was here to take care of you." I was glad too.

—Lauren Motzkin, Staff reporter for the *Yale Daily News*

At some point most college students will get sick... and then get better...and then get sick again. That's just what happens. It's just a lot more dramatic when you can't reach out and touch your child's forehead (although video chat can at least let you see him). One thing that can help is knowing that your child has good medical care. The health center can be a great resource, but it's also comforting to have a go-to doctor in the community. The more comfortable you are with your child's medical care,

One time I was sick with the flu, so my boyfriend took me to student health. I called my mom to ask about some information for the forms I had to fill out first. She thought I sounded really bad and disoriented, so she found my boyfriend's phone number from my phone bill and called him to make sure he was taking care of me. I felt like this was a little over the top and a lot embarrassing.

—Katherine, junior

The best thing a parent can do is send a kid to school with a mini medicine cabinet. Three weeks ago I got really sick with an awful cough and fever. I had only brought some ibuprofen. Big mistake! When I went home for the weekend, the first thing I had my mom do was to make me my own mini medicine cabinet with all the meds, cough syrup, and stuff you need when you're sick.

—Caitlin, freshman

Have the number to the local Chinese take-outs near school, and send wonton or noodle soup! Pay for it and have it just arrive to the room as a "free" surprise.

—Patricia, sophomore

the better you can sleep at night. If you're thinking about making a surprise visit to help him heal, it's nice to have a professional opinion (assuming you're authorized to get medical information) before making the trek.

Hearing your child's voice will mean wanting to see the face that goes with it. If you're lucky enough to Skype, seeing that face should help you. This still won't allow you to reach out and touch his forehead. But at least you can rest easy knowing that you sent him off to school with a bucket of medicine, a thermometer, and the essentials. You did send him off with this, right?

Sick kids like to be spoiled. They are big babies. If you can baby your child without visiting him, that makes him feel very happy and loved.

Sick kids don't want parents surprising them or rushing to see them unless they ask for it or a doctor recommends it.

And don't worry—most of them will call when they need you. I was a brave college student who tried to battle it out with mono on my own. That is, until I was so sick I couldn't stand it. I asked my mom to please come and get me. Three and a half hours later, she was there to get me (that was record time). Mom saved me. Your child will let you know when he needs you. Showing up without his asking will just make it seem like you think he can't take care of himself, and that's not the message you want to send. (Although if it's a situation where he doesn't have a roommate, an RA, or anyone to take care of him, you might need to show up uninvited.)

> The least helpful thing my mother does when I'm sick is start over-reacting and thinking I'm going to end up in the hospital and die just because I'm sick and we're in two different states. She didn't trust that Lafayette, Indiana, had a hospital until I sent her a link to the website.
>
> —Jennifer, senior

> I never felt more homesick than the day I had a stomach virus and had to hang out in my room wishing my mom were there to take care of me! It was in the middle of orientation week too, and I hadn't adapted to college yet. It's so much nicer to get sick at home!
>
> —Freshman

One of the biggest obstacles a parent faces when helping a sick child is HIPAA and FERPA. Your eighteen-year-old's medical and academic file may be protected from you. A mom shared a story with me about how her daughter got mono at school. The daughter went to the doctor and couldn't remember what the doctor had told her. She was too out of it to remember. She asked her mom to call and find out what her suggested treatment plan was. When Mom called, the health center wouldn't tell her anything because of HIPAA laws. The person on the other end of the phone did offer to share the information if her sick daughter walked across campus to fill out an authorization. Eventually, the woman allowed a verbal okay from the daughter and released the information.

Just know you must be authorized to get medical information and to get professionals to share sensitive information about your child. If he is sick and you need to communicate with the health care provider, make sure your child has granted you permission.

MENTAL HEALTH: AWARENESS AND ACCEPTANCE

College can be overwhelming and difficult at times. Here's what students are feeling.

WHO FEELS OVERWHELMED?

- 77.4 % of male students reported that they felt overwhelmed by all they had to do any time within the last 12 months
- 91.9 % of female students reported that they felt overwhelmed by all they had to do any time within the last 12 months

WHO FEELS HOPELESS?

- 39.1 % of male students reported that they felt things were hopeless any time within the last 12 months

According to the Association for University and College Counseling Center Directors Annual Survey, in 2009 80 percent of directors reported that they believe the number of students with severe psychological problems on campus had increased in the past year. Ninety-six percent of directors reported that the number of students with significant psychological problems was a growing concern in their center or on campus. Eighty-three percent of centers reported that there had been an increase in the past year in the number of students coming for counseling who are already taking psychotropic medications.

Too many times, problems that come up during college are seen as a student's not caring, being immature, or being irresponsible. But some of the stumbles may be signs of something deeper. Some parents don't want to think about mental health issues, and some don't know to think about it. But all parents need to know and think about these issues.

Even if your child isn't coming to school with a mental health issue, she may start exhibiting symptoms that you need to know about. Parents who are aware and accepting that any child can have an anxiety disorder, depression, attention deficit disorder, or other mental health issues can be on the lookout for these symptoms. For example:

- When mental health issues are on your radar, poor grades, mood swings, and a lack of interest in the things your child once loved can be seen as something more than just the transition to college.
- When mental health issues are on your radar, a student with a history of not getting in trouble who gets written up for drinking violations could be more than a person who is out of control, but a person who is battling a bigger, more serious issue.
- When mental health issues are on your radar, a student who has gained or lost a lot of weight isn't a student who provokes a joke, but rather some concerns because the weight might be a symptom of something much deeper happening.
- When mental health issues are on your radar, a student who is constantly running out of money isn't financially irresponsible and careless, but rather a student who might be buying drugs, alcohol, or gambling.

> Parents can start the conversation about mental health with their children even before they think there are mental health concerns. Open up, let your kids know that you're there for them at all times, that there are issues they may be facing or may face in the future that are affecting their everyday lives and that you are there for them to talk to. Let them know that they don't have to be in crisis to get help, and that you love and support them always.
>
> —Alison Malmon Mahowald,
> Founder/Director of Active Minds
> (www.activeminds.org)

If you ever have a concern, the counseling services on campus should be able to help your child, often free of charge. If you're not familiar with the counseling center, the following information should be helpful:

FIVE THINGS PARENTS MIGHT NOT KNOW ABOUT COLLEGE COUNSELING SERVICES

By Brian Van Brunt,
Director of Counseling and Testing Center, Western Kentucky University, President-Elect of the American College Counseling Association

1. Free. Counseling is often free or at least covered as part of the tuition costs. This expense often costs $75 to $100 an hour for outpatient care outside of the college community.

2. Counselors and psychologists **can** talk to you if they are seeing your student. It requires that your student sign a release giving you permission to talk to them. Talk to your son or daughter and see if they are ok with you checking in with their therapist if you are concerned. Don't pry into their life, but be aware of what is going on if they are struggling.

3. Some colleges and universities may limit the number of sessions your student can access. It may be helpful to find this out before they start therapy.

4. Some counselors are good; some are not. Help your student find a counselor or psychologist who fits best with their needs and personality. Don't expect them to find the perfect connection on their first try—encourage them to try a different therapist if things don't seem to be working out.

5. Therapy isn't just for people with major mental health problems. Most of the students seen in counseling are coming in to talk to a person about everyday problems like relationships, sadness, and stress.

Identifying the Symptoms

How can a parent distinguish between the normal behavior and emotions associated with the transition to college and something more serious? Below are symptoms of common mental health disorders as defined by the National

Institute of Mental Health. (For a complete list, visit www.nimh.nih.gov/health.)

Symptoms of Depression
(source: http://www.nimh .nih.gov/health)

The severity, frequency, and duration of symptoms [of depression] will vary depending on the individual and his or her particular illness. Symptoms include:

If your child tells you he or she feels depressed, don't have the "you'll snap out of it" attitude like most people do. Not everyone snaps out of it, and some of them have a legitimate health problem. Ask if your child thinks he/she needs help, and don't take it lightly. Be as supportive as you can. Offer to help find a good psychiatrist or counselor, let your child know you love him/her, and keep the lines of communication open. Without my parents, I doubt I'd be alive to say this today.

—Melissa, senior

- Persistent sad, anxious, or "empty" feelings
- Feelings of hopelessness and/or pessimism
- Feelings of guilt, worthlessness, and/or helplessness
- Irritability, restlessness
- Loss of interest in activities or hobbies once pleasurable, including sex
- Fatigue and decreased energy
- Difficulty concentrating, remembering details, and making decisions
- Insomnia, early-morning wakefulness, or excessive sleeping
- Overeating, or appetite loss
- Thoughts of suicide, suicide attempts
- Persistent aches or pains, headaches, cramps, or digestive problems that do not ease even with treatment

Symptoms of Bipolar Disorder
(source: http://www.nimh.nih.gov/health)
People with bipolar disorder experience unusually intense emotional states that occur in distinct periods called "mood episodes." An overly joyful or overexcited state is called a manic episode, and an extremely sad or hopeless state is called a depressive episode. Sometimes a mood episode includes symptoms of both mania and depression. This is called a mixed state. People with bipolar disorder also may be explosive and irritable during a mood episode.

Extreme changes in energy, activity, sleep, and behavior go along with these changes in mood. It is possible for someone with bipolar disorder to experience a long-lasting period of unstable moods rather than discrete episodes of depression or mania.

A person may be having an episode of bipolar disorder if he or she has a number of manic or depressive symptoms for most of the day, nearly every day, for at least one or two weeks. Sometimes symptoms are so severe that the person cannot function normally at work, school, or home.

Symptoms of General Anxiety Disorder
(source: http://www.nimh.nih.gov/health)
People with generalized anxiety disorder (GAD) go through the day filled with exaggerated worry and tension, even though there is little or nothing to provoke it. They anticipate disaster and are overly concerned about health issues, money, family problems, or difficulties at work.

Sometimes just the thought of getting through the day produces anxiety.

GAD is diagnosed when a person worries excessively about a variety of everyday problems for at least six months. People with GAD can't seem to get rid of their concerns, even though they usually realize that their anxiety is more intense than the situation warrants. They can't relax, startle easily, and have difficulty concentrating. Often they have trouble falling asleep or staying asleep. Physical symptoms that often accompany the anxiety include fatigue, headaches, muscle tension, muscle aches, difficulty swallowing, trembling, twitching, irritability, sweating, nausea, lightheadedness, having to go to the bathroom frequently, feeling out of breath, and hot flashes.

Symptoms of Attention Deficit Hyperactivity Disorder

Inattention, hyperactivity, and impulsivity are the key behaviors of ADHD. It is normal for all children to be

There are some very bright students whose ADHD was not identified when they were younger. Perhaps their strong intelligence helped them compensate; maybe their schools provided great support or their parents were wonderful at being their children's executive secretaries. But with college and the increased load of tasks that require strong executive functions, these students' ADHD becomes apparent. These students should be evaluated by a suitable mental health professional and encouraged to seek college accommodations.

Students already identified as having ADHD should pursue accommodations through their school's disabilities office even before they begin classes. Many accommodations colleges provide are invisible (like priority registration) and can make the critical difference between failing and passing.

—Stephen M. Butnik, PhD,
Licensed Clinical Psychologist

inattentive, hyperactive, or impulsive sometimes, but for children with ADHD these behaviors are more severe and occur more often. To be diagnosed with the disorder, a child must have symptoms for six or more months and to a degree that is greater than other children of the same age.

Students who have symptoms of **inattention** may:

- Be easily distracted, miss details, forget things, and frequently switch from one activity to another
- Have difficulty focusing on one thing
- Become bored with a task after only a few minutes, unless they are doing something enjoyable
- Have difficulty focusing attention on organizing and completing a task or learning something new
- Have trouble completing or turning in homework assignments, often losing things (e.g., pencils, assignments) needed to complete tasks or activities
- Not seem to listen when spoken to
- Daydream, become easily confused, and move slowly
- Have difficulty processing information as quickly and accurately as others
- Struggle to follow instructions.

Be Aware of Self-Injurers

(source: http://www.nimh.nih.gov/health)

Every year I get flooded with mail from students who hurt themselves. They cut, puncture, and cause physical self-harm. The intense physical pain can cover up the emotional pain of feeling lonely, angry, hopeless, unloved, or excluded.

Self-injurers may also have an eating disorder or an alcohol or drug problem, or may have been victims of abuse. While most self-injurers don't want to commit suicide, sometimes the injuries can lead to illness or accidental death.

Here are signs that your child may be self-injuring:

- Cuts or scars on the arms or legs
- Hiding cuts or scars by wearing long-sleeved shirts or pants, even in hot weather
- Making poor excuses about how the injuries happened

If your child is exhibiting symptoms of any mental health issue that concerns you, do not hesitate to get your child help. At the very least, send your child to the health center or a doctor's office to get a mental health screening. This will give your child some answers and access to support, in case things get worse or other issues surface later in the year.

How Your Kid Can Help Friends Get Help

It's common for students to have a friend or two who is secretly suffering from depression or other mental health issues. A lot of students want to help the friend and fix it. There are ways to help, but most friends are not qualified to fix it. The best advice for someone who wants to help is to get their friend in touch with a professional. This means contacting a residence life professional, a therapist in the counseling office, or a crisis hotline. A lot of students don't think crisis hotlines are for the people who want to help, but they are there to guide them too.

Also, let your child know about Active Minds (www.activeminds.org). Active Minds was founded in 2001 by Alison Malmon after the suicide of her older brother, Brian. In the middle of his senior year at the University of Pennsylvania, he returned home and began receiving treatment for what was later diagnosed as schizoaffective disorder. For years he had kept his symptoms a secret. In the spring of Alison's freshman year at Penn, her brother ended his life. Active Minds is committed to removing the stigma of mental illness and encouraging students to get help. There are more than two hundred chapters across the country. Your child can start a chapter if there isn't one already on campus.

BE AWARE OF FORCED HOSPITALIZATIONS

In some states, a student who shows suicidal tendencies can be hospitalized against his or her wishes. The state of Florida is one of them.

Suicide Prevention

Suicide is the third leading cause of death among fifteen- to twenty-four-year-olds. If you are even a little concerned about your child and suicide, contact the health center, contact the residence hall professional staff, and make a trip to campus. Families with a history of suicide, mental health disorders, substance abuse, and family violence are particularly at risk.

Behaviors Exhibited by People in Need of Help

Feeling hopeless; feeling rage or uncontrolled anger or seeking revenge; acting reckless or engaging in risky activities (seemingly without thinking); feeling trapped—like there's no way out; increasing alcohol or drug use; withdrawing from friends, family, and society; feeling anxious, agitated, or unable to sleep or sleeping all the time; experiencing dramatic mood changes; seeing no reason for living or having no sense of purpose in life; threatening to hurt or kill oneself or talking about wanting to hurt or kill oneself; looking for ways to kill oneself by seeking access to firearms, pills, or other means; talking or writing about death, dying, or suicide when these actions are out of the ordinary for the person.

If you're not familiar with the Jed Foundation, check it out and share this resource with other parents and their children. The Jed Foundation (www.jedfoundation.org) was founded in 2000 by Donna and Phil Satow. After they lost their son Jed to suicide, they discovered that college students and parents are in urgent need of resources to help students, colleges, and parents recognize and address signs of emotional distress and suicide. The foundation started ULifeline (http://Ulifeline.org). This resource launched in 2000 and has become a widely used online resource for college mental health with campus-specific information for over 1,250 schools. The site includes a self-evaluator to assist students in finding help on their particular campus. The site greets students with the message:

"ULifeline is an ANONYMOUS online resource where you can learn more about emotional health and ways to help yourself or a friend if you are struggling with your thoughts or feelings. We ask you to select your school so that we can provide you with information about resources at your school."

Your child's campus should also have a suicide prevention program with hotlines and services. Check the website and make sure he or she has the number, just in case. Another resource to pass along is the National Suicide Prevention Hotline at 1-800-273-TALK (8255). This hotline is helpful for anyone who feels sad, hopeless, or suicidal. It's also open to family and friends who are concerned about a loved one.

I was fourteen when I was first diagnosed with depression. Four years later, I was about to start my first semester at University of New Orleans. My psychiatrist and I decided to start easing me off my antidepressants. A couple of weeks later, Hurricane Katrina hit and disrupted my entire semester and my hometown. I pulled through it as well as I could, feeling down here and there but still feeling like myself, so I continued to decrease my meds as I had been told to.

In August of 2006 I was starting my sophomore year, thankfully at UNO. I had had a lousy summer break because of chronic migraines. I was feeling worse and worse mentally as well, until one day I snapped. I immediately called my best friend, telling him that, though I didn't want to, I felt like dying. I barely had the motivation to get out of bed in the morning. I knew it was back and called my mom. She was incredibly supportive. I have been back on my antidepressants for almost four years now, and I feel like me again.

—Melissa, senior

Who can possibly think that after making a drastic life change, like, say, moving away from home, living with total strangers, eating entirely new foods, and changing one's sleep patterns, a good choice to make would be to stop taking a prescription medication without the advice of a medical professional? Want to get off your meds? Fine. Go to the health center on your campus (that you are paying for) and talk to them! After years of working with college students and witnessing friends and relatives try this move, stopping meds without medical supervision brings three words to mind: Crash And Burn. Make sure starting fresh doesn't include ignoring medical care.

—Erika, housing professional

Make Sure They Stay on Their Meds

There's this phenomenon that happens when a student who was previously on medication goes to college. For some reason there's this sudden feeling that they don't need their meds. It's a fresh start, and that means stopping their meds. But this is absolutely not the time for them to stop. If you have a child who is on meds, make sure he is closely supervised and has a psychiatrist near campus should there be an unexpected situation. If he wants to make changes, make it essential that he is under the close supervision of a doctor on or near campus.

WHAT ARE THE SIDE EFFECTS OF ANTIDEPRESSANTS?

The most common side effects associated with antidepressants include:

1. **Headache**: usually temporary and will subside.

2. **Nausea**: temporary and usually short–lived.

3. **Insomnia and nervousness (trouble falling asleep or waking often during the night)**: may occur during the first few weeks but often subside over time or if the dose is reduced.

4. **Agitation**: feeling jittery.

5. **Sexual problems**: both men and women can experience sexual problems, including reduced sex drive, erectile dysfunction, delayed ejaculation, or inability to have an orgasm.

—Source: www.nimh.nih.gov

WARNING SIGNS OF PROBLEM TEEN GAMBLING

· Carries or possesses gambling materials (dice, playing cards, scratch tickets)

· Missing money or possessions in the house

· Steals from family to get money for gambling

· Uses "other money" (lunch, bus) to gamble; weight loss may become evident

· Personality changes; frequent mood swings

· Gambles to escape worries, frustration or disappointments

· Displaying unexplained wealth

· Unusual interest in sports scores and point spreads over favorite teams and who wins

—Source: http://wellness.missouri.edu/
Gambling/parents.html

The Costs: Make Sure They Know the Facts

A lot of students (and parents) are concerned about the costs of care and won't get help. Most schools offer free counseling and services to students. When students use up the free sessions, the costs can be minimal. Make sure you know what's covered and tell your child what's covered. Therapy can be on a sliding scale. Also, make sure he knows that it's confidential. Unless he is a threat to himself or those around him, care has to be kept confidential—even from you (unless there is consent).

ADDICTION

According to the National Institute on Drug Abuse, addiction is defined as "a chronic, relapsing brain disease that is characterized by compulsive drug seeking and use, despite harmful consequences. It is considered a brain disease because drugs change the brain—they change its structure and how it works. These brain changes can be long-lasting and can lead to the harmful behaviors seen in people who abuse drugs." Teenagers are especially vulnerable to developing addictive behaviors.

In addition to drug or alcohol addiction, other types of addiction can develop during the college years, including Internet addiction, sex addiction, love addiction, gambling addiction, and video game addiction. Addictions can often be associated with other mental health issues. They often interfere with a student's daily routine, causing irregular sleep, affecting grades, causing weight loss or weight gain, and interfering with friendships. Internet addiction, gambling addiction, and sex addiction are all behaviors that are getting increased attention.

College health centers offer programs and groups for a wide range of addictions. A student who is coming to campus with an addiction should make sure help and support are available on campus or in the community.

For a list of hotlines and resources, visit www.HappiestKidonCampus.com.

A HEALTHY FINISH

This tip is about the gritty and real part of college experience that is rarely mentioned. Struggling during the college years isn't always about not trying hard enough or being imperfect; it can be the result of a medical condition. Understanding this can mean exploring problems, getting help, and learning how to thrive regardless of the diagnosis. Self-awareness combined with loving and supportive parents can remove the stigma and turn the unhappiest kid on campus into the happiest and healthiest.

QUESTIONS AND ANSWERS

Q: What are some ways parents can help their sick students?

A: If you can't be there to do the cooking, do the next best thing. Have a local place deliver food. You can even have a grocery store deliver food. Assuming it's just a regular cold or flu, send food. You can also send a care package with the best over-the-counter medications, magazines, and snacks.

Q: When is family counseling a good idea?

A: If you're having a problem communicating with your child, having a third party in the room can make the difference. If she asks you to participate in family counseling, it's absolutely a good idea. If you think family counseling will help, then there is every reason to do it. It's especially helpful when one parent isn't as open and comfortable dealing with mental health issues.

Q: If a student is diagnosed with a mental health disorder, can that student get special accommodations?

A: Yes, a student who has a diagnosis can register with the office of disabilities services. Depending on the illness, special accommodations and support can be made available.

Q: Any other advice for parents with sick kids?

A: Try not to panic. The more you heighten the situation, the more alarmed your child will become. The goal is to help alleviate the tension and teach her to take care of herself, not freak out and scream "Mommeeeeee!"

Have a question? Want to answer another parent's question?

Post your questions and answers; visit *The Happiest Kid on Campus* Parent Forum: www.HappiestKidonCampus.com.

TIP #24 THE STUDENT BODY IMAGE

Gaining It, Losing It, and Being Treated For It

The Tip

Always look for the writing on the wall.

The Story

(Originally published in the *Indiana Daily Student*, by Rachel Stark. The following is an excerpt of the story.)

Ballantine Hall, first floor, across the hall and down a short way from the computer lab, first stall on the left—my go-to bathroom stall. Mondays, Wednesdays, and Fridays when I make this pit stop, I usually get in and get out and on to my gender studies class. This day was different. I pushed through the swinging door and marched to my stall and let my backpack slam to the ground with a thud. Then I noticed it—a large circle of notes in an array of handwriting and colors located right next to the toilet paper dispenser. Oh, typical graffiti, I thought. But this was unusual. I had read the "(So and so) is a slut" and "I hate the world" comments on this stall before—one-liners that we've all read so many times we just roll our eyes when we see them. No, this jumble of notes initially caught my eye because of the large area it consumed on the stall, but what hooked my interest was the one sentence that had triggered a flurry of responses: "I'm becoming bulimic and don't know how to stop." Questions flooded my mind. Who is this woman? Why, of all places, did she reach for help on a bathroom stall? Did she scribble that note on the cold, gray stall after throwing up her lunch? Is she OK?

I was disgusted when I read the first response. "That sucks" was all one person had written. But I read on and realized I wasn't the only one who worried about this woman. The clutter of notes that followed had turned this first-floor bathroom stall into a forum, the writers anonymous but connected. "Don't shut down or isolate yourself...talk to people. Don't feel scared or ashamed. Your true friends will still love you. They won't judge you. Good luck!" The messages were written in red, blue, black ink. Some were in bubbly printed handwriting, some in scribbled cursive. "Ask a friend for help. If they judge you, they're not good friends anyway. (I know...I used to be anorexic.)" Some, like this one, ended with a smiley face. "Don't ruin your life or body! You are beautiful and unique—don't deprive the world of what only you can offer. There are many who struggle with the same battle and win—you can do it! Believe in yourself!" These encouragements captivated me. It became routine to check in to see the latest updates on the stall. "PRAY," one woman had written. With an arrow leading away from the one-word message, another woman wrote, "and take control." Someone went beyond the advice everyone else gave by suggesting a specific person for her to visit: "I would suggest seeing Dr. Stockton at CAPS—she's a great psychologist. But get help before it's too late… Please." One woman seemed to echo my exact thoughts on the stall in two brief sentences: "I love the support people show here. If only it was true everywhere in life."

(To read the complete story, please visit www. HappiestKidonCampus.com.)

* * *

THE STUDENT BODY IMAGE

Some students gain the freshman fifteen, some the freshman fifty, and some come home for Thanksgiving and look like they've taken the all-you-can-eat buffet literally (one parent actually told this to her daughter—no, this is not recommended). And others just look the same but are keeping a big secret inside. This tip explores college eating disorders, as well as regular weight issues, and what you can do (or should not do) to help your child.

EATING DISORDERS ON CAMPUS

A few years ago after a new student event that a student came up to me with an RA after the program and mentioned that she was going to get help for her eating disorder. She had just told her RA her secret. She had been hiding her eating disorder through high school and didn't want to get help because she didn't want her parents to worry about her. Now that she was in college, she was ready to finally face her eating disorder.

A lot of students come to campus with eating disorders that their parents don't know about. And some will develop disorders in college. The lack of control that's part of the college experience can mean turning their focus onto controlling the one thing that is manageable—weight and body image.

> Women and girls are much more likely than males to develop an eating disorder. Men and boys account for an estimated 5 to 15 percent of patients with anorexia or bulimia and an estimated 35 percent of those with binge-eating disorder. Eating disorders are real, treatable medical illnesses with complex underlying psychological and biological causes. They frequently coexist with other psychiatric disorders such as depression, substance abuse, or anxiety disorders.
>
> —Source: http://www.nimh.nih.gov/ health/publications/eating-disorders

Spotting the Symptoms

Hiding eating disorders from a parent can be easy in college. A child can eat during short visits home, secretly purge after a meal, or exercise for many hours after eating. It's *easy* for you to be fooled.

But even though they can trick you, they can't fool themselves, and they can't fully hide the symptoms. Eating disorders are most often associated with anxiety, depression, or other mental health issues. If you can spot some of the other symptoms, the eating disorder will be treated with the other issues. (This is where Tip #23 can be very helpful.) Below are the most common eating disorders and the associated symptoms to be on the lookout for. (See www. nimh.nih.gov for more information on eating disorders.)

Anorexia Nervosa

Anorexia nervosa is characterized by emaciation, a relentless pursuit of thinness and unwillingness to maintain a normal or healthy weight, a distortion of body image and intense fear of gaining weight, a lack of menstruation among girls and women, and extremely disturbed eating behavior. Some people with anorexia lose weight by dieting and exercising excessively; others lose weight by self-induced vomiting or misusing laxatives, diuretics, or enemas.

Symptoms of Anorexia

- Thinning of the bones (osteopenia or osteoporosis)
- Brittle hair and nails
- Dry and yellowish skin
- Growth of fine hair over body (e.g., lanugo)
- Mild anemia, muscle weakness and loss
- Severe constipation
- Low blood pressure, slowed breathing and pulse
- Drop in internal body temperature, causing a person to feel cold all the time
- Lethargy

IF THEY NEED HELP AND SUPPORT

Contact the counseling and psychological services on campus. Visit online and call. Ask about hotlines, therapy, and resources available on and around campus.

Contact the National Association of Anorexia and Associated Eating Disorders (ANAD). The ANAD Helpline number is 630-577-1330 (open Monday through Friday 9 AM to 5 PM Central Time). ANAD also has a special email

Bulimia Nervosa

Bulimia nervosa is characterized by recurrent and frequent episodes of eating unusually large amounts of food (e.g., binge eating) and feeling a lack of control over the eating. This binge eating is followed by a type of behavior that compensates for the binge, such as purging (e.g., vomiting, excessive use of laxatives or diuretics), fasting, and/or excessive exercise.

Symptoms of Bulimia

- Chronically inflamed and sore throat
- Swollen glands in the neck and below the jaw
- Worn tooth enamel and increasingly sensitive and decaying teeth as a result of exposure to stomach acids
- Gastroesophageal reflux disorder
- Intestinal distress and irritation from laxative abuse
- Kidney problems from diuretic abuse
- Severe dehydration from purging of fluids

Binge Eating Disorder

Binge eating disorder is characterized by recurrent binge eating episodes during which a person feels a loss of control over his or her eating. Unlike with bulimia, binge eating episodes are not followed by purging, excessive exercise, or fasting. As a result, people with binge eating disorder often are overweight or obese. They also experience guilt, shame, and/or distress about the binge eating, which can lead to more binge eating.

Getting Support

If your child is going to school and has already been diagnosed and treated for an eating disorder, make sure she has local support before setting foot on campus. Identify a therapist or counselor with whom she can build a relationship before she needs it.

If you suspect your child has an eating disorder but don't know for sure, take comfort in knowing that campuses are equipped to help. Most schools have dedicated resources to help students identify and manage eating disorders.

FROM DARTMOUTH UNIVERSITY

The philosophy behind Dartmouth's Eating Disorders Program is one of treating the whole student. Eating disorders affect people emotionally, socially, and physically. Therefore, individualized treatment utilizes the expertise of a variety of clinical specialists:

- **Psychologists** for counseling, body image, stress, depression, anxiety, and worries about friends.
- **Psychiatrists** for bingeing, obsessive thoughts, sleep problems, and depression.
- **Nutritionists** for advice on developing a healthy campus eating plan, achieving/maintaining healthy weight, and controlling chaotic eating, purging, and over-exercise.
- **Physicians/Physician Assistants/Nurse Practitioners** for medical evaluations, irregular menses, bone health, and anemia.
- **In-patient Staff** for a short-term infirmary stay to help structure meals and not purge.

Source: http://www.dartmouth.edu/~chd/resources/eating/index.html

---

If your son or daughter thinks a roommate or friend has an eating disorder, instead of just listening, direct your child to the resident assistant or counseling services. Before you consider reaching out to the other child's parent, make sure the parent is someone who will help and not hurt the situation. Some parents are less than accepting of the truth. That can get uncomfortable.

THE FRESHMAN FIFTEEN

My mom said I looked "full" when I came home for Thanksgiving.

—Kass, recent grad

Full disclosure: I've gained and lost a lot of weight in my life. In fact, I gained ten pounds while writing this book and then lost three. I know what it's like to have pants that are way too tight, too loose, and way too tight again (bummer).

College students can gain weight pretty easily. Having an international buffet available with ten food stations can take some time to figure out. Students who were extremely active in high school may find themselves less active and eating too much of the wrong foods at the wrong time. Eating breadsticks, wings, and pizza at 3:00 a.m. can pack on the pounds fast. However, weight gain or loss can also be a sign of stress, anxiety, depression, or an underlying condition. Gaining weight can be a sign of something more than a student eating too much and moving too little.

Students know when they have gained weight. If your kid comes home for Thanksgiving break and looks like he gained weight, don't make a joke (although it might be tempting). A lot of parents have weight issues themselves, and thus freak out when their child gains weight.

If you do feel the need to comment on your child's weight, do it from a place of concern. No jokes. When he sees his friends, there will be plenty of comments and jokes. He doesn't need it from you too.

If it's a dramatic weight gain, then ask him what you can do to help. You can even do a little research and offer access to a nutritionist or pass along the information of a nutritionist on campus. There are a lot of students who have never had to manage their own diets, because they always ate at home. They don't know how to make healthy choices, because the choices have always been made for them. What was served was what they ate. And when they did make not-so-healthy choices, they were active enough that it didn't matter. So connecting a student with a nutritionist can have life-long implications. What's really cool is that a lot of

> You know people talk about the freshman fifteen—I have lost ten pounds and haven't even tried. I'm definitely not complaining though.
>
> —Jake, freshman

schools have free nutritional services available to students (you gotta love college). If your child is looking for advice and wants to be active, point him in the direction of intramural sports, club sports, and classes at the recreational center. He might even take kick-boxing as an elective class.

On the other side of the spectrum are students who lose too much weight. Sometimes people get anxious at college or are too active to eat enough. (Sometimes it's an underlying emotional or physical issue; see the the discussion earlier in this chapter for information on eating disorders.) If your child is losing weight, the answer can be changing his meal plan, moving him to a location with a dining hall that works better with his schedule, or getting a to-go box from the dining center. A happy student who is losing weight might need to take some of the 3:00 a.m. breadsticks from the student who is gaining weight.

Most students will lose the weight once they form a routine and start becoming more active on campus. It takes a few months to realize how to manage this new lifestyle. Morning bagels, endless cereal, multiple helpings of french fries, pizza, and chicken fingers are delicious the first few months—until that trip home for Thanksgiving when friends see them for the first time and offer some candid observations. Friends don't hold back (one more reason you do not need to joke). That's usually when the salad bar, stir-fry station, and roasted chicken become staples. And if a student wants to enjoy some beverages and late-night snacks, a daily trip to the gym or a pick-up game of basketball will make its way into his routine. If he continues to gain weight through winter break, a doctor's visit and nutritionist may help.

QUESTIONS AND ANSWERS

Q: What's the best way for a parent to communicate a child's weight gain? Please give some examples.

A: The best way is to not looked shocked, not make strange gasping noises, and not ask if she ate her roommate. She knows she's gained weight. All she wants to know is that she is loved. Make sure she's not dealing with an emotional or physical illness. And give her a big hug—the biggest one ever.

And don't just take it from me. Here's some advice directly from the students themselves.

The best ways for a parent to comment about college weight gain:

- Unless we seem upset about it, please don't give advice unless we seek it. We might not care, and telling us will make it a bigger deal.
- Suggest we work out together as a way to reconnect and bond (my mom and I started doing zumba on my college breaks).
- Discreetly and tactfully pointing out that you've put on a few pounds yourself, whether it be from eating the wrong foods or drinking too much.
- Talk to your child about perhaps seeing a nutritionist for tips on maintaining a healthy weight.
- Don't say anything. There is a very good chance that we know we've gained fifteen pounds and are feeling pretty shitty about it.

The worst ways for a parent to comment about college weight gain:

- Saying, "Those pants are looking a bit tight...do you want a new pair?"

- Slapping your belly at the family Thanksgiving dinner and saying, "We ought to just cook her up instead...we could eat for months..."
- Pointing out the obvious: "Well, looks like somebody took the all-you-can-eat buffet a little too literally..."
- Slipping a diet book under my pillow...and never actually saying a word to me.
- Making a public announcement about my weight gain in any way, shape, or form is forbidden.
- Not trying to hide the obvious look of surprise on your face.
- Telling me, "There is a difference between fitting in your jeans fine and exploding in them."
- Making jokes or negative comments about the weight I've gained.

Have a question? Want to answer another parent's question?

Post your questions and answers; visit *The Happiest Kid on Campus* Parent Forum: www.HappiestKidonCampus.com.

TIP #25 TRANSFERRING

Coming or Going for All the Right Reasons (or Wrong Reasons)

The Tip

Sometimes our dream school can be an eye-opening experience. If it's not the right fit, please listen to your child and support her. She will be grateful.

The Story

My parents and I have always been close; I guess that comes from being an only child. My mother is a brilliant artist, and my father is a hardworking, respected administrator at the college I will graduate from. We were all confused when the school I chose out of high school didn't work out. I was discouraged, but they were always there to listen and provide guidance, without being disappointed in me (which they weren't, and which I was). While a senior in high school, I applied to a number of colleges, both in-state and out. I did not apply to the school that my father has spent the last forty-two years working at. I felt that I had already spent most of my life on that campus, and that it was time to go off on my own. Thanks to that aforementioned time spent at the local school, I always had a very specific idea of what college was going to be like for me. I pictured kids with their arms full of books, drinking coffee under big, castle-like buildings. I imagined making friends with cultured, interesting people who wanted to see the world. Instead, I was thrust into a freshman dorm where most kids were overwhelmed with being on their own for the first time. Girls drank, passed out, did drugs, slept around, didn't make it to class, and after a while they generally looked (and probably felt) like shit but claimed to be having a great time. I consider myself an outgoing, personable individual, but I didn't make any friends. I just couldn't relate to the behaviors and feelings that, apparently, came with being a freshman, and it was devastating. My parents were pleased when I returned home to finish my undergraduate education—and it turned out to be the right place. The decisions I made were my own, but they were always there to support me. I can't wait for the day that I walk across the stage at commencement, because my mom will be in the crowd, and my dad will be on the stage. I want nothing more than to give them back all they have given me by having the best life I can.

—Anna, senior

* * *

Some students spend a year on campus and transfer. Some spend a few months. And others spend only a few days (it's more common than you'd think). Deciding to transfer and find a place in a new school where everyone is already in place can be a struggle. It helps to have a parent who is familiar with the process and can help a student ask the right questions in order to make sure transferring is the right decision.

Too many times students think transferring is the answer but just end up taking their old problems with them. These tips will give you essential information to help guide your child through the decision-making process and help you help them to make a smooth transition to his or her new campus and become (you know it's coming) the happiest kid on campus.

TRANSFERRING: I DID IT

I started at the University of Wisconsin in Madison and ended up at Indiana University in Bloomington, Indiana. But I think if I had started at Indiana University, I might have transferred to U–Madison. It wasn't the school; it was me. I'm grateful for that year I had in Madison, because it was one of the most valuable, emotional, and powerful years of my life. A tough year can be one of the best ones. What I learned went way beyond the classroom. I learned how to survive on my own.

Unless there are extenuating circumstances, health issues, or a financial crisis that forces your child to leave school, I encourage you to encourage her to stick it out at her school for at least a year. A few months on campus isn't a full representation of the college experience. It's too new, and things are moving too fast. The second half of the year is when things settle into place and she can gauge what feels right and what feels wrong.

There's another important reason why she shouldn't transfer in less than a year. If your child wants to transfer successfully, she needs to be able to answer the following questions:

- What specifically went wrong this year?
- What is it that I want that my current campus can't provide?
- What will be different the next time?
- What can I do differently to make it happen?

Until she goes through the full cycle, it's hard to have those answers. So while there are of course exceptions, encourage her to stick it out for a year if she can.

And I'll tell you a secret—if you give her permission to leave but ask her to stick around for the rest of the year, something cool might happen. It's what happened to me.

The moment I decided to leave was the moment I stopped trying so hard to be liked by everyone. I stopped caring what people thought. I gave them permission to not always like me. It didn't matter. I put myself in rooms with people I didn't know. I met people who I wanted to meet instead of waiting for people to want to meet me.

Over the course of the second half of the year, I made good friends. Once I stopped trying so hard and got comfortable with the uncomfortable, life changed. I still transferred to Indiana University, because I wanted a fresh start, but the strong finish during my first year gave me confidence that carried over into my second college experience.

GIVE THEM PERMISSION TO LEAVE

Transferring can be tough on parents. They are great when the acceptance letters come in the mail, but when a student wants to transfer they are less than enthusiastic. A lot of parents don't like the idea of transferring, because they see it as giving up. They see it as their own failure. Some find it embarrassing and don't want to have to explain to their friends. While it's understandable for parents to be disappointed and confused, it doesn't really address the reason why your child hasn't found his place on campus and wants to leave.

Sometimes a school that appears to be the best choice turns out to be the wrong fit. Just like a pair of shoes, walking on campus regularly is different than trying it on for a day. Call it the Universal Rejection Truth of the College Experience—not all students thrive on campus. It can be confusing and disappointing for your child and for you, but try not to force it. Give him permission to be uncomfortable on campus.

> Transferring was a big deal in my household. I was at a big state school and wanted to switch to a smaller liberal arts institution (i.e., a school more than twice as expensive). My parents, being the parents of my younger siblings as well, weren't going to pay all of that difference. That was ok, I understood. The part that was a real problem was that they also weren't willing to allow me to take on the loans and debts that I would then need. I'll make the story simple: they lost that battle. And yeah, the amount of money I have pledged to my name is daunting (college prices, my goodness), but I had to step up and do what was necessary for my health, my happiness, and my education. To me, it's worth it, but I know letting me be an adult and make this decision is one of the hardest things my parents have done.
>
> —Kelsey, sophomore

Instead of fighting it, accepting it will help him figure out what doesn't fit. Accepting that he is uncomfortable means being in his corner while he figures out what went wrong.

The irony is that the more you give him permission to explore transferring, he will have the freedom to explore his feelings and discover the reasons why things went wrong on campus. And it's during this search for answers that he might just realize that his current campus isn't so bad. Also, if you're not forcing him to be happy, the focus isn't on you. It's on what he can do to make himself happy.

REASONS TO TRANSFER (AND QUESTIONS TO RAISE)

Some students pick the wrong school for the wrong reasons. Some pick the right school but find it's the wrong fit. Some pick the right school but end up living in the wrong place or meeting the wrong people. Given that approximately one in four students transfer to another school their second year, there are a lot of students with a lot of reasons. Here are some of the most common reasons students transfer, and some questions you can bring up to make sure your child is leaving for the right reasons:

It's Expensive

Paying for one year doesn't mean being able to pay for four, five, or six. Before accepting that it's too expensive, suggest that your child go to the financial aid office and discuss options. Special arrangements could be made. There might

The cost of my school forced me to have to transfer to a different school. If I hadn't transferred, I would have come out of school as a teacher with loans higher than my salary. My parents were not as supportive as I wanted them to be; however, in the end they are just happy I'm still in school.

—Gabby, freshman

be a new grant or scholarship available. She could consider an opportunity to become an RA or take on a leadership position that could decrease expenses and make it work. When contemplating a transfer, she must first check to see if the other school will accept all of the credit hours she has earned so far. Transferring might seem like a better deal, but it can also mean having to stick around in college for another year or two.

It's the Wrong Fit

Sometimes it's just not the right campus. If so, you need to get your child to ask himself questions. What went wrong? What can he do next year to make it right? Why will the next school be any different? A student who is looking for the right fit needs to pinpoint what went wrong so he can make it fit the next time. Sometimes it's not the school, but the student. Like bad body odor, problems will just stick to students when they transfer unless they can pinpoint the problem and come in with a fresh, new approach.

I chose my school on a whim. I thought it would be a good idea to go to the "best" school I got into, but I did it without much thinking and now I'm stuck. For financial reasons, I can't transfer (I have a prepaid plan for this school), but I wish I could go back and better consider what it would have been like at other schools.

—Bailey, freshman

It's Too Big or Too Small

It's possible to get lost in a big school, and it's possible to feel confined in a small one. It's not so much the size that matters but what a student does on campus to make a big campus small enough to feel at home, and a small campus big enough to grow. If your child is at a big school and wants to transfer to a smaller campus, ask what she's done to make her big campus smaller. Then ask what she plans to do to make her smaller campus big enough to explore her interests.

I had to transfer to a different school because of grades and money. I was paying out-of-state tuition for a college and didn't know if I wanted to go there anymore. I'd changed my major six times and couldn't keep my grades up. I moved back to my home state and started at the community college with support from my dad. Hopefully I'll make it this time.

—Connie, sophomore

It's Not the Right Academic Fit

Most students change their major, and not all schools offer a major that reflects a new interest. A student who changes majors and decides a current campus is the wrong one needs to make sure that it's the right choice before transferring. This means getting a part-time job, an internship, or some kind of hands-on experience to make sure he's chosen the right major. If not, changing majors again will mean changing schools again.

It's Too Far from Home

Some students realize being so far from home isn't as great as they thought it would be. Before transferring closer to home, ask your child what he's done to make his new school feel like home. Moving close to home might make you smile with delight, but being too close to home can make it too easy for your child to avoid doing the work it takes to make his new campus feel like home. Coming home every weekend might be fun for a while, but it's not going to help him learn how to create a life for himself. Being just far enough away to have a life but still have dinner with parents can work too.

It's Too Far from a Significant Other

This one really bothers me. I get it, but it bugs me. If someone doesn't know how to create an independent life away from a significant other, chances are it's not going to happen on the same campus. Bring up the hypothetical situation of what would happen if they broke up. Would your child transfer again? College is about options and creating a life for yourself. If you can negotiate, encourage your child to wait an extra year before committing to the transfer, or to go to a school near a significant other instead of attending the same school.

THREE THINGS TO DO BEFORE GIVING YOUR BLESSING

Before you run out to buy yourself the officially licensed warm-up suit of your child's new school, there are some things she needs to do:

1. Make sure she can get into another school. Applying doesn't mean she will get accepted.

2. Make sure she knows exactly which credit hours will transfer and which won't.

Transferring wasn't so hard. The worst part was not having all of my credits transfer. I wish there was a better system for that.

—Daniel, sophomore

This means talking to an admissions counselor or academic adviser at the school that interests her.

3. Make sure she isn't running away from problems rather than toward new opportunities. This means being able to pinpoint why she is leaving and what will be different this time around. You never know— there might be a bigger emotional or mental health issue at the source.

Transferring is far from a tragedy. In fact, it can be a blessing. I want to share a letter with you (see sidebar). It came from a first-year student who had just applied to transfer from her dream school to another school closer to home. Clearly, the wrong fit can bring the richest rewards.

SUPPORTING THE TRANSFER STUDENT

Going from one school to a new one means having to do the first year over again. As a transfer student who went through

I spent my entire high school career working to get into my dream school. When I arrived on campus, it was nothing like I expected. I learned that things aren't easy, happiness isn't handed to you—YOU have to be the one to find it. It takes experience and opportunities to realize what kind of person you are. And I have found that the person I truly am wants to be close to my family, yet be myself and be a college student and become responsible. I also learned that who you were

continued on page 594

continued from page 593

in high school doesn't matter. College is about making a new name for yourself, experiencing new things, and creating memories and bonds that will last a lifetime. You can aspire to be something bigger and something better, and find your own happiness, which is exactly what I am doing. Life is tough, and it is even harder when you allow it to be. I want to transfer because happiness is important to me, my family is important to me, and most of all, staying true to myself is important to me.

I am very grateful that I have had the opportunity to dream and chase those dreams, and thankful for my experience here, but it's just not for me. At least I don't think. Maybe there will be some strange fate that restricts me from transferring and I'll return here next fall. If that is the case, then I am going to do what I'm doing now: make the most of my experience and never quit dreaming. I have remained positive throughout this experience, because I am happy here. However, I just know I can be happier somewhere else. And I am determined to find my highest level of happiness, wherever that might be.

—Mackenzie, freshman

this, I didn't expect my second "first-year experience" to be filled with so many of the same experiences. There's finding friends, dealing with roommates, sitting with strangers in the cafeteria, new classes, new teachers, and so many other new experiences. The only thing that made it easier was knowing that this was all normal and would pass. I knew what was beyond it. The 10 percent difficult didn't consume as much time or energy the second time around.

Knowing college might be uncomfortable at times, being patient, planning how I would get involved, creating a world of options, getting help before I needed it, and using the lessons learned from my first college experience made all the difference. It wasn't the new university that made the difference; it was my ability to take risks and take advantage of the amazing opportunities that made it work.

The most difficult part about transferring, for me, was feeling completely alone on my new campus. I knew nobody, but since everybody knew each other, that made it even more difficult for me to approach anyone. Everybody seemed to cling to the people they knew and didn't really care about meeting new people. I ended up clinging to the first person to approach me, which happened to be a guy who was absolutely no good for me. He ended up causing me five months of trouble.

—Shayna, junior

Transfer students, especially freshman transfer students, are some of the most at-risk students. Students transferring in their second or third year of college can also face the emotional stress, financial pressures, and feelings of not belonging or being too old to get involved. A lot of transfer students take their problems with them, transferring them from one campus to another, but yet they expect everything to change. It's for this reason that all transfer students need to plan, map out a path, and work to create a new world of options.

Whether your child is transferring from a community college to a four-year school or from one university to another, the most important thing you can do is encourage your child to plug in to programs designed specifically for transfer students. And she

ATTENTION PARENTS OF TRANSFER STUDENTS

Plug yourself in to all the parent resources at the new school. Do it all over again. Attend orientation events for parents. Move them in. Get familiar with all the resources, support services, and people who can help your child transition.

should also attend the school's first-year programs. Even if she is a second- or third-year student, the first year at a new school means following all the advice given to first-year students (including the advice in this book). If your child doesn't like this idea, a helpful way to frame it is to remind her that having experience and knowing what college is about puts her in a place to help others. She can be the older expert.

With one year under her belt, making a plan and mapping out a path should be even easier. As a transfer student, she'll know what's coming. She just might need your help preparing. Help her get comfortable with the uncomfortable part of college life.

Here are some essential things transfer students should keep in mind when making the move:

- A transfer student needs to find three activities and organizations to join (one should be a group or organization for transfer students).
- A transfer student needs to get involved quickly and have a distinct plan before arriving on campus.
- A transfer student needs to be patient (harder to do when the clock is running).
- A transfer student needs to have a close relationship with an academic adviser (there's no time to learn by trial and error).
- A transfer student should live in the residence halls (being in the heart of campus will help make it easier to find connections).

- A transfer student needs to get help sooner rather than later when stumbling academically (there's no time to feel stupid; get help fast).
- A transfer student needs to get comfortable with the uncomfortable and have parents who will do the same (the 10 percent uncomfortable can only take up 10 percent of their time considering how little time there is to waste).
- A transfer student needs a mentor on campus as soon as possible. He can start with the professional staff and then connect with student leaders on campus.
- A transfer student with educated and informed parents is like a chef with a powerful sous chef. It's all about helping your student get the right ingredients to cook up the best possible college experience as efficiently as possible.

THE RIGHT REASONS AND THE RIGHT FIT

Transferring for the right reasons can be the right move. It just takes some work to figure out that it's the right move. I think that if more students take more time during the college search process to figure out why a school is the right fit, and knew to map out a path before arriving on campus, there wouldn't be a need to transfer. A student who understands the college experience before arriving on campus is a student who is set up to become the happiest kid on campus.

QUESTIONS AND ANSWERS

Q: How can uncomfortable parents explain to their friends why their son or daughter is transferring?

A: Just say it wasn't the right fit. You can leave it at that. If someone asks for more details, you can just say he or she "wasn't comfortable."

Q: Do all four-year institutions accept transfer students?

A: The vast majority do, but the requirements to get in vary. The best approach is to check with the admissions office and find out the transfer requirements. Some schools that are options for first-year students might not be options for third-year students.

Q: Is it easier to be accepted as a transfer student?

A: It depends. If your child is transferring from a community college, the admissions process can be much easier. Some colleges and universities have arrangements with schools that offer admission to students completing certain requirements. When transferring from one four-year school to another, acceptance requirements and available spots will vary.

Q: What happens if a school will not accept credit hours?

A: I wish there were a way to sell them on eBay, but if your child transfers and the new school won't accept his credit hours, consider it extra knowledge. Perhaps he will go on a game show and will correctly answer the ten-thousand-dollar question using knowledge from that extra class.

Q: When does a student need to apply to transfer?

A: Some schools have rolling admissions (meaning admission is open all year long). Other schools have a window of time and deadlines. Encourage your child to apply as soon as possible, but make it clear that she doesn't have to transfer just because she's applying. It's all about having options.

Have a question? Want to answer another parent's question?

Post your questions and answers; visit *The Happiest Kid on Campus* Parent Forum: www.HappiestKidonCampus.com.

THE HAPPIEST ENDING

FINAL HAPPY WORDS

Hi, Parents,

I just wanted to thank you one more time for taking the time to read this book! I hope the last 599 pages have helped you feel better prepared and more comfortable than ever about your child's (and your) college experience. I look forward to continuing this relationship with you and sharing the latest facts, statistics, and information to help your child be the happiest kid on campus.

Thanks again,

Harlan Cohen

THE HAPPIEST KID ON CAMPUS ONLINE

Find resources, support services, helpful websites, participate in online discussions, read advice, and share your feedback:

Website:
www.HappiestKidonCampus.com

Facebook fan page:
www.Facebook.com/HappiestKidonCampus

Twitter:
http://Twitter.com/HappiestKid

THE NAKED ROOMMATE AND THE AUTHOR ONLINE

Find resources, participate in online discussions, read advice, and share your feedback:

Connect with *The Naked Roommate* online:
- Website: www.NakedRoommate.com
- Facebook: www.Facebook.com/TNRfanpage
- Twitter: http://Twitter.com/NakedRoommate

Connect with Harlan online:
- Website: www.HelpMeHarlan.com
- Facebook: www.Facebook.com/Harlan.Cohen
- Twitter: http://Twitter.com/HarlanCohen
- Email: Harlan@HelpMeHarlan.com

AUTHOR SPEAKING EVENTS

KEYNOTES, WORKSHOPS, AND LIVE EVENTS

Harlan Cohen is a nationally recognized speaker who has presented on hundreds of campuses across the country. Harlan delivers keynotes, facilitates workshops, and can be found participating in a wide variety of events. He can host your:

- College night event
- Conference keynote
- Graduation keynote
- Parent programs (high school and college)
- High school programs (sophomores, juniors, and seniors)
- Professional development workshop (for high school and college professionals)

For more information on Harlan's keynotes, workshops, and events, visit:

www.HelpMeHarlan.com/speak.html

www.HappiestKidonCampus.com

READ "HELP ME, HARLAN!" IN YOUR LOCAL OR COLLEGE NEWSPAPER

He's like "Dear Abby," only younger, hairier, and a man. Harlan's syndicated "Help Me, Harlan!" advice column can be read in local daily and college newspapers in the United States, Canada, and around the world. His column is distributed by King Features Syndicate.

If he's not published in your newspaper and you would like to read his advice column, please email your newspaper editor and ask them to run "Help Me, Harlan!" Also, feel free to send a note to syndication@HelpMeHarlan.com, and we'll pass along the word for you. In the meantime, Harlan's archived advice can be read online at www.HelpMeHarlan.com.

ABOUT THE AUTHOR

Harlan Cohen is the bestselling author of four books, a professional speaker, a musician, and one of the most widely read and respected male syndicated advice columnists in the country.

Harlan's writing career began at Indiana University's school newspaper, the *Indiana Daily Student*. He shifted his path toward advice after interning at *The Tonight Show with Jay Leno* in the summer of 1995. Harlan was inspired to begin writing his column after meeting a writer who had penned a similar column while in college. When he returned to campus, Harlan immediately launched his "Help Me, Harlan!" advice column. At first he wrote questions and answers to himself. When he started to help himself, he knew he was good. Then real letters started rolling in. Harlan's balance of honest advice, helpful resources, and sharp humor turned the column into an instant success on and off campus. As the column spread, Harlan began writing books, speaking on college campuses, and creating original music to bring the topics addressed in his writing to life.

Harlan is the bestselling author of the books *The Happiest Kid on Campus* (Sourcebooks), *Dad's Pregnant Too!* (Sourcebooks), *The Naked Roommate: And 107 Other*

Issues You Might Run Into in College (Sourcebooks), and *Campus Life Exposed: Advice from the Inside* (Peterson's). Harlan is a contributor to *Chicken Soup for the Teenage Soul III* and has been featured as an expert offering advice in the *New York Times, Wall Street Journal Classroom Edition, Real Simple, Seventeen, Psychology Today,* and hundreds of other newspapers and publications. King Features Syndicate distributes Harlan's "Help Me, Harlan!" advice column worldwide. Harlan is a frequent guest on television programs across the country and has appeared on hundreds of radio programs. Harlan is a professional speaker who has visited over four hundred college campuses. He is an expert who addresses teen issues, college life, parenting, pregnancy, dating, relationships, sex/no sex, rejection, risk taking, leadership, women's issues, and a variety of other topics.

Harlan is the founder of the websites www.HappiestKidonCampus.com, www.NakedRoommate.com, www.DadsPregnant.com, and www.HelpMeHarlan.com. He is the producer, lead singer, and musician on his album *Fortunate Accidents.* He is also the founder and president of Rejection Awareness Week (February 7–14 annually) and the International Risk-Taking Project.

He lives in Chicago, Illinois, with his wife and two young children. In his spare time he thinks about how little spare time he has (and then his spare time is over, leaving him thinking about how he squandered his spare time, eating up more spare time).

THE NAKED SUITE OF PRODUCTS

THE NAKED ROOMMATE: AND 107 OTHER ISSUES YOU MIGHT RUN INTO IN COLLEGE

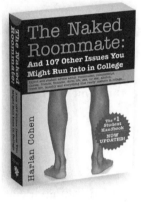

- The #1 going-to-college book
- Required reading on college campuses across the country
- Over 250,000 copies in print

Advice columnist Harlan Cohen's *The Naked Roommate and 107 Other Issues You Might Run Into in College* is a friendly, funny, and wise guide to making the most of college.

—Sarah Lindner, *American-Statesman*

Used As Required Reading on College Campuses across the Country

The laughter and real-life honesty of the book's presentation helps students realize that their experiences are not unique to them and that everyone is in the same boat.

—Beverly Dolinsky, VP Student Affairs,
Endicott College

It (*The Naked Roommate*) doesn't recommend excessive drinking, illegal drug-taking and random sexual hookups, but it recognizes that such things happen in college and offers sensible tips about what to do if you or your friends get in a jam.

—Charles McGrath, *New York Times*

THE NAKED SUITE OF PRODUCTS

The Naked Roommate book

The Naked Roommate workbook

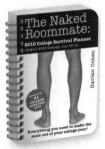

The Naked Roommate planner

The Naked Roommate boxed calendar

The NAKED daily (free daily email dispatch)

The Naked Roommate instructor's guide

The Naked Roommate speaking tour

The Naked Roommate professional training (live seminar for instructors using the book as first-year experience text)

Harlan thought the greatest transition in life was going to college...then he got married and started a family.

Dad's Pregnant Too! is what happens when *The Naked Roommate* gets someone pregnant. It's everything and anything expectant dads and their partners need to know about having a baby.

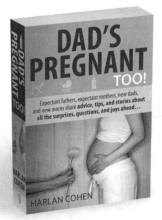

Index